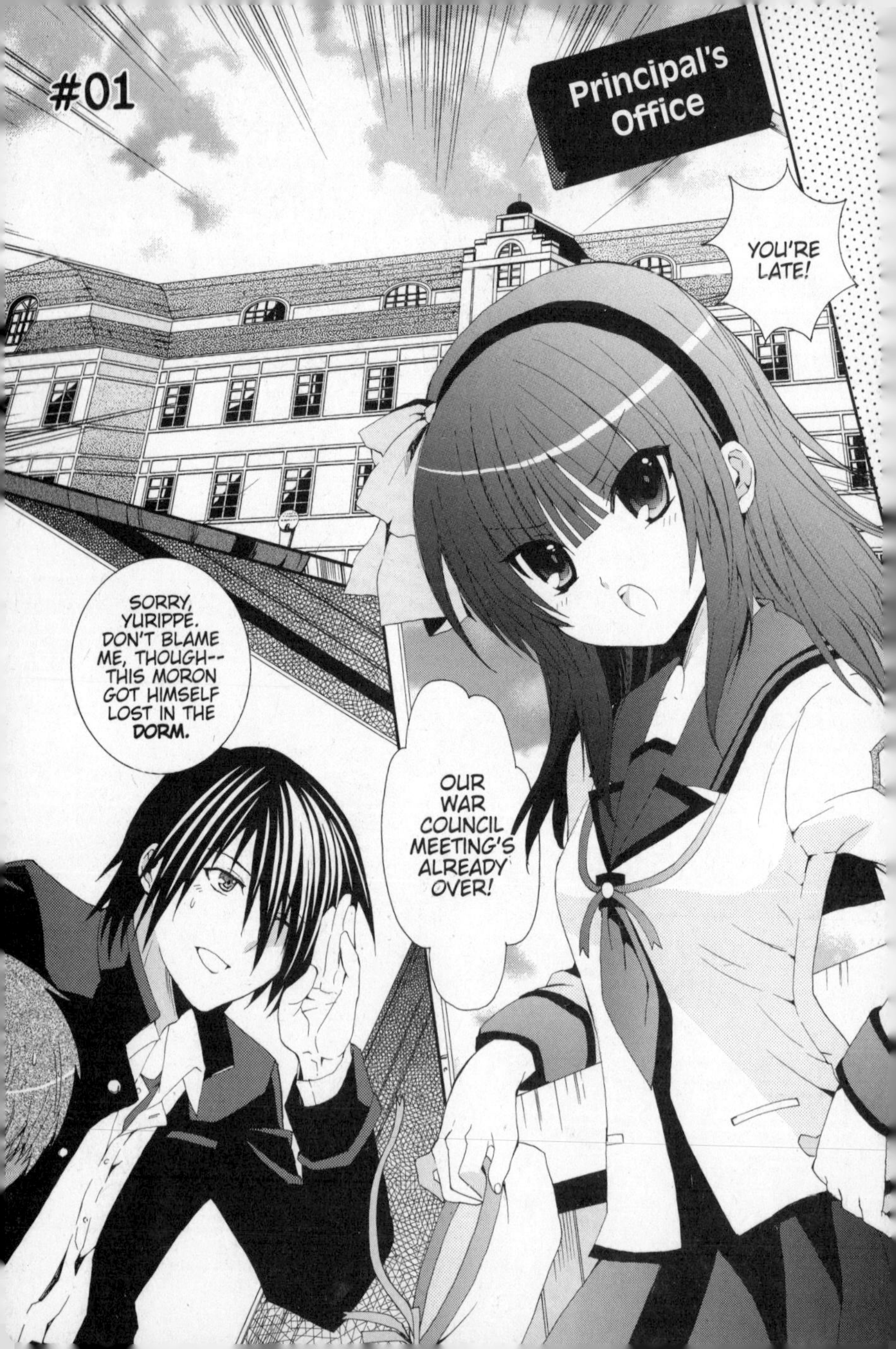
#01
Principal's Office
YOU'RE LATE!
OUR WAR COUNCIL MEETING'S ALREADY OVER!
SORRY, YURIPPE. DON'T BLAME ME, THOUGH-- THIS MORON GOT HIMSELF LOST IN THE DORM.

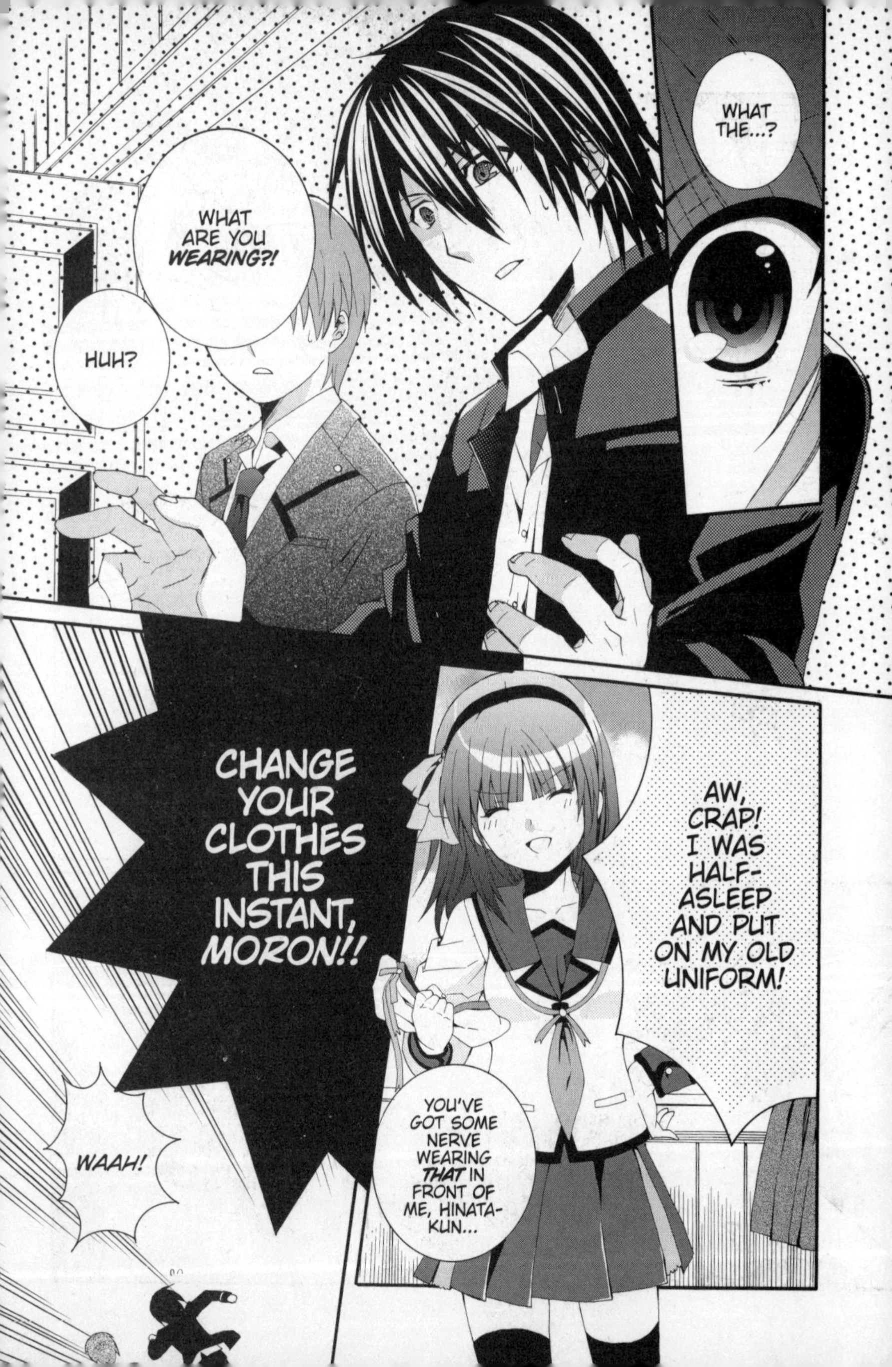
WHAT THE...?
WHAT ARE YOU *WEARING?!*
HUH?
AW, CRAP! I WAS HALF-ASLEEP AND PUT ON MY OLD UNIFORM!
YOU'VE GOT SOME NERVE WEARING ***THAT*** IN FRONT OF ME, HINATA-KUN...
CHANGE YOUR CLOTHES THIS INSTANT, *MORON!!*
WAAH!

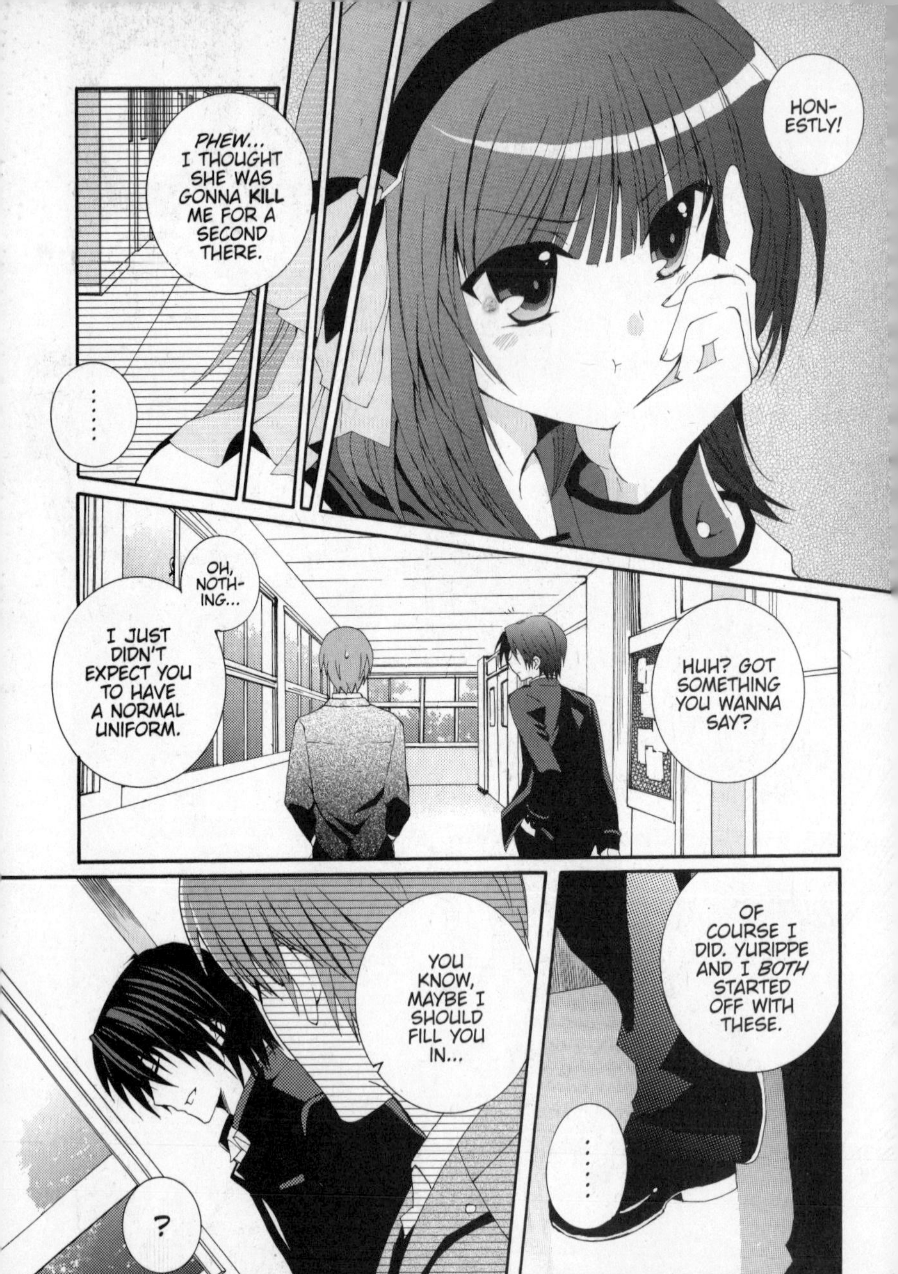
HON-ESTLY!
PHEW... I THOUGHT SHE WAS GONNA KILL ME FOR A SECOND THERE.
......
HUH? GOT SOMETHING YOU WANNA SAY?
OH, NOTHING...
I JUST DIDN'T EXPECT YOU TO HAVE A NORMAL UNIFORM.
OF COURSE I DID. YURIPPE AND I *BOTH* STARTED OFF WITH THESE.
......
YOU KNOW, MAYBE I SHOULD FILL YOU IN...
?

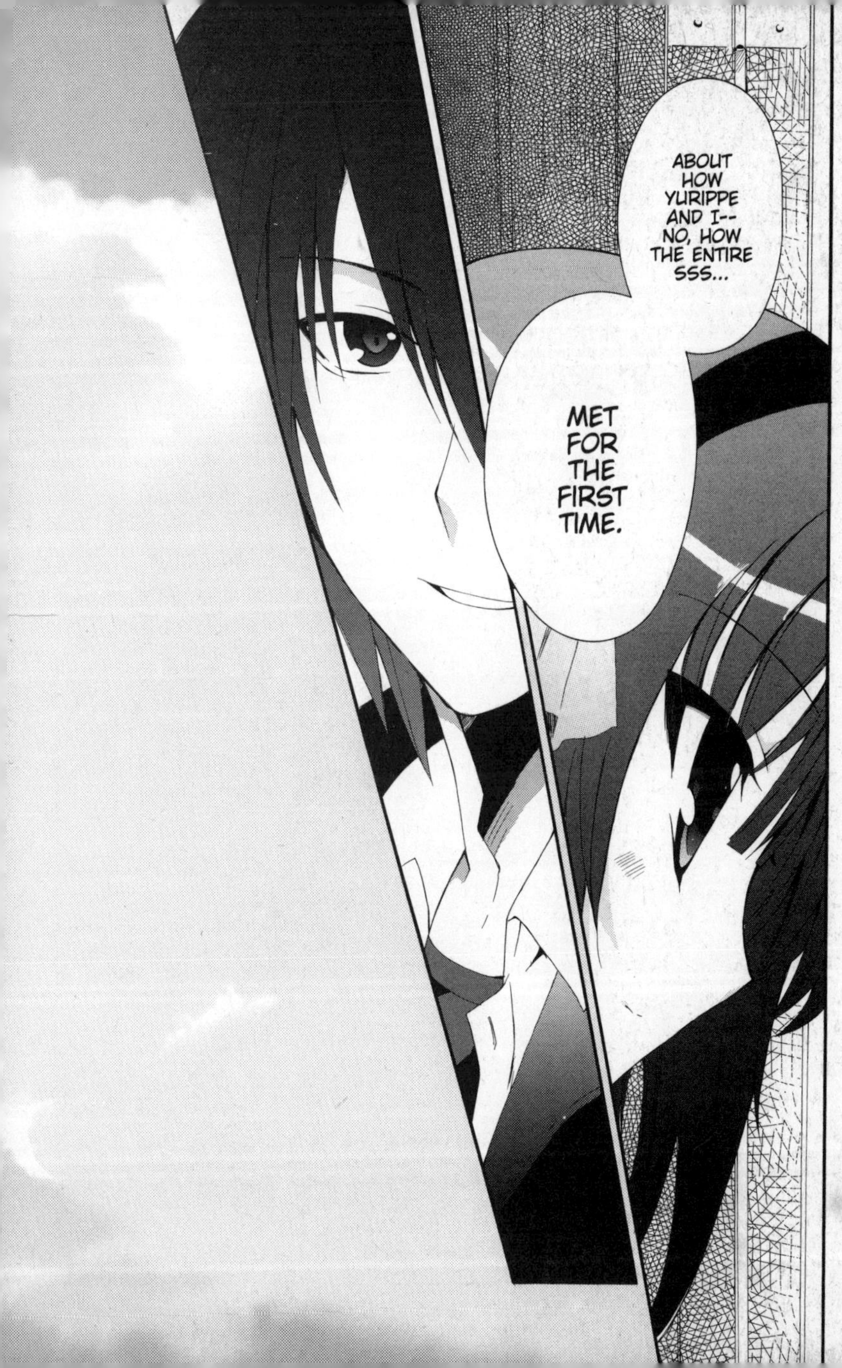
ABOUT HOW YURIPPE AND I-- NO, HOW THE ENTIRE SSS...
MET FOR THE FIRST TIME.

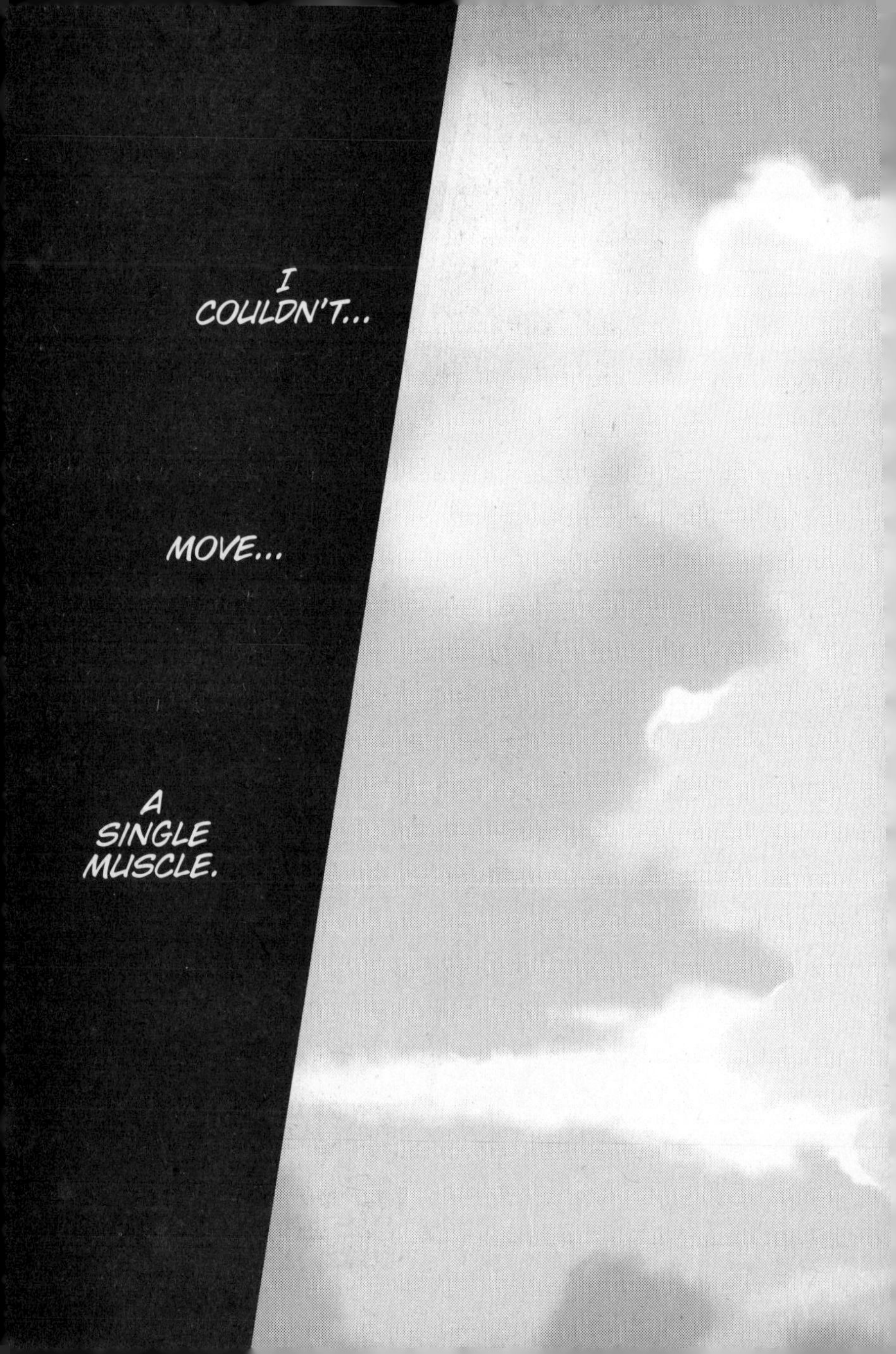
I COULDN'T...
MOVE...
A SINGLE MUSCLE.

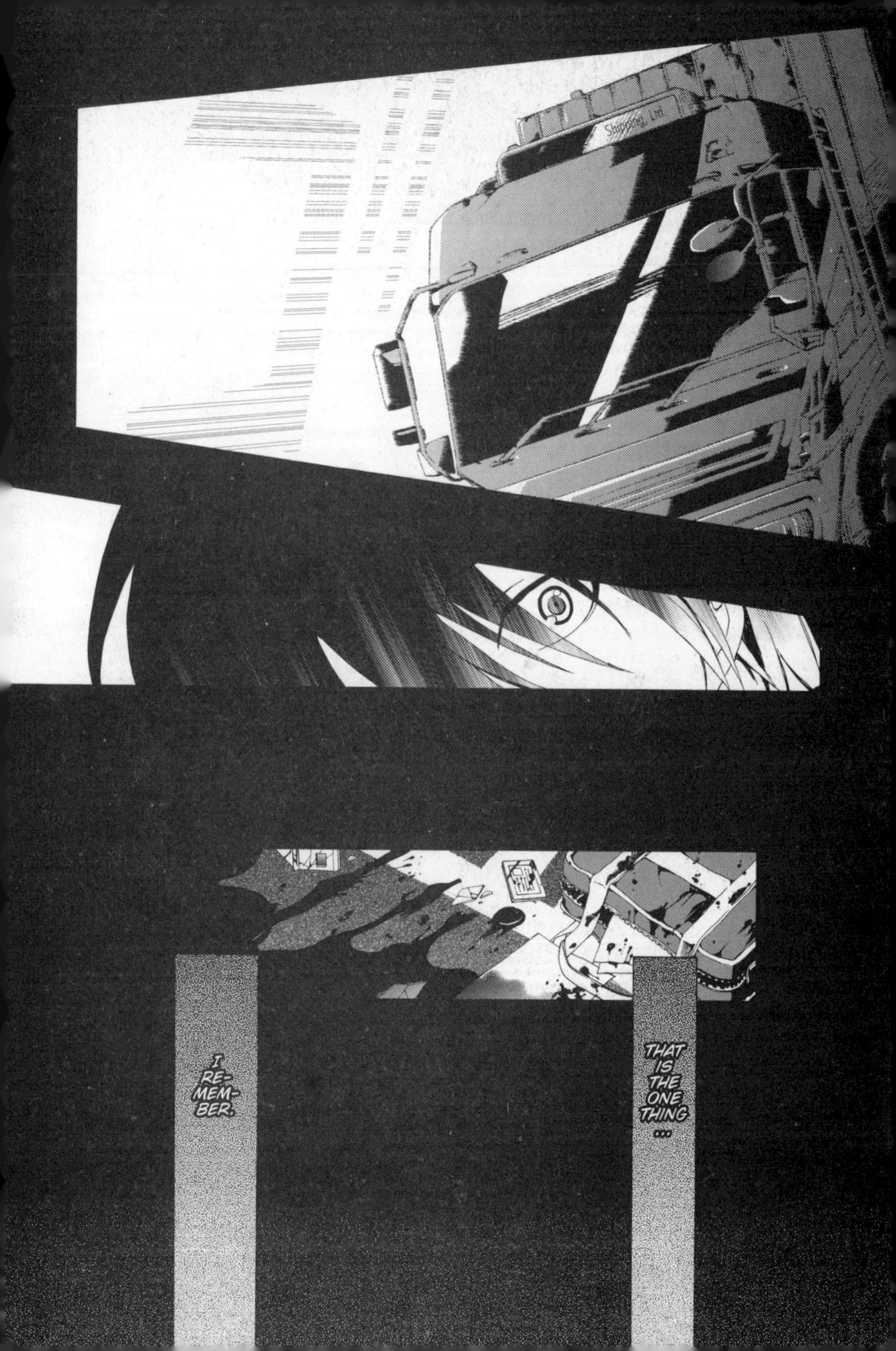
Shipping, Ltd.
THAT IS THE ONE THING...
I RE-MEM-BER.

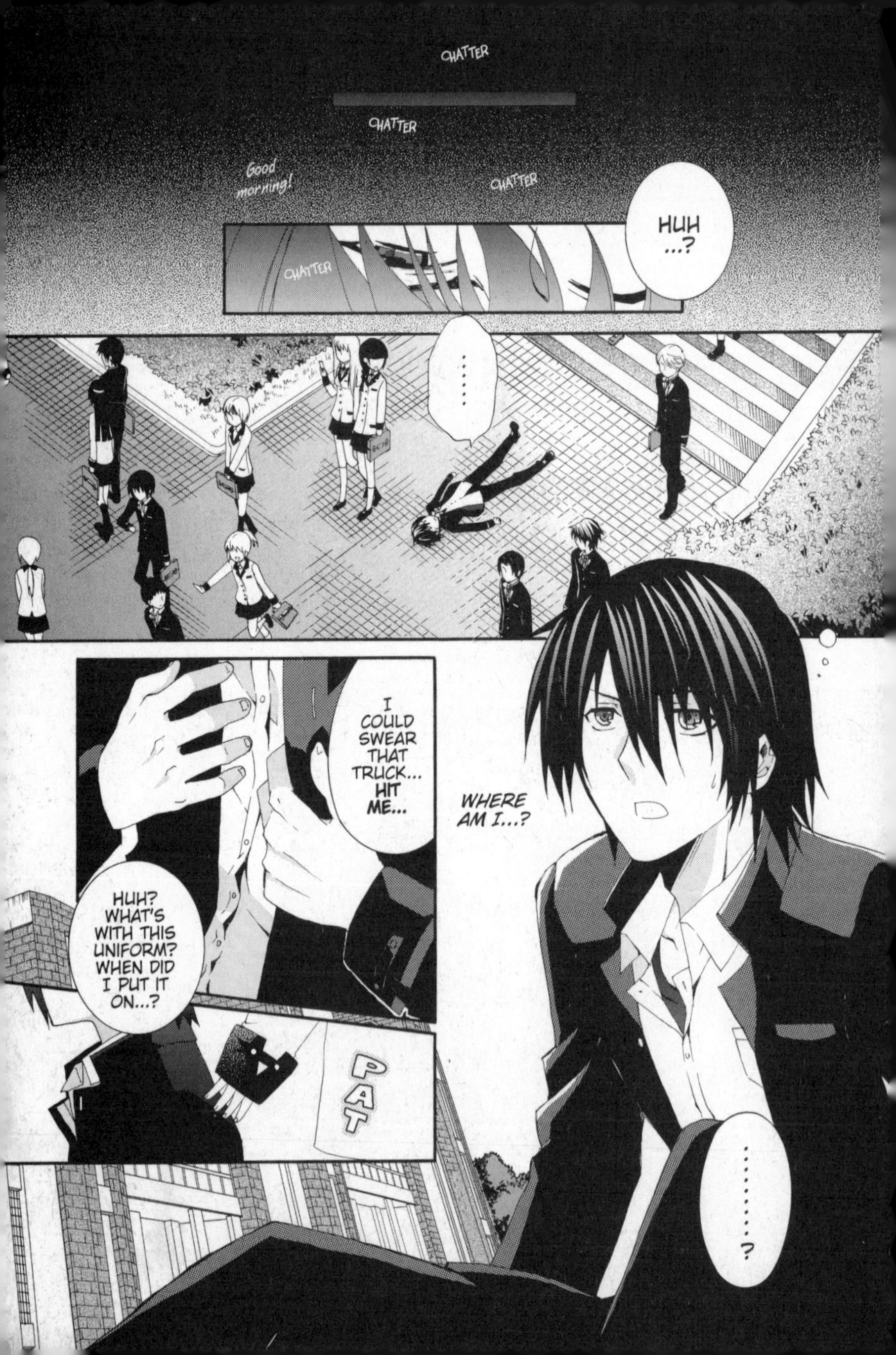
CHATTER
CHATTER
CHATTER
Good morning!
HUH ...?
CHATTER
......
WHERE AM I...?
......?
I COULD SWEAR THAT TRUCK... HIT ME...
HUH? WHAT'S WITH THIS UNIFORM? WHEN DID I PUT IT ON...?
PAT

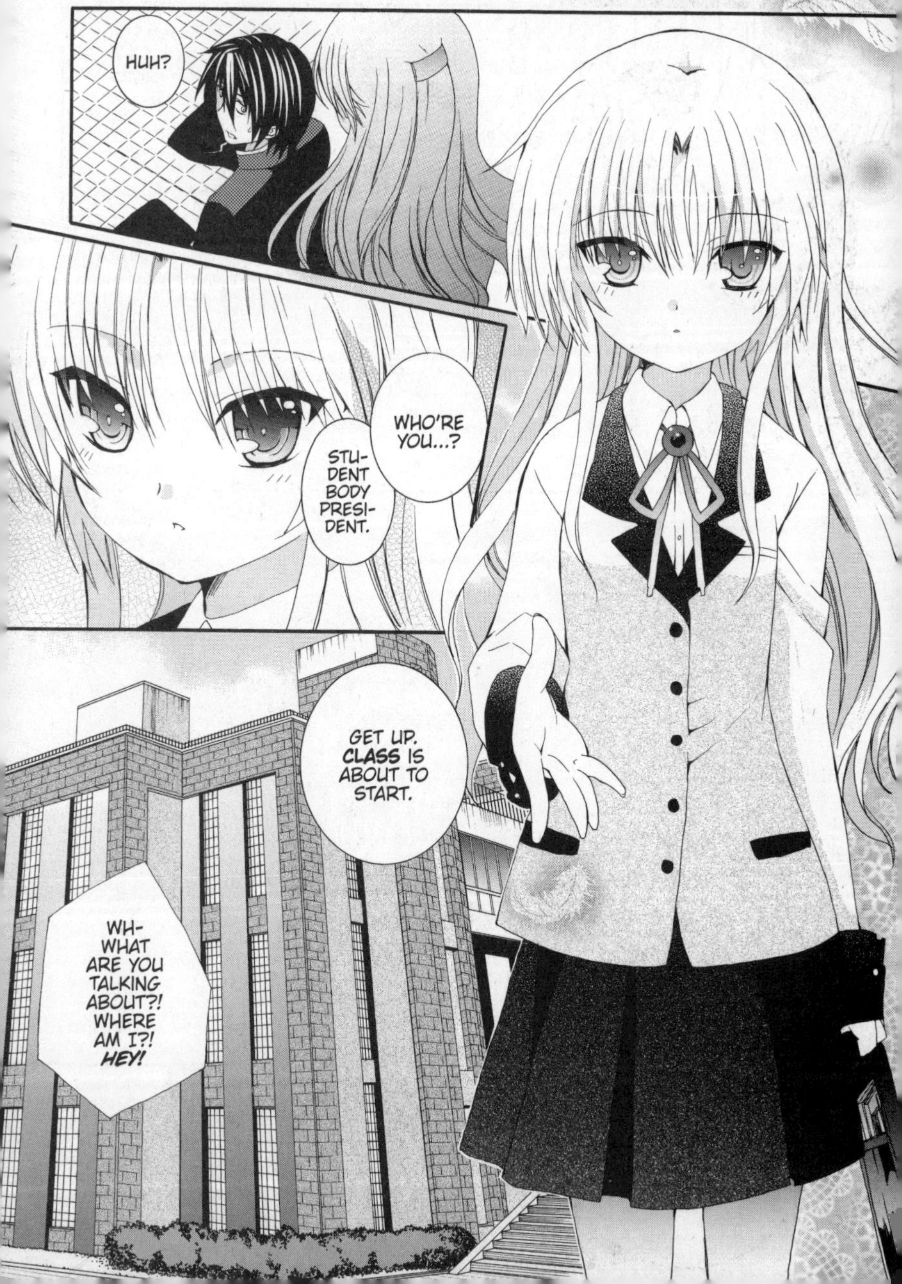
HUH?
WHO'RE YOU...?
STU-DENT BODY PRESI-DENT.
GET UP. **CLASS** IS ABOUT TO START.
WH-WHAT ARE YOU TALKING ABOUT?! WHERE AM I?! ***HEY!***

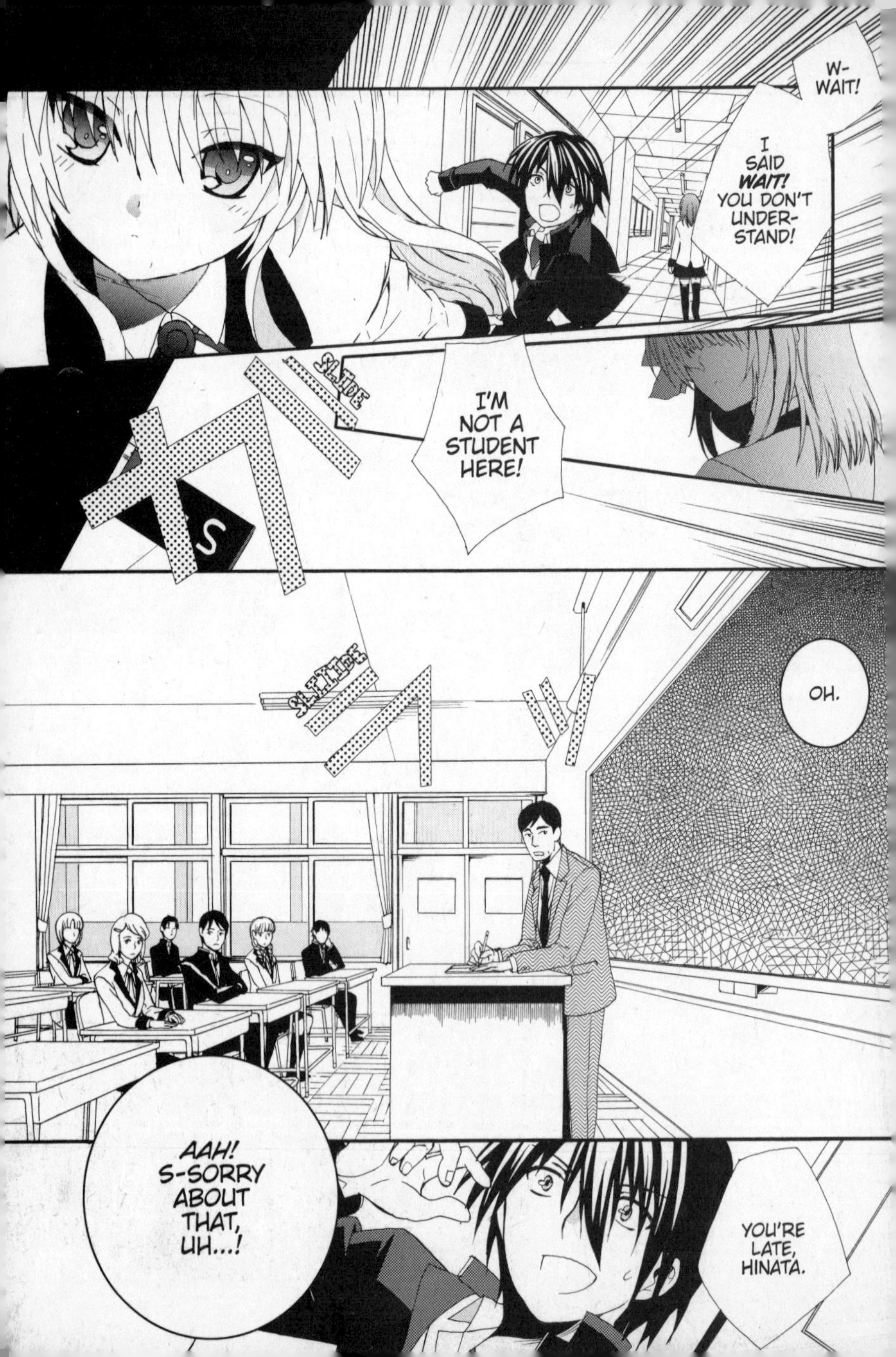
W-WAIT!
I SAID *WAIT!* YOU DON'T UNDER-STAND!
SLIDE
I'M NOT A STUDENT HERE!
SLIIIDE
OH.
YOU'RE LATE, HINATA.
AAH! S-SORRY ABOUT THAT, UH...!

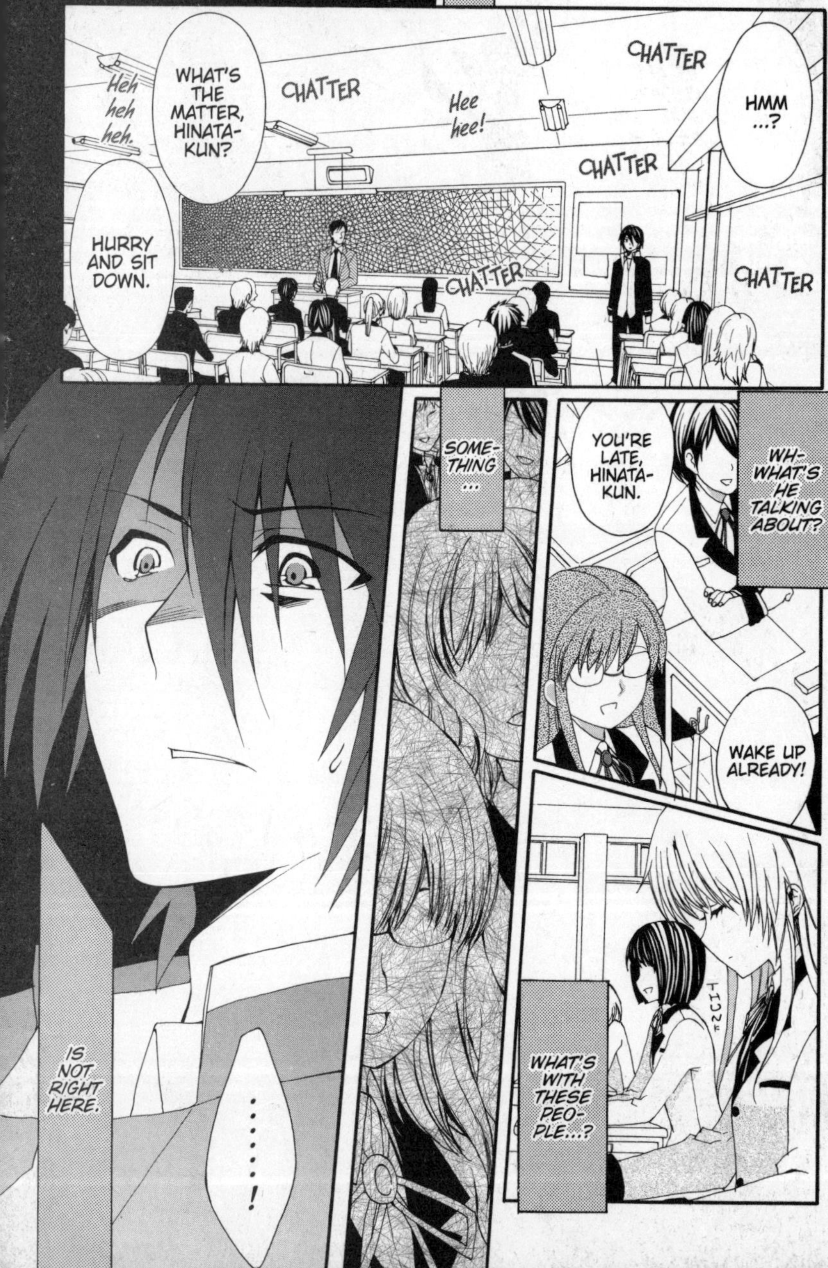
CHATTER
HMM ...?
CHATTER
Hee hee!
CHATTER
WHAT'S THE MATTER, HINATA-KUN?
Heh heh heh.
CHATTER
CHATTER
HURRY AND SIT DOWN.
WH-WHAT'S HE TALKING ABOUT?
YOU'RE LATE, HINATA-KUN.
WAKE UP ALREADY!
THUNK
WHAT'S WITH THESE PEO-PLE...?
SOME-THING...
IS NOT RIGHT HERE.
......!

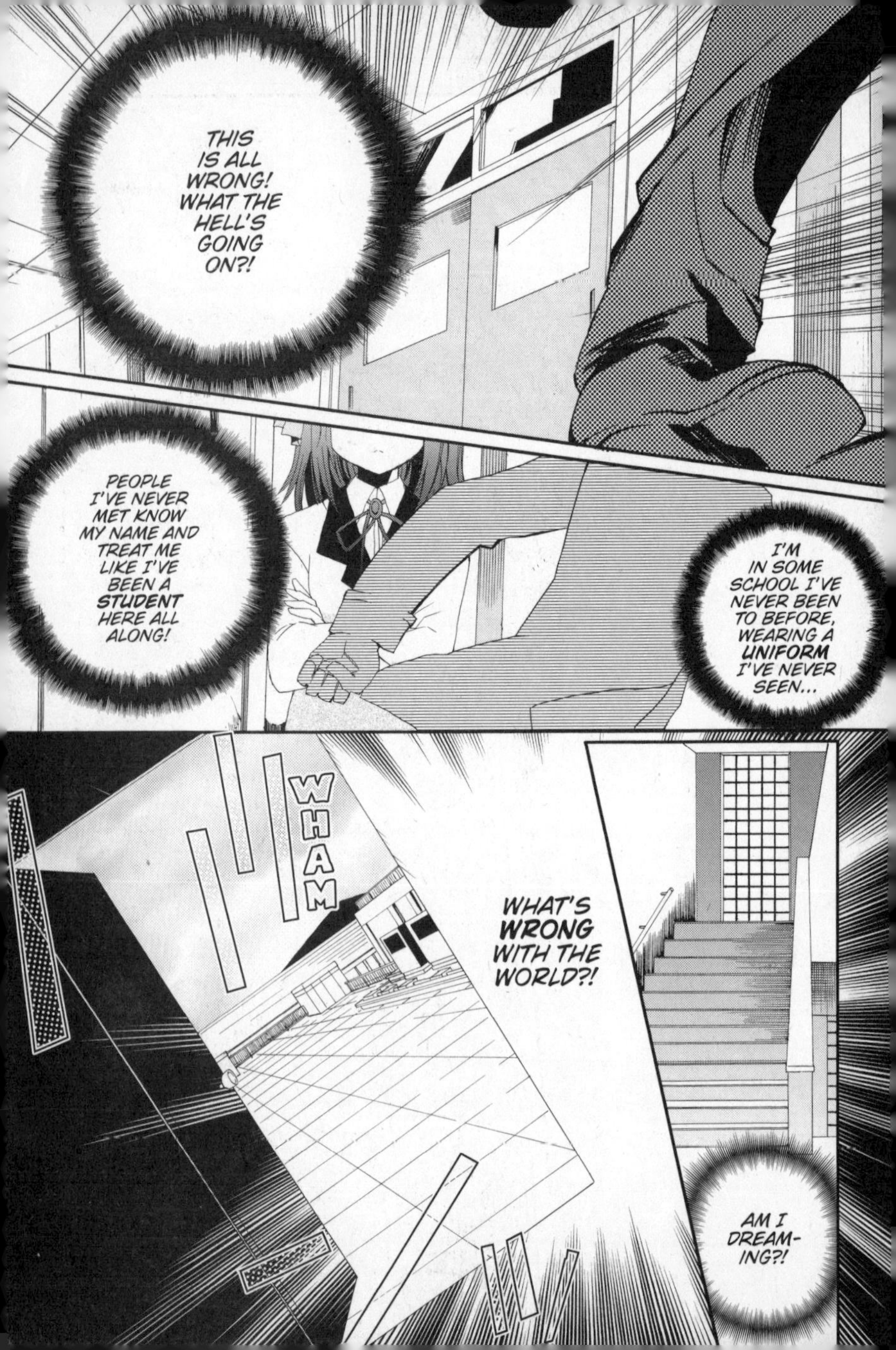
THIS IS ALL WRONG! WHAT THE HELL'S GOING ON?!
I'M IN SOME SCHOOL I'VE NEVER BEEN TO BEFORE, WEARING A **UNIFORM** I'VE NEVER SEEN...
PEOPLE I'VE NEVER MET KNOW MY NAME AND TREAT ME LIKE I'VE BEEN A **STUDENT** HERE ALL ALONG!
AM I DREAM-ING?!
WHAM
WHAT'S **WRONG** WITH THE WORLD?!

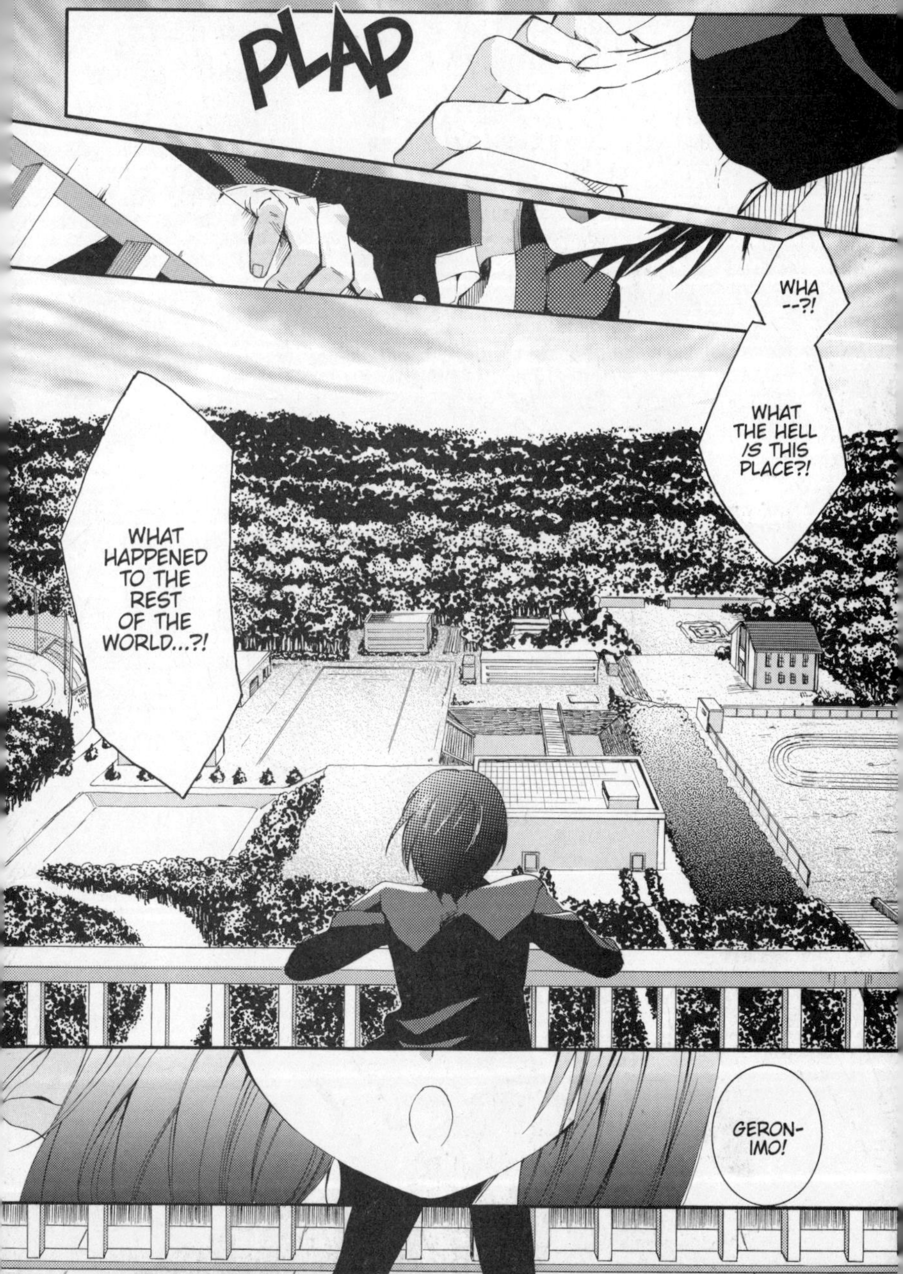
PLAP
WHA--?!
WHAT THE HELL *IS* THIS PLACE?!
WHAT HAPPENED TO THE REST OF THE WORLD...?!
GERON-IMO!

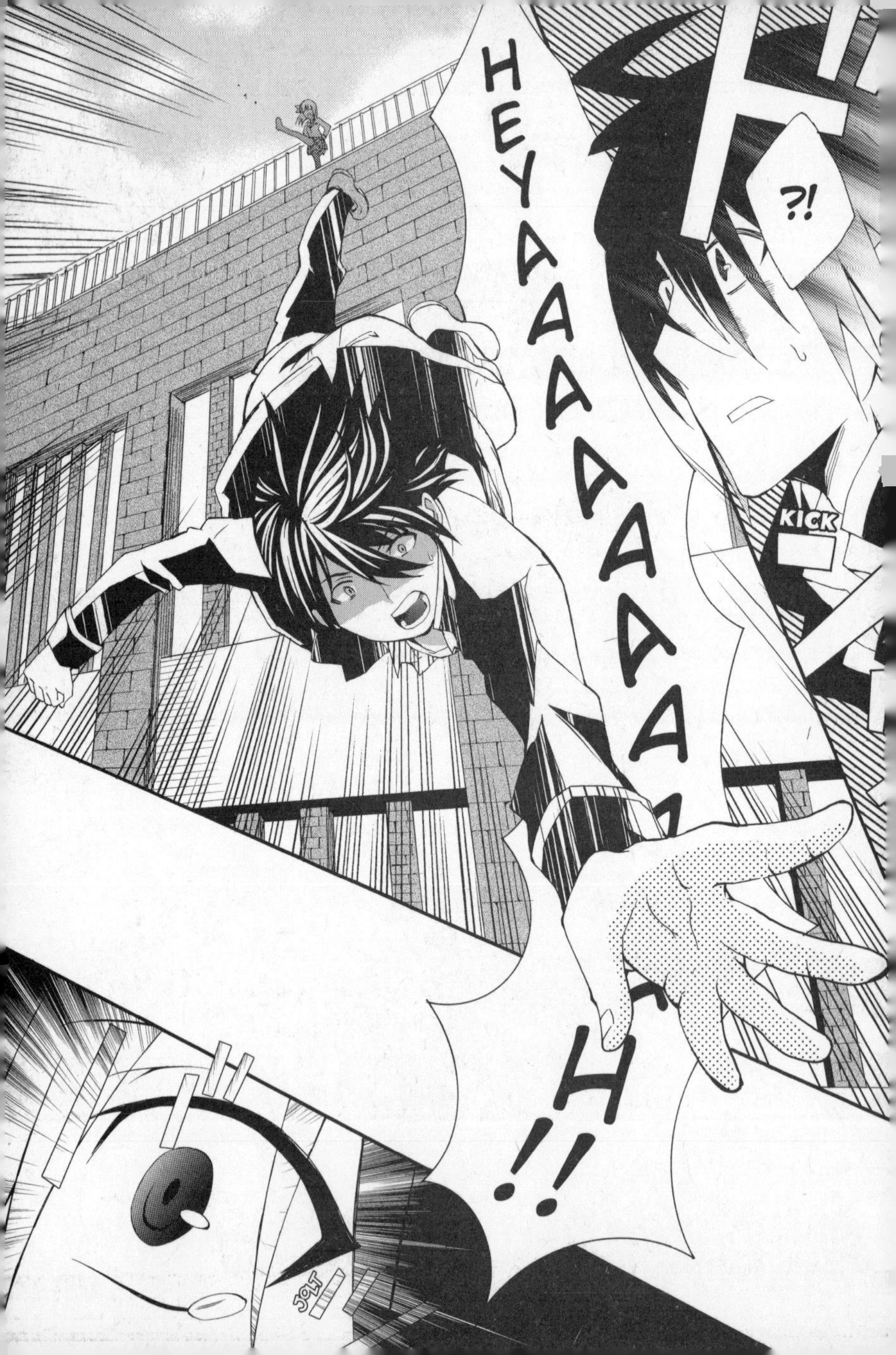
?!
HEYAAAAAAAAH!!
KICK
JOLT

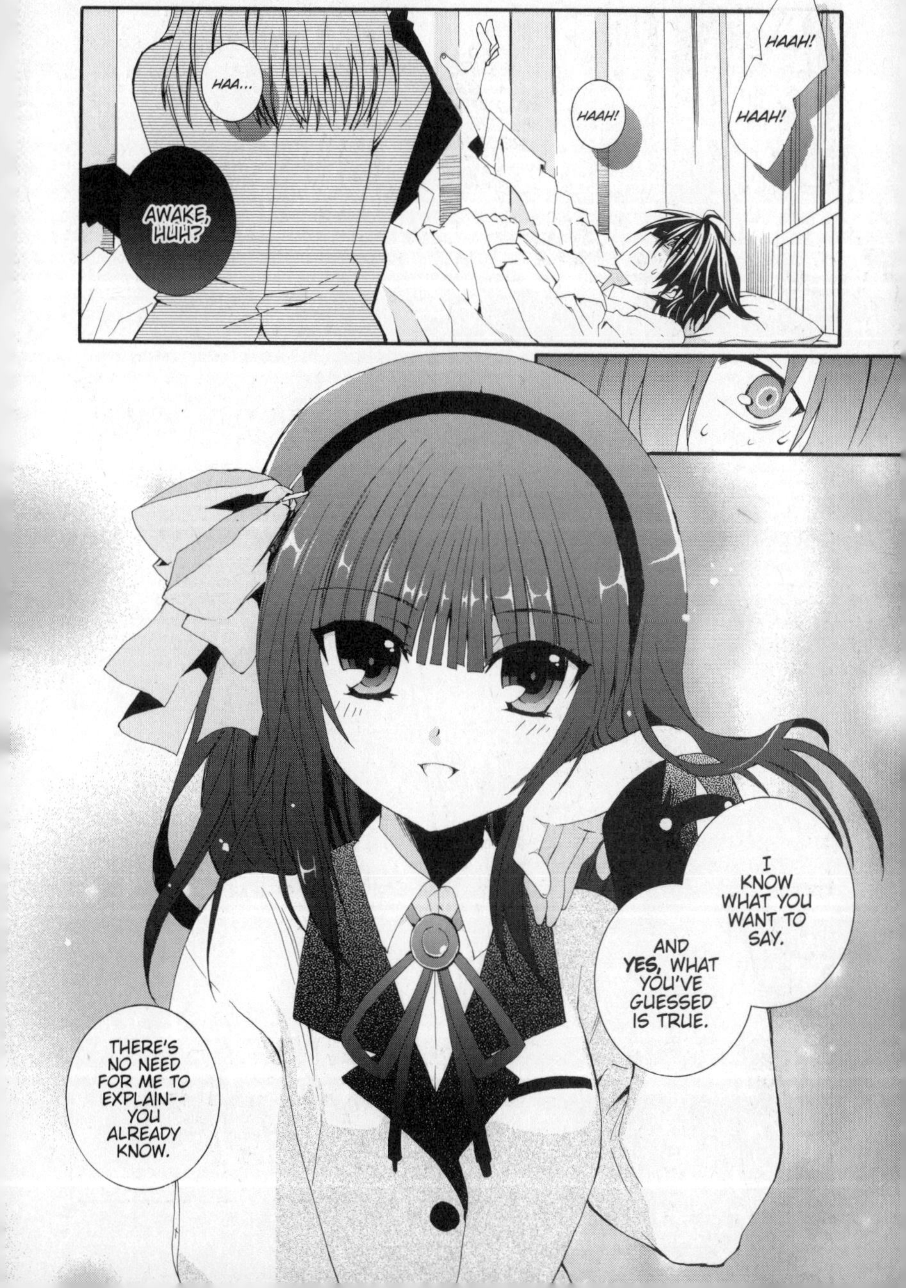
HAAH!
HAAH!
HAAH!
HAA...
AWAKE, HUH?
I KNOW WHAT YOU WANT TO SAY.
AND **YES,** WHAT YOU'VE GUESSED IS TRUE.
THERE'S NO NEED FOR ME TO EXPLAIN-- YOU ALREADY KNOW.

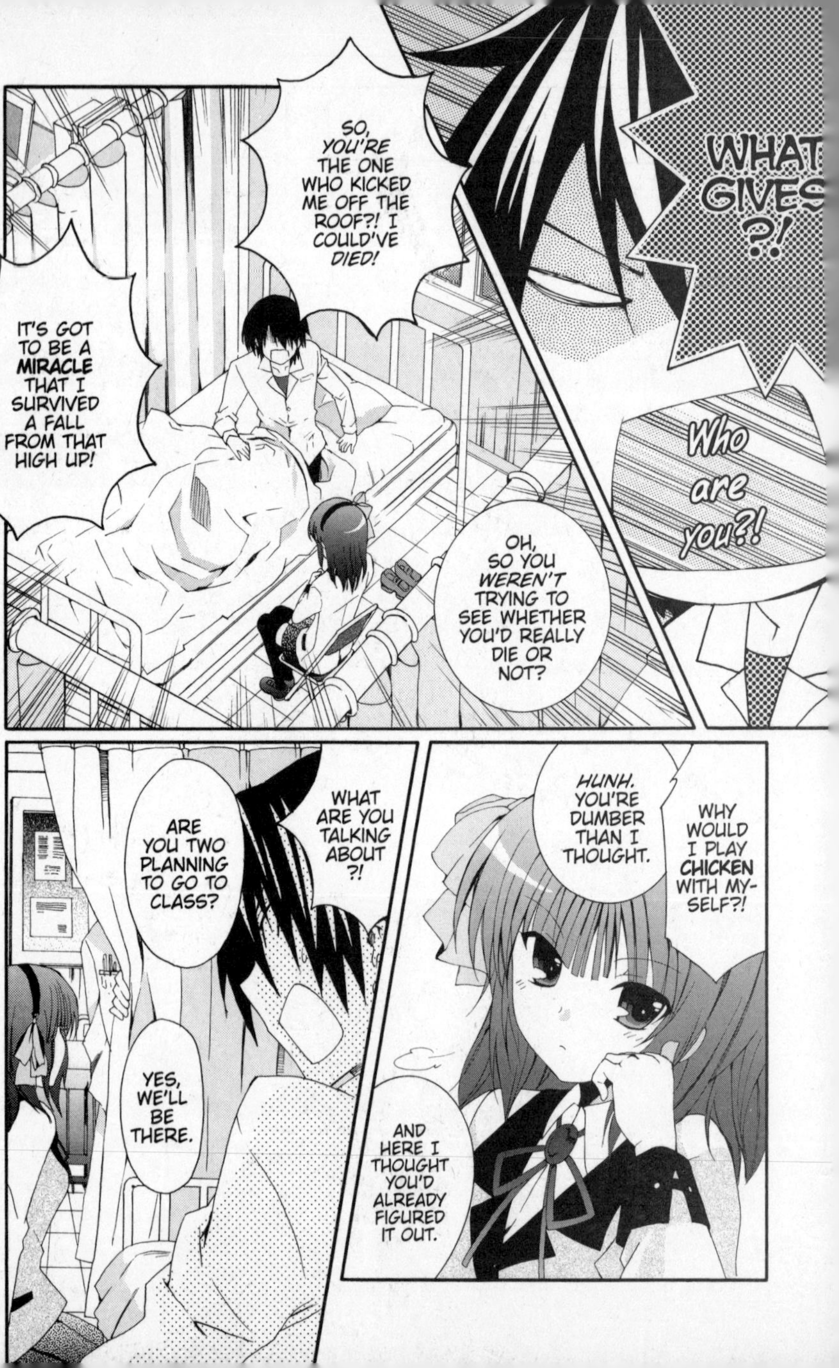
WHAT GIVES?!
Who are you?!
SO, YOU'RE THE ONE WHO KICKED ME OFF THE ROOF?! I COULD'VE DIED!
IT'S GOT TO BE A MIRACLE THAT I SURVIVED A FALL FROM THAT HIGH UP!
OH, SO YOU WEREN'T TRYING TO SEE WHETHER YOU'D REALLY DIE OR NOT?
HUNH. YOU'RE DUMBER THAN I THOUGHT.
WHY WOULD I PLAY CHICKEN WITH MY-SELF?!
AND HERE I THOUGHT YOU'D ALREADY FIGURED IT OUT.
WHAT ARE YOU TALKING ABOUT?!
ARE YOU TWO PLANNING TO GO TO CLASS?
YES, WE'LL BE THERE.

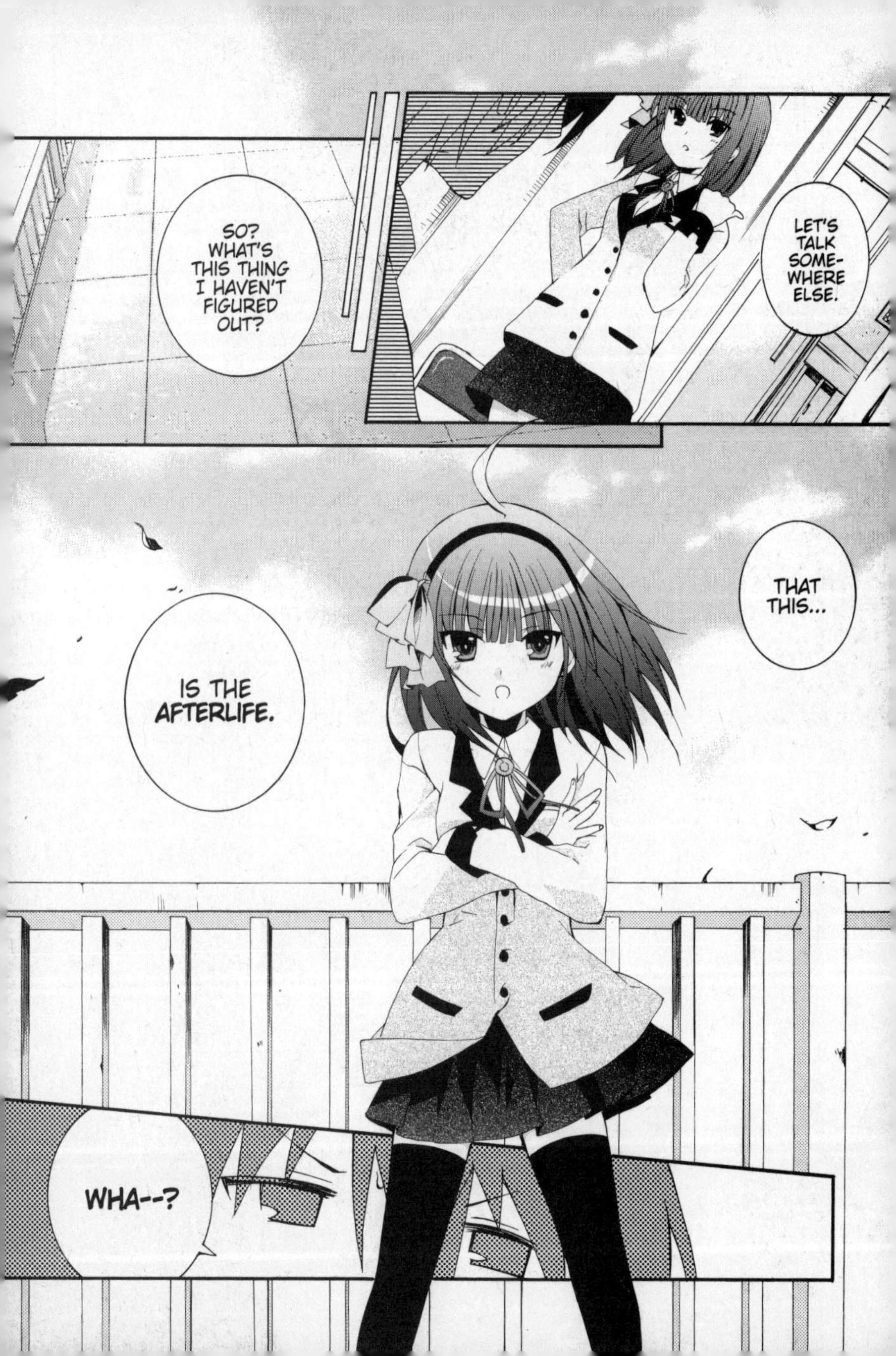
LET'S TALK SOME-WHERE ELSE.
SO? WHAT'S THIS THING I HAVEN'T FIGURED OUT?
THAT THIS...
IS THE AFTERLIFE.
WHA--?

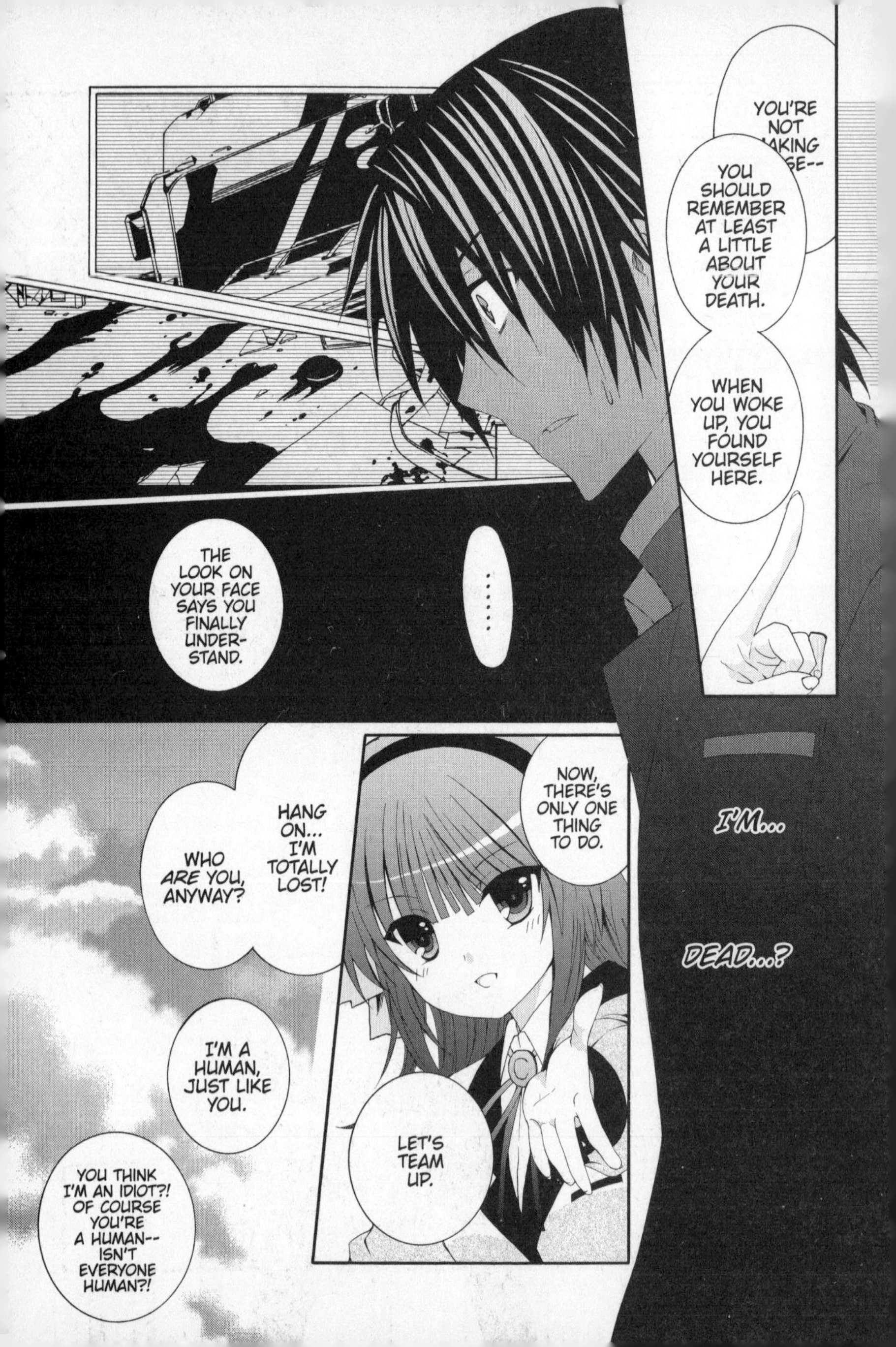
YOU'RE NOT
YOU SHOULD REMEMBER AT LEAST A LITTLE ABOUT YOUR DEATH.
WHEN YOU WOKE UP, YOU FOUND YOURSELF HERE.
......
THE LOOK ON YOUR FACE SAYS YOU FINALLY UNDERSTAND.
I'M...
DEAD...?
NOW, THERE'S ONLY ONE THING TO DO.
LET'S TEAM UP.
HANG ON... I'M TOTALLY LOST!
WHO *ARE* YOU, ANYWAY?
I'M A HUMAN, JUST LIKE YOU.
YOU THINK I'M AN IDIOT?! OF COURSE YOU'RE A HUMAN--ISN'T EVERYONE HUMAN?!

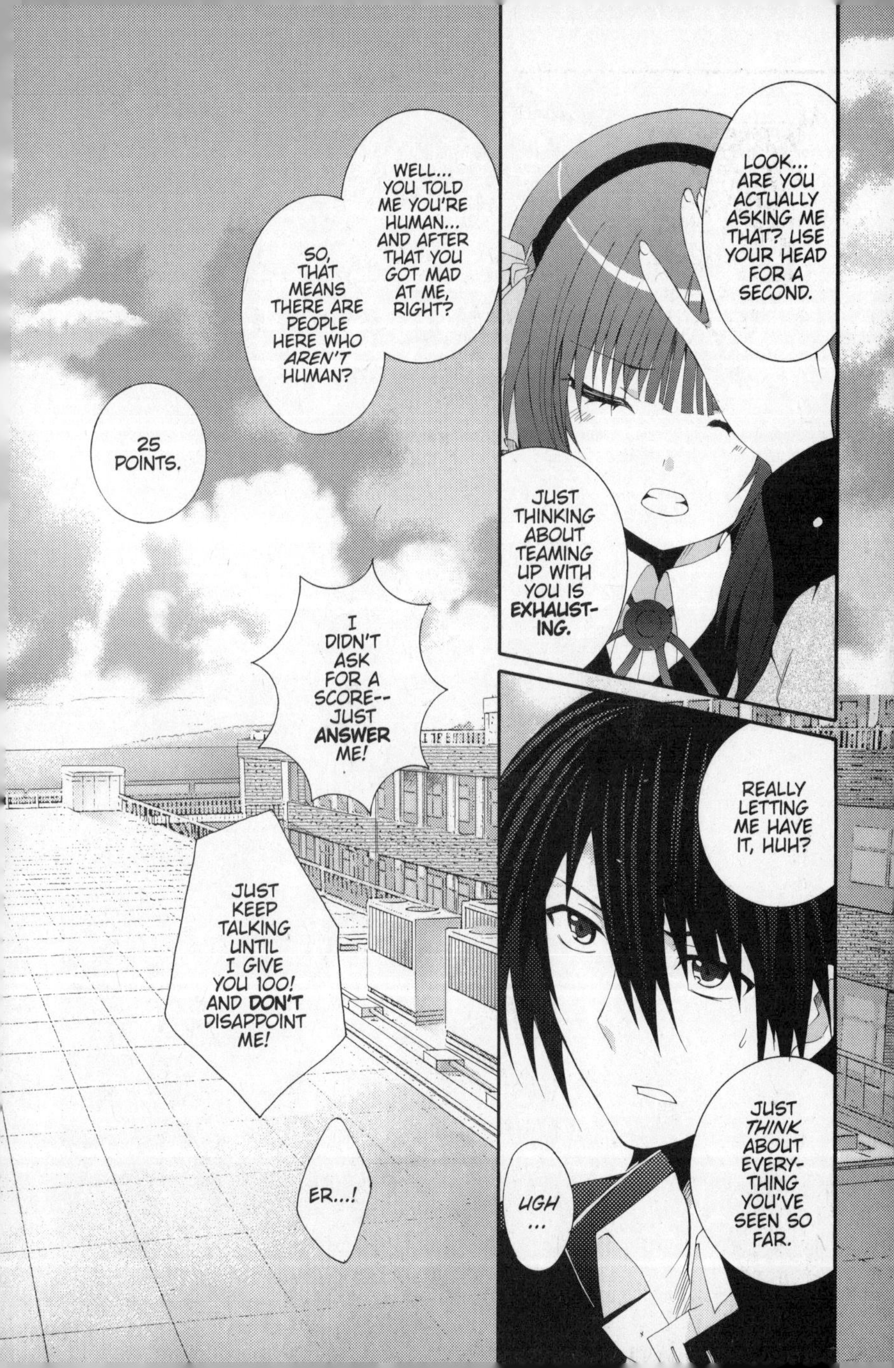
LOOK... ARE YOU ACTUALLY ASKING ME THAT? USE YOUR HEAD FOR A SECOND.
JUST THINKING ABOUT TEAMING UP WITH YOU IS **EXHAUSTING.**
REALLY LETTING ME HAVE IT, HUH?
JUST *THINK* ABOUT EVERYTHING YOU'VE SEEN SO FAR.
UGH ...
WELL... YOU TOLD ME YOU'RE HUMAN... AND AFTER THAT YOU GOT MAD AT ME, RIGHT?
SO, THAT MEANS THERE ARE PEOPLE HERE WHO *AREN'T* HUMAN?
25 POINTS.
I DIDN'T ASK FOR A SCORE-- JUST **ANSWER** ME!
JUST KEEP TALKING UNTIL I GIVE YOU 100! AND **DON'T** DISAPPOINT ME!
ER...!

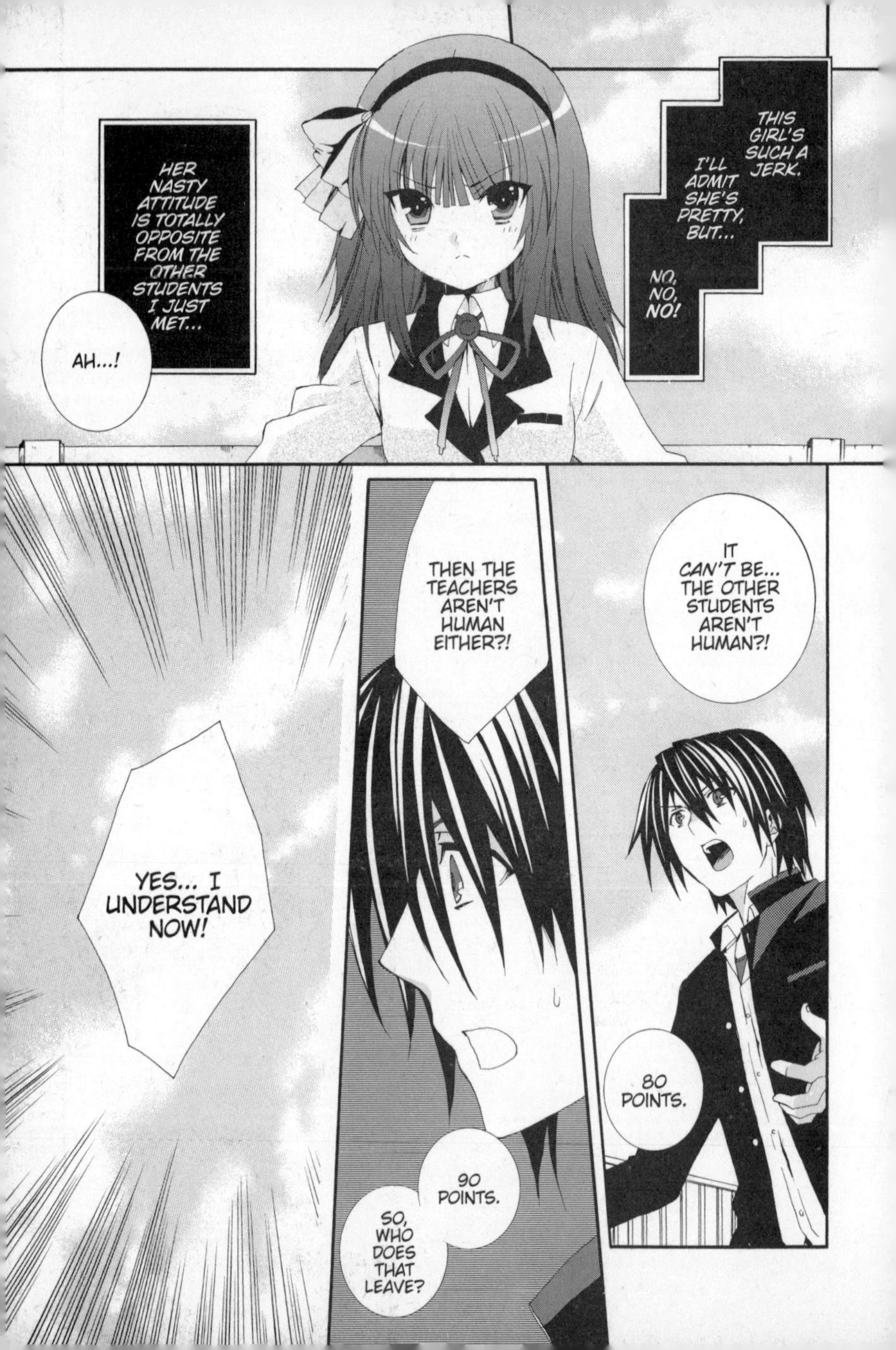
THIS GIRL'S SUCH A JERK.
I'LL ADMIT SHE'S PRETTY, BUT...
NO, NO, NO!
HER NASTY ATTITUDE IS TOTALLY OPPOSITE FROM THE OTHER STUDENTS I JUST MET...
AH...!
IT CAN'T BE... THE OTHER STUDENTS AREN'T HUMAN?!
80 POINTS.
THEN THE TEACHERS AREN'T HUMAN EITHER?!
90 POINTS.
SO, WHO DOES THAT LEAVE?
YES... I UNDERSTAND NOW!

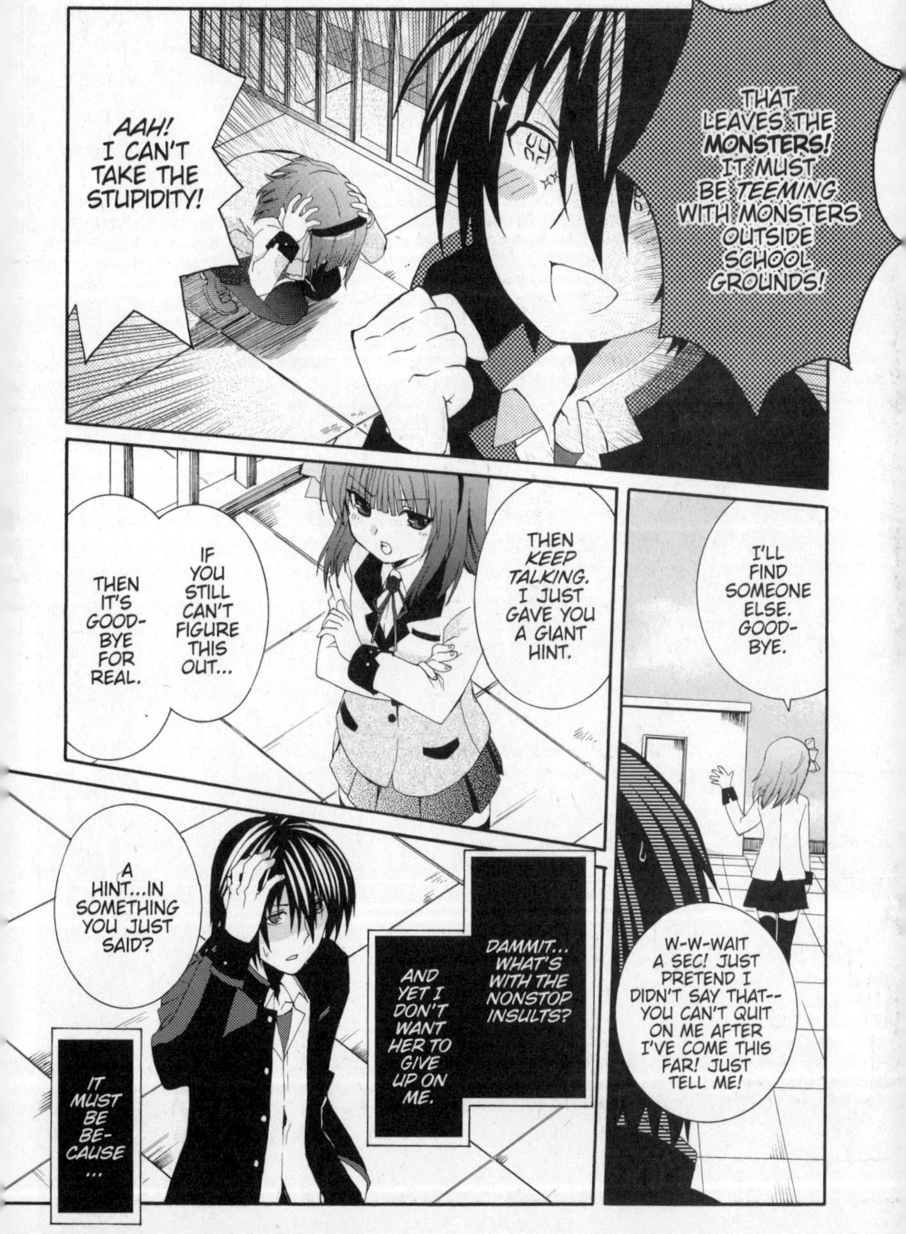
THAT LEAVES THE **MONSTERS!** IT MUST BE *TEEMING* WITH MONSTERS OUTSIDE SCHOOL GROUNDS!
AAH! I CAN'T TAKE THE STUPIDITY!
I'LL FIND SOMEONE ELSE. GOOD-BYE.
W-W-WAIT A SEC! JUST PRETEND I DIDN'T SAY THAT-- YOU CAN'T QUIT ON ME AFTER I'VE COME THIS FAR! JUST TELL ME!
THEN *KEEP TALKING*. I JUST GAVE YOU A GIANT HINT.
IF YOU STILL CAN'T FIGURE THIS OUT...
THEN IT'S GOOD-BYE FOR REAL.
DAMMIT... WHAT'S WITH THE NONSTOP INSULTS?
AND YET I DON'T WANT HER TO GIVE UP ON ME.
A HINT...IN SOMETHING YOU JUST SAID?
IT MUST BE BE-CAUSE...

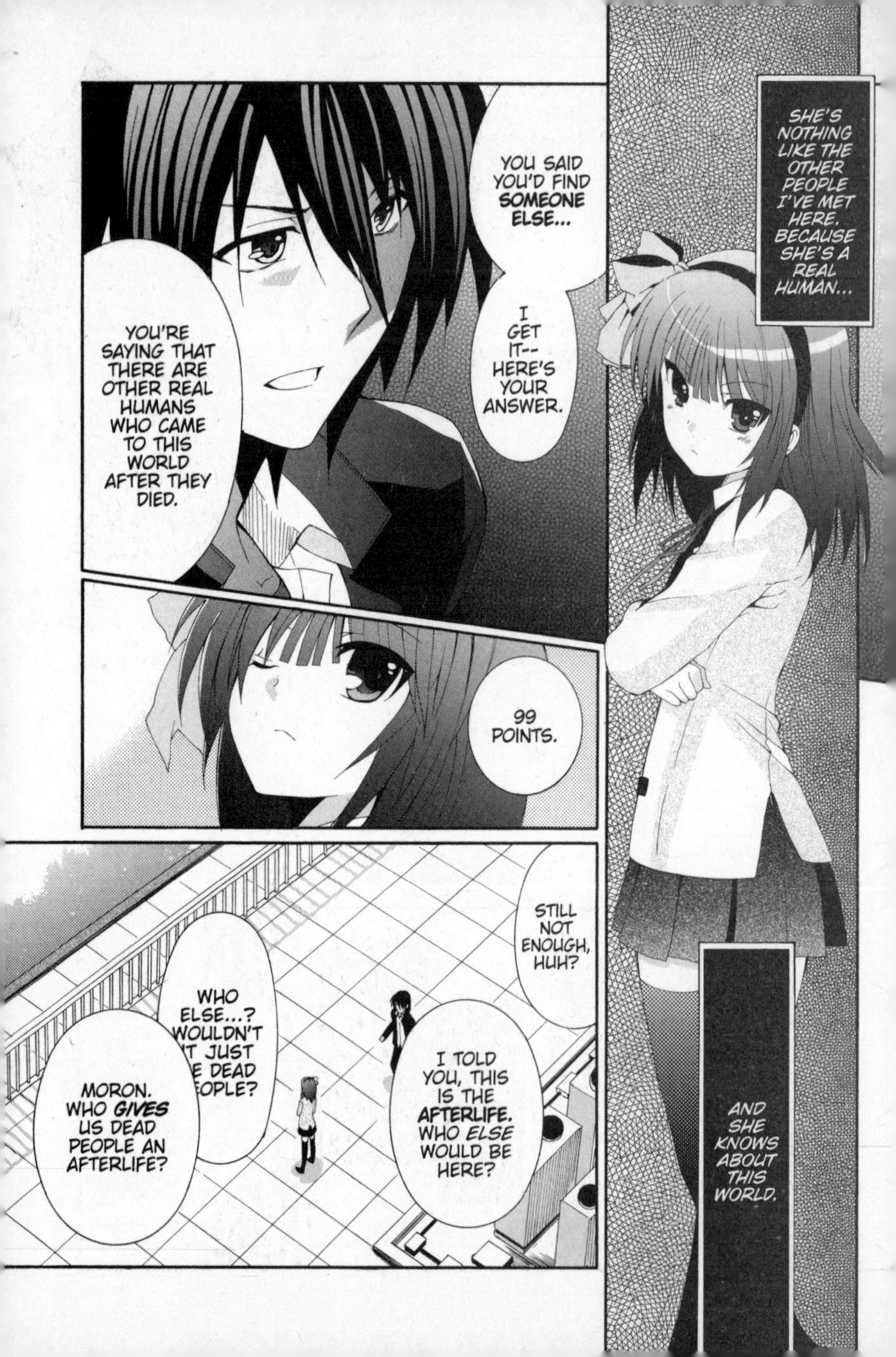
SHE'S NOTHING LIKE THE OTHER PEOPLE I'VE MET HERE. BECAUSE SHE'S A REAL HUMAN...
AND SHE KNOWS ABOUT THIS WORLD.
YOU SAID YOU'D FIND **SOMEONE ELSE...**
I GET IT-- HERE'S YOUR ANSWER.
YOU'RE SAYING THAT THERE ARE OTHER REAL HUMANS WHO CAME TO THIS WORLD AFTER THEY DIED.
99 POINTS.
STILL NOT ENOUGH, HUH?
I TOLD YOU, THIS IS THE **AFTERLIFE.** WHO *ELSE* WOULD BE HERE?
WHO ELSE...? WOULDN'T IT JUST E DEAD EOPLE?
MORON. WHO ***GIVES*** US DEAD PEOPLE AN AFTERLIFE?

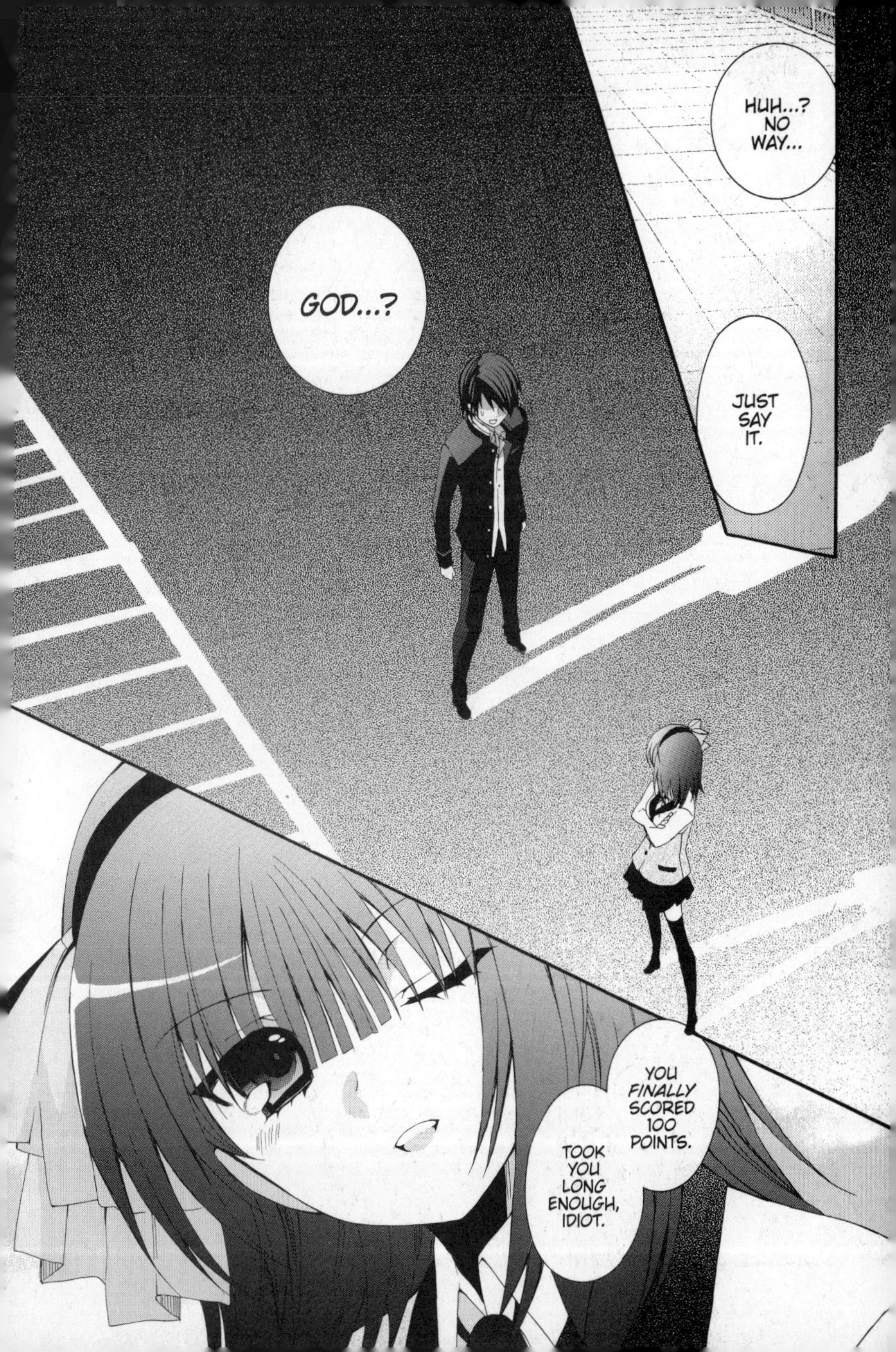
HUH...? NO WAY...
JUST SAY IT.
GOD...?
YOU FINALLY SCORED 100 POINTS.
TOOK YOU LONG ENOUGH, IDIOT.

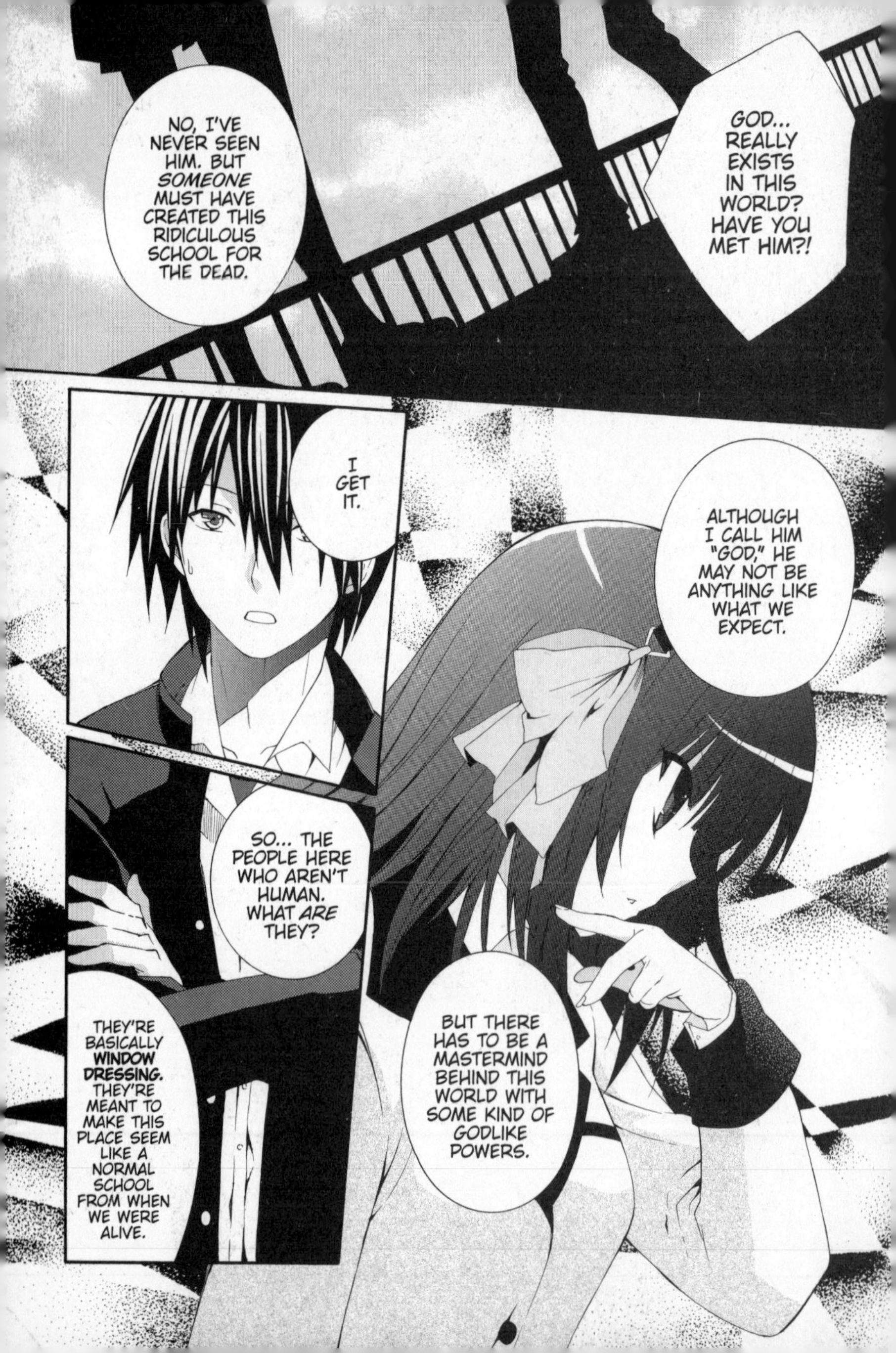

GOD... REALLY EXISTS IN THIS WORLD? HAVE YOU MET HIM?!
NO, I'VE NEVER SEEN HIM. BUT *SOMEONE* MUST HAVE CREATED THIS RIDICULOUS SCHOOL FOR THE DEAD.
ALTHOUGH I CALL HIM "GOD," HE MAY NOT BE ANYTHING LIKE WHAT WE EXPECT.
BUT THERE HAS TO BE A MASTERMIND BEHIND THIS WORLD WITH SOME KIND OF GODLIKE POWERS.
I GET IT.
SO... THE PEOPLE HERE WHO AREN'T HUMAN. WHAT *ARE* THEY?
THEY'RE BASICALLY **WINDOW DRESSING.** THEY'RE MEANT TO MAKE THIS PLACE SEEM LIKE A NORMAL SCHOOL FROM WHEN WE WERE ALIVE.

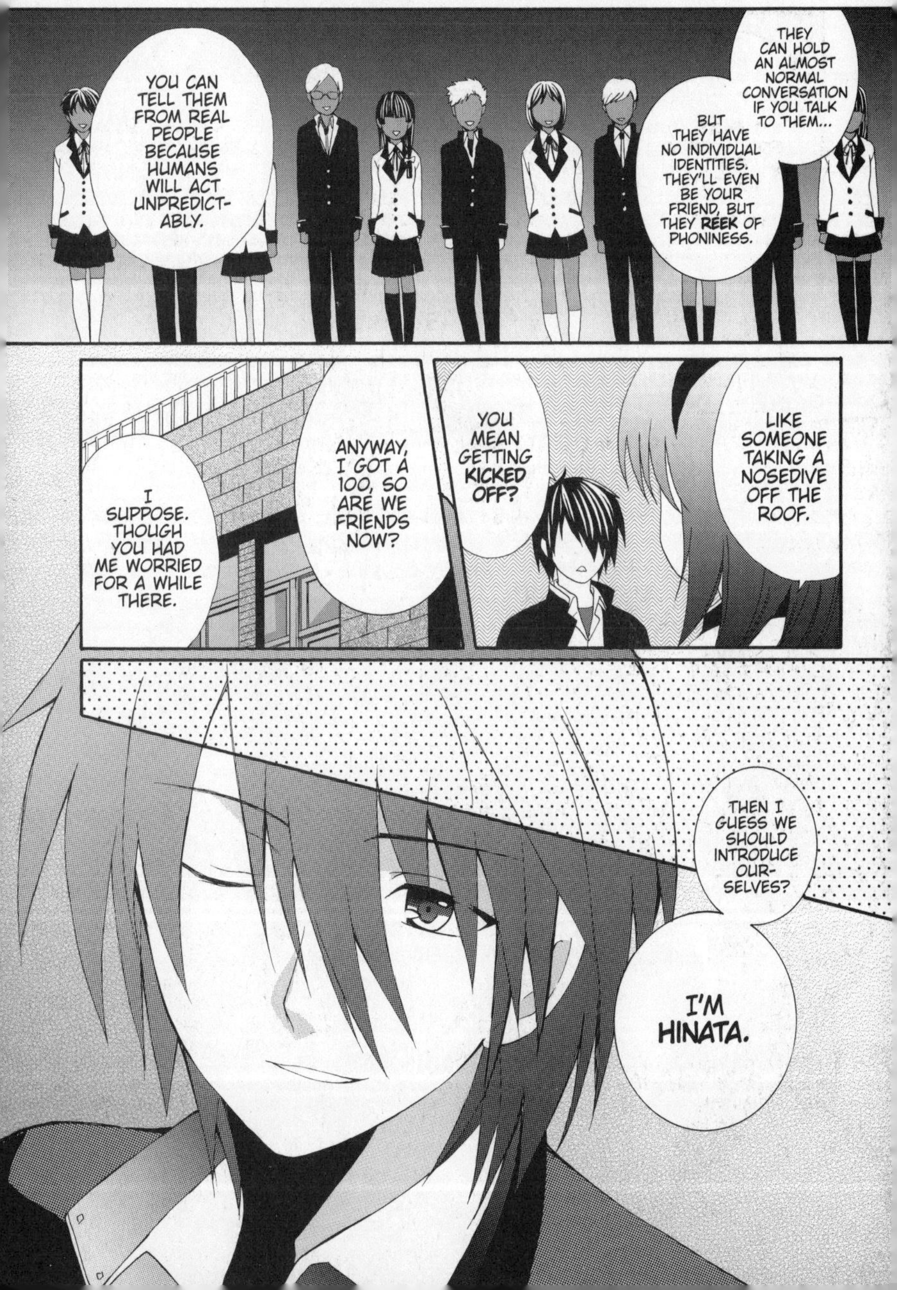
THEY CAN HOLD AN ALMOST NORMAL CONVERSATION IF YOU TALK TO THEM...
BUT THEY HAVE NO INDIVIDUAL IDENTITIES. THEY'LL EVEN BE YOUR FRIEND, BUT THEY **REEK** OF PHONINESS.
YOU CAN TELL THEM FROM REAL PEOPLE BECAUSE HUMANS WILL ACT UNPREDICT-ABLY.
LIKE SOMEONE TAKING A NOSEDIVE OFF THE ROOF.
YOU MEAN GETTING **KICKED** OFF?
ANYWAY, I GOT A 100, SO ARE WE FRIENDS NOW?
I SUPPOSE. THOUGH YOU HAD ME WORRIED FOR A WHILE THERE.
THEN I GUESS WE SHOULD INTRODUCE OUR-SELVES?
I'M **HINATA.**

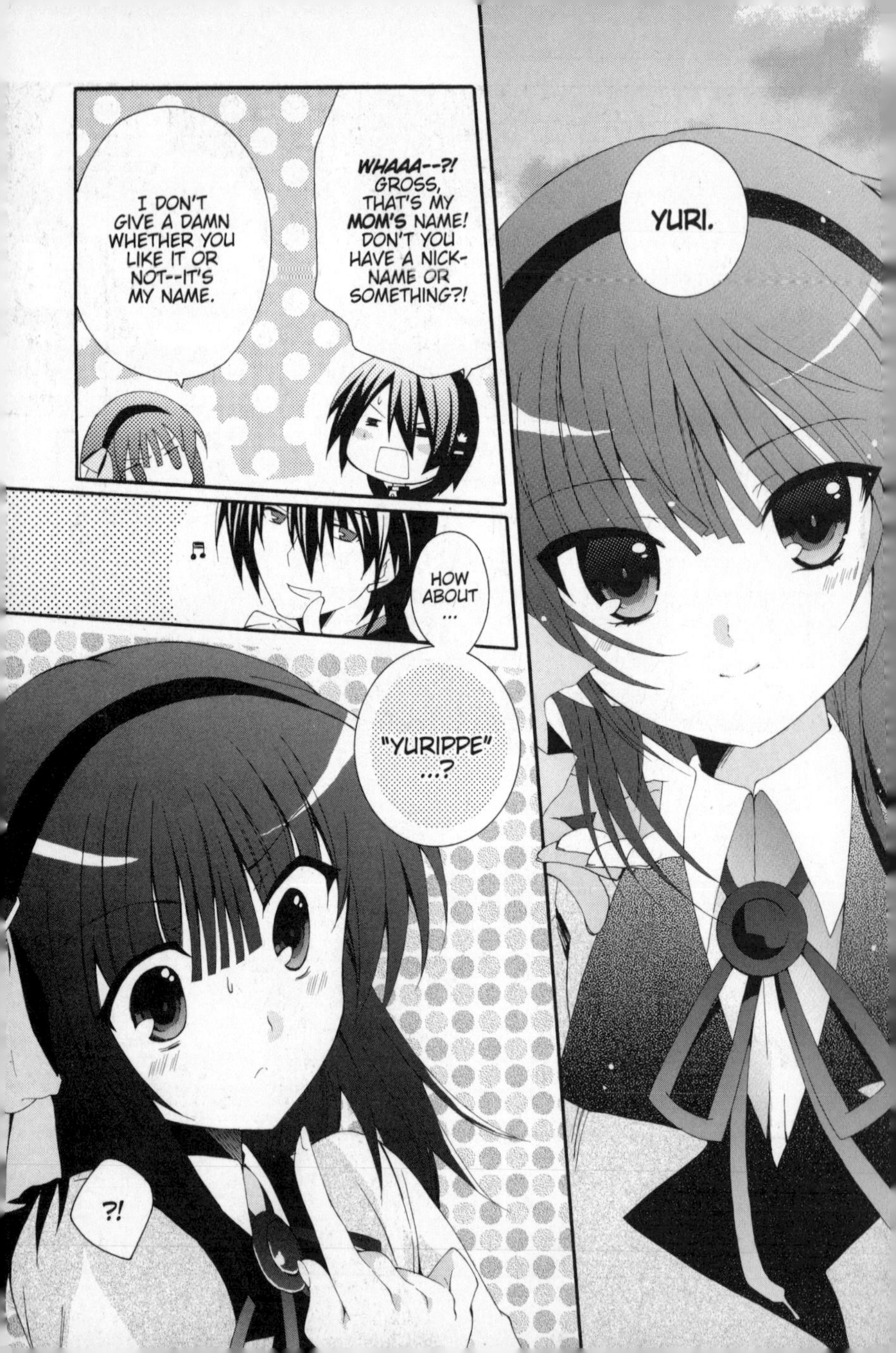
YURI.
WHAAA--?! GROSS, THAT'S MY MOM'S NAME! DON'T YOU HAVE A NICK-NAME OR SOMETHING?!
I DON'T GIVE A DAMN WHETHER YOU LIKE IT OR NOT--IT'S MY NAME.
HOW ABOUT ...
"YURIPPE" ...?
?!

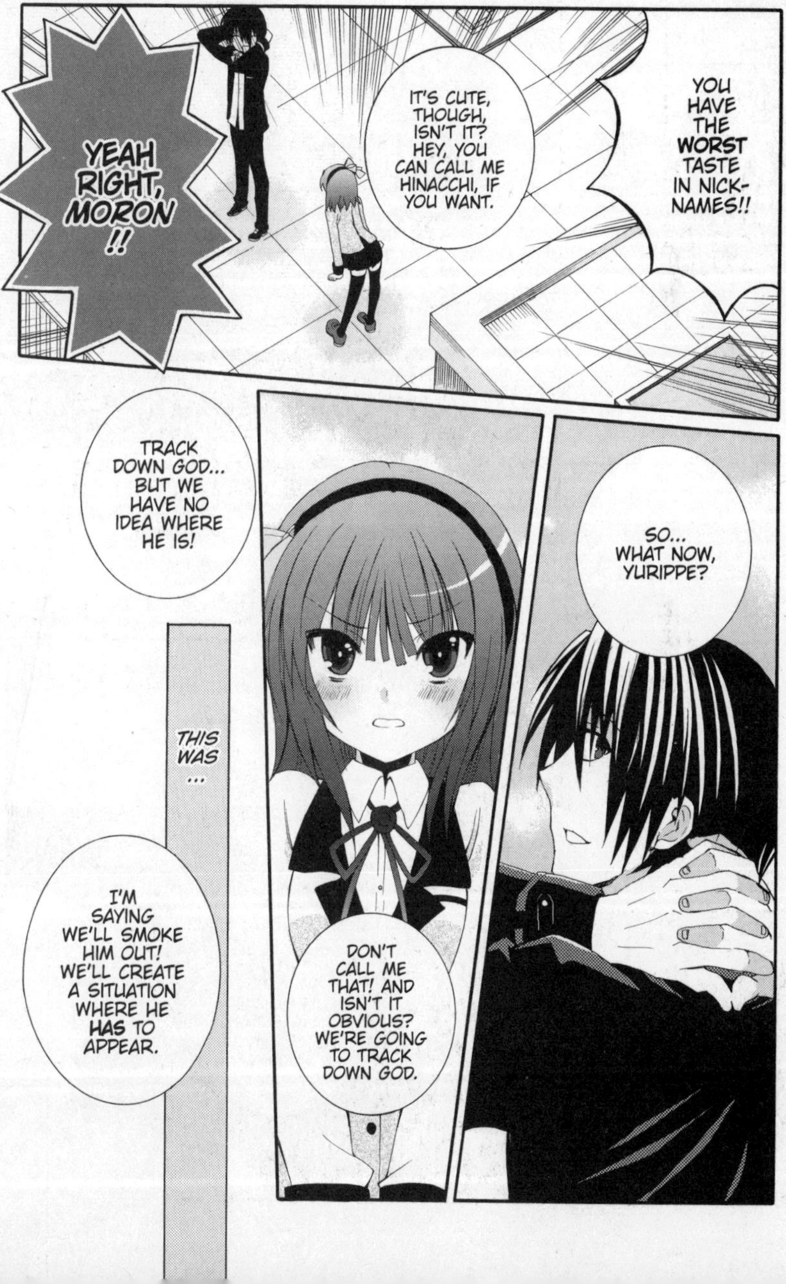
YOU HAVE THE WORST TASTE IN NICK-NAMES!!
IT'S CUTE, THOUGH, ISN'T IT? HEY, YOU CAN CALL ME HINACCHI, IF YOU WANT.
YEAH RIGHT, MORON!!
SO... WHAT NOW, YURIPPE?
DON'T CALL ME THAT! AND ISN'T IT OBVIOUS? WE'RE GOING TO TRACK DOWN GOD.
TRACK DOWN GOD... BUT WE HAVE NO IDEA WHERE HE IS!
THIS WAS ...
I'M SAYING WE'LL SMOKE HIM OUT! WE'LL CREATE A SITUATION WHERE HE HAS TO APPEAR.

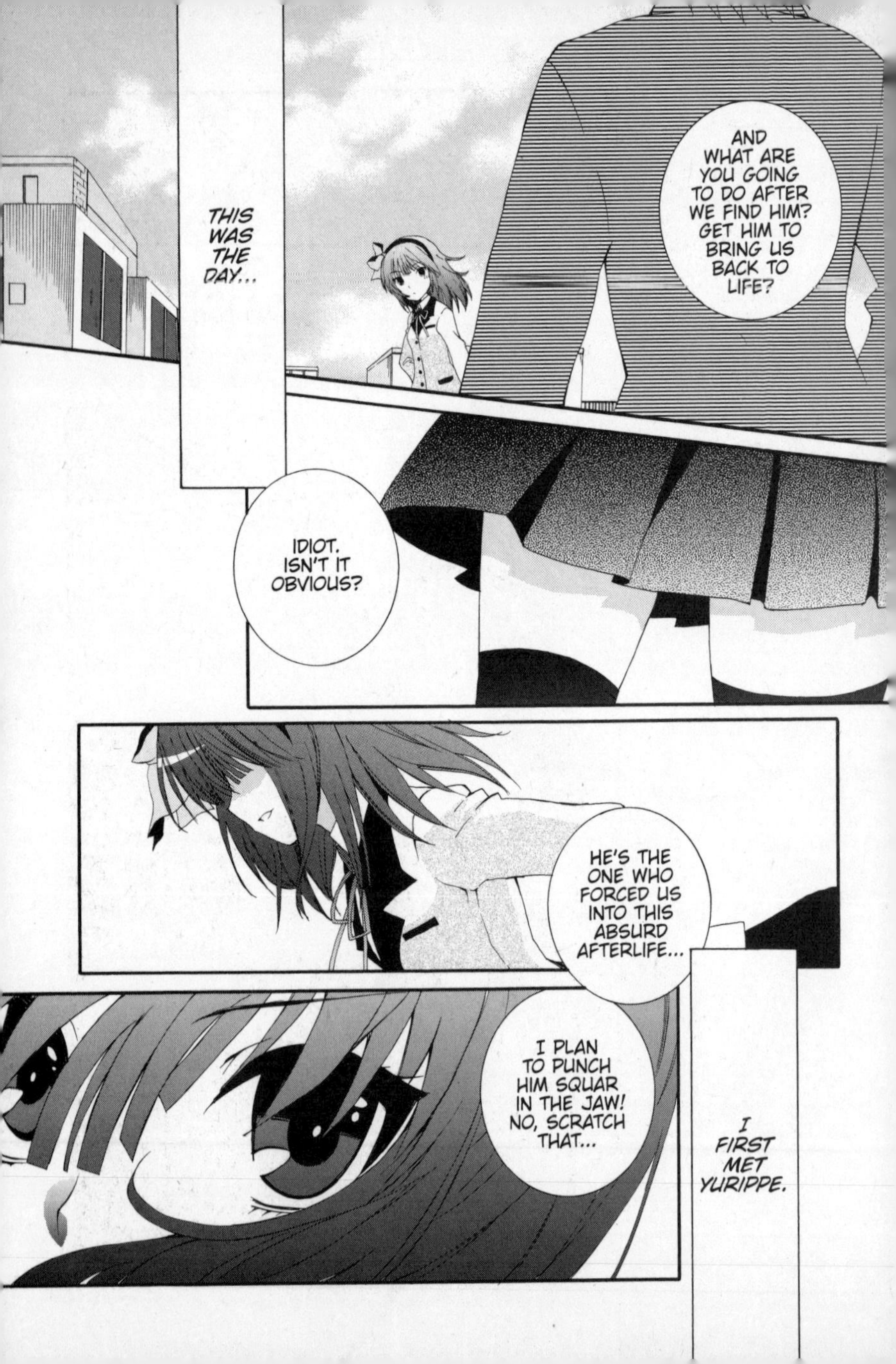
AND WHAT ARE YOU GOING TO DO AFTER WE FIND HIM? GET HIM TO BRING US BACK TO LIFE?
THIS WAS THE DAY...
IDIOT. ISN'T IT OBVIOUS?
HE'S THE ONE WHO FORCED US INTO THIS ABSURD AFTERLIFE...
I FIRST MET YURIPPE.
I PLAN TO PUNCH HIM SQUAR IN THE JAW! NO, SCRATCH THAT...

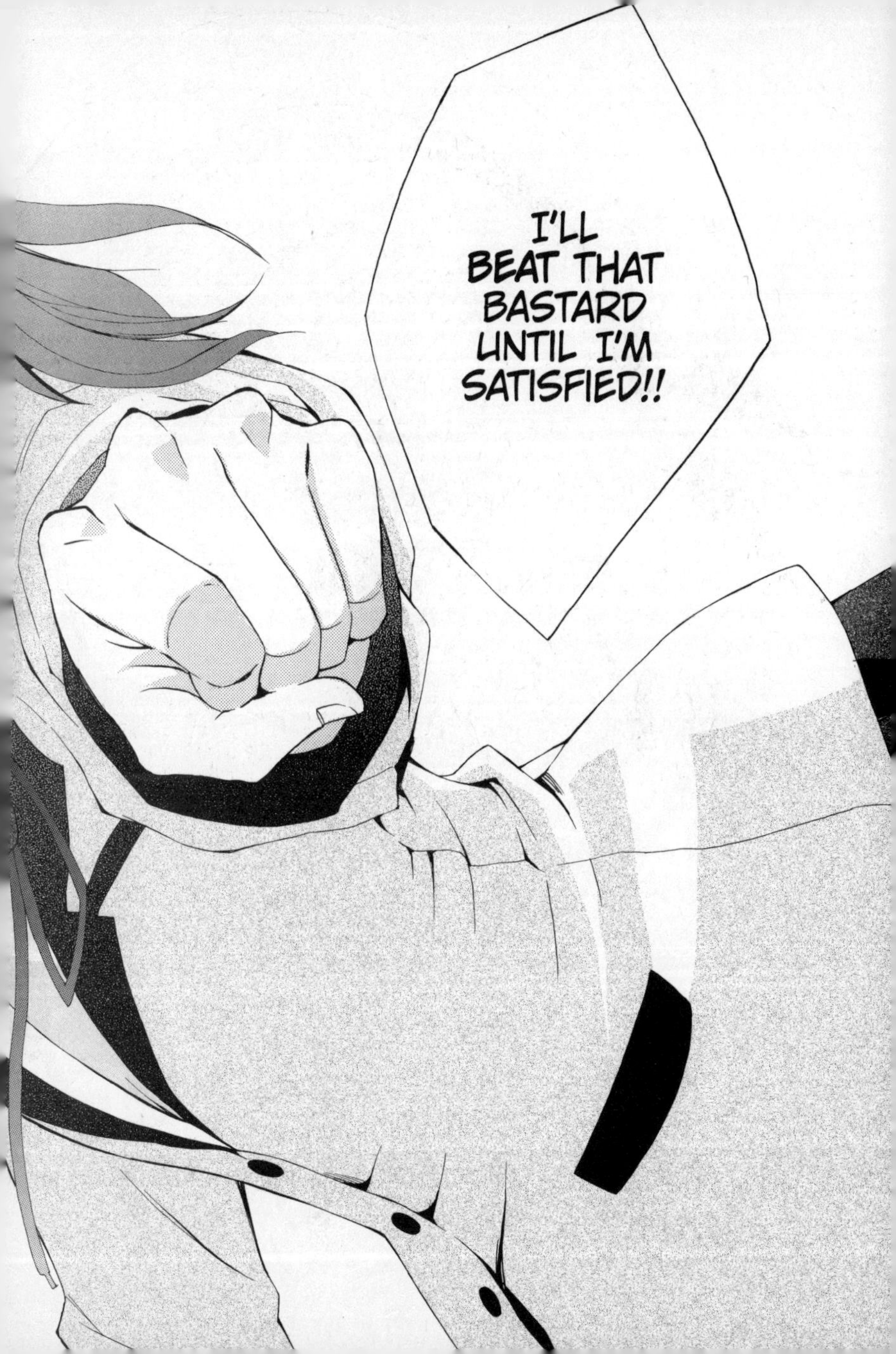
I'LL BEAT THAT BASTARD UNTIL I'M SATISFIED!!

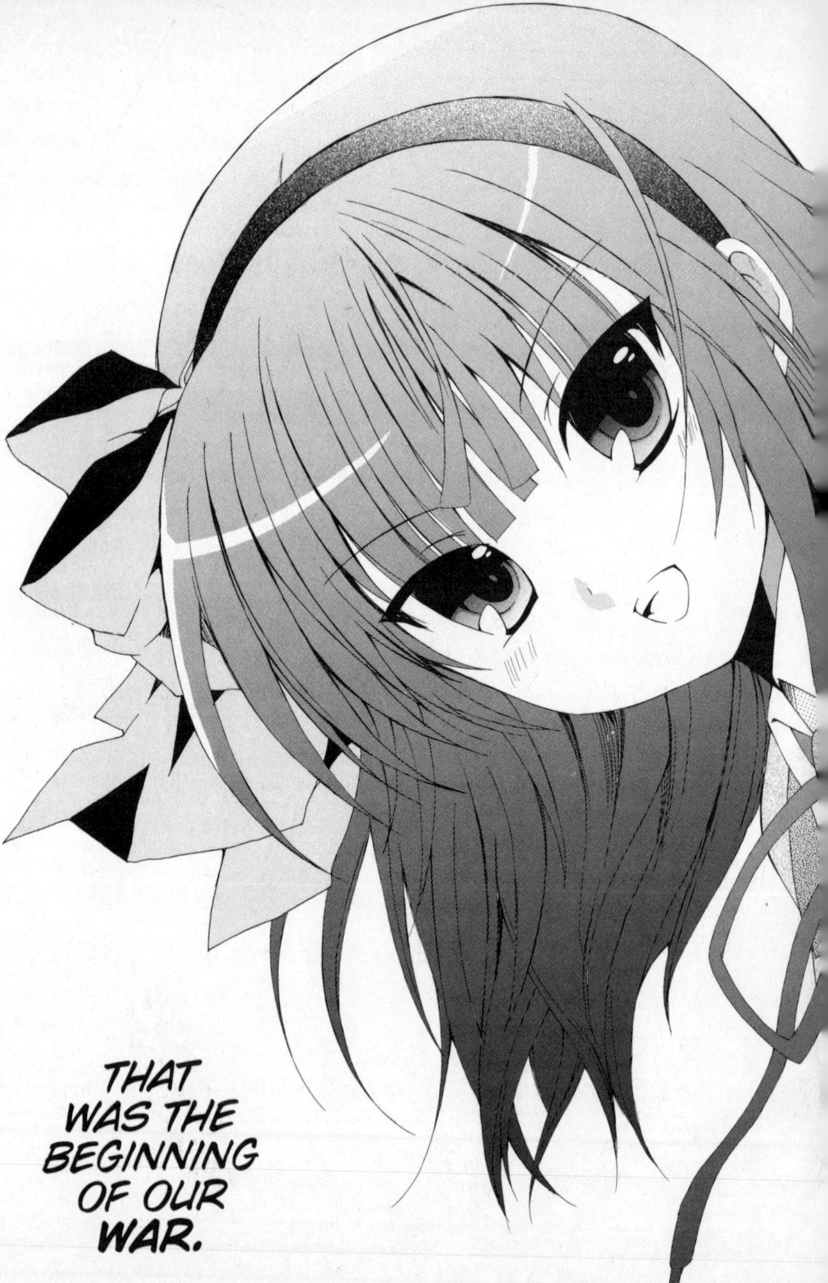
THAT WAS THE BEGINNING OF OUR WAR.

Angel Beats!
Heaven's Door

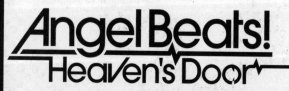

#02

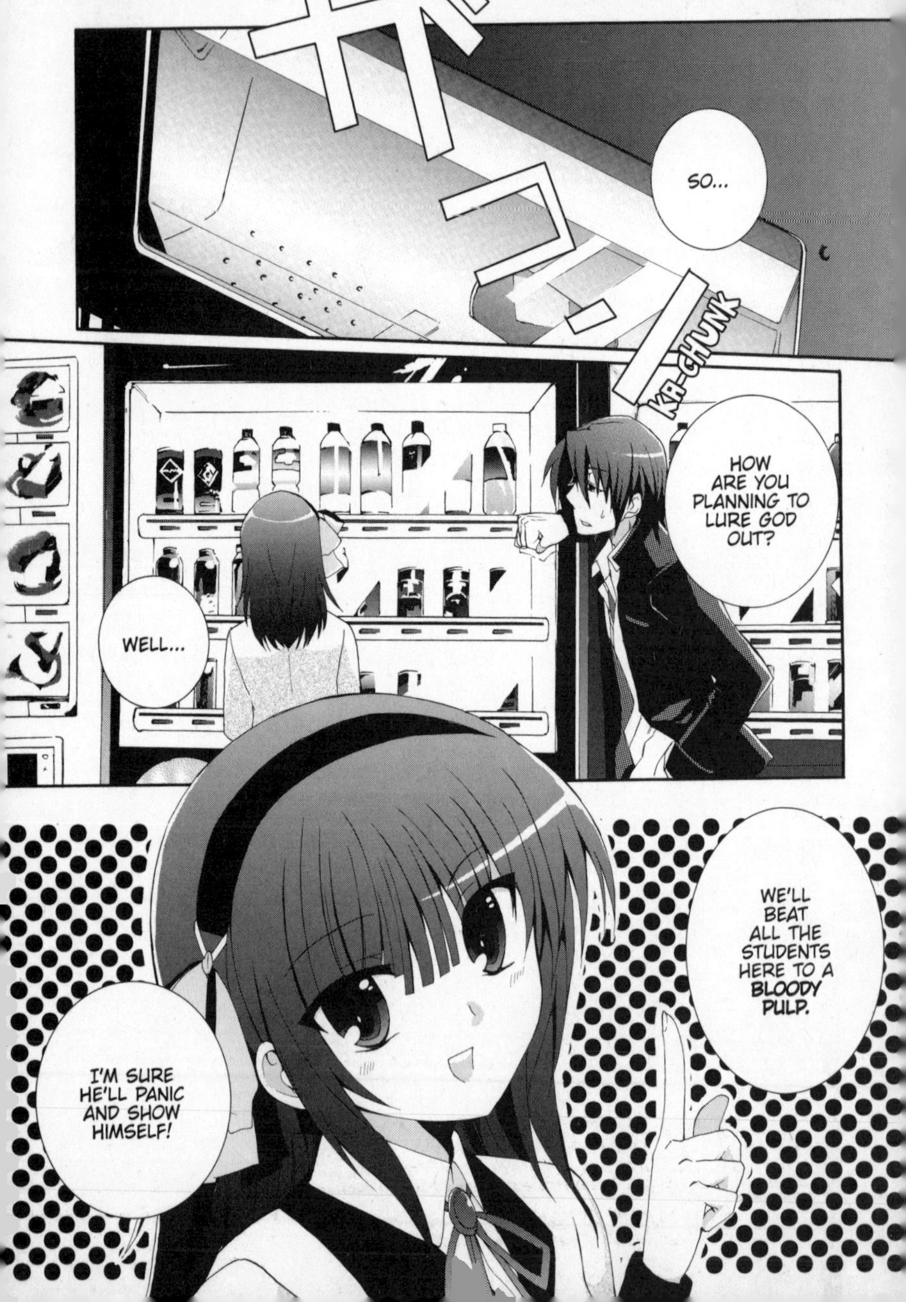
SO...
KA-CHUNK
HOW ARE YOU PLANNING TO LURE GOD OUT?
WELL...
WE'LL BEAT ALL THE STUDENTS HERE TO A **BLOODY PULP.**
I'M SURE HE'LL PANIC AND SHOW HIMSELF!

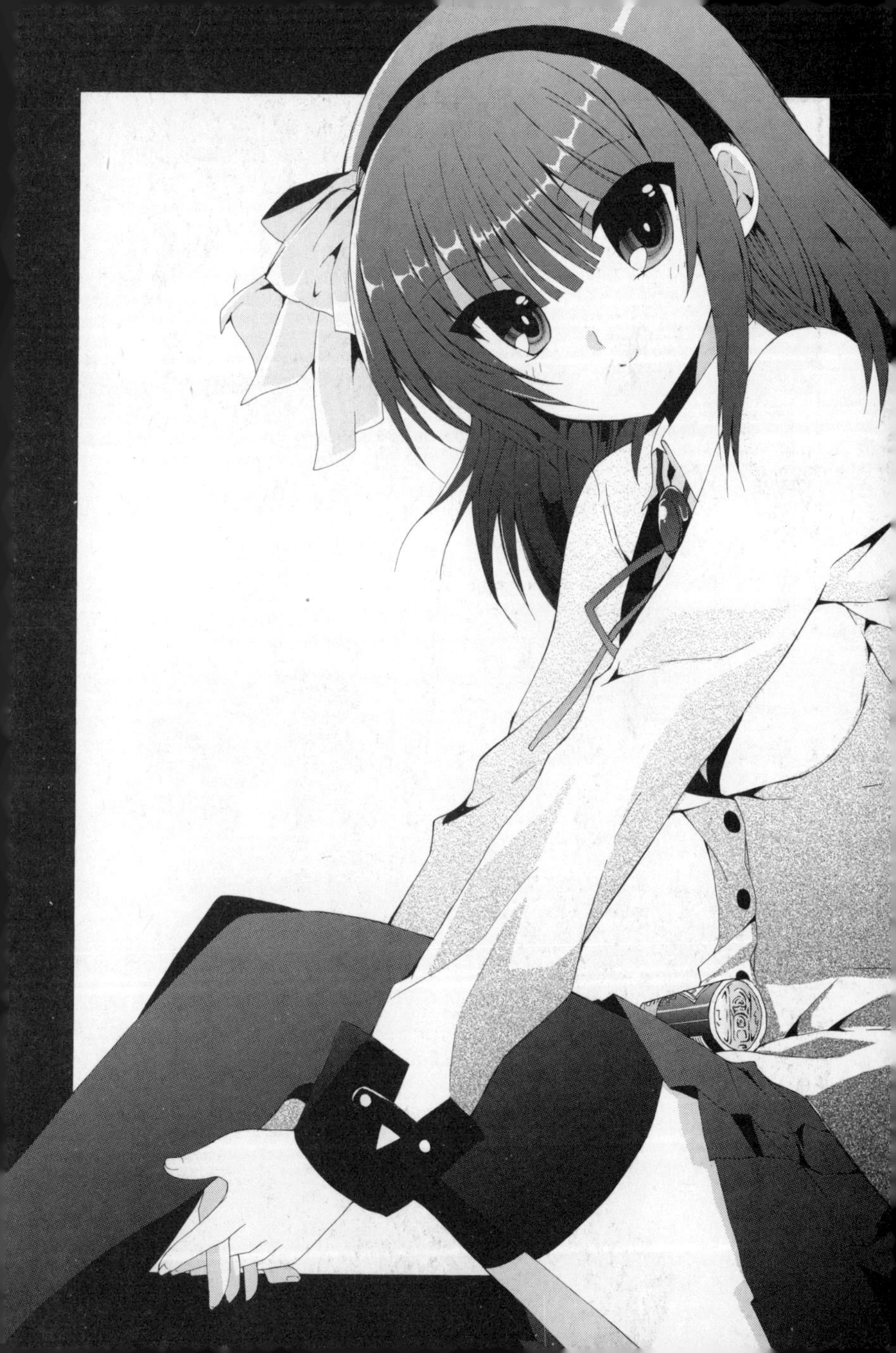

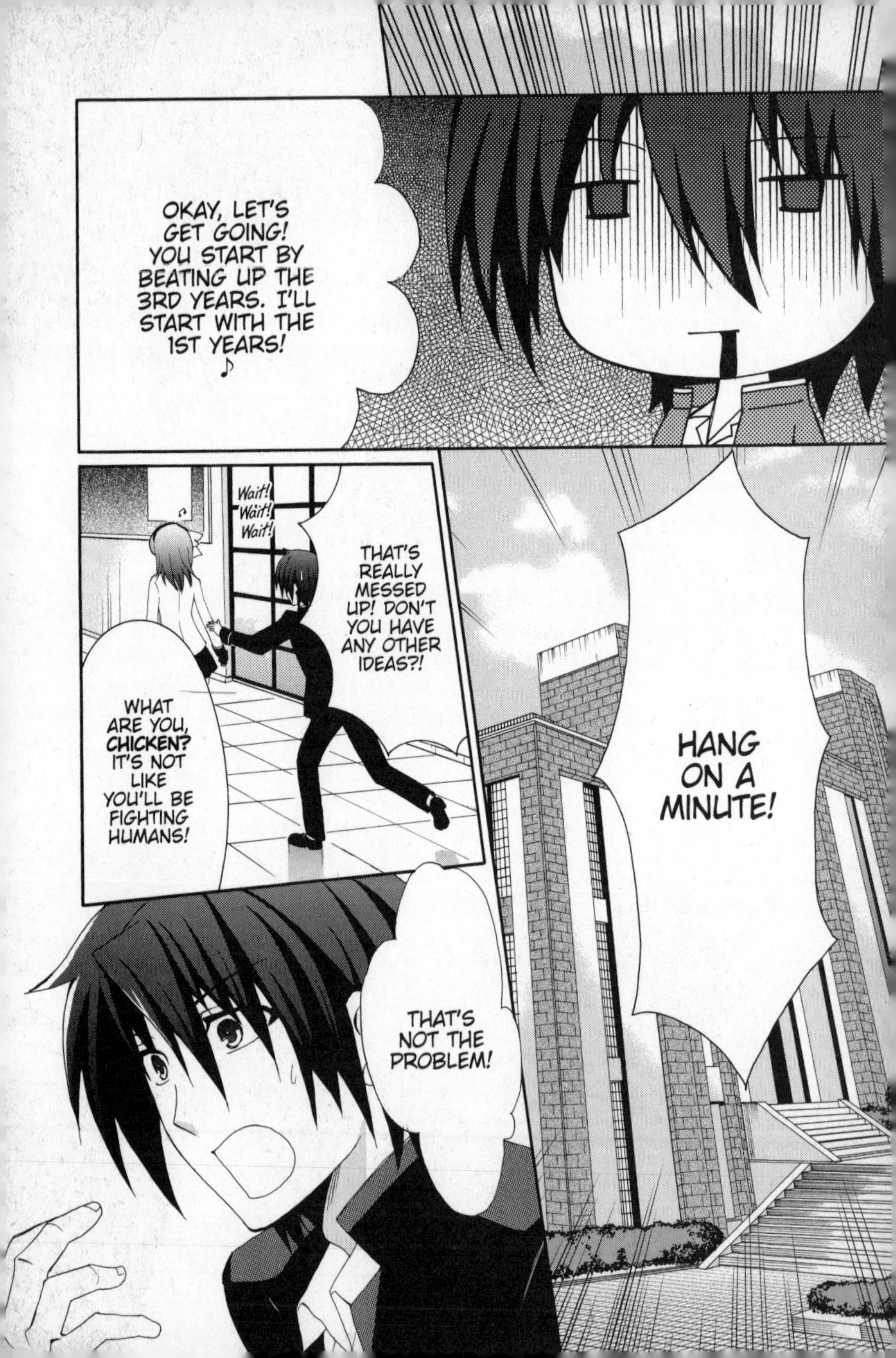
OKAY, LET'S GET GOING! YOU START BY BEATING UP THE 3RD YEARS. I'LL START WITH THE 1ST YEARS! ♪
HANG ON A MINUTE!
Wait! Wait! Wait!
THAT'S REALLY MESSED UP! DON'T YOU HAVE ANY OTHER IDEAS?!
WHAT ARE YOU, **CHICKEN?** IT'S NOT LIKE YOU'LL BE FIGHTING HUMANS!
THAT'S NOT THE PROBLEM!

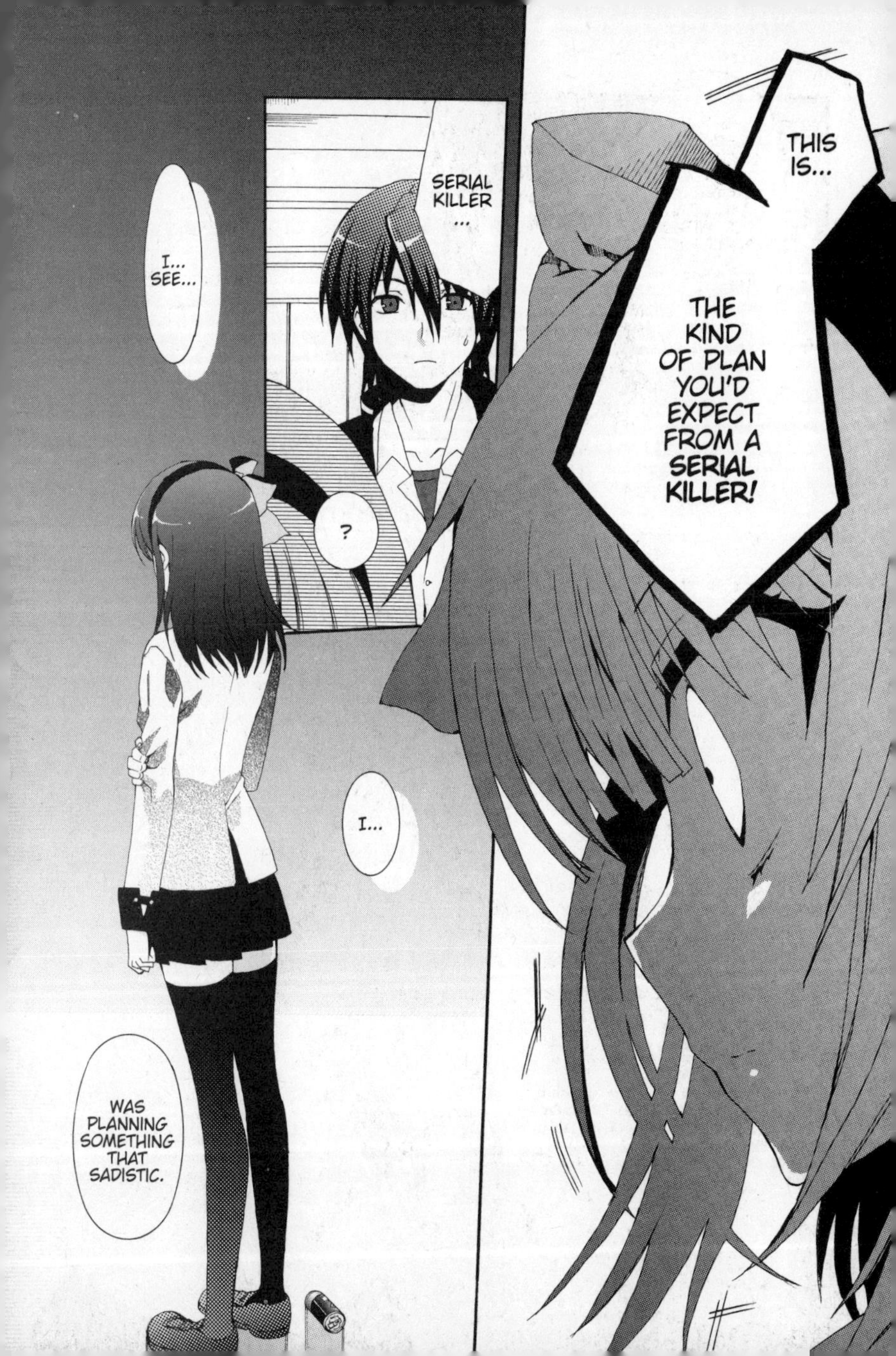
THIS IS...
THE KIND OF PLAN YOU'D EXPECT FROM A SERIAL KILLER!
SERIAL KILLER ...
I... SEE...
?
I...
WAS PLANNING SOMETHING THAT SADISTIC.

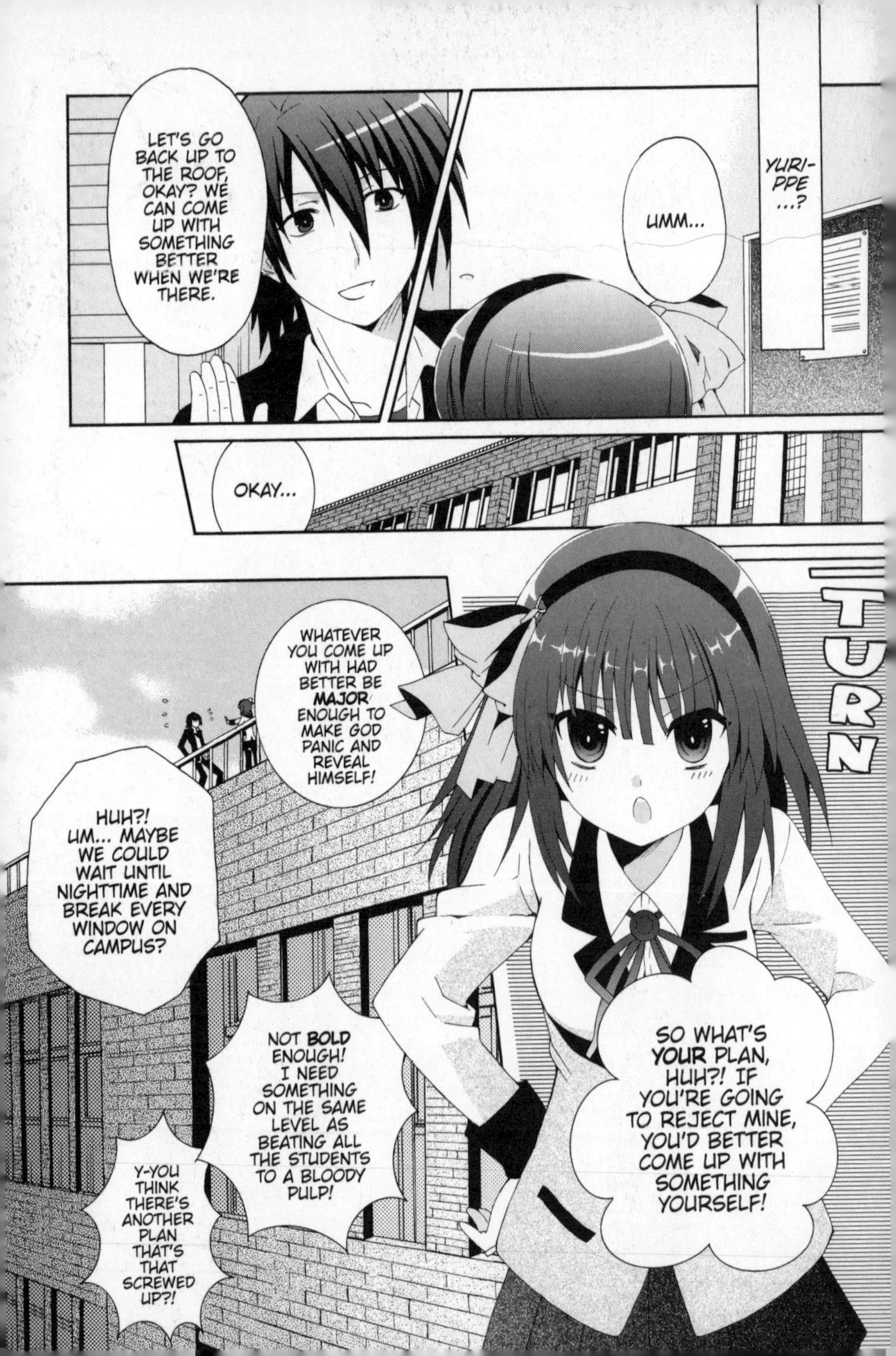
YURI-PPE ...?
UMM...
LET'S GO BACK UP TO THE ROOF, OKAY? WE CAN COME UP WITH SOMETHING BETTER WHEN WE'RE THERE.
OKAY...
TURN
WHATEVER YOU COME UP WITH HAD BETTER BE MAJOR ENOUGH TO MAKE GOD PANIC AND REVEAL HIMSELF!
HUH?! UM... MAYBE WE COULD WAIT UNTIL NIGHTTIME AND BREAK EVERY WINDOW ON CAMPUS?
NOT BOLD ENOUGH! I NEED SOMETHING ON THE SAME LEVEL AS BEATING ALL THE STUDENTS TO A BLOODY PULP!
Y-YOU THINK THERE'S ANOTHER PLAN THAT'S THAT SCREWED UP?!
SO WHAT'S YOUR PLAN, HUH?! IF YOU'RE GOING TO REJECT MINE, YOU'D BETTER COME UP WITH SOMETHING YOURSELF!

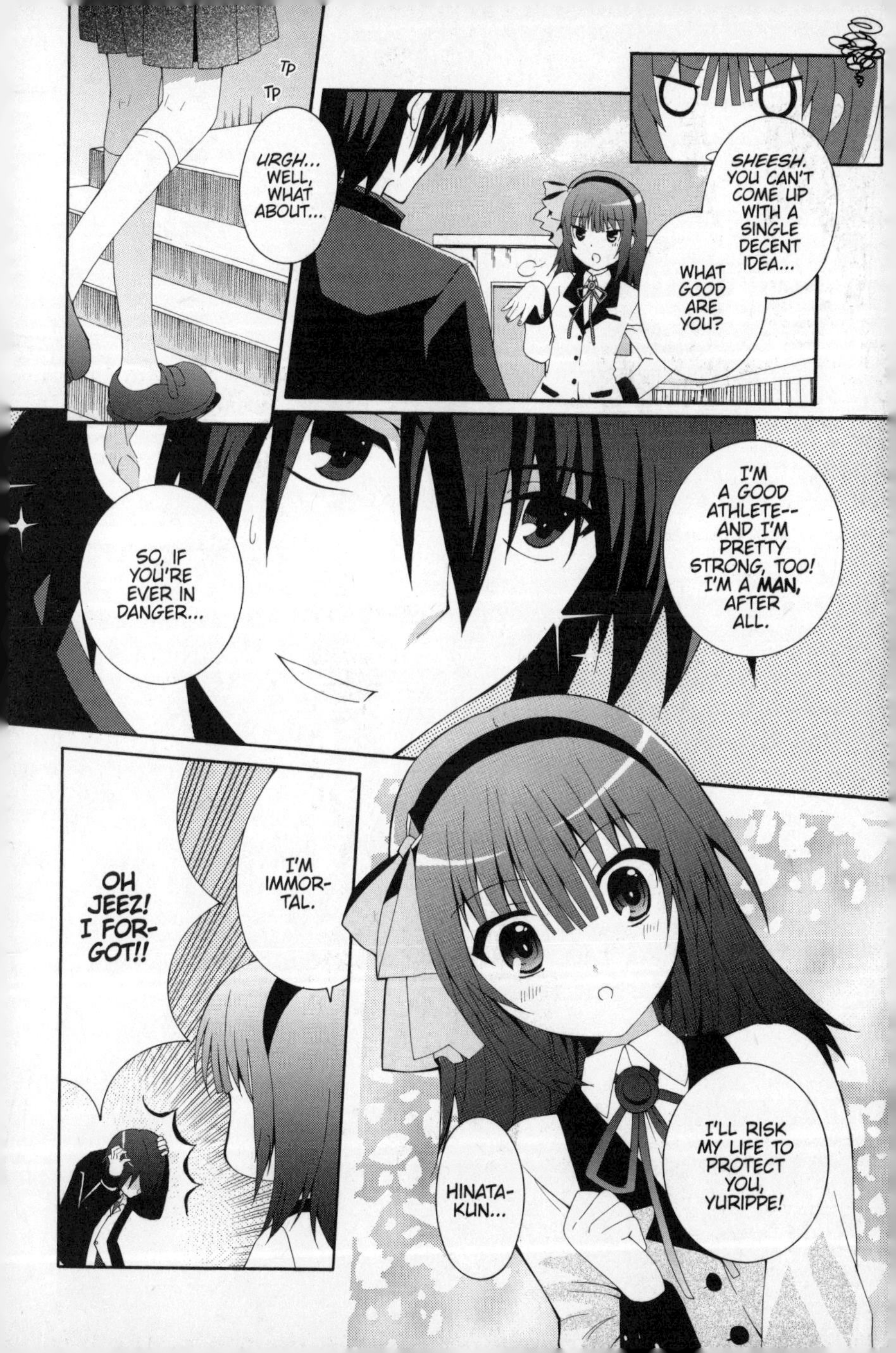
SHEESH. YOU CAN'T COME UP WITH A SINGLE DECENT IDEA...
WHAT GOOD ARE YOU?
URGH... WELL, WHAT ABOUT...
TP
TP
I'M A GOOD ATHLETE-- AND I'M PRETTY STRONG, TOO! I'M A **MAN**, AFTER ALL.
SO, IF YOU'RE EVER IN DANGER...
I'LL RISK MY LIFE TO PROTECT YOU, YURIPPE!
HINATA-KUN...
I'M IMMOR-TAL.
OH JEEZ! I FOR-GOT!!

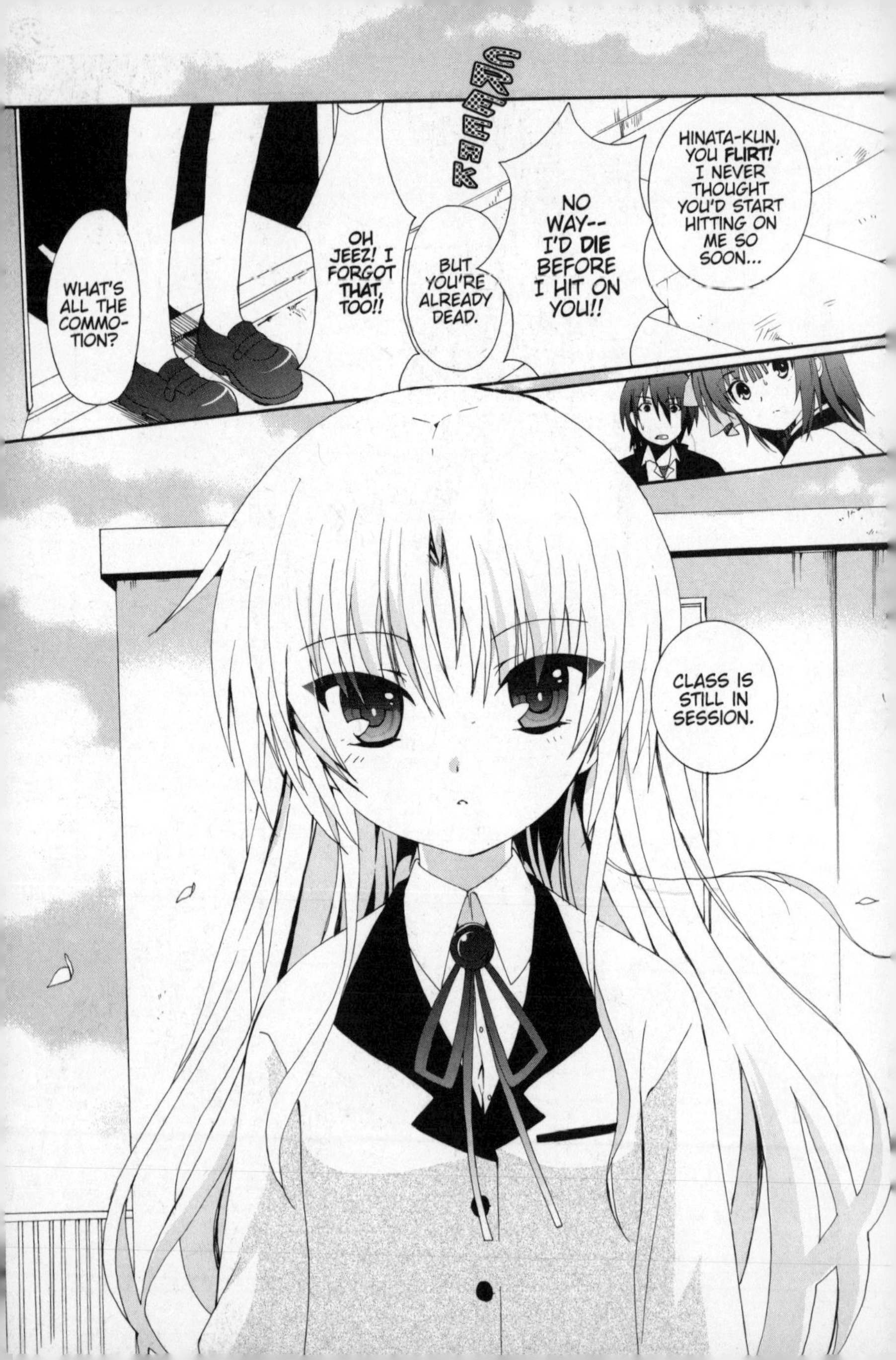
HINATA-KUN, YOU FLIRT! I NEVER THOUGHT YOU'D START HITTING ON ME SO SOON...
NO WAY-- I'D DIE BEFORE I HIT ON YOU!!
BUT YOU'RE ALREADY DEAD.
OH JEEZ! I FORGOT THAT, TOO!!
CREERK
WHAT'S ALL THE COMMOTION?
CLASS IS STILL IN SESSION.

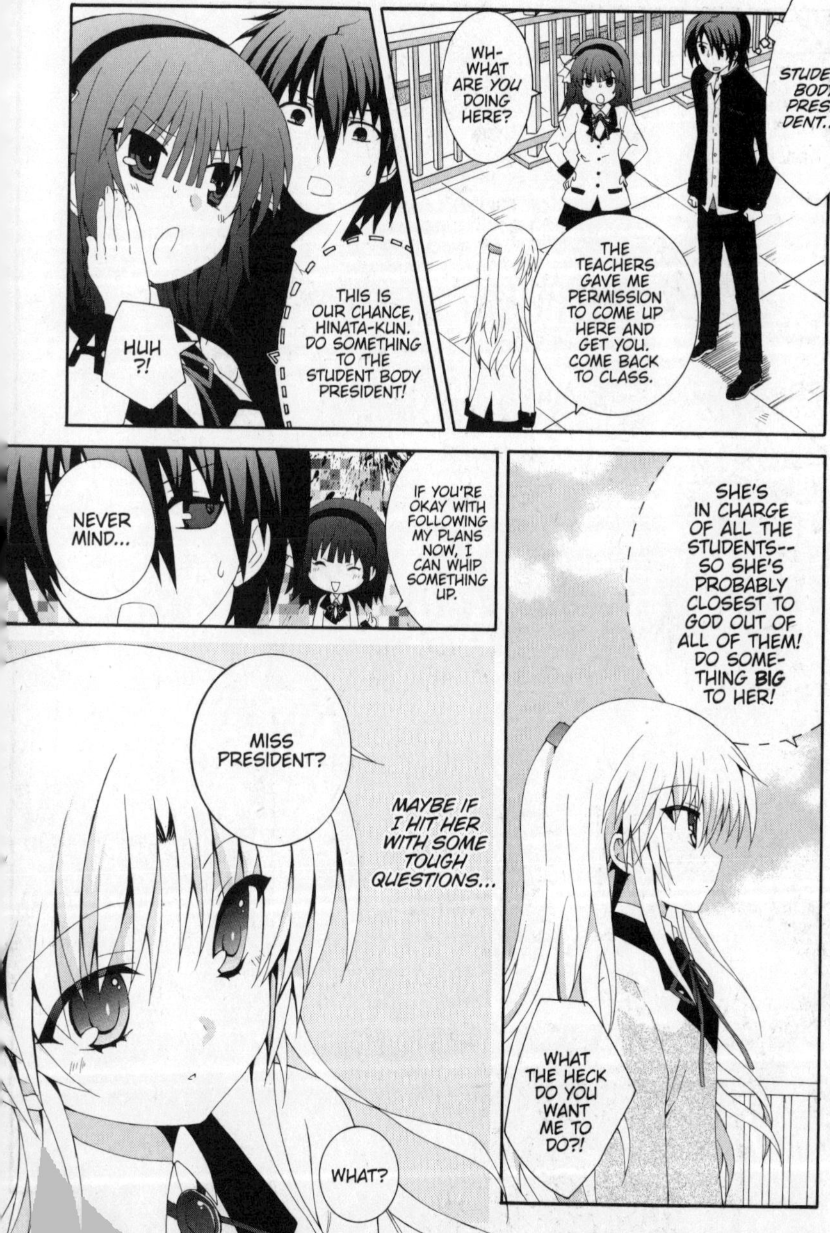
STUDENT BODY PRESI-DENT...!
WH-WHAT ARE YOU DOING HERE?
THE TEACHERS GAVE ME PERMISSION TO COME UP HERE AND GET YOU. COME BACK TO CLASS.
THIS IS OUR CHANCE, HINATA-KUN. DO SOMETHING TO THE STUDENT BODY PRESIDENT!
HUH?!
SHE'S IN CHARGE OF ALL THE STUDENTS-- SO SHE'S PROBABLY CLOSEST TO GOD OUT OF ALL OF THEM! DO SOME-THING **BIG** TO HER!
WHAT THE HECK DO YOU WANT ME TO DO?!
IF YOU'RE OKAY WITH FOLLOWING MY PLANS NOW, I CAN WHIP SOMETHING UP.
NEVER MIND...
MISS PRESIDENT?
MAYBE IF I HIT HER WITH SOME TOUGH QUESTIONS...
WHAT?

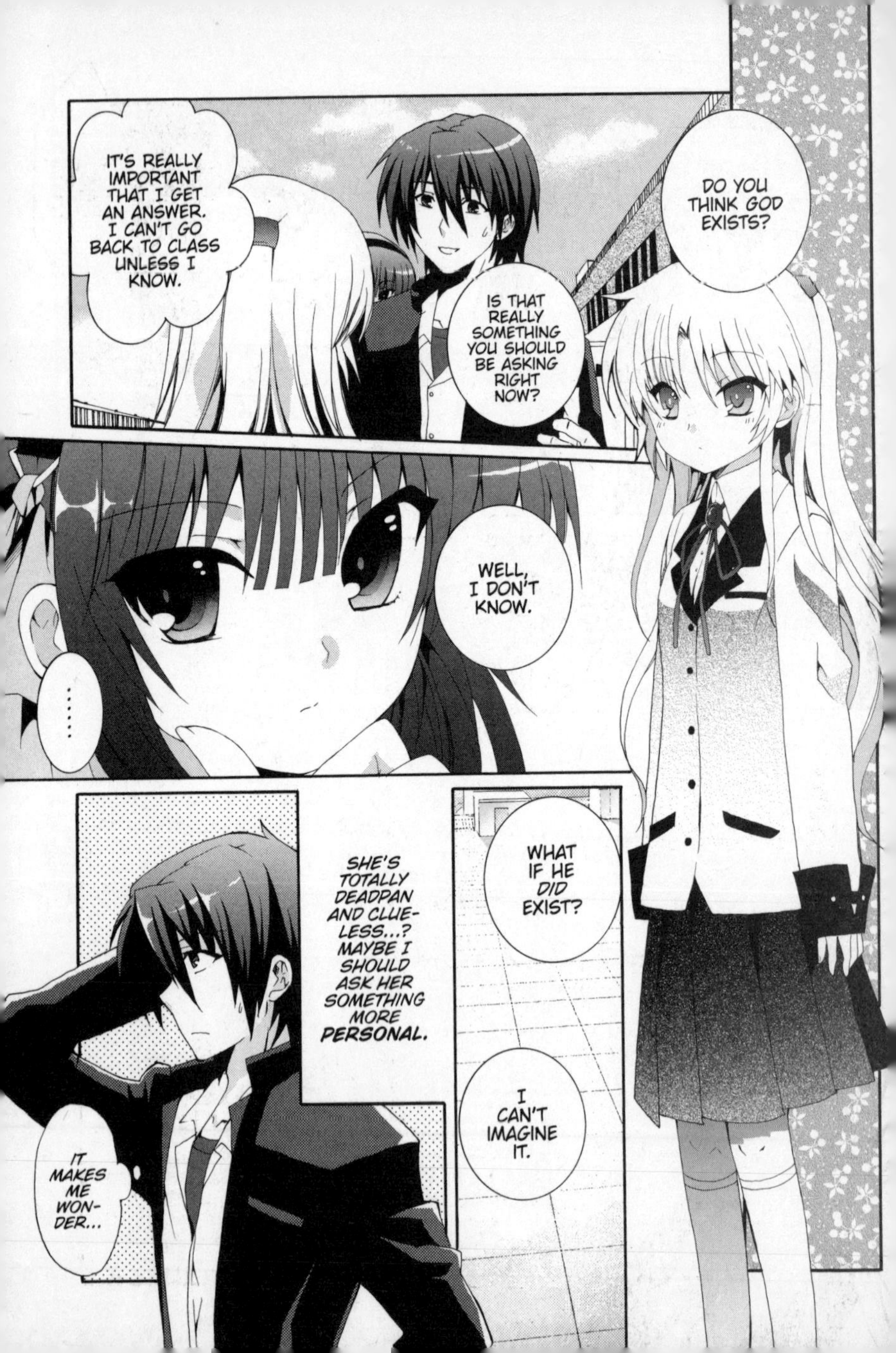
DO YOU THINK GOD EXISTS?
IS THAT REALLY SOMETHING YOU SHOULD BE ASKING RIGHT NOW?
IT'S REALLY IMPORTANT THAT I GET AN ANSWER. I CAN'T GO BACK TO CLASS UNLESS I KNOW.
WELL, I DON'T KNOW.
......
WHAT IF HE DID EXIST?
I CAN'T IMAGINE IT.
SHE'S TOTALLY DEADPAN AND CLUELESS...? MAYBE I SHOULD ASK HER SOMETHING MORE PERSONAL.
IT MAKES ME WONDER...

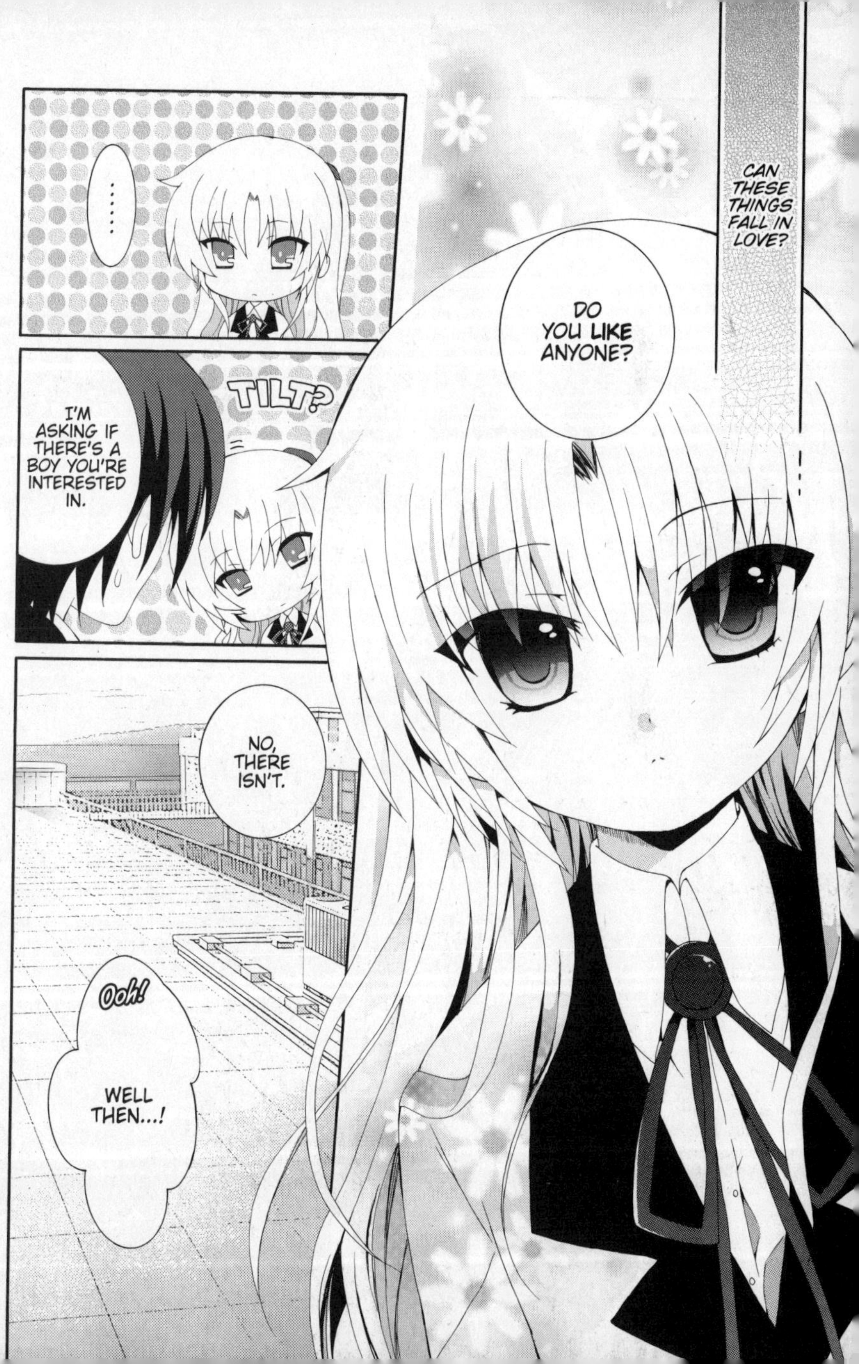
CAN THESE THINGS FALL IN LOVE?
DO YOU LIKE ANYONE?
......
TILT?
I'M ASKING IF THERE'S A BOY YOU'RE INTERESTED IN.
NO, THERE ISN'T.
Ooh!
WELL THEN...!

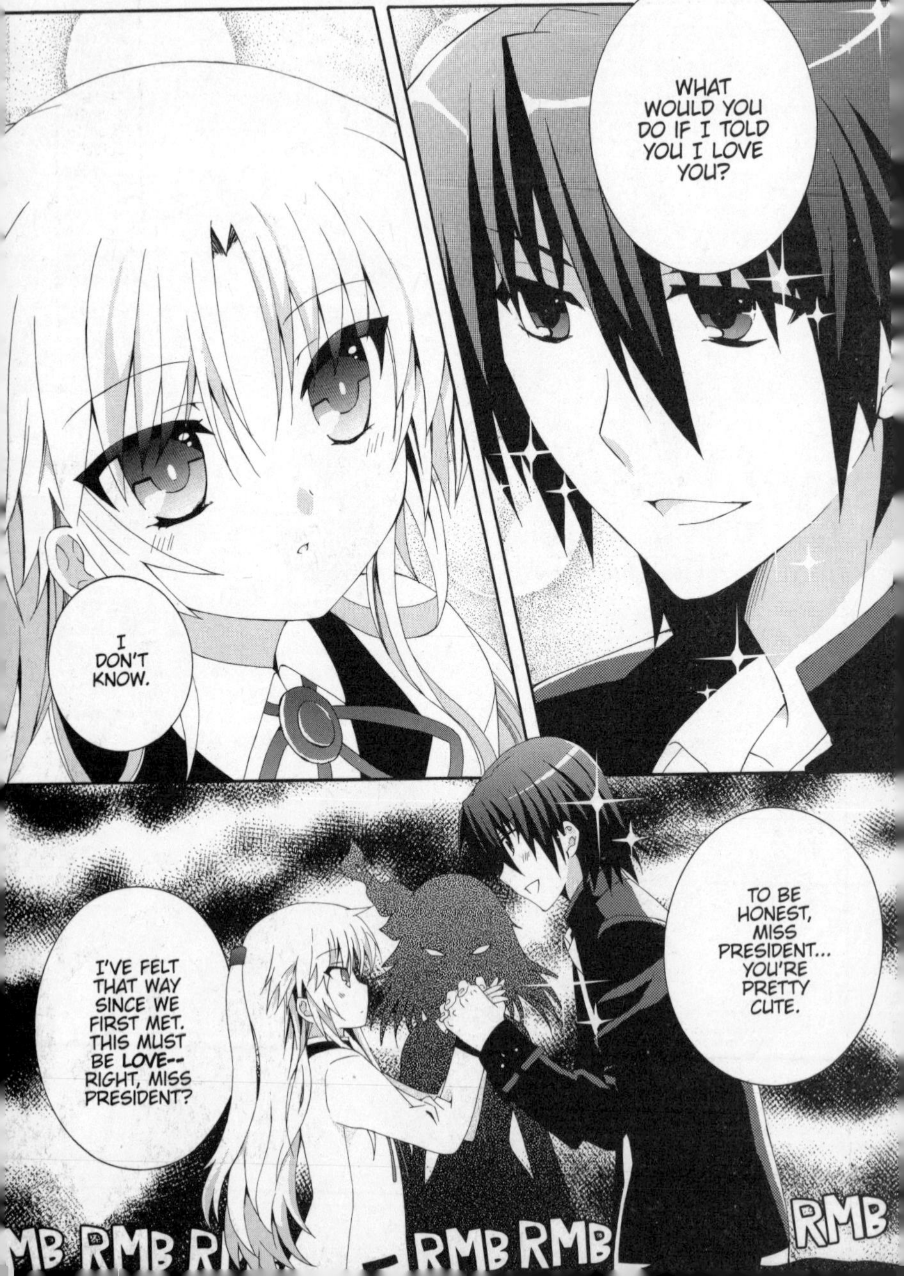
WHAT WOULD YOU DO IF I TOLD YOU I LOVE YOU?
I DON'T KNOW.
TO BE HONEST, MISS PRESIDENT... YOU'RE PRETTY CUTE.
I'VE FELT THAT WAY SINCE WE FIRST MET. THIS MUST BE LOVE-- RIGHT, MISS PRESIDENT?
RMB
RMB RMB
MB RMB R

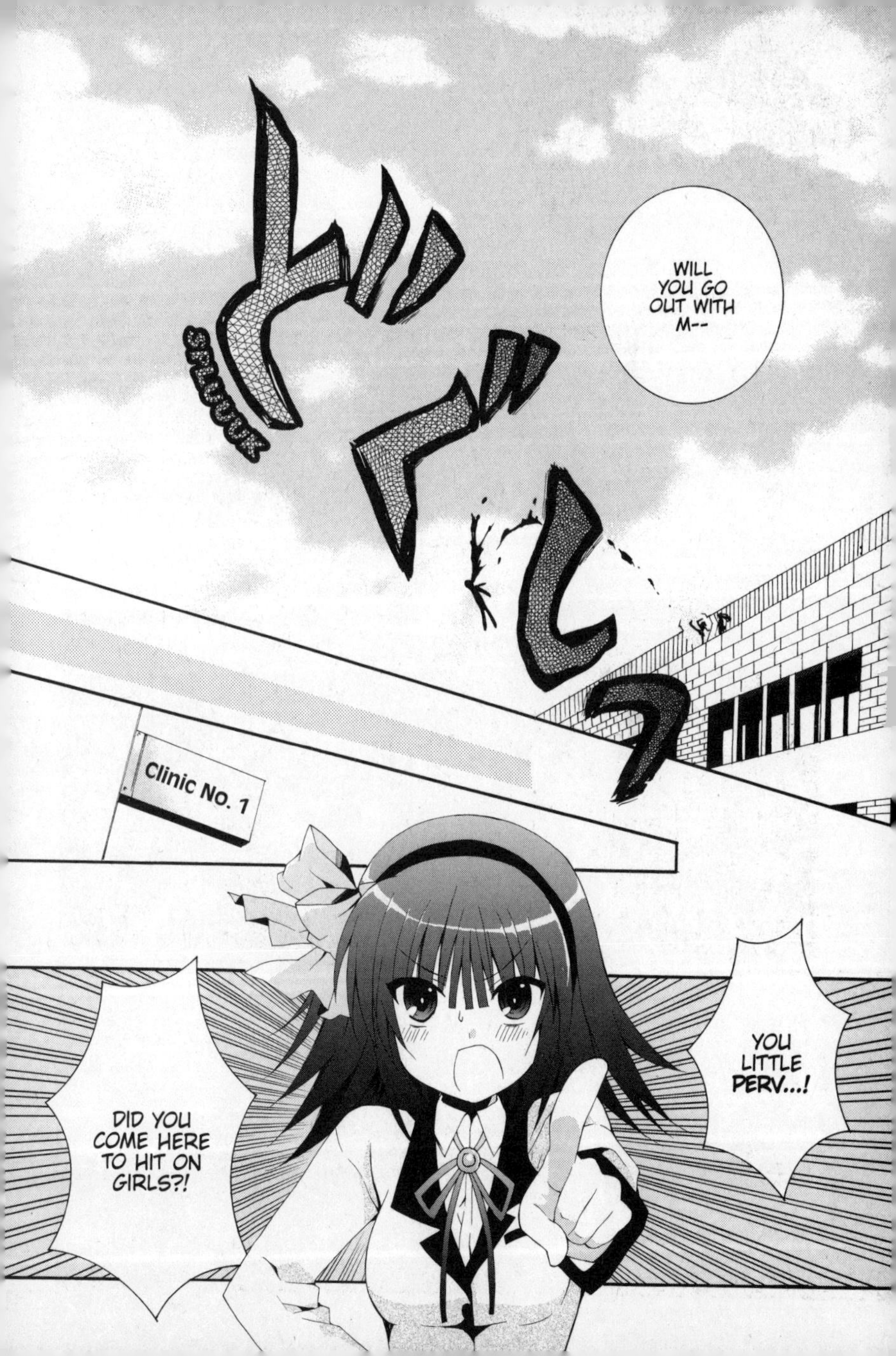
WILL YOU GO OUT WITH M--
SPLUUUK
Clinic No. 1
YOU LITTLE PERV...!
DID YOU COME HERE TO HIT ON GIRLS?!

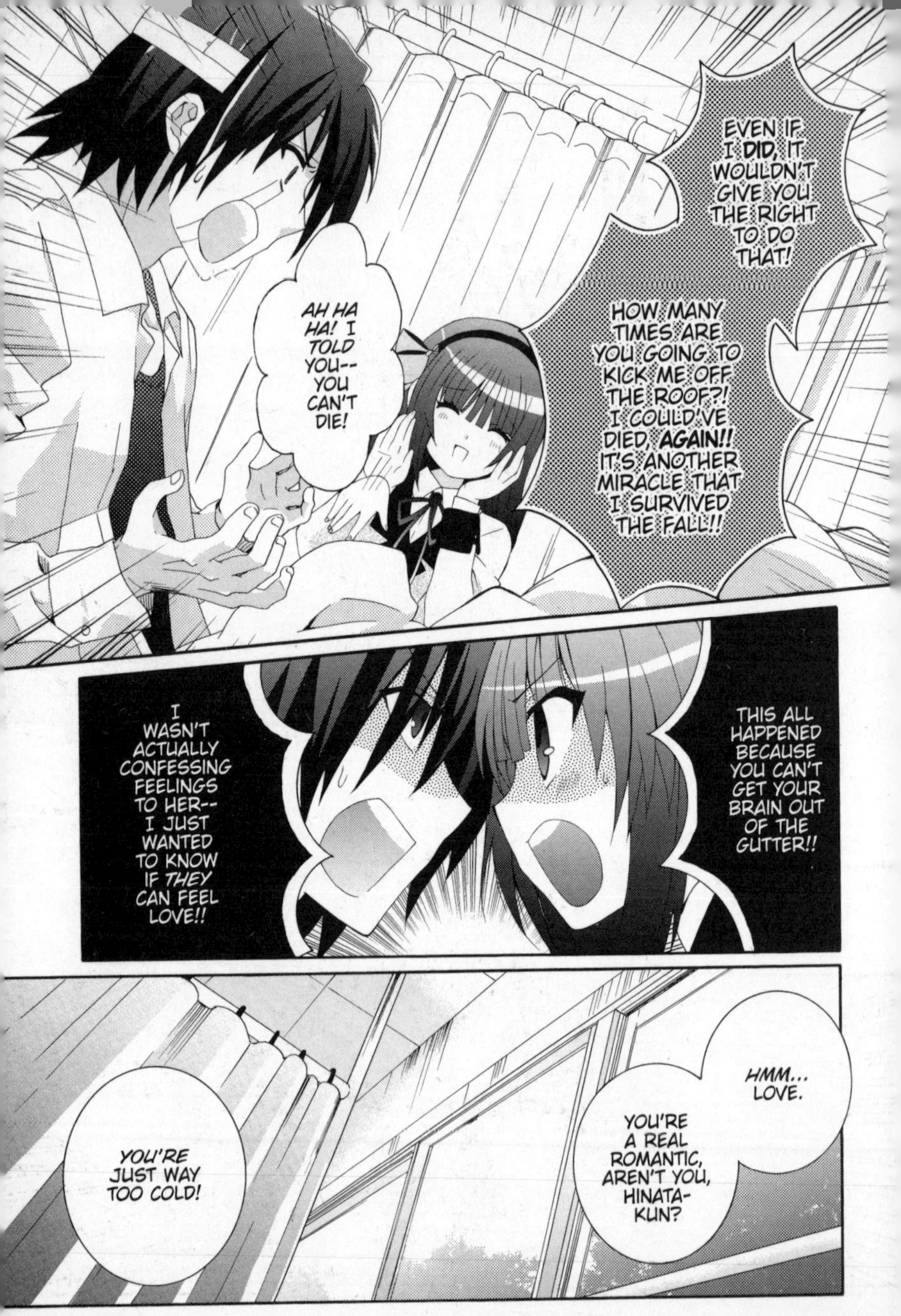
EVEN IF I **DID**, IT WOULDN'T GIVE YOU THE RIGHT TO DO THAT!
HOW MANY TIMES ARE YOU GOING TO KICK ME OFF THE ROOF?! I COULD'VE DIED, **AGAIN!!** IT'S ANOTHER MIRACLE THAT I SURVIVED THE FALL!!
AH HA HA! I TOLD YOU-- YOU CAN'T DIE!
THIS ALL HAPPENED BECAUSE YOU CAN'T GET YOUR BRAIN OUT OF THE GUTTER!!
I WASN'T ACTUALLY CONFESSING FEELINGS TO HER-- I JUST WANTED TO KNOW IF *THEY* CAN FEEL LOVE!!
HMM... LOVE.
YOU'RE A REAL ROMANTIC, AREN'T YOU, HINATA-KUN?
YOU'RE JUST WAY TOO COLD!

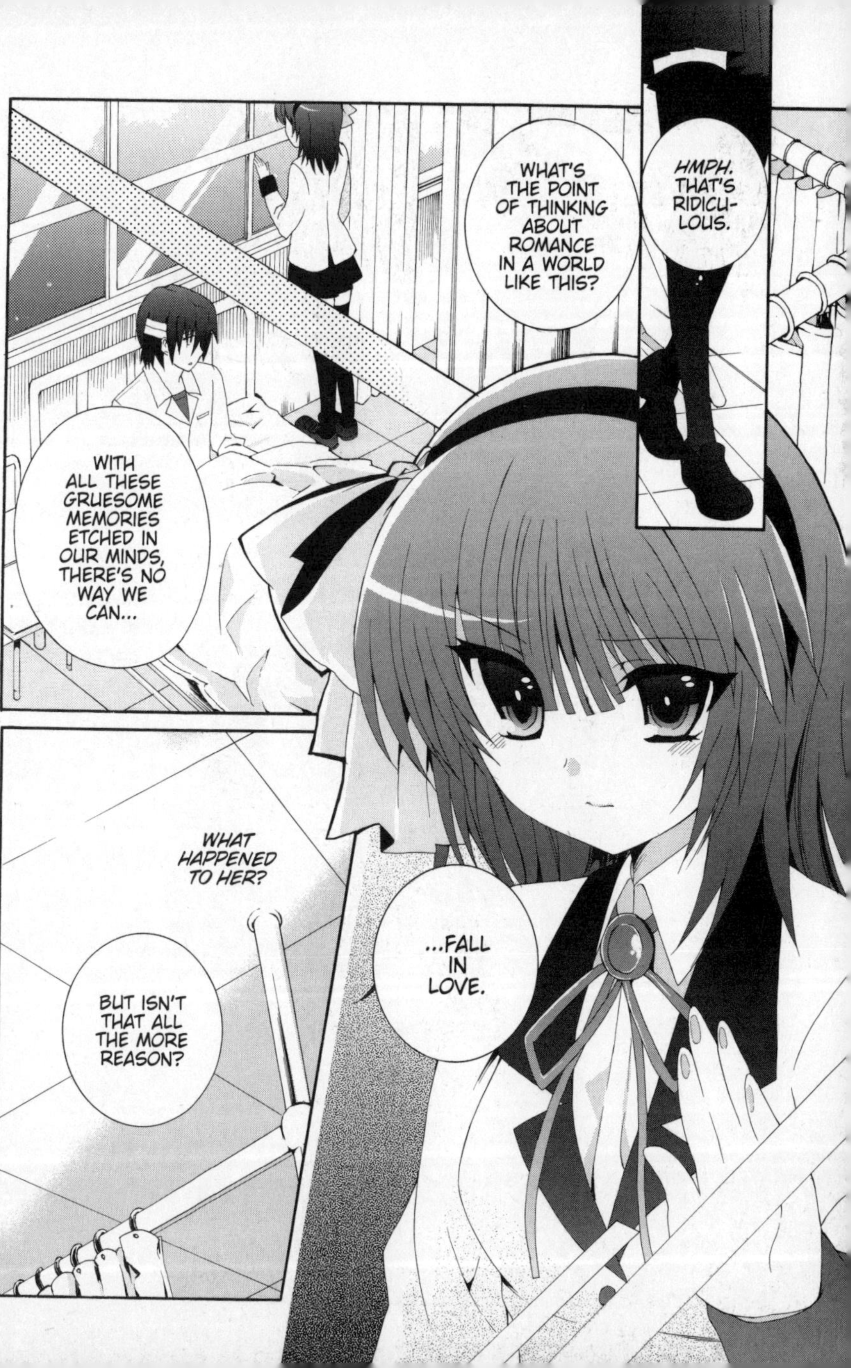
HMPH. THAT'S RIDICULOUS.
WHAT'S THE POINT OF THINKING ABOUT ROMANCE IN A WORLD LIKE THIS?
WITH ALL THESE GRUESOME MEMORIES ETCHED IN OUR MINDS, THERE'S NO WAY WE CAN...
...FALL IN LOVE.
WHAT HAPPENED TO HER?
BUT ISN'T THAT ALL THE MORE REASON?

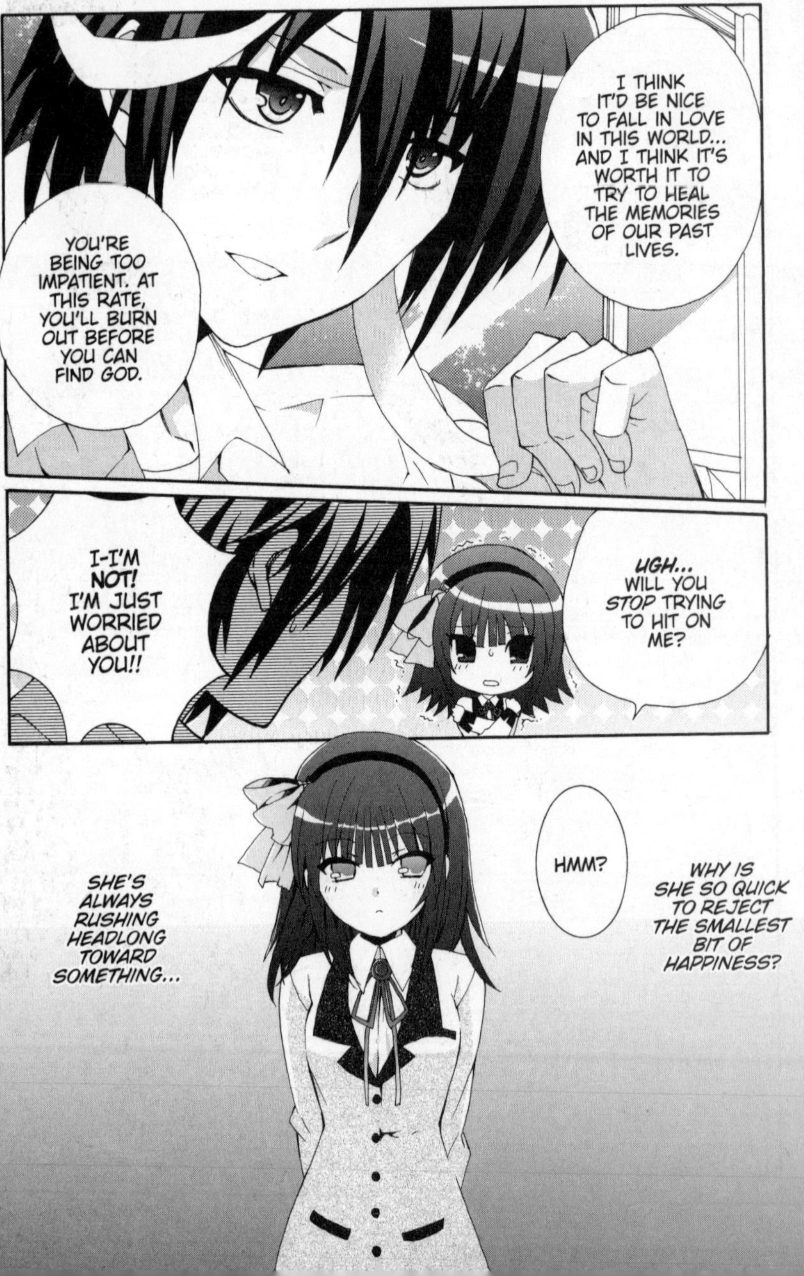
I THINK IT'D BE NICE TO FALL IN LOVE IN THIS WORLD... AND I THINK IT'S WORTH IT TO TRY TO HEAL THE MEMORIES OF OUR PAST LIVES.
YOU'RE BEING TOO IMPATIENT. AT THIS RATE, YOU'LL BURN OUT BEFORE YOU CAN FIND GOD.
UGH... WILL YOU STOP TRYING TO HIT ON ME?
I-I'M NOT! I'M JUST WORRIED ABOUT YOU!!
HMM?
WHY IS SHE SO QUICK TO REJECT THE SMALLEST BIT OF HAPPINESS?
SHE'S ALWAYS RUSHING HEADLONG TOWARD SOMETHING...

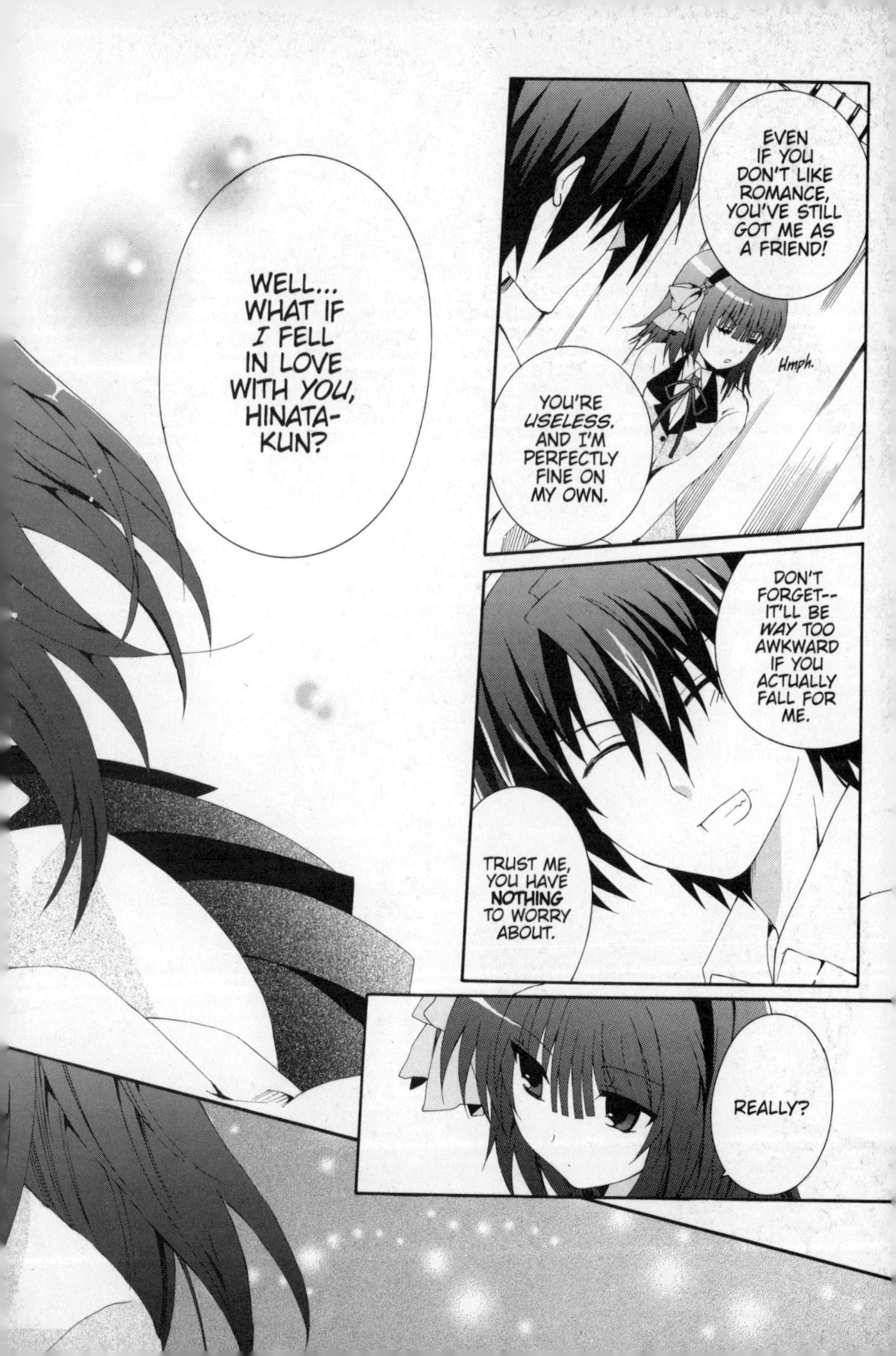
EVEN IF YOU DON'T LIKE ROMANCE, YOU'VE STILL GOT ME AS A FRIEND!
Hmph.
YOU'RE *USELESS.* AND I'M PERFECTLY FINE ON MY OWN.
DON'T FORGET-- IT'LL BE *WAY* TOO AWKWARD IF YOU ACTUALLY FALL FOR ME.
TRUST ME, YOU HAVE **NOTHING** TO WORRY ABOUT.
REALLY?
WELL... WHAT IF *I* FELL IN LOVE WITH *YOU*, HINATA-KUN?

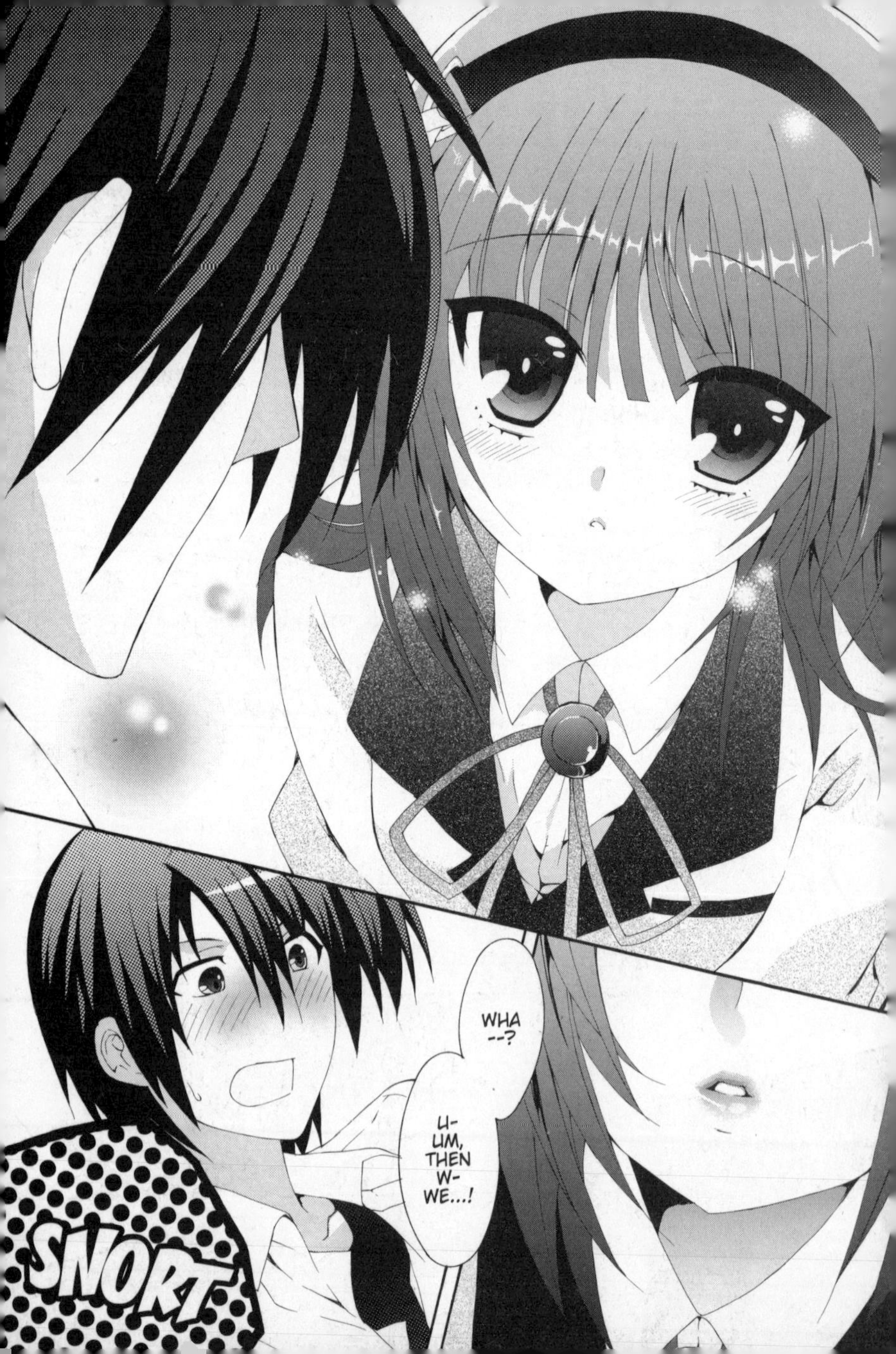
WHA --?
U-UM, THEN W-WE...!
SNORT

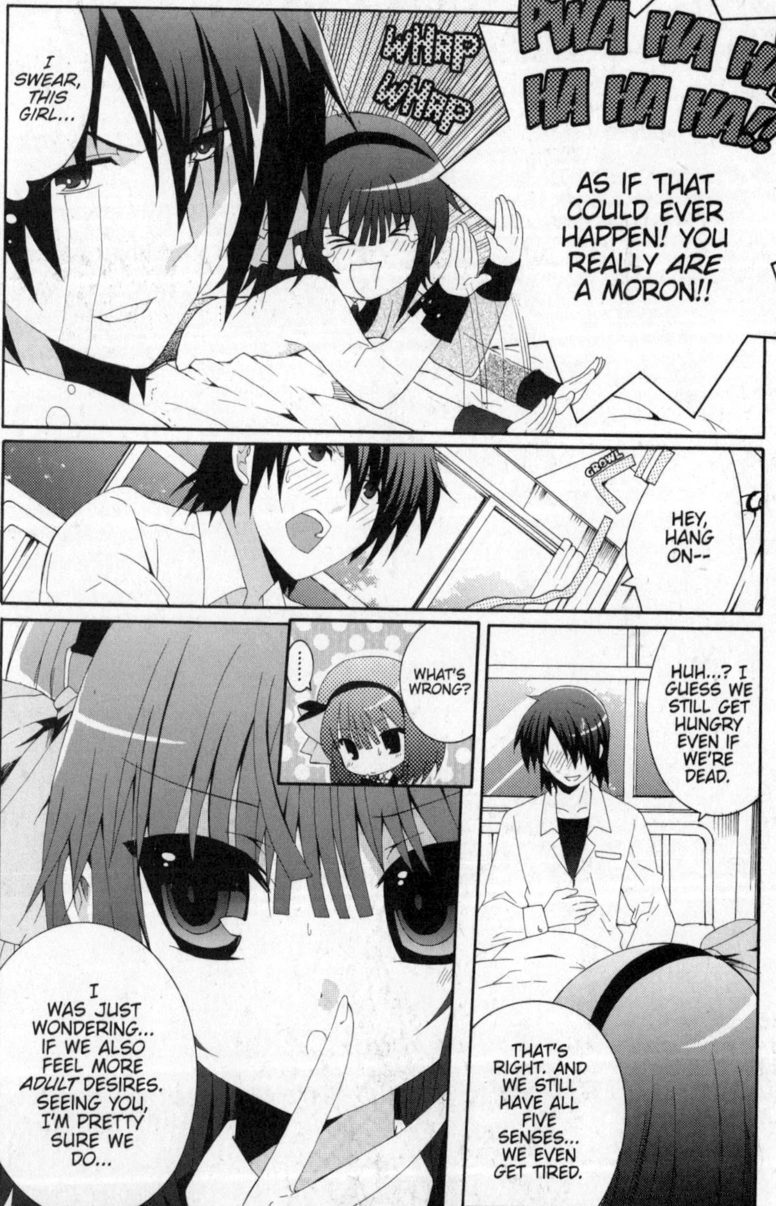
PWA HA HA HA HA HA!!
AS IF THAT COULD EVER HAPPEN! YOU REALLY ARE A MORON!!
WHAP WHAP
I SWEAR, THIS GIRL...
GROWL
HEY, HANG ON--
HUH...? I GUESS WE STILL GET HUNGRY EVEN IF WE'RE DEAD.
THAT'S RIGHT. AND WE STILL HAVE ALL FIVE SENSES... WE EVEN GET TIRED.
......
WHAT'S WRONG?
I WAS JUST WONDERING... IF WE ALSO FEEL MORE ADULT DESIRES. SEEING YOU, I'M PRETTY SURE WE DO...

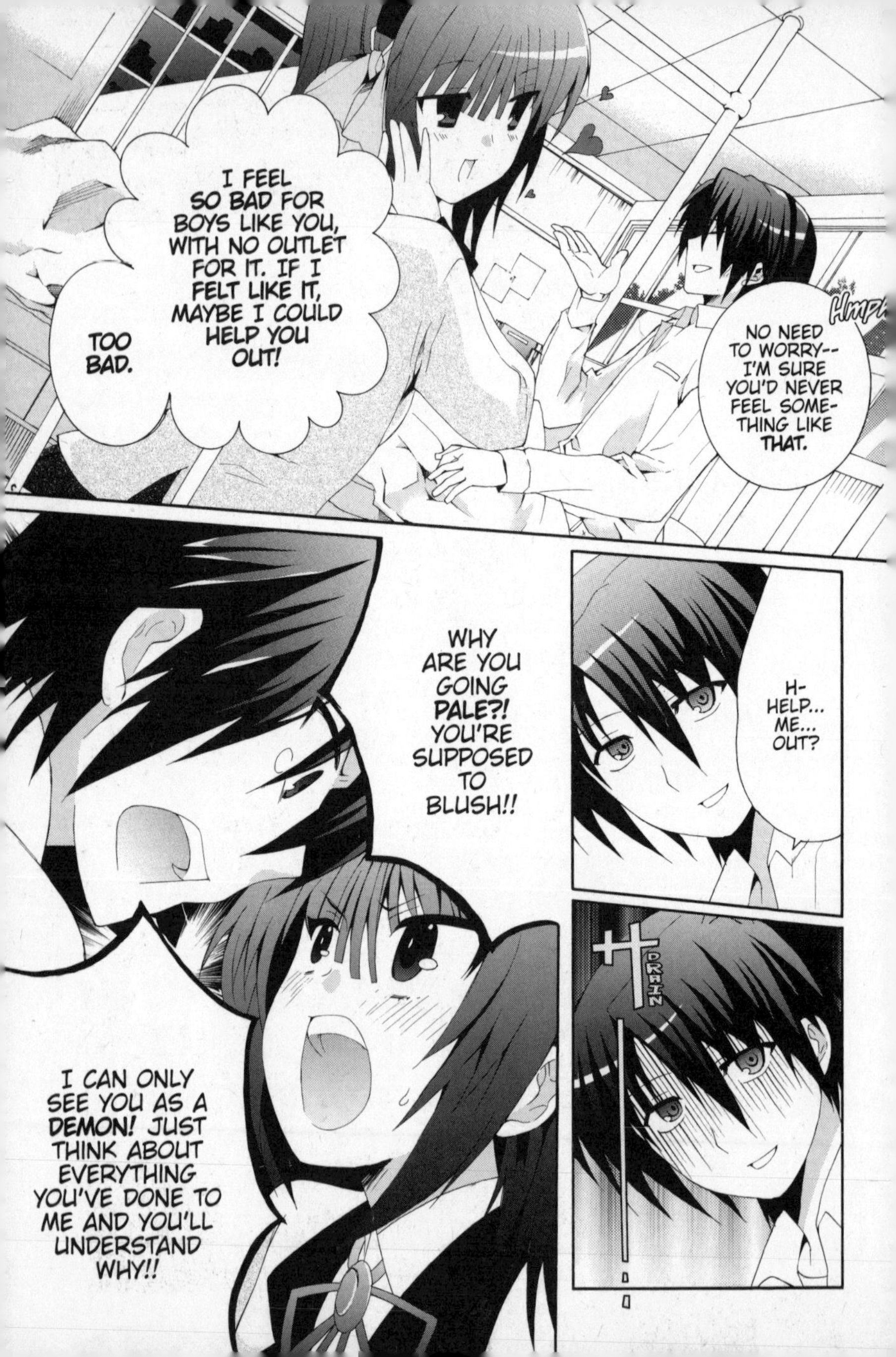
I FEEL SO BAD FOR BOYS LIKE YOU, WITH NO OUTLET FOR IT. IF I FELT LIKE IT, MAYBE I COULD HELP YOU OUT!
TOO BAD.
Hmph
NO NEED TO WORRY-- I'M SURE YOU'D NEVER FEEL SOME-THING LIKE THAT.
H- HELP... ME... OUT?
DRAIN
WHY ARE YOU GOING PALE?! YOU'RE SUPPOSED TO BLUSH!!
I CAN ONLY SEE YOU AS A DEMON! JUST THINK ABOUT EVERYTHING YOU'VE DONE TO ME AND YOU'LL UNDERSTAND WHY!!

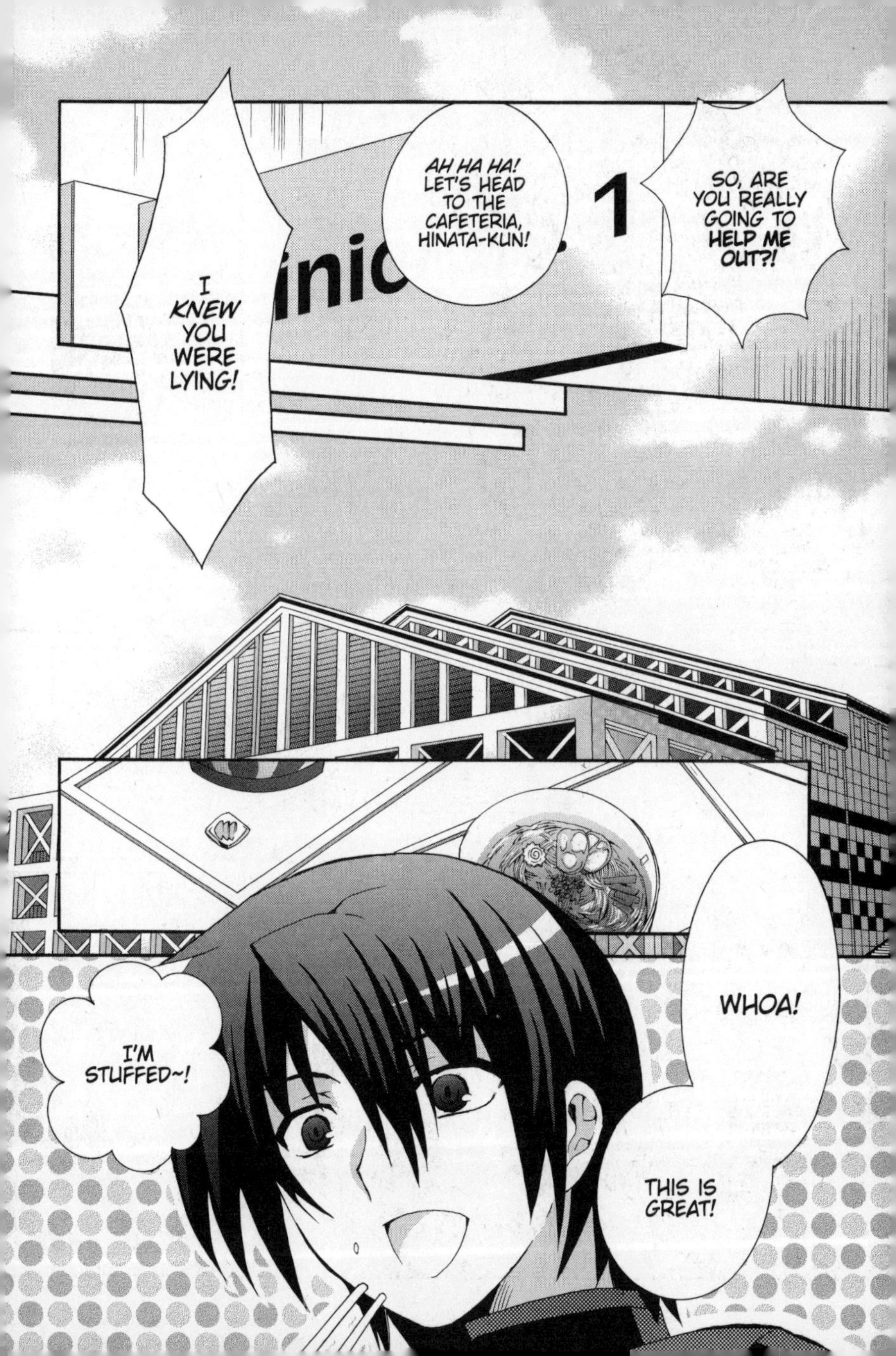
SO, ARE YOU REALLY GOING TO HELP ME OUT?!
AH HA HA! LET'S HEAD TO THE CAFETERIA, HINATA-KUN!
I KNEW YOU WERE LYING!
WHOA!
THIS IS GREAT!
I'M STUFFED~!

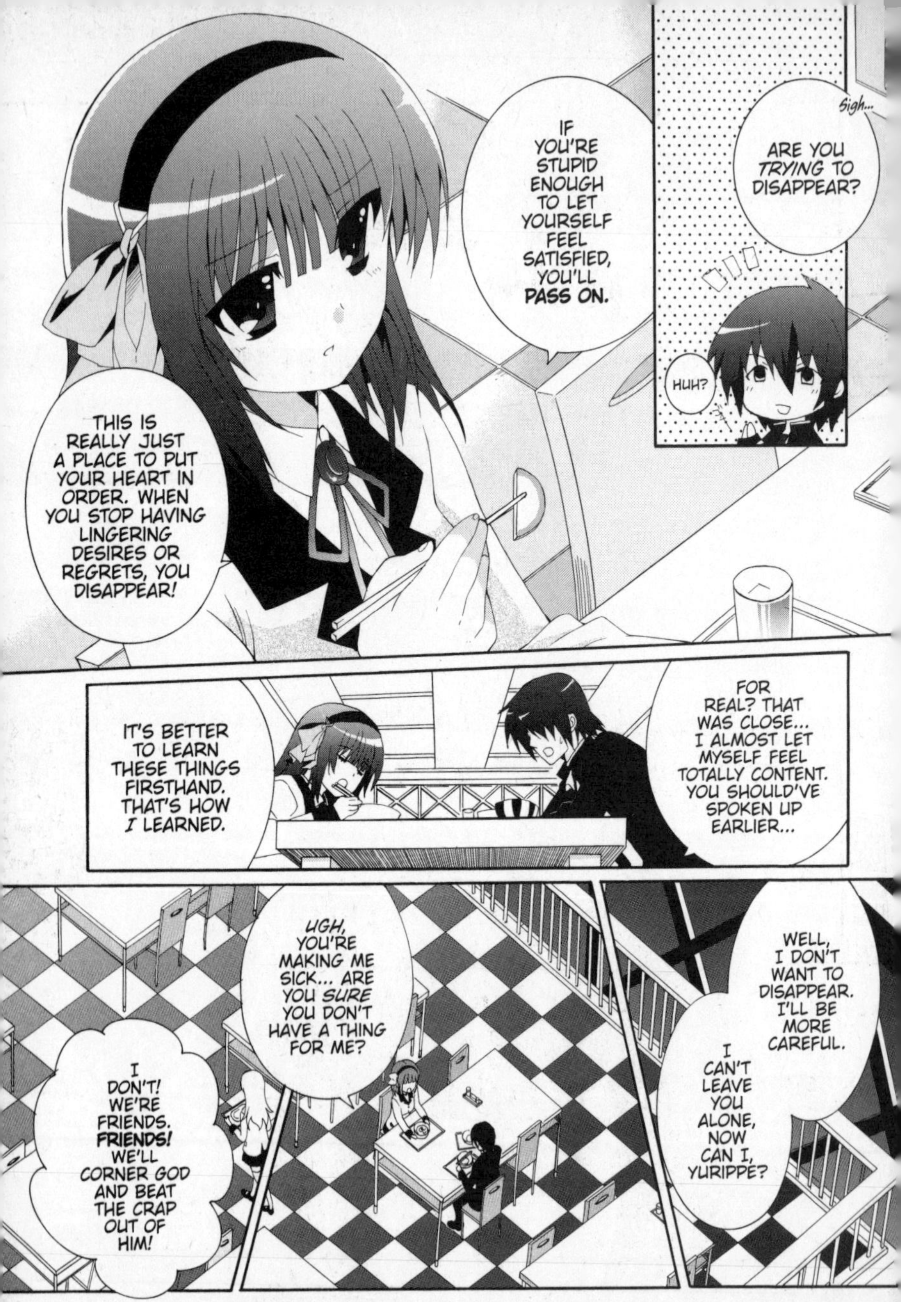
Sigh...
ARE YOU *TRYING* TO DISAPPEAR?
HUH?
IF YOU'RE STUPID ENOUGH TO LET YOURSELF FEEL SATISFIED, YOU'LL **PASS ON.**
THIS IS REALLY JUST A PLACE TO PUT YOUR HEART IN ORDER. WHEN YOU STOP HAVING LINGERING DESIRES OR REGRETS, YOU DISAPPEAR!
FOR REAL? THAT WAS CLOSE... I ALMOST LET MYSELF FEEL TOTALLY CONTENT. YOU SHOULD'VE SPOKEN UP EARLIER...
IT'S BETTER TO LEARN THESE THINGS FIRSTHAND. THAT'S HOW *I* LEARNED.
WELL, I DON'T WANT TO DISAPPEAR. I'LL BE MORE CAREFUL.
I CAN'T LEAVE YOU ALONE, NOW CAN I, YURIPPE?
UGH, YOU'RE MAKING ME SICK... ARE YOU *SURE* YOU DON'T HAVE A THING FOR ME?
I DON'T! WE'RE FRIENDS. **FRIENDS!** WE'LL CORNER GOD AND BEAT THE CRAP OUT OF HIM!

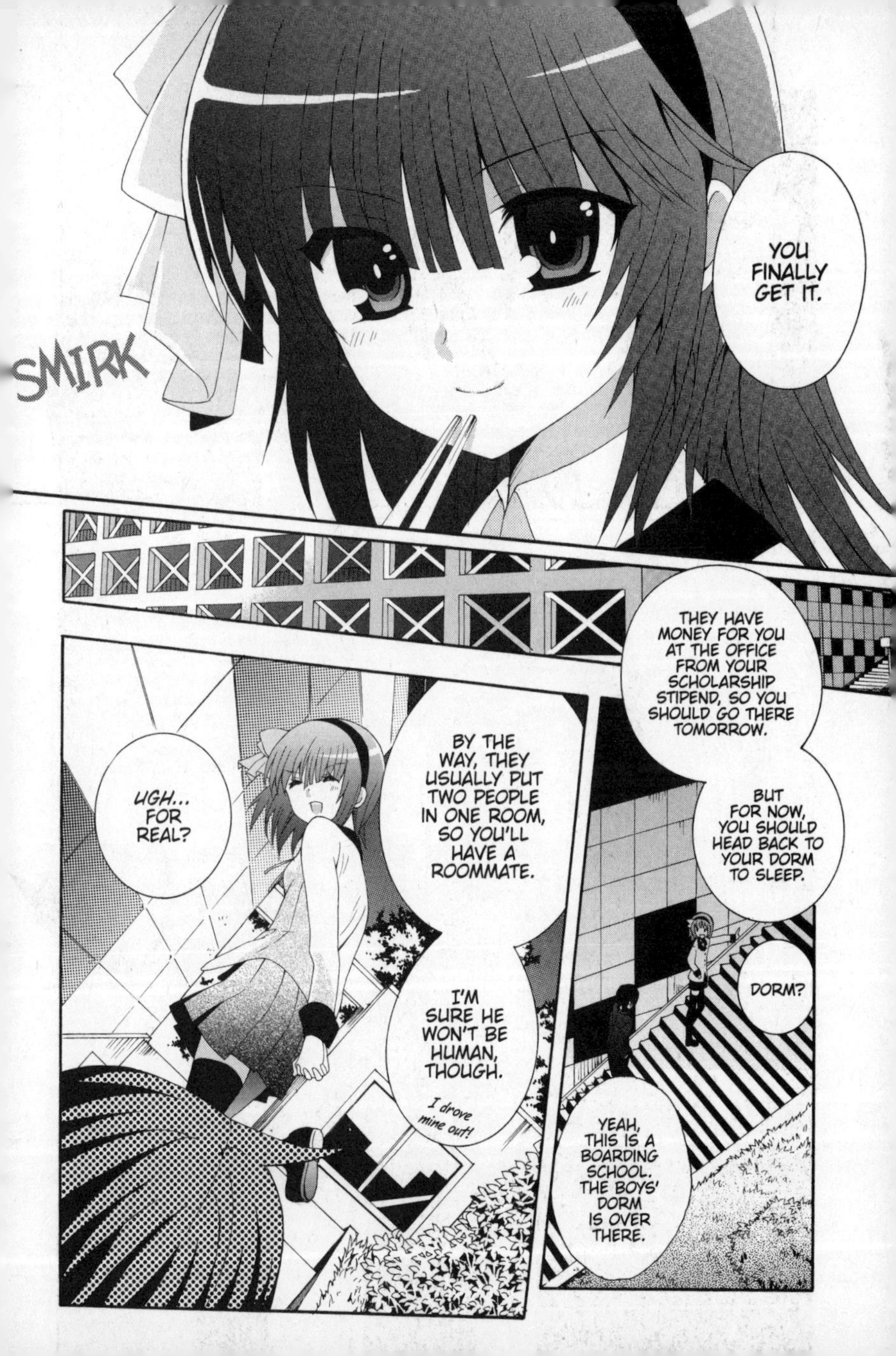
YOU FINALLY GET IT.
SMIRK
THEY HAVE MONEY FOR YOU AT THE OFFICE FROM YOUR SCHOLARSHIP STIPEND, SO YOU SHOULD GO THERE TOMORROW.
BUT FOR NOW, YOU SHOULD HEAD BACK TO YOUR DORM TO SLEEP.
DORM?
YEAH, THIS IS A BOARDING SCHOOL. THE BOYS' DORM IS OVER THERE.
BY THE WAY, THEY USUALLY PUT TWO PEOPLE IN ONE ROOM, SO YOU'LL HAVE A ROOMMATE.
UGH... FOR REAL?
I'M SURE HE WON'T BE HUMAN, THOUGH.
I drove mine out!

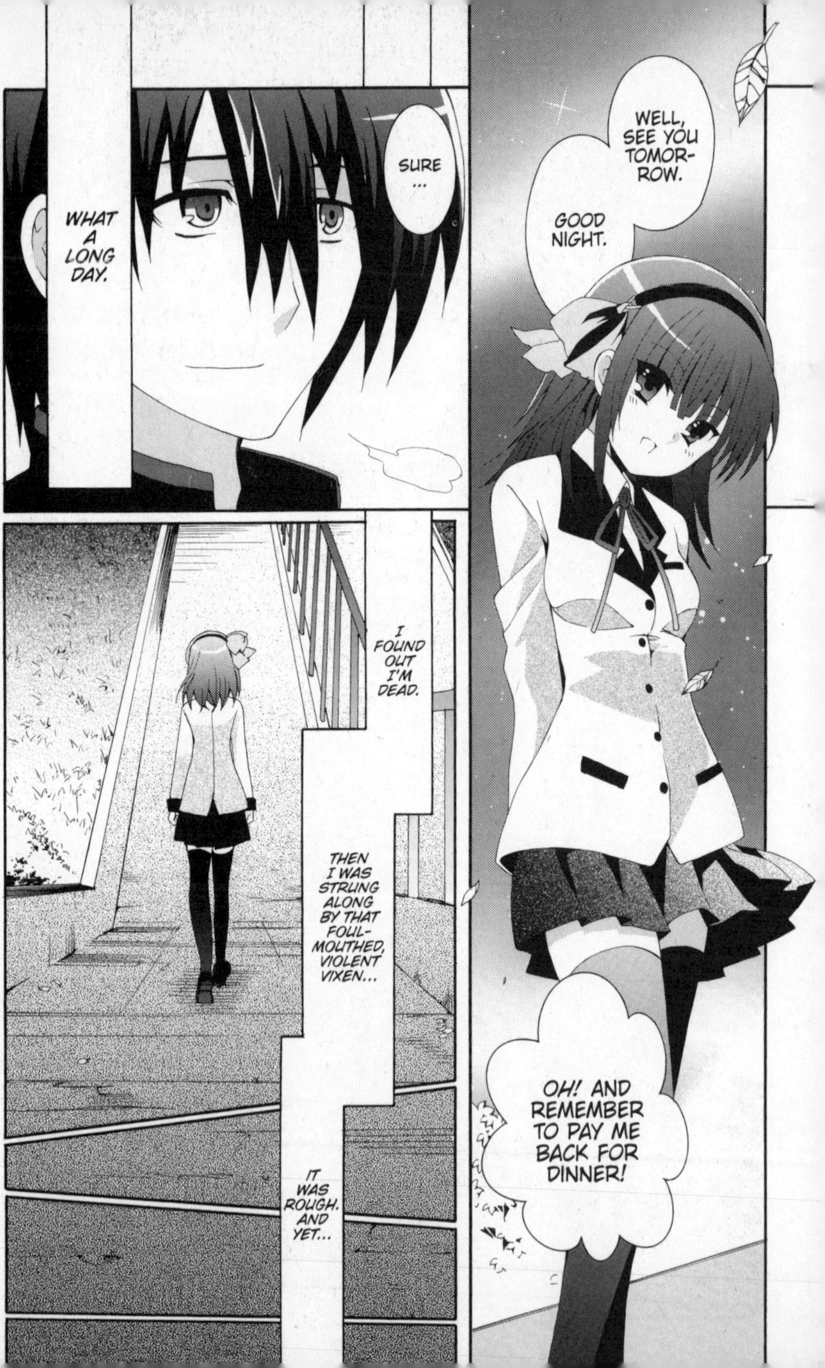
WELL, SEE YOU TOMOR-ROW.
GOOD NIGHT.
OH! AND REMEMBER TO PAY ME BACK FOR DINNER!
SURE ...
WHAT A LONG DAY.
I FOUND OUT I'M DEAD.
THEN I WAS STRUNG ALONG BY THAT FOUL-MOUTHED, VIOLENT VIXEN...
IT WAS ROUGH. AND YET...

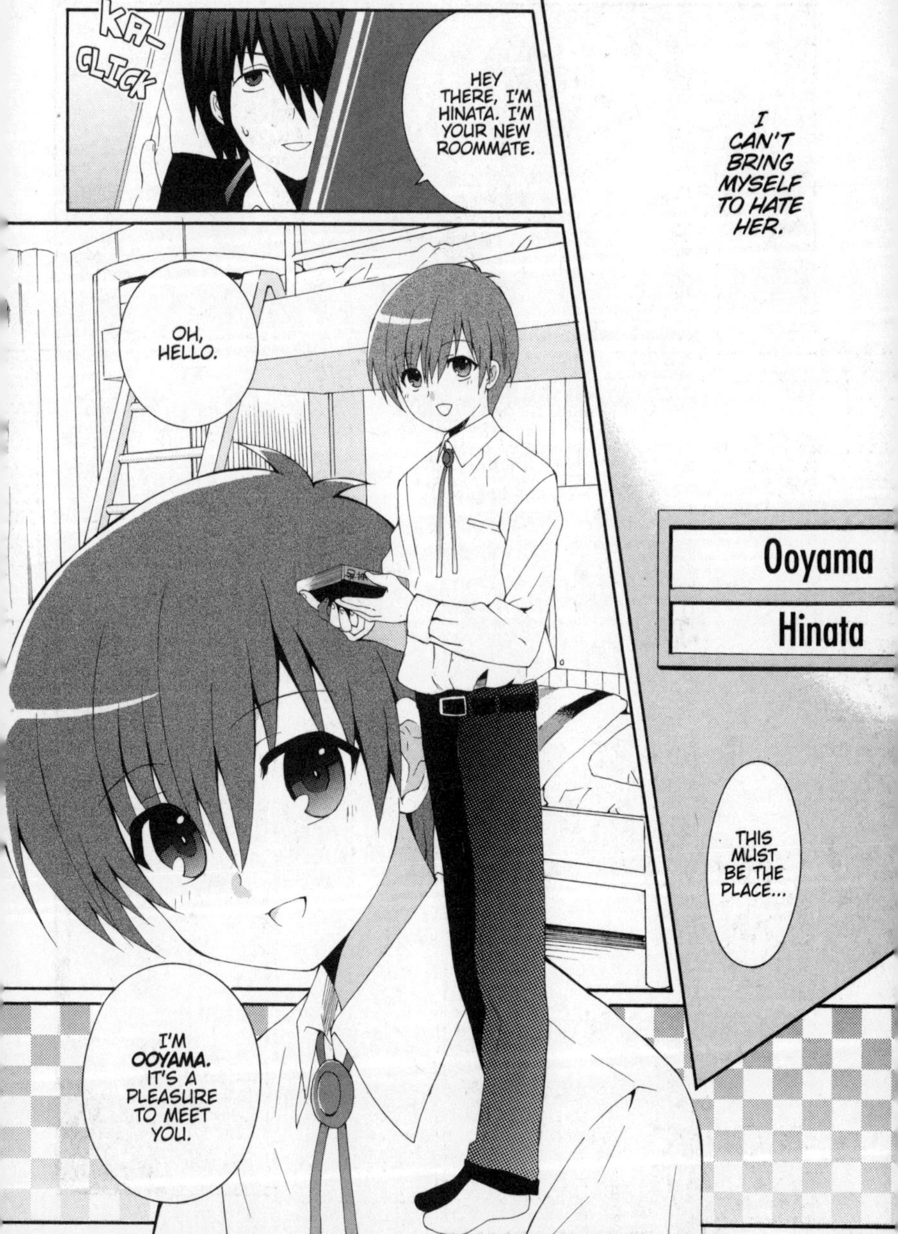
I CAN'T BRING MYSELF TO HATE HER.
Ooyama
Hinata
THIS MUST BE THE PLACE...
KA-CLICK
HEY THERE, I'M HINATA. I'M YOUR NEW ROOMMATE.
OH, HELLO.
I'M OOYAMA. IT'S A PLEASURE TO MEET YOU.

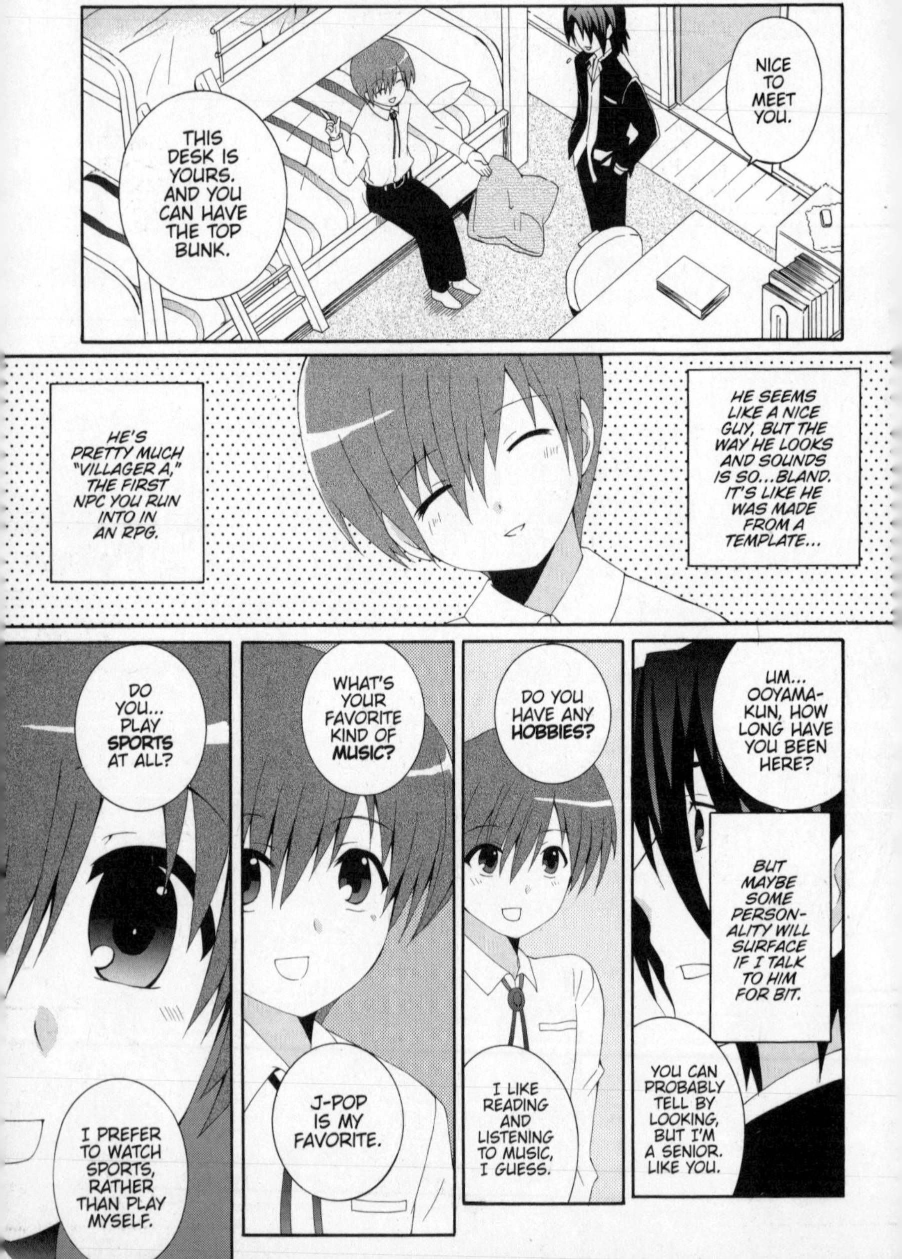
NICE TO MEET YOU.
THIS DESK IS YOURS. AND YOU CAN HAVE THE TOP BUNK.
HE SEEMS LIKE A NICE GUY, BUT THE WAY HE LOOKS AND SOUNDS IS SO...BLAND. IT'S LIKE HE WAS MADE FROM A TEMPLATE...
HE'S PRETTY MUCH "VILLAGER A," THE FIRST NPC YOU RUN INTO IN AN RPG.
UM... OOYAMA-KUN, HOW LONG HAVE YOU BEEN HERE?
BUT MAYBE SOME PERSON-ALITY WILL SURFACE IF I TALK TO HIM FOR BIT.
YOU CAN PROBABLY TELL BY LOOKING, BUT I'M A SENIOR. LIKE YOU.
DO YOU HAVE ANY **HOBBIES?**
I LIKE READING AND LISTENING TO MUSIC, I GUESS.
WHAT'S YOUR FAVORITE KIND OF **MUSIC?**
J-POP IS MY FAVORITE.
DO YOU... PLAY **SPORTS** AT ALL?
I PREFER TO WATCH SPORTS, RATHER THAN PLAY MYSELF.

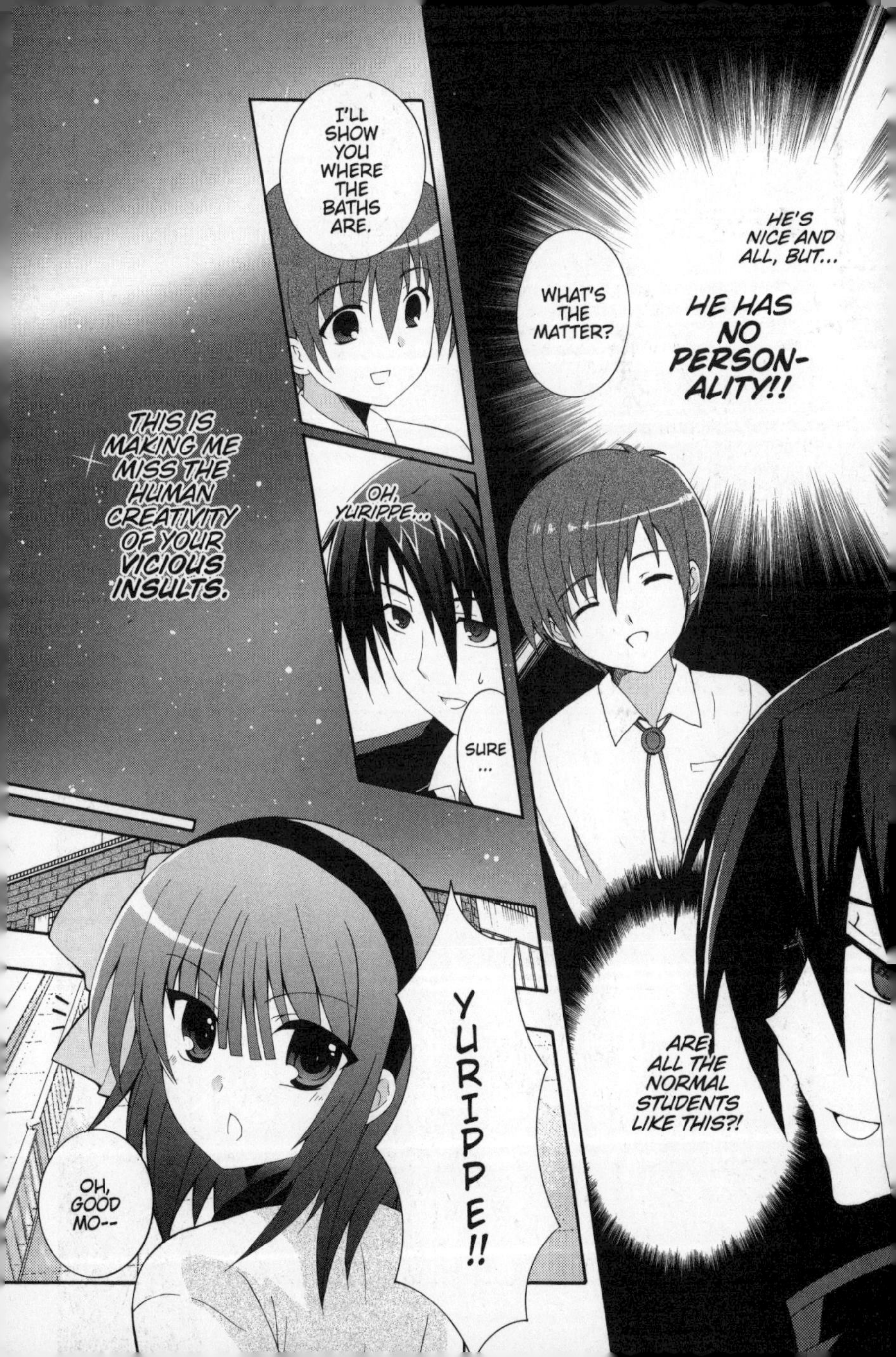
HE'S NICE AND ALL, BUT...
HE HAS NO PERSONALITY!!
WHAT'S THE MATTER?
ARE ALL THE NORMAL STUDENTS LIKE THIS?!
I'LL SHOW YOU WHERE THE BATHS ARE.
SURE...
THIS IS MAKING ME MISS THE HUMAN CREATIVITY OF YOUR VICIOUS INSULTS.
OH, YURIPPE...
YURIPPE!!
OH, GOOD MO--

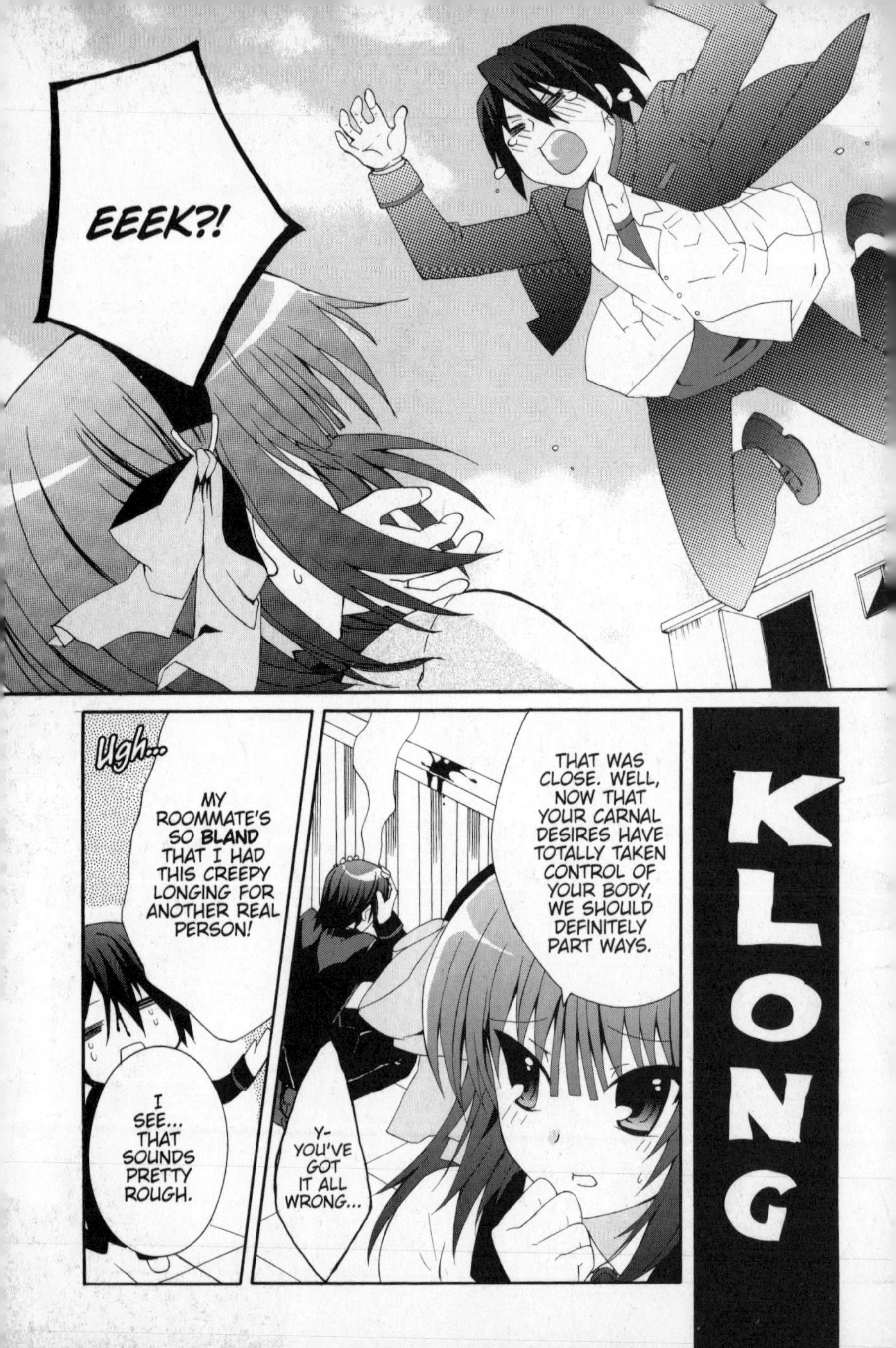
EEEK?!
KLONG
THAT WAS CLOSE. WELL, NOW THAT YOUR CARNAL DESIRES HAVE TOTALLY TAKEN CONTROL OF YOUR BODY, WE SHOULD DEFINITELY PART WAYS.
Y-YOU'VE GOT IT ALL WRONG...
Ugh...
MY ROOMMATE'S SO BLAND THAT I HAD THIS CREEPY LONGING FOR ANOTHER REAL PERSON!
I SEE... THAT SOUNDS PRETTY ROUGH.

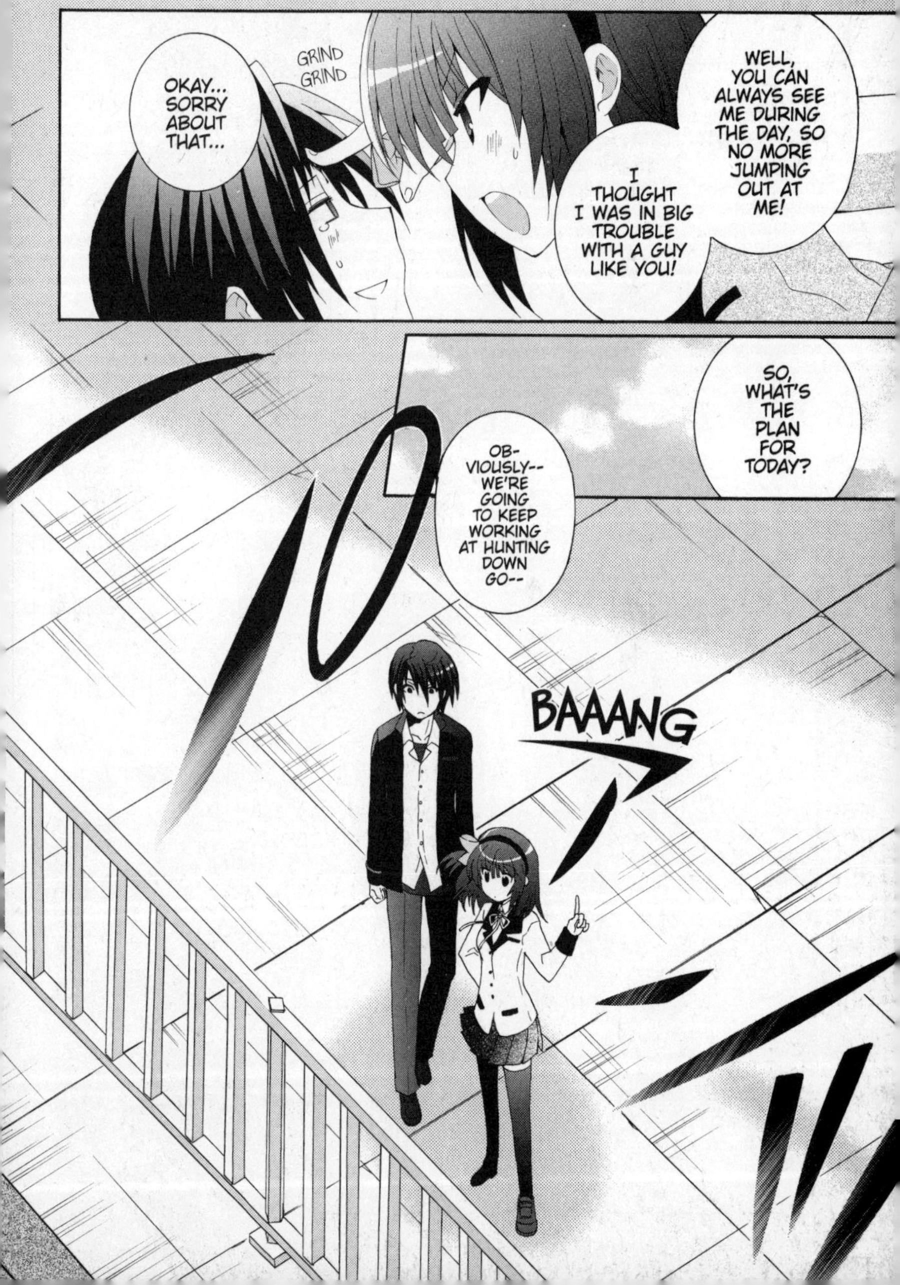
WELL, YOU CAN ALWAYS SEE ME DURING THE DAY, SO NO MORE JUMPING OUT AT ME!
I THOUGHT I WAS IN BIG TROUBLE WITH A GUY LIKE YOU!
GRIND GRIND
OKAY... SORRY ABOUT THAT...
SO, WHAT'S THE PLAN FOR TODAY?
OB-VIOUSLY-- WE'RE GOING TO KEEP WORKING AT HUNTING DOWN GO--
BAAANG

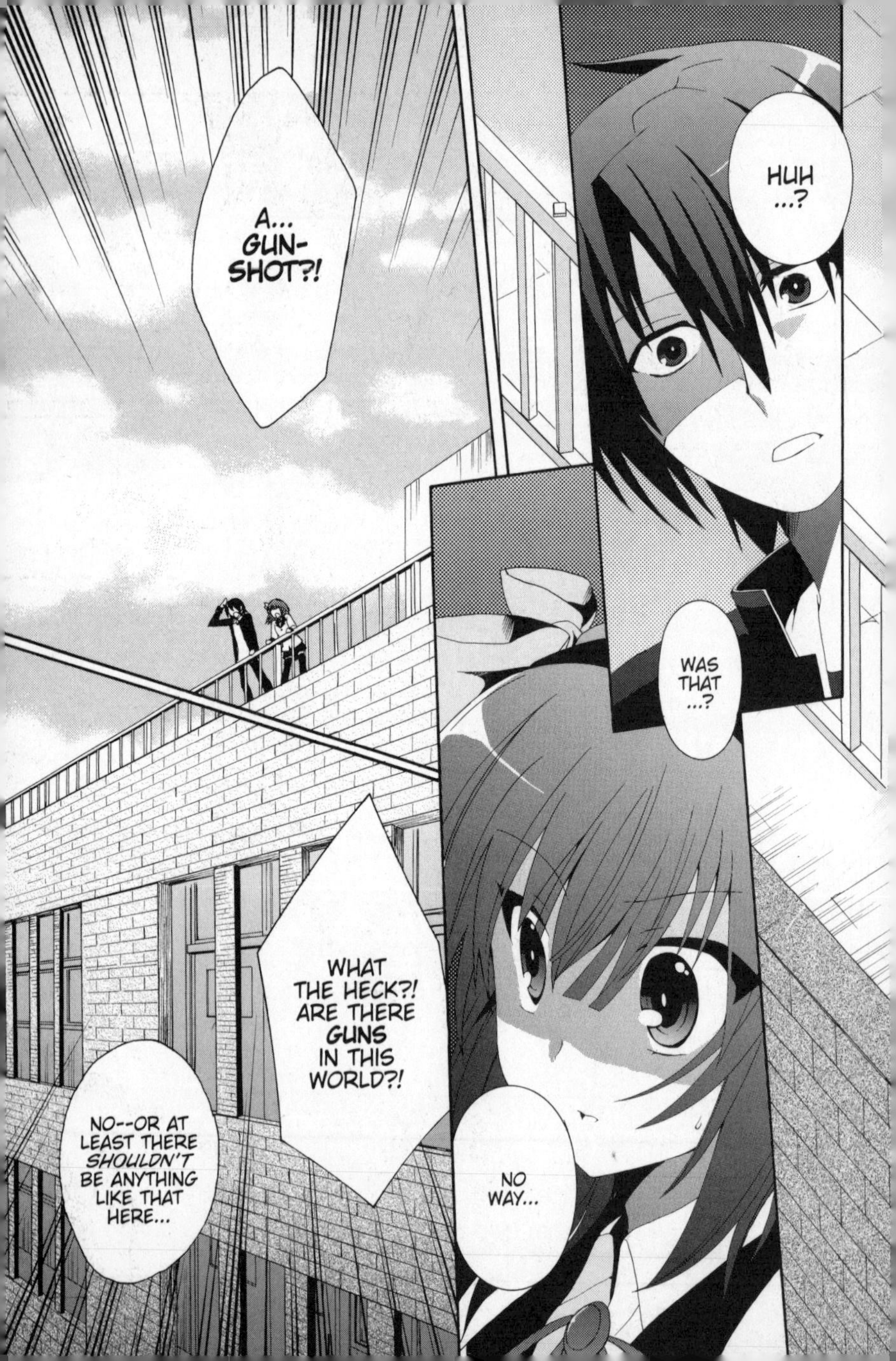
HUH ...?
WAS THAT ...?
NO WAY...
A... GUN-SHOT?!
WHAT THE HECK?! ARE THERE **GUNS** IN THIS WORLD?!
NO--OR AT LEAST THERE *SHOULDN'T* BE ANYTHING LIKE THAT HERE...

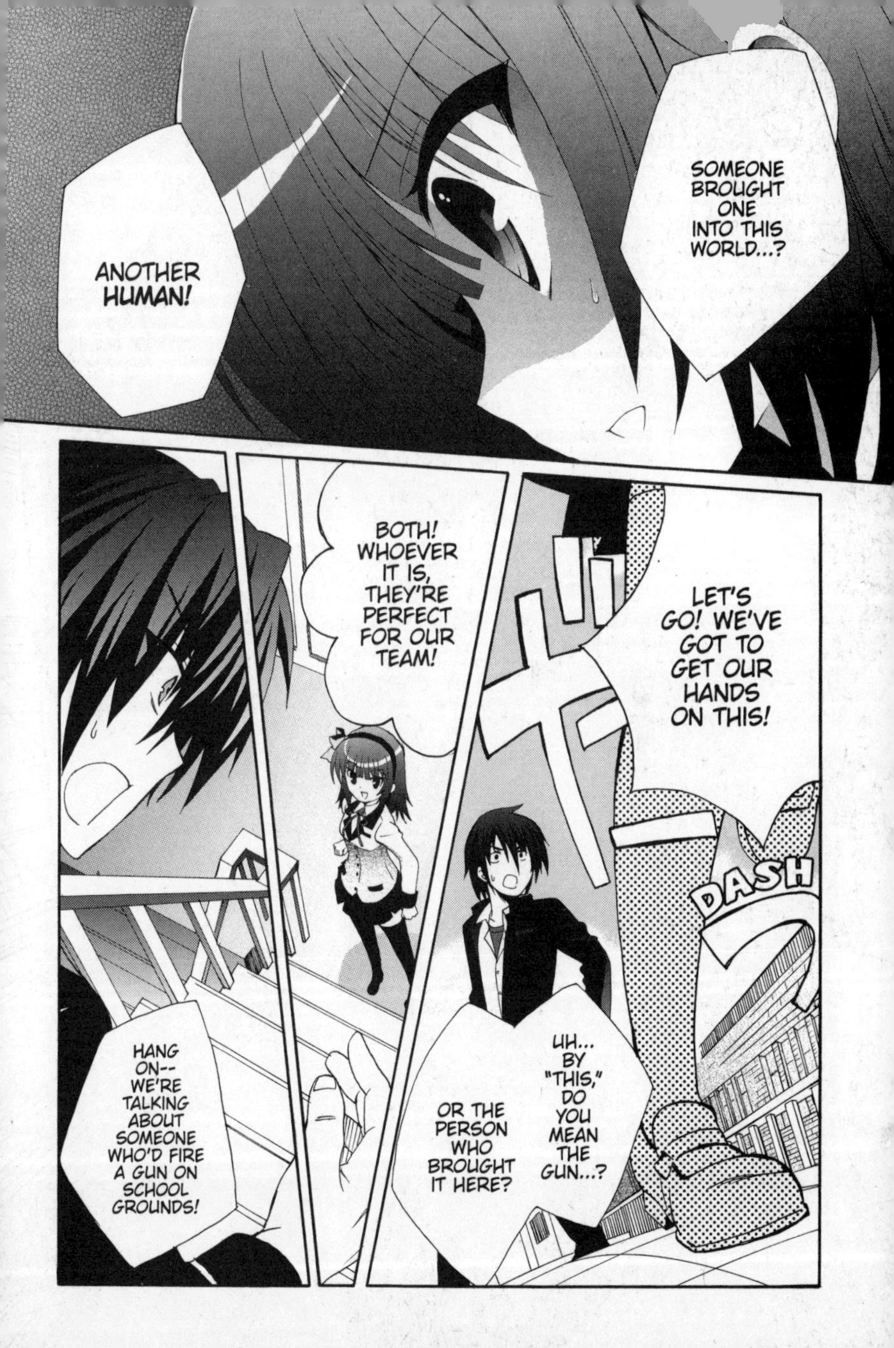
SOMEONE BROUGHT ONE INTO THIS WORLD...?
ANOTHER HUMAN!
LET'S GO! WE'VE GOT TO GET OUR HANDS ON THIS!
DASH
UH... BY "THIS," DO YOU MEAN THE GUN...?
OR THE PERSON WHO BROUGHT IT HERE?
BOTH! WHOEVER IT IS, THEY'RE PERFECT FOR OUR TEAM!
HANG ON-- WE'RE TALKING ABOUT SOMEONE WHO'D FIRE A GUN ON SCHOOL GROUNDS!

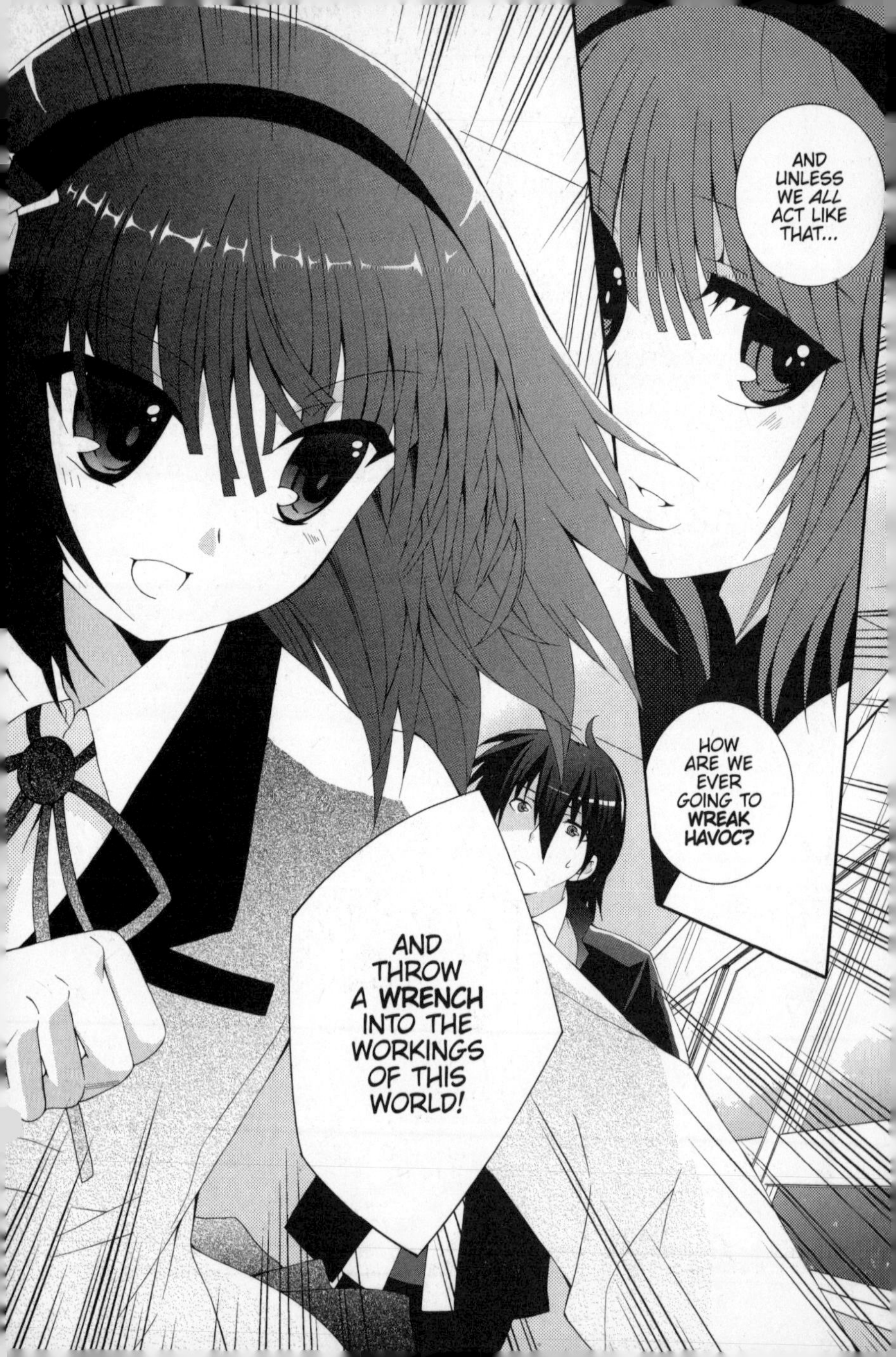
AND UNLESS WE *ALL* ACT LIKE THAT...
HOW ARE WE EVER GOING TO **WREAK HAVOC?**
AND THROW A **WRENCH** INTO THE WORKINGS OF THIS WORLD!

Angel Beats!
Heaven's Door

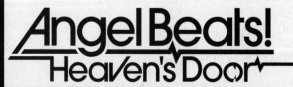

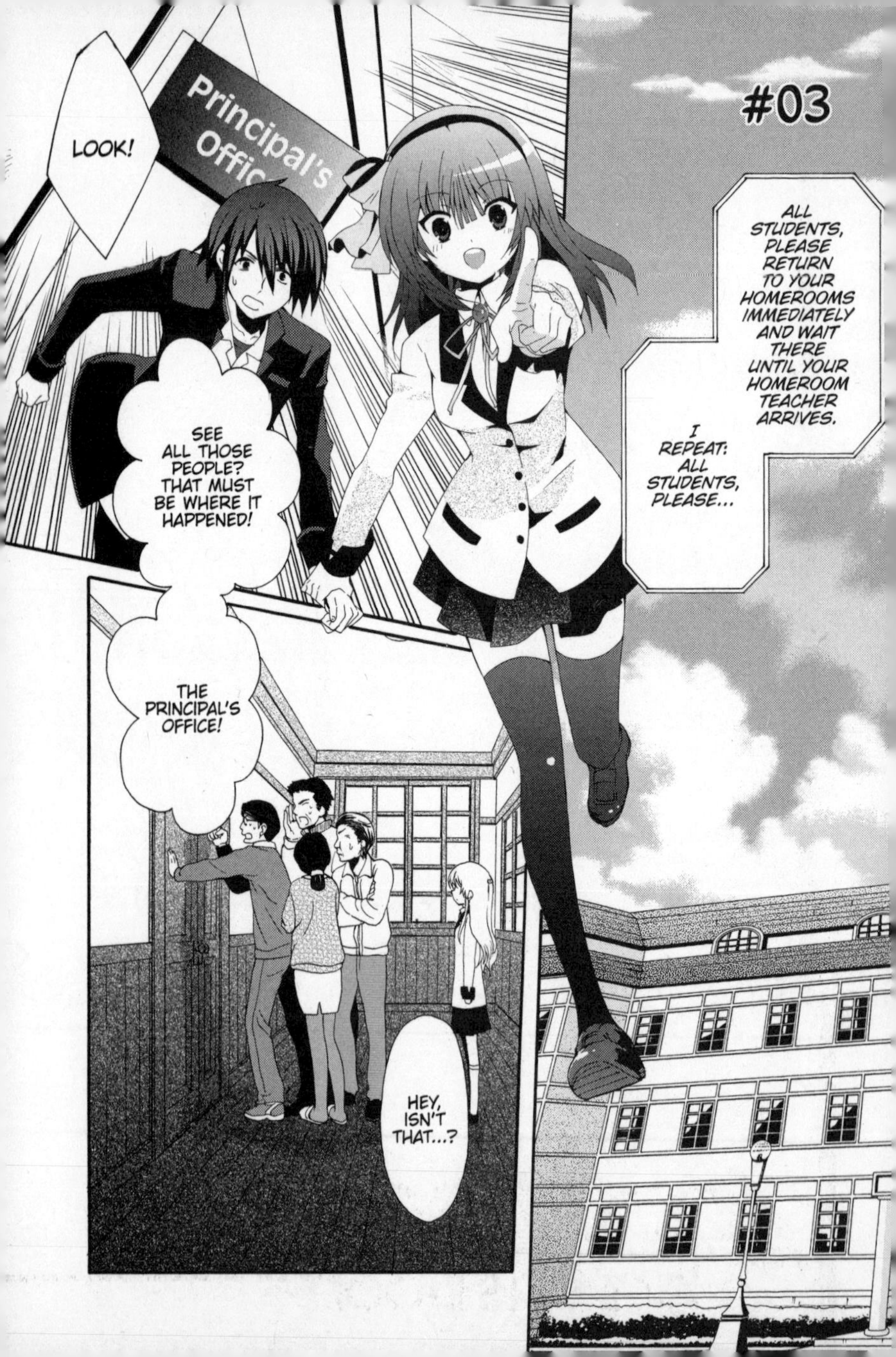
#03
ALL STUDENTS, PLEASE RETURN TO YOUR HOMEROOMS IMMEDIATELY AND WAIT THERE UNTIL YOUR HOMEROOM TEACHER ARRIVES.
I REPEAT: ALL STUDENTS, PLEASE...
LOOK!
Principal's
SEE ALL THOSE PEOPLE? THAT MUST BE WHERE IT HAPPENED!
THE PRINCIPAL'S OFFICE!
HEY, ISN'T THAT...?

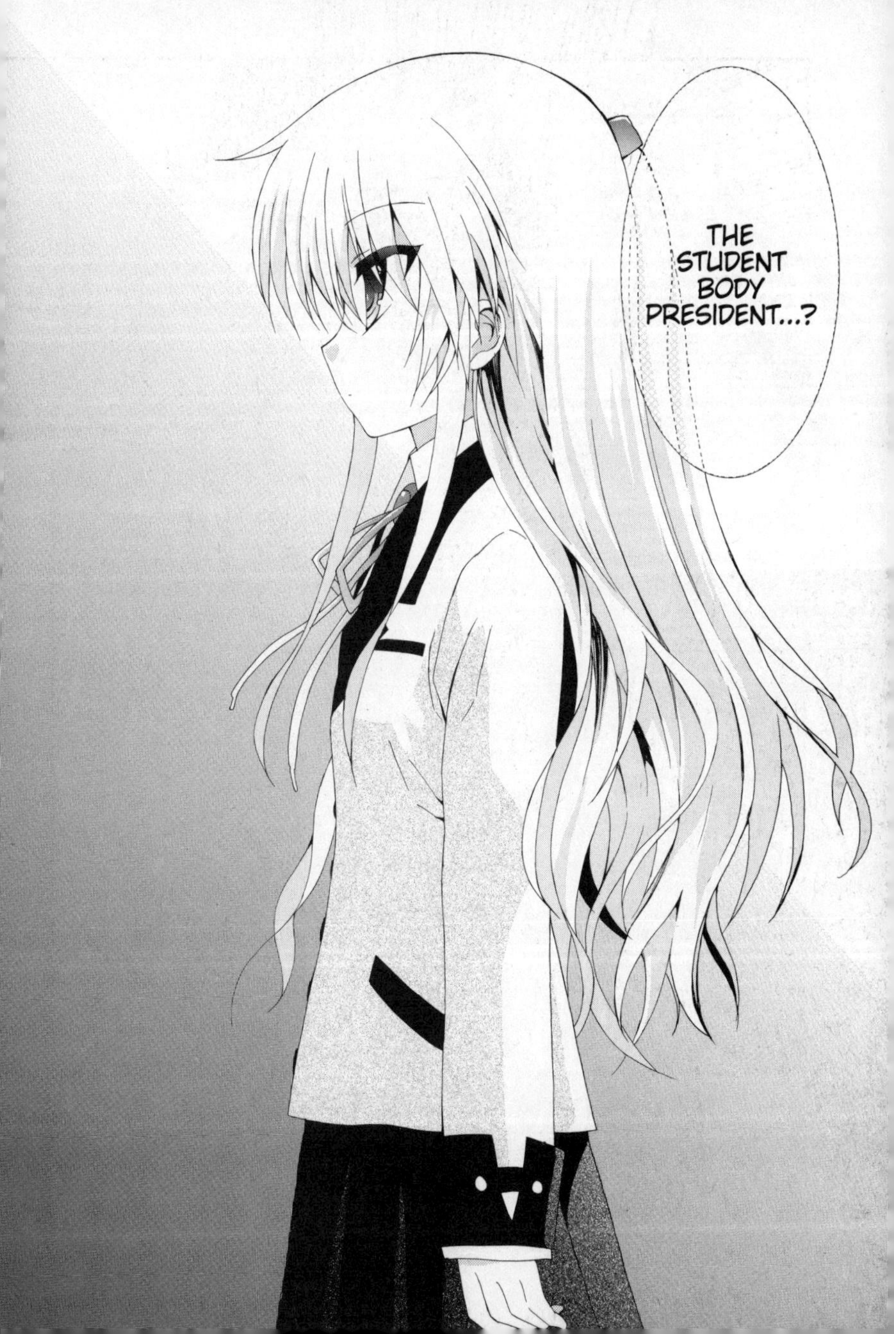
THE STUDENT BODY PRESIDENT...?

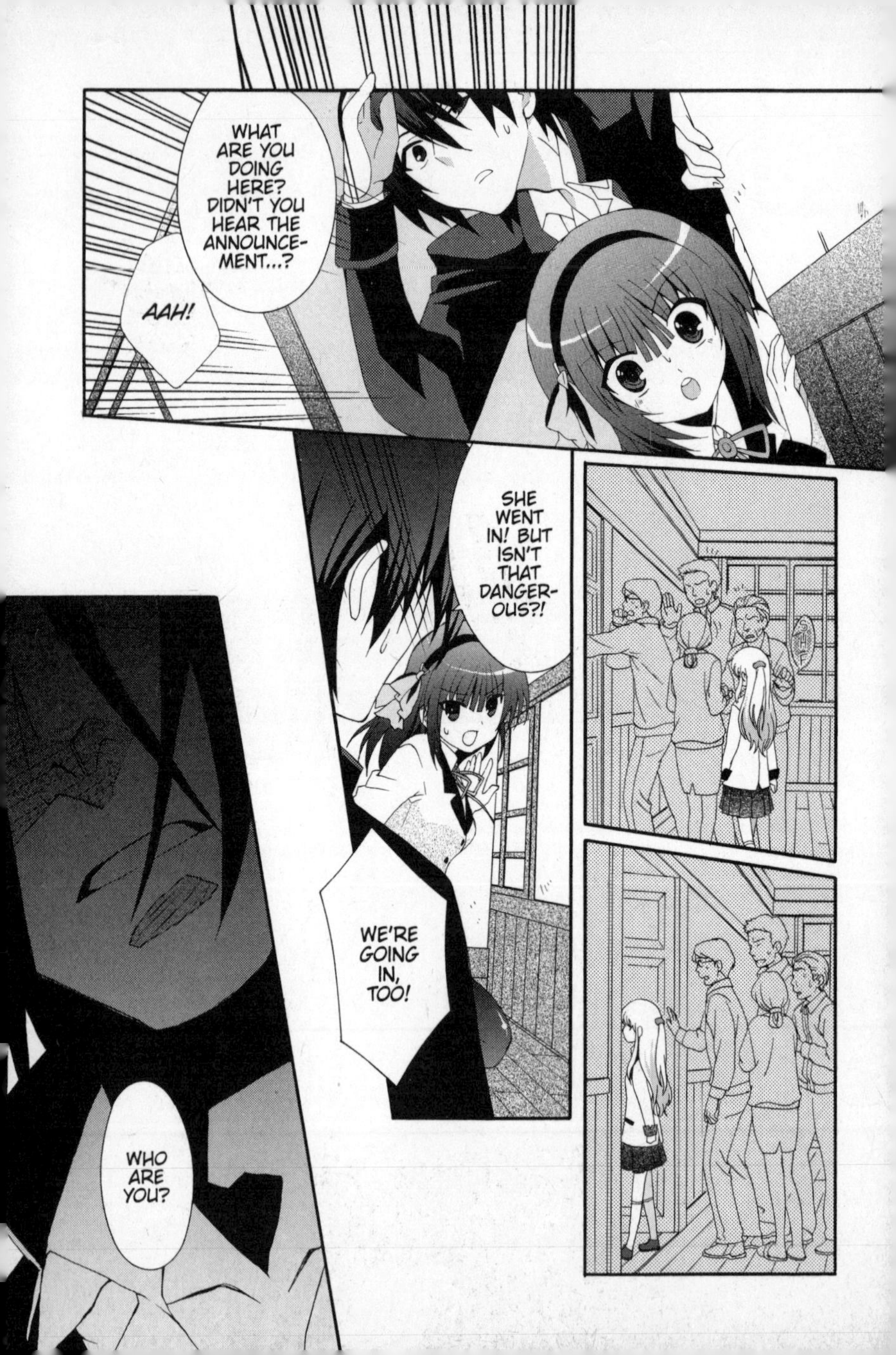
WHAT ARE YOU DOING HERE? DIDN'T YOU HEAR THE ANNOUNCE-MENT...?
AAH!
SHE WENT IN! BUT ISN'T THAT DANGER-OUS?!
WE'RE GOING IN, TOO!
WHO ARE YOU?

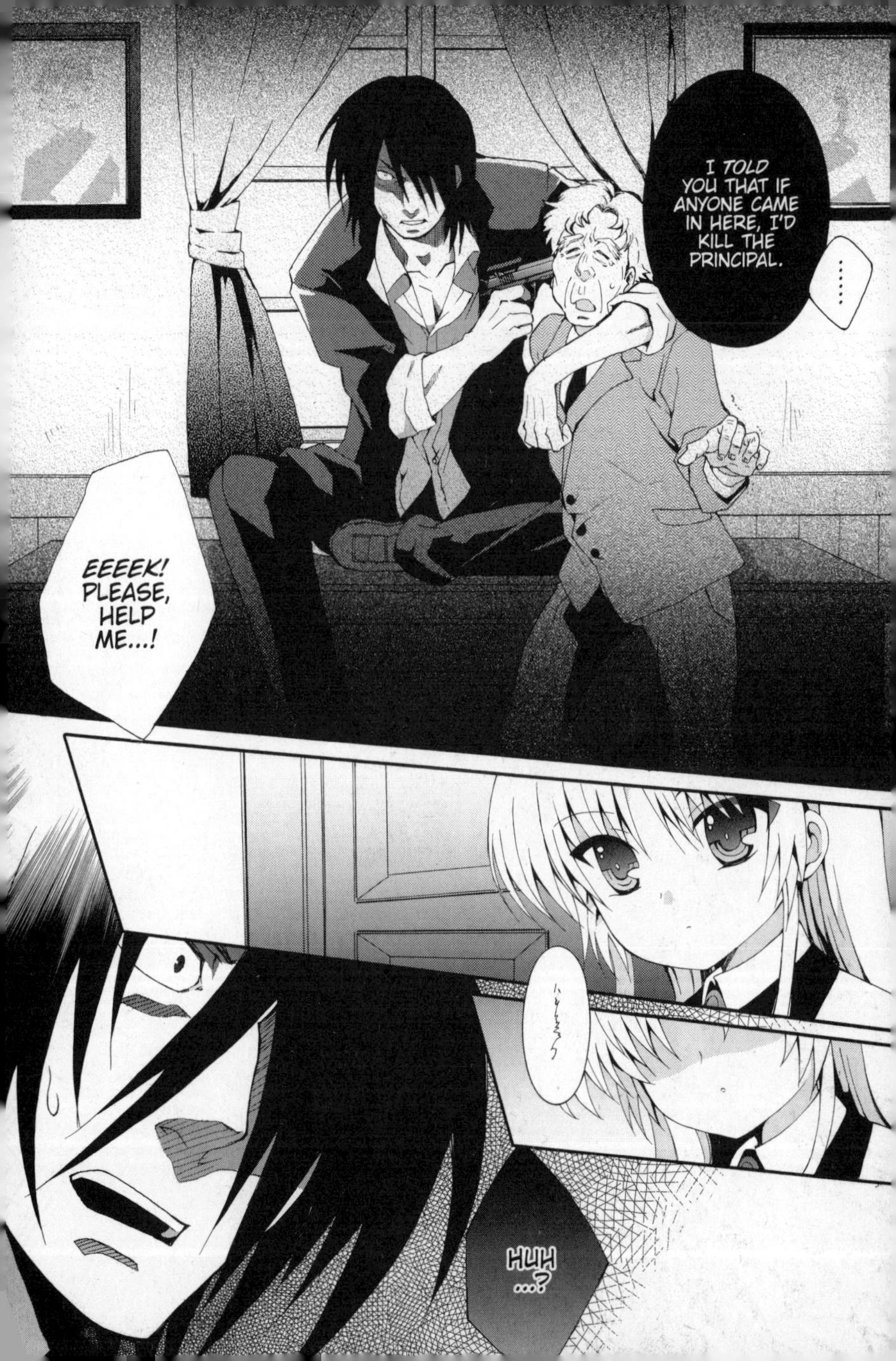
I *TOLD* YOU THAT IF ANYONE CAME IN HERE, I'D KILL THE PRINCIPAL.
......
EEEEK! PLEASE, HELP ME...!
HUH ...?

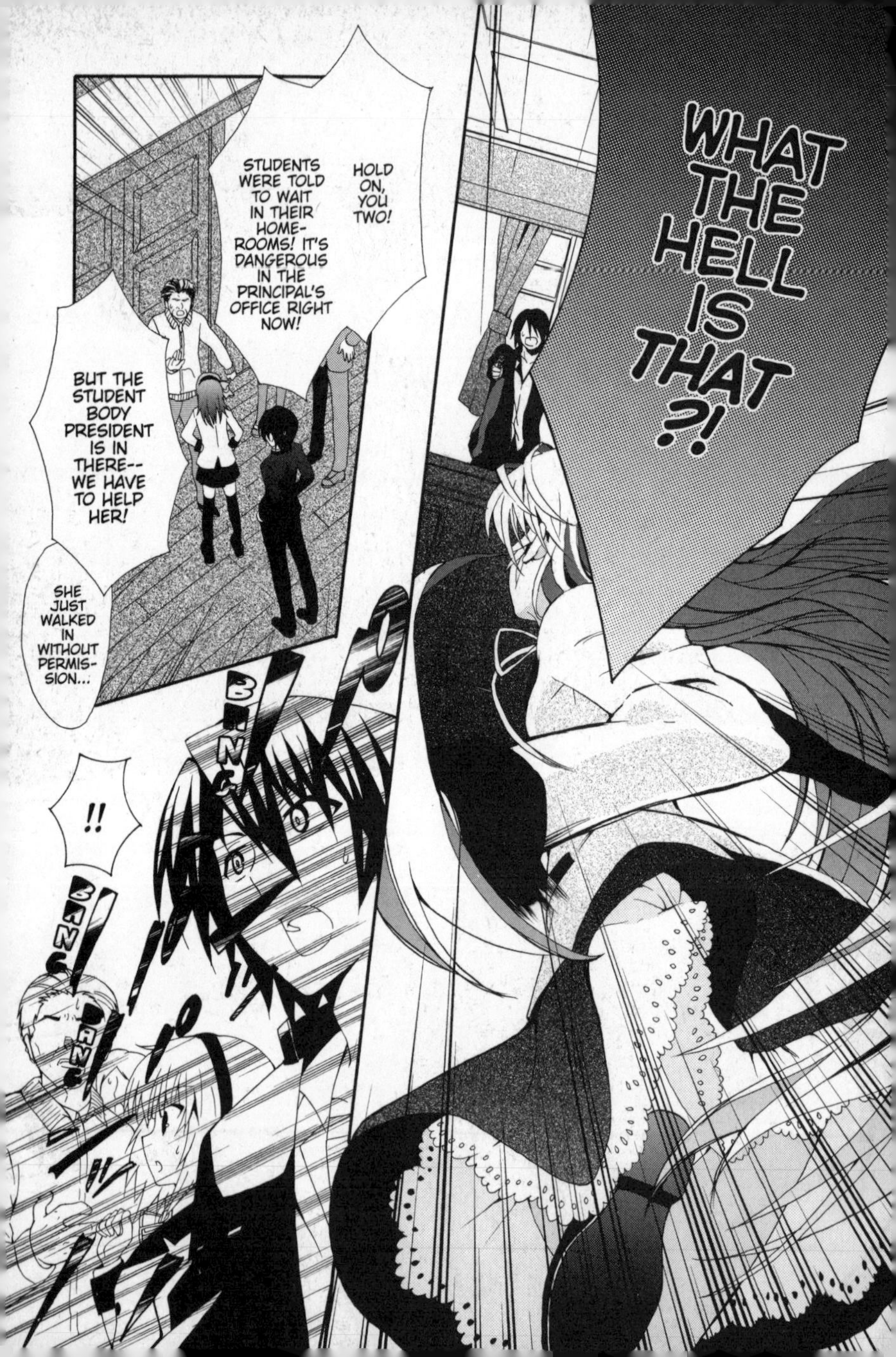
WHAT THE HELL IS THAT?!
HOLD ON, YOU TWO!
STUDENTS WERE TOLD TO WAIT IN THEIR HOME-ROOMS! IT'S DANGEROUS IN THE PRINCIPAL'S OFFICE RIGHT NOW!
BUT THE STUDENT BODY PRESIDENT IS IN THERE-- WE HAVE TO HELP HER!
SHE JUST WALKED IN WITHOUT PERMIS-SION...
BANG
!!
BANG
BANG

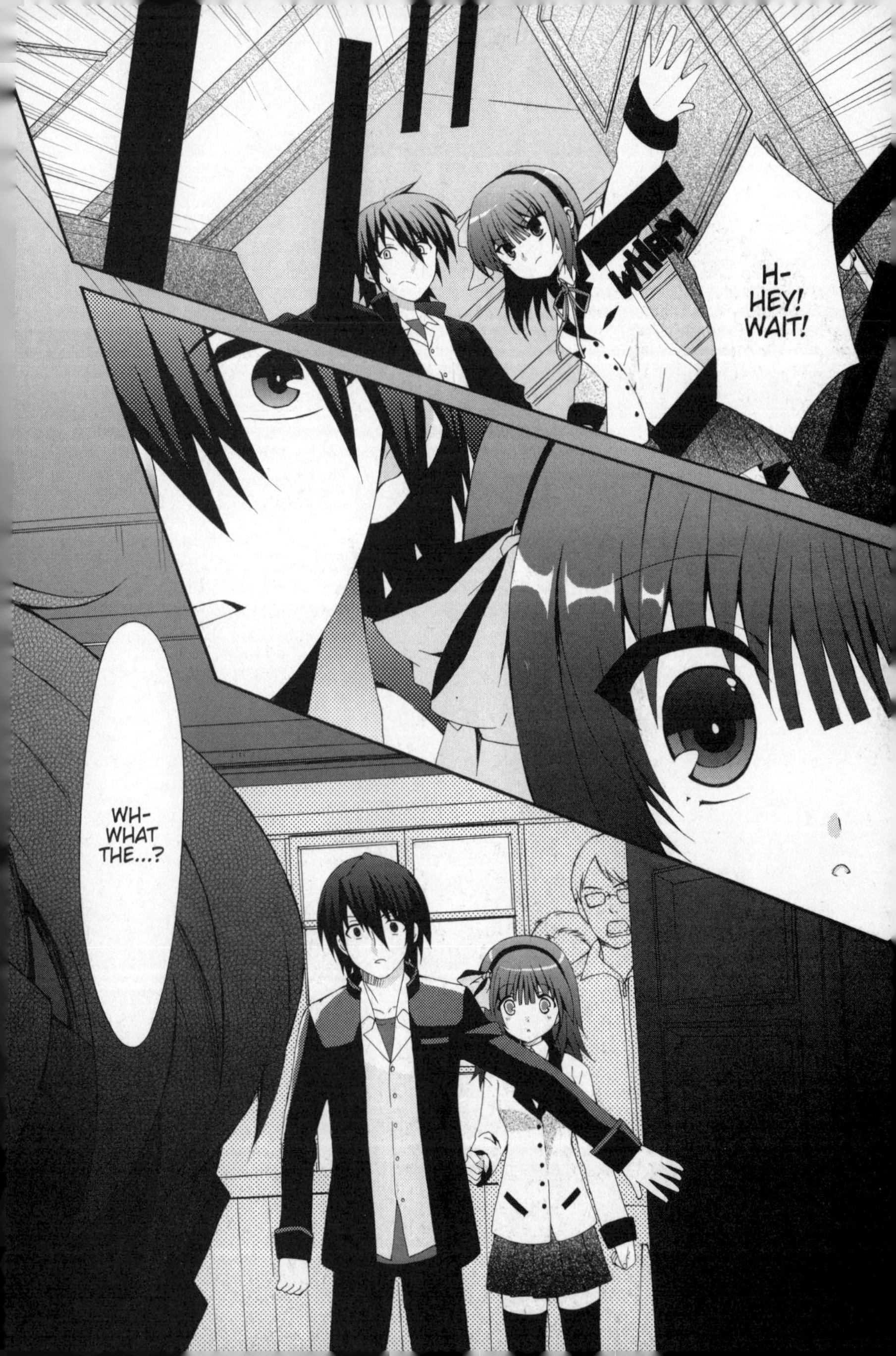
WHAM
H- HEY! WAIT!
WH- WHAT THE...?

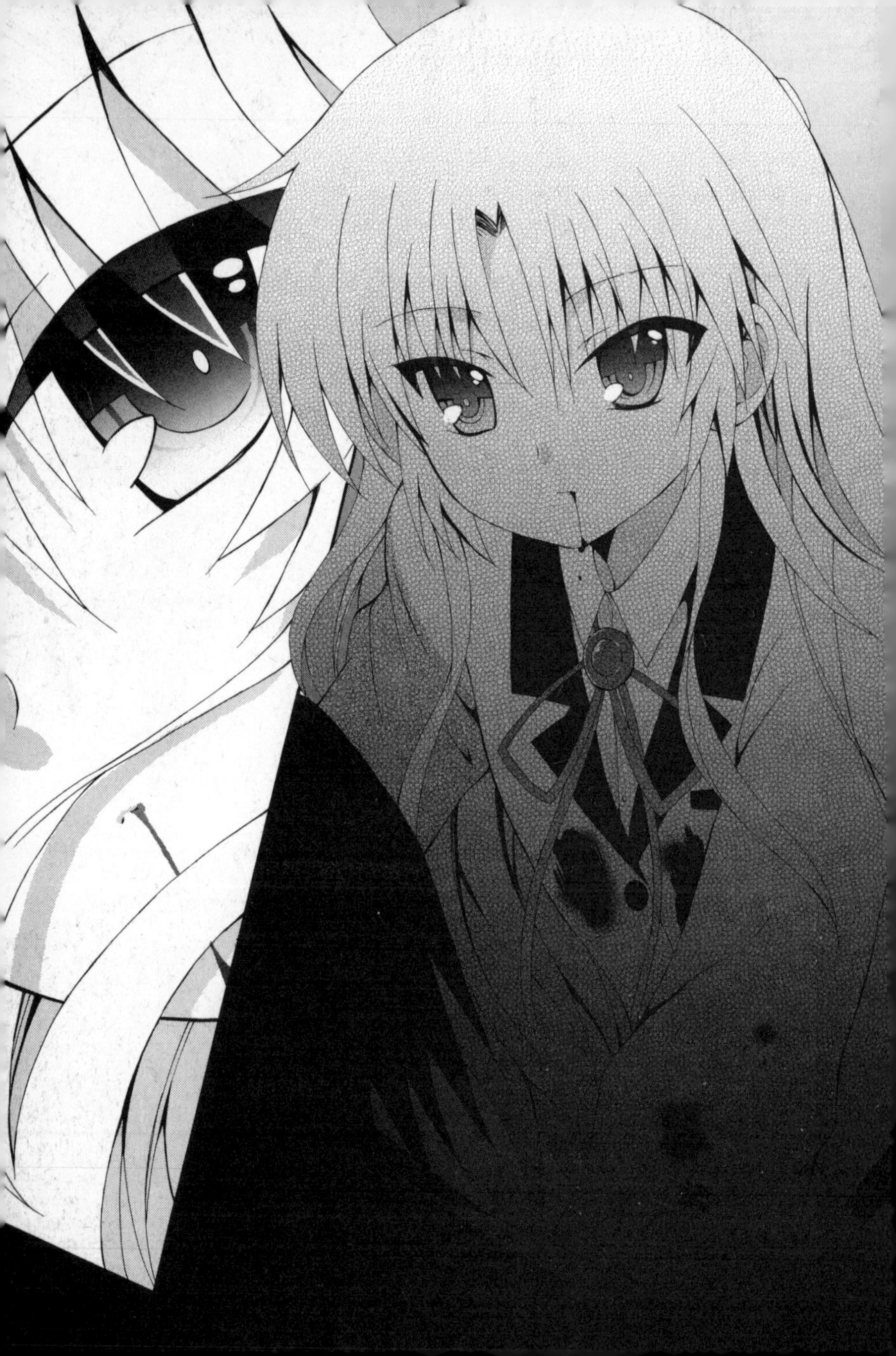

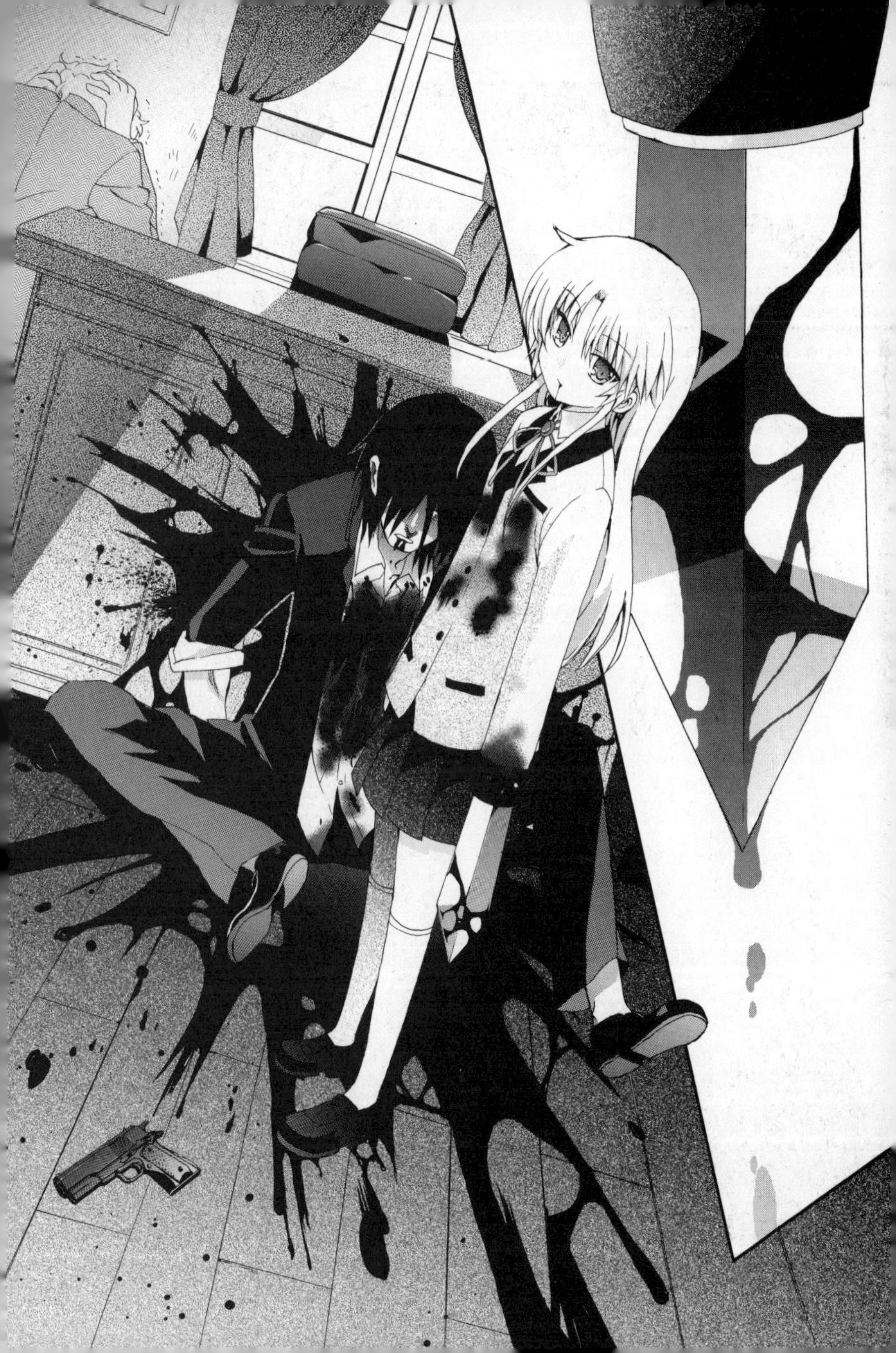

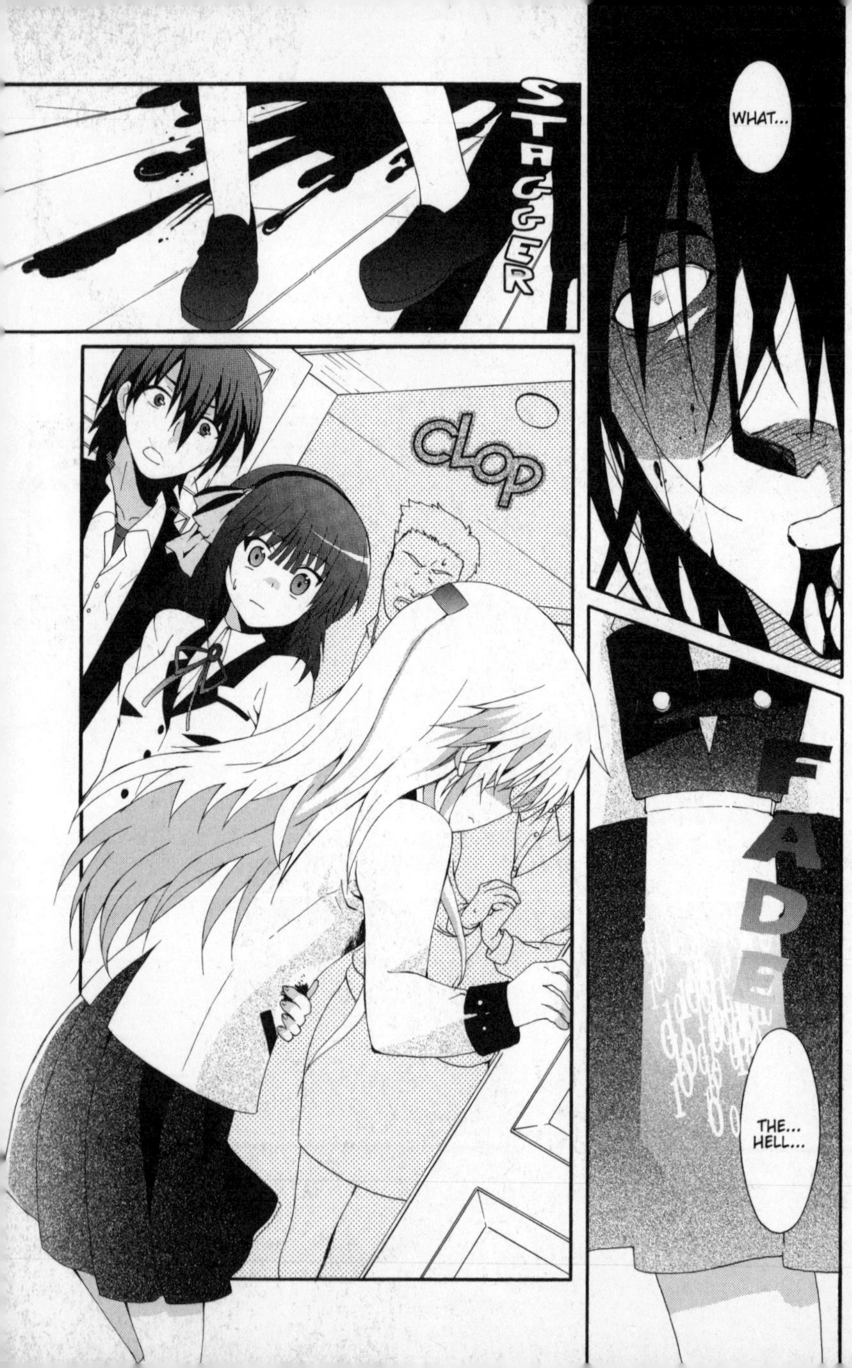
WHAT...
STAGGER
CLOP
FADE
THE... HELL...

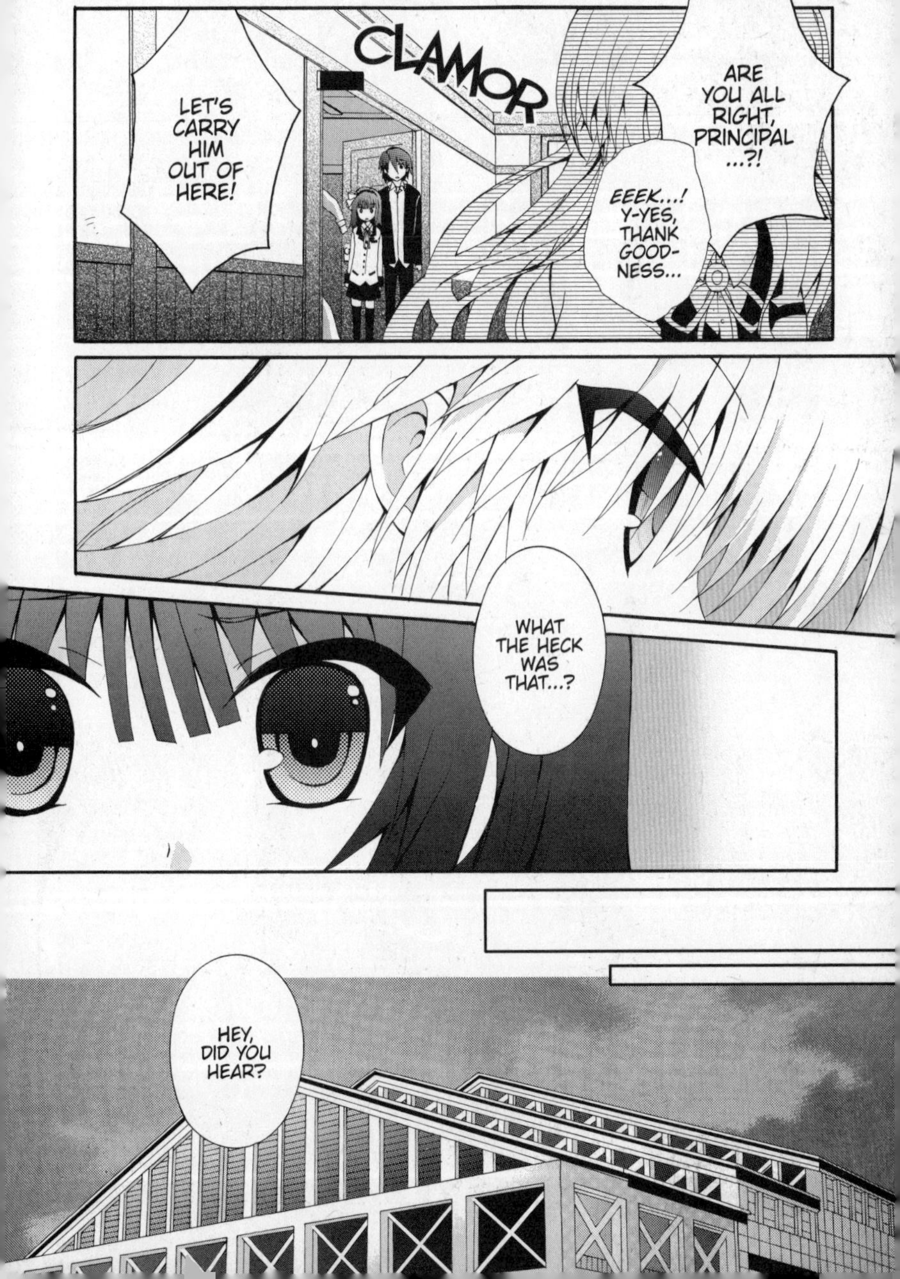
ARE YOU ALL RIGHT, PRINCIPAL ...?!
CLAMOR
EEEK...! Y-YES, THANK GOOD-NESS...
LET'S CARRY HIM OUT OF HERE!
WHAT THE HECK WAS THAT...?
HEY, DID YOU HEAR?

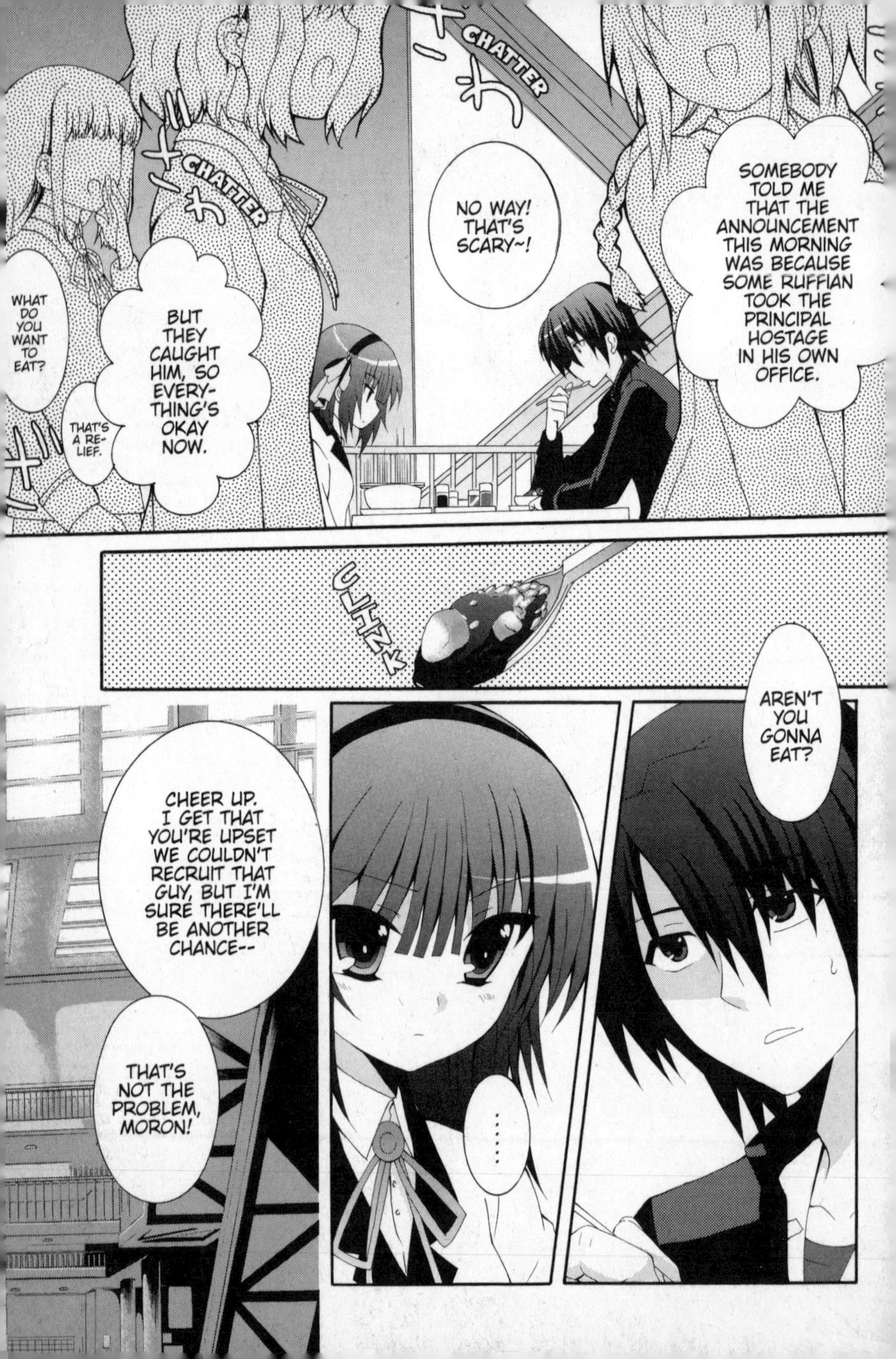
SOMEBODY TOLD ME THAT THE ANNOUNCEMENT THIS MORNING WAS BECAUSE SOME RUFFIAN TOOK THE PRINCIPAL HOSTAGE IN HIS OWN OFFICE.
CHATTER
NO WAY! THAT'S SCARY~!
CHATTER
BUT THEY CAUGHT HIM, SO EVERY-THING'S OKAY NOW.
THAT'S A RE-LIEF.
WHAT DO YOU WANT TO EAT?
CLINK
AREN'T YOU GONNA EAT?
......
CHEER UP. I GET THAT YOU'RE UPSET WE COULDN'T RECRUIT THAT GUY, BUT I'M SURE THERE'LL BE ANOTHER CHANCE--
THAT'S NOT THE PROBLEM, MORON!

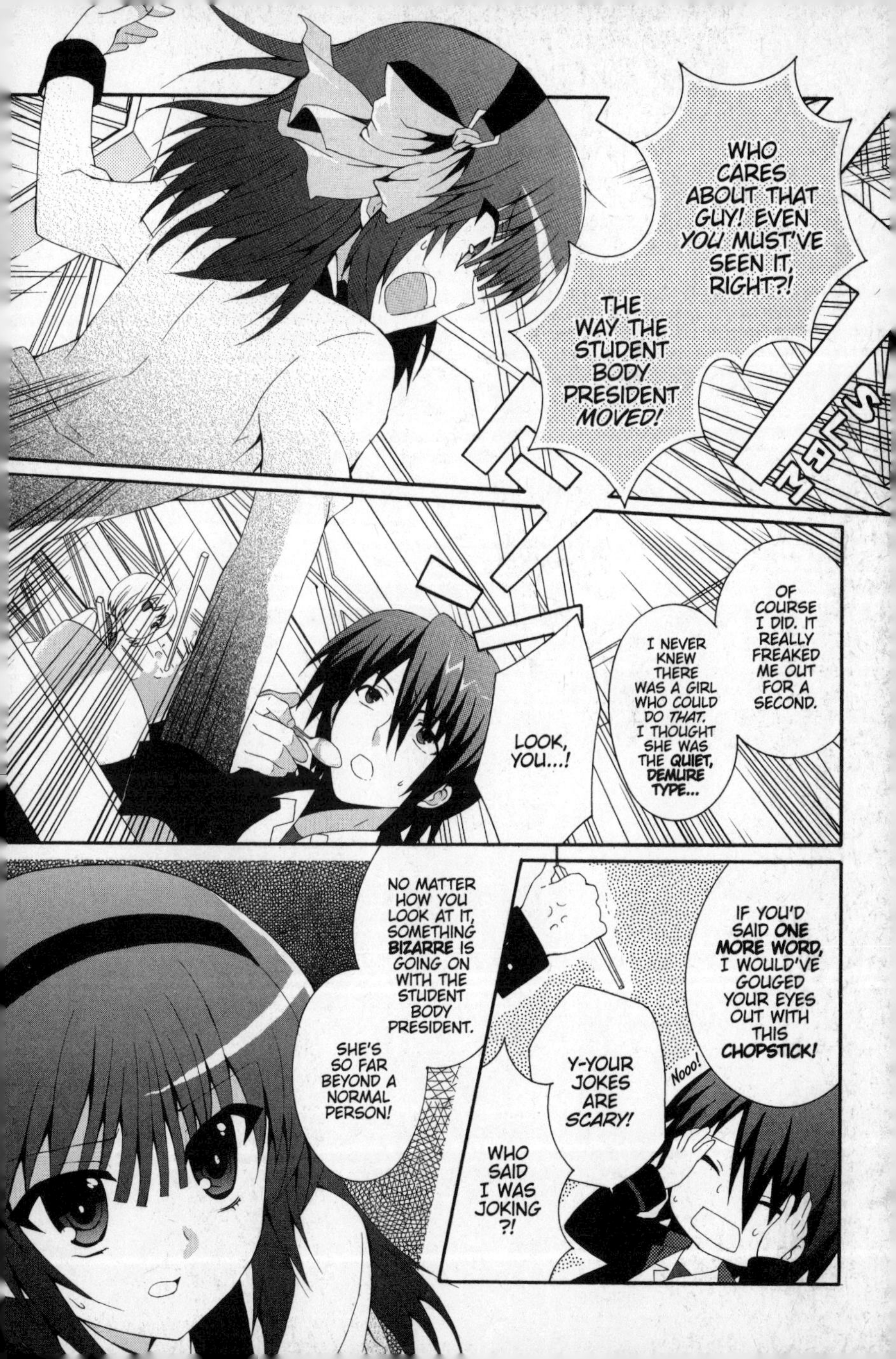
WHO CARES ABOUT THAT GUY! EVEN YOU MUST'VE SEEN IT, RIGHT?!
THE WAY THE STUDENT BODY PRESIDENT MOVED!
SLAM
OF COURSE I DID. IT REALLY FREAKED ME OUT FOR A SECOND.
I NEVER KNEW THERE WAS A GIRL WHO COULD DO THAT. I THOUGHT SHE WAS THE QUIET, DEMURE TYPE...
LOOK, YOU...!
IF YOU'D SAID ONE MORE WORD, I WOULD'VE GOUGED YOUR EYES OUT WITH THIS CHOPSTICK!
Nooo!
Y-YOUR JOKES ARE SCARY!
WHO SAID I WAS JOKING?!
NO MATTER HOW YOU LOOK AT IT, SOMETHING BIZARRE IS GOING ON WITH THE STUDENT BODY PRESIDENT.
SHE'S SO FAR BEYOND A NORMAL PERSON!

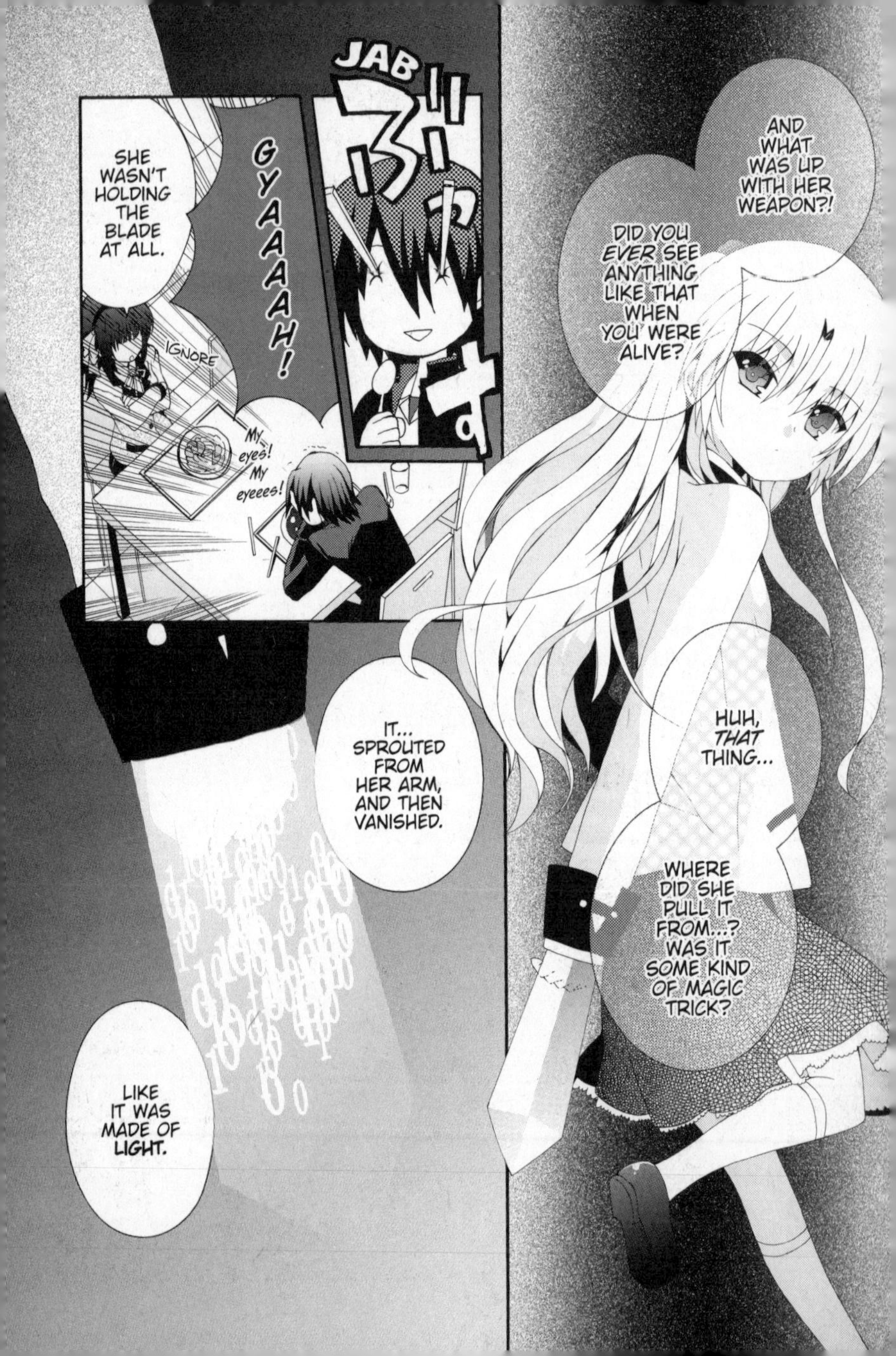
AND WHAT WAS UP WITH HER WEAPON?!
DID YOU EVER SEE ANYTHING LIKE THAT WHEN YOU WERE ALIVE?
HUH, THAT THING...
WHERE DID SHE PULL IT FROM...? WAS IT SOME KIND OF MAGIC TRICK?
JAB
GYAAAAAH!
SHE WASN'T HOLDING THE BLADE AT ALL.
IGNORE
My eyes! My eyeees!
IT... SPROUTED FROM HER ARM, AND THEN VANISHED.
LIKE IT WAS MADE OF LIGHT.

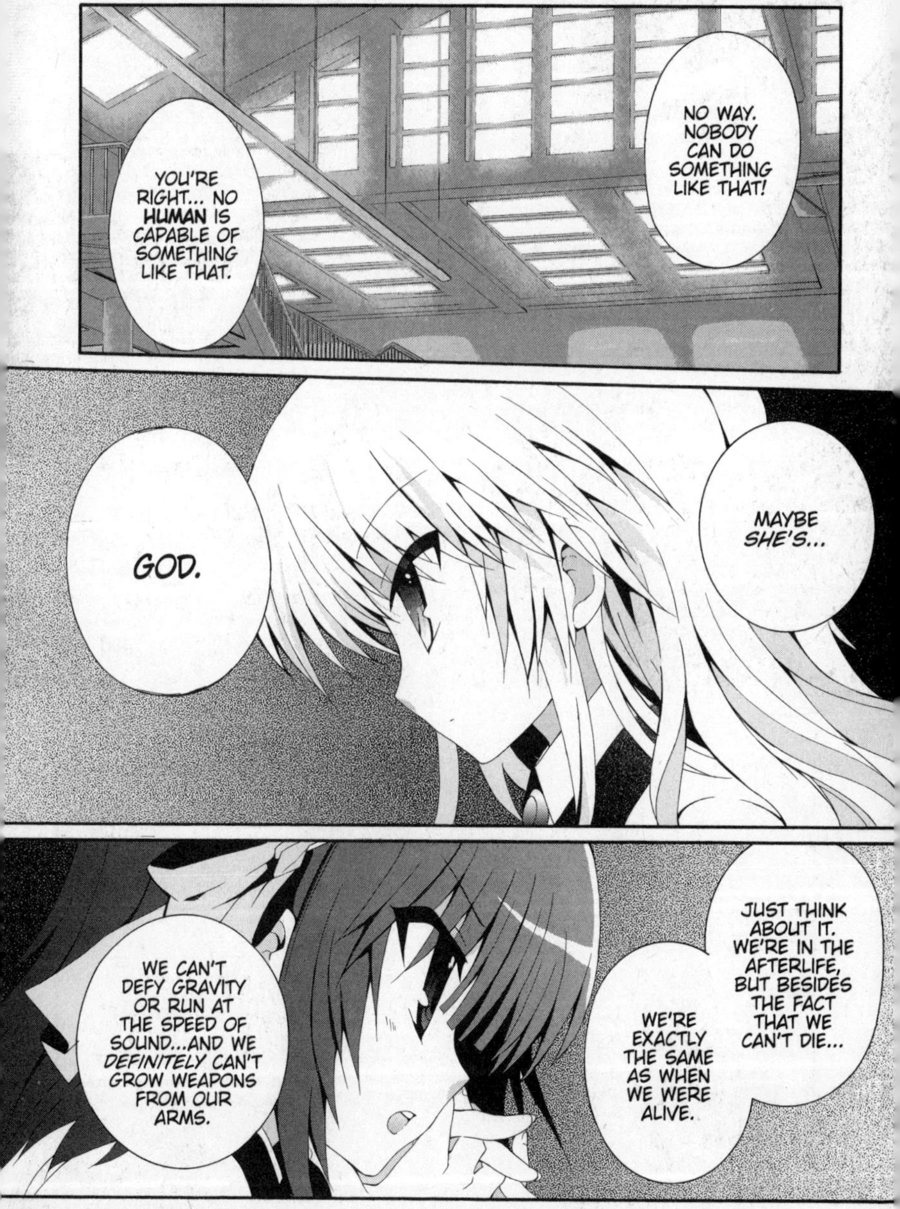
NO WAY. NOBODY CAN DO SOMETHING LIKE THAT!
YOU'RE RIGHT... NO HUMAN IS CAPABLE OF SOMETHING LIKE THAT.
MAYBE SHE'S...
GOD.
JUST THINK ABOUT IT. WE'RE IN THE AFTERLIFE, BUT BESIDES THE FACT THAT WE CAN'T DIE...
WE'RE EXACTLY THE SAME AS WHEN WE WERE ALIVE.
WE CAN'T DEFY GRAVITY OR RUN AT THE SPEED OF SOUND...AND WE DEFINITELY CAN'T GROW WEAPONS FROM OUR ARMS.

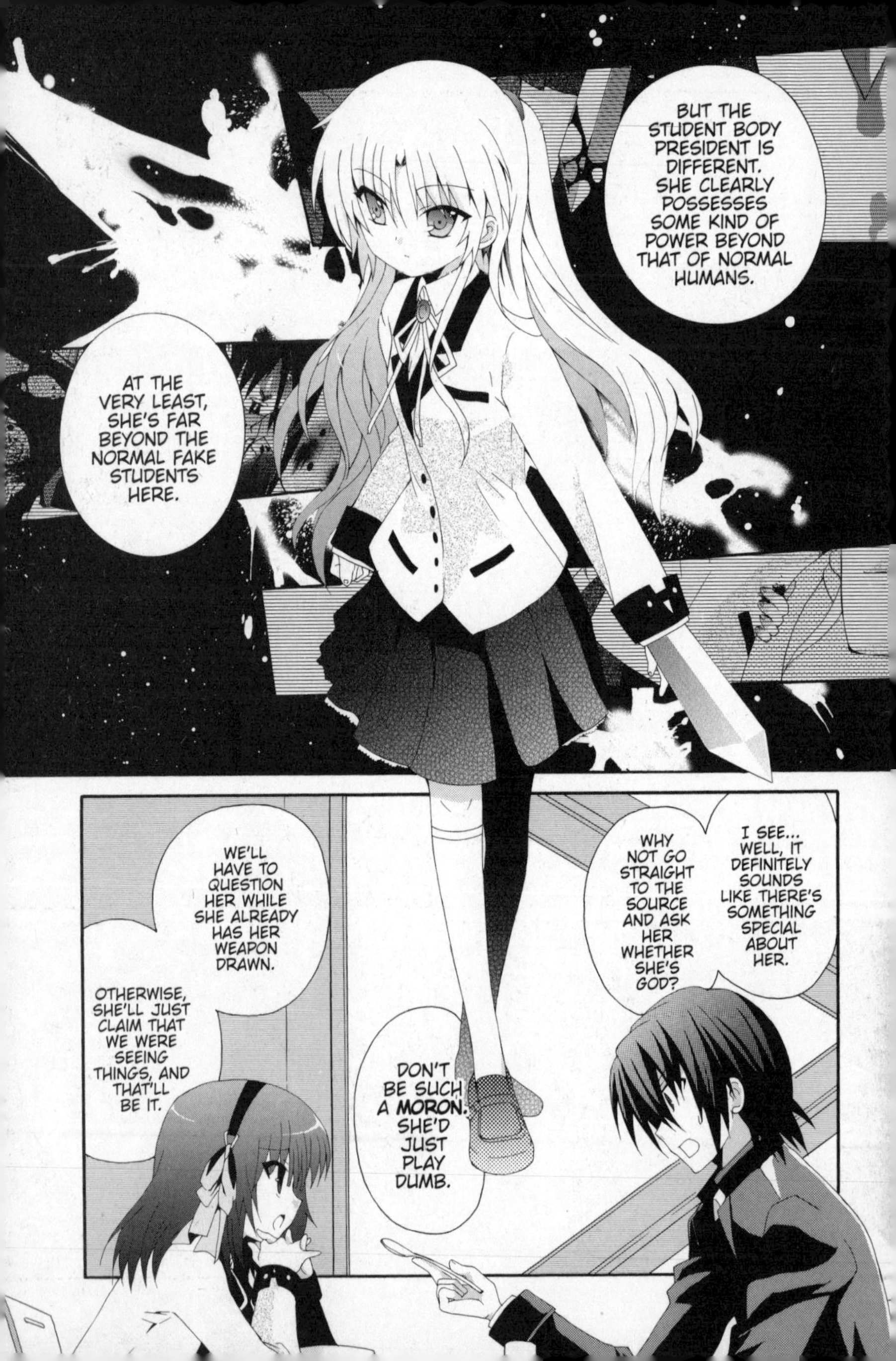
BUT THE STUDENT BODY PRESIDENT IS DIFFERENT. SHE CLEARLY POSSESSES SOME KIND OF POWER BEYOND THAT OF NORMAL HUMANS.
AT THE VERY LEAST, SHE'S FAR BEYOND THE NORMAL FAKE STUDENTS HERE.
I SEE... WELL, IT DEFINITELY SOUNDS LIKE THERE'S SOMETHING SPECIAL ABOUT HER.
WHY NOT GO STRAIGHT TO THE SOURCE AND ASK HER WHETHER SHE'S GOD?
DON'T BE SUCH A **MORON**. SHE'D JUST PLAY DUMB.
WE'LL HAVE TO QUESTION HER WHILE SHE ALREADY HAS HER WEAPON DRAWN.
OTHERWISE, SHE'LL JUST CLAIM THAT WE WERE SEEING THINGS, AND THAT'LL BE IT.

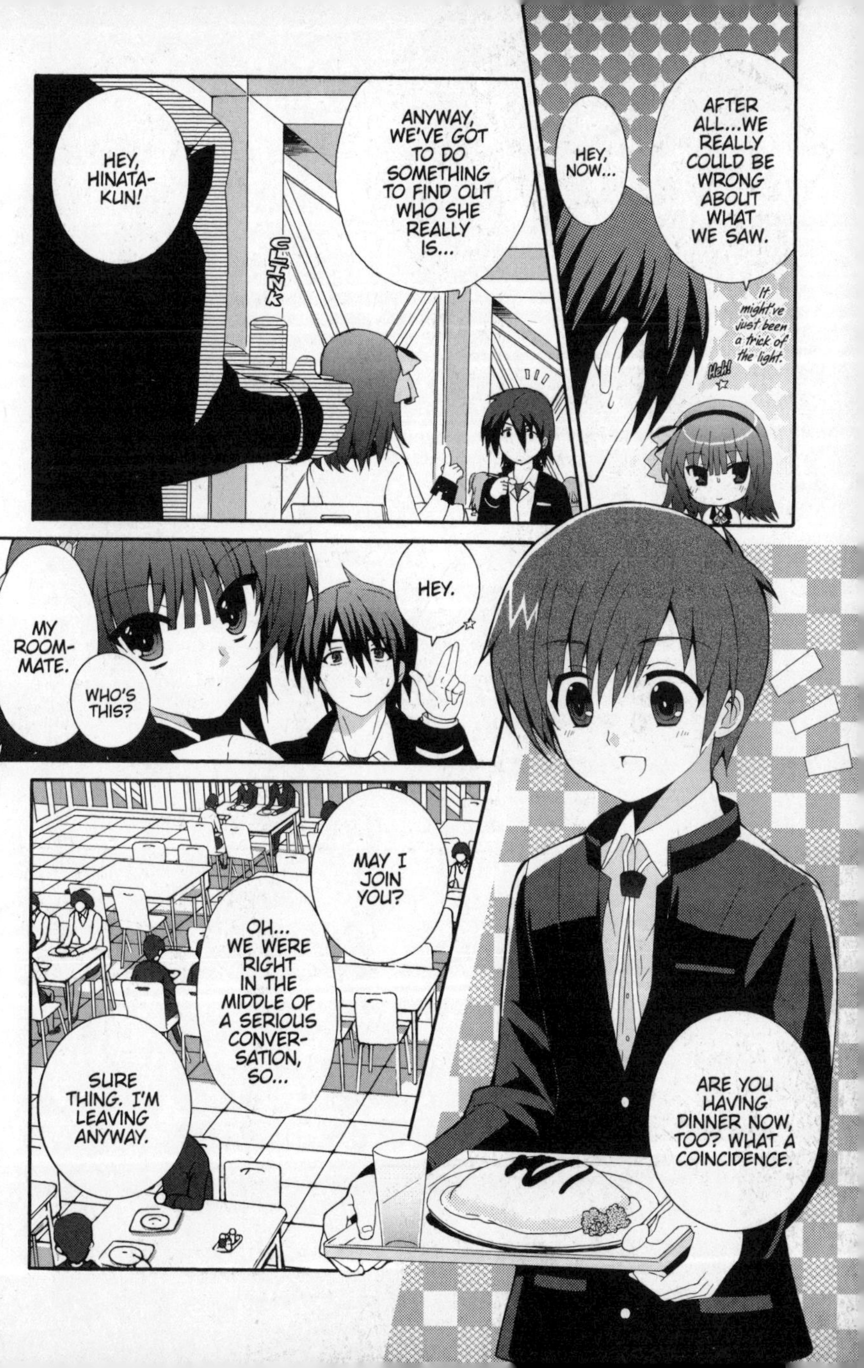

AFTER ALL...WE REALLY COULD BE WRONG ABOUT WHAT WE SAW.
HEY, NOW...
It might've just been a trick of the light.
Heh!
ANYWAY, WE'VE GOT TO DO SOMETHING TO FIND OUT WHO SHE REALLY IS...
CLINK
HEY, HINATA-KUN!
ARE YOU HAVING DINNER NOW, TOO? WHAT A COINCIDENCE.
HEY.
MY ROOMMATE.
WHO'S THIS?
MAY I JOIN YOU?
OH... WE WERE RIGHT IN THE MIDDLE OF A SERIOUS CONVERSATION, SO...
SURE THING. I'M LEAVING ANYWAY.

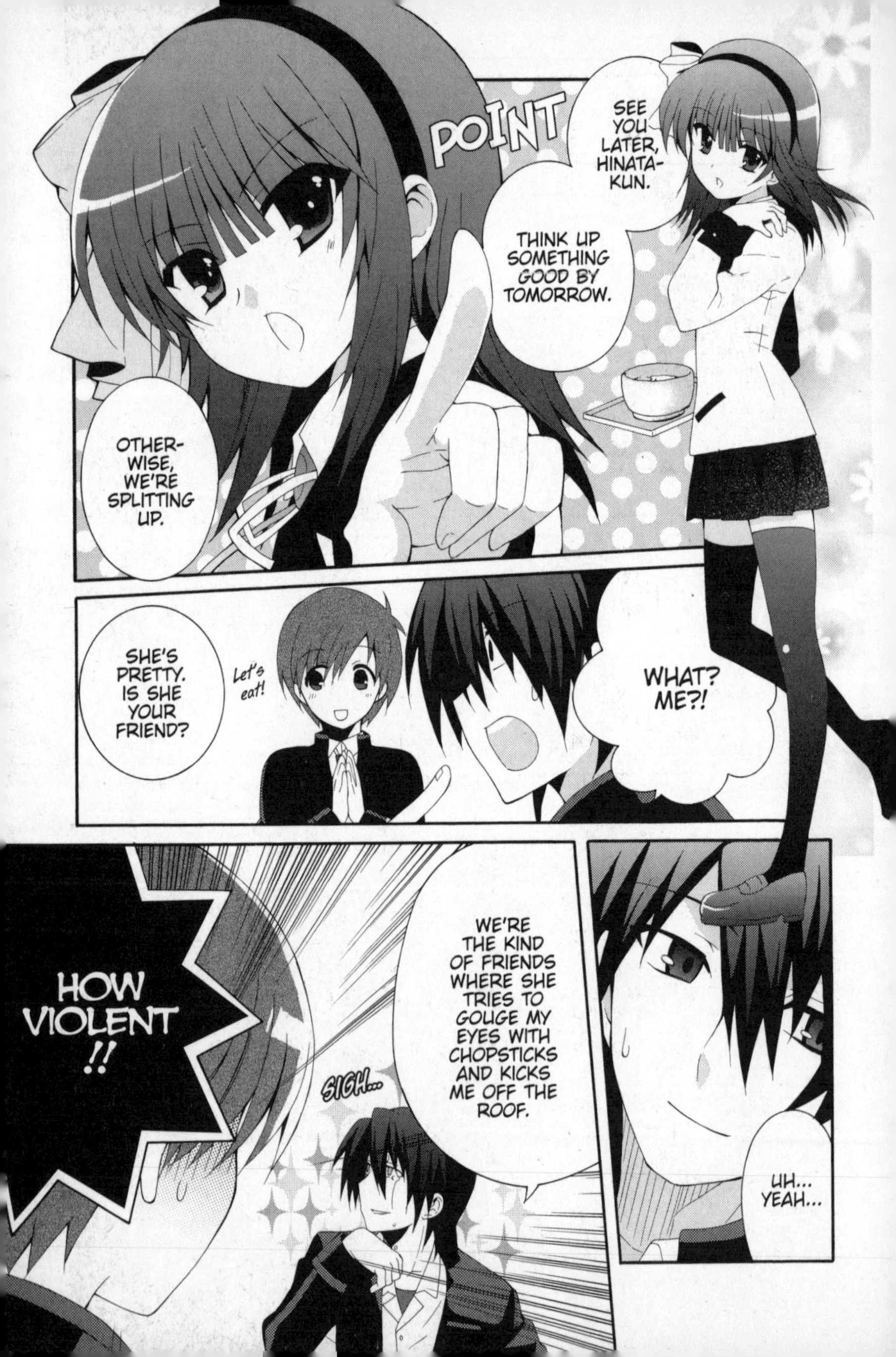
SEE YOU LATER, HINATA-KUN.
THINK UP SOMETHING GOOD BY TOMORROW.
POINT
OTHER-WISE, WE'RE SPLITTING UP.
WHAT? ME?!
SHE'S PRETTY. IS SHE YOUR FRIEND?
Let's eat!
UH... YEAH...
WE'RE THE KIND OF FRIENDS WHERE SHE TRIES TO GOUGE MY EYES WITH CHOPSTICKS AND KICKS ME OFF THE ROOF.
SIGH...
HOW VIOLENT!!

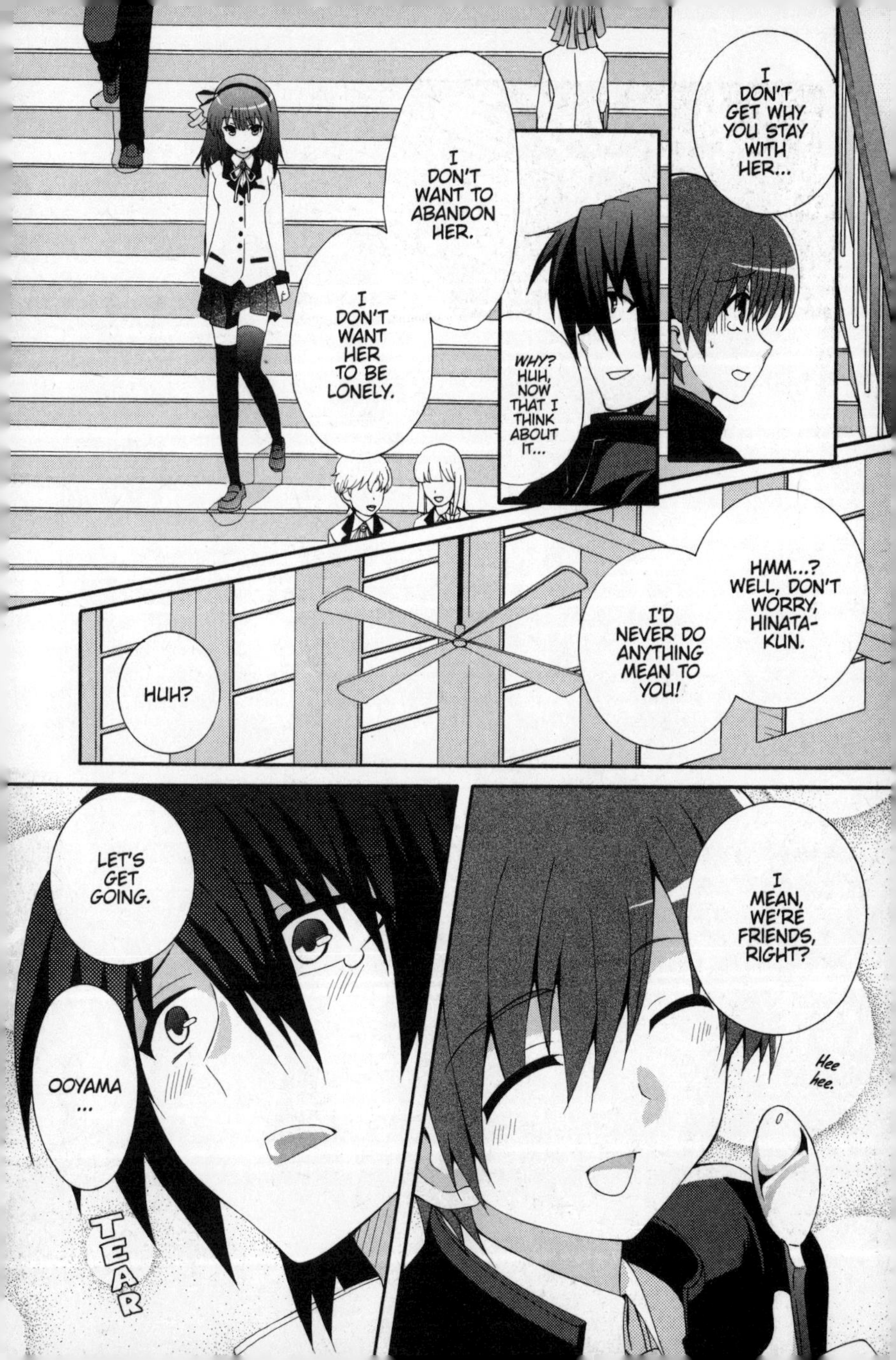
I DON'T GET WHY YOU STAY WITH HER...
WHY? HUH, NOW THAT I THINK ABOUT IT...
I DON'T WANT TO ABANDON HER.
I DON'T WANT HER TO BE LONELY.
HMM...? WELL, DON'T WORRY, HINATA-KUN.
I'D NEVER DO ANYTHING MEAN TO YOU!
HUH?
I MEAN, WE'RE FRIENDS, RIGHT?
Hee hee.
LET'S GET GOING.
OOYAMA ...
TEAR

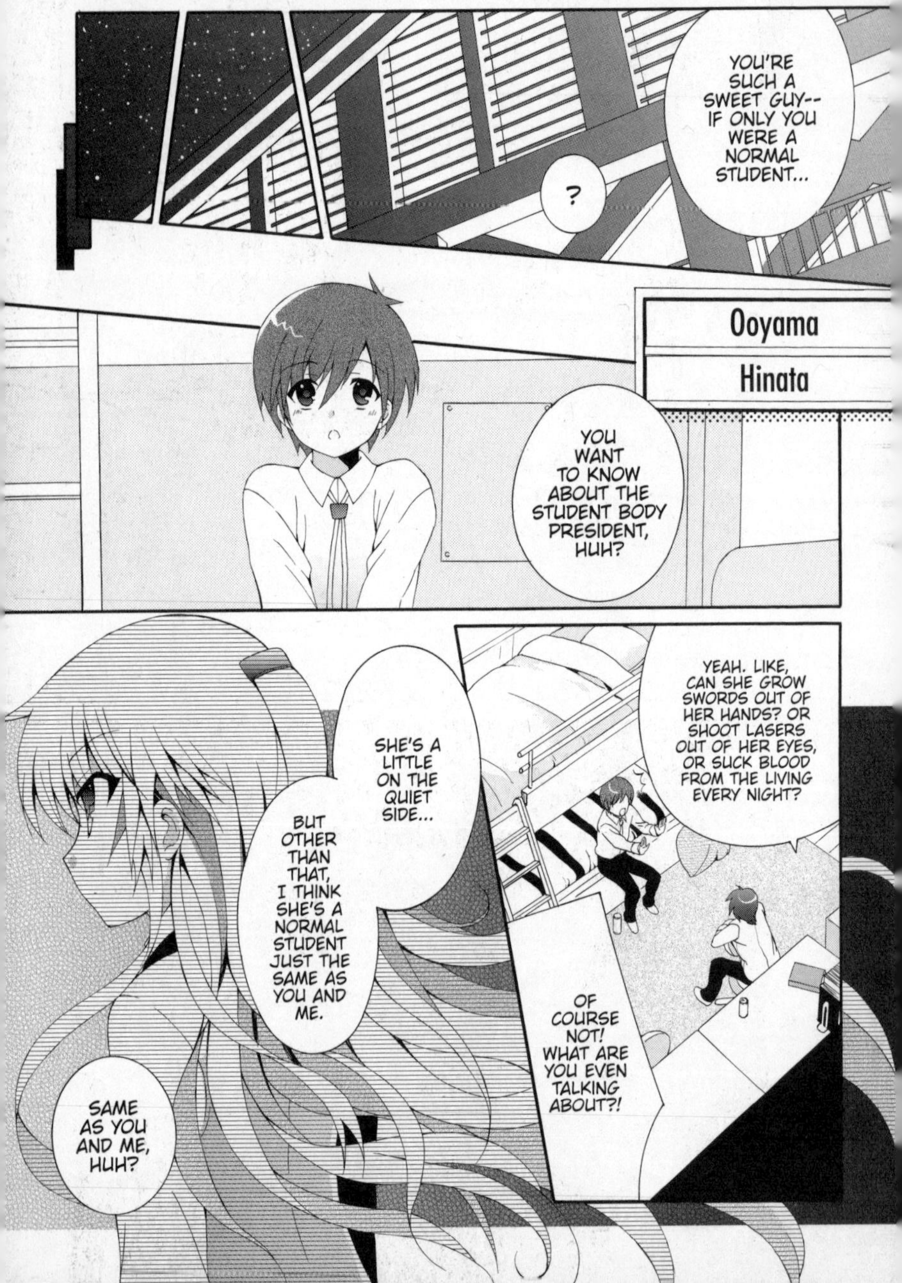
YOU'RE SUCH A SWEET GUY-- IF ONLY YOU WERE A NORMAL STUDENT...
?
Ooyama
Hinata
YOU WANT TO KNOW ABOUT THE STUDENT BODY PRESIDENT, HUH?
YEAH. LIKE, CAN SHE GROW SWORDS OUT OF HER HANDS? OR SHOOT LASERS OUT OF HER EYES, OR SUCK BLOOD FROM THE LIVING EVERY NIGHT?
OF COURSE NOT! WHAT ARE YOU EVEN TALKING ABOUT?!
SHE'S A LITTLE ON THE QUIET SIDE...
BUT OTHER THAN THAT, I THINK SHE'S A NORMAL STUDENT JUST THE SAME AS YOU AND ME.
SAME AS YOU AND ME, HUH?

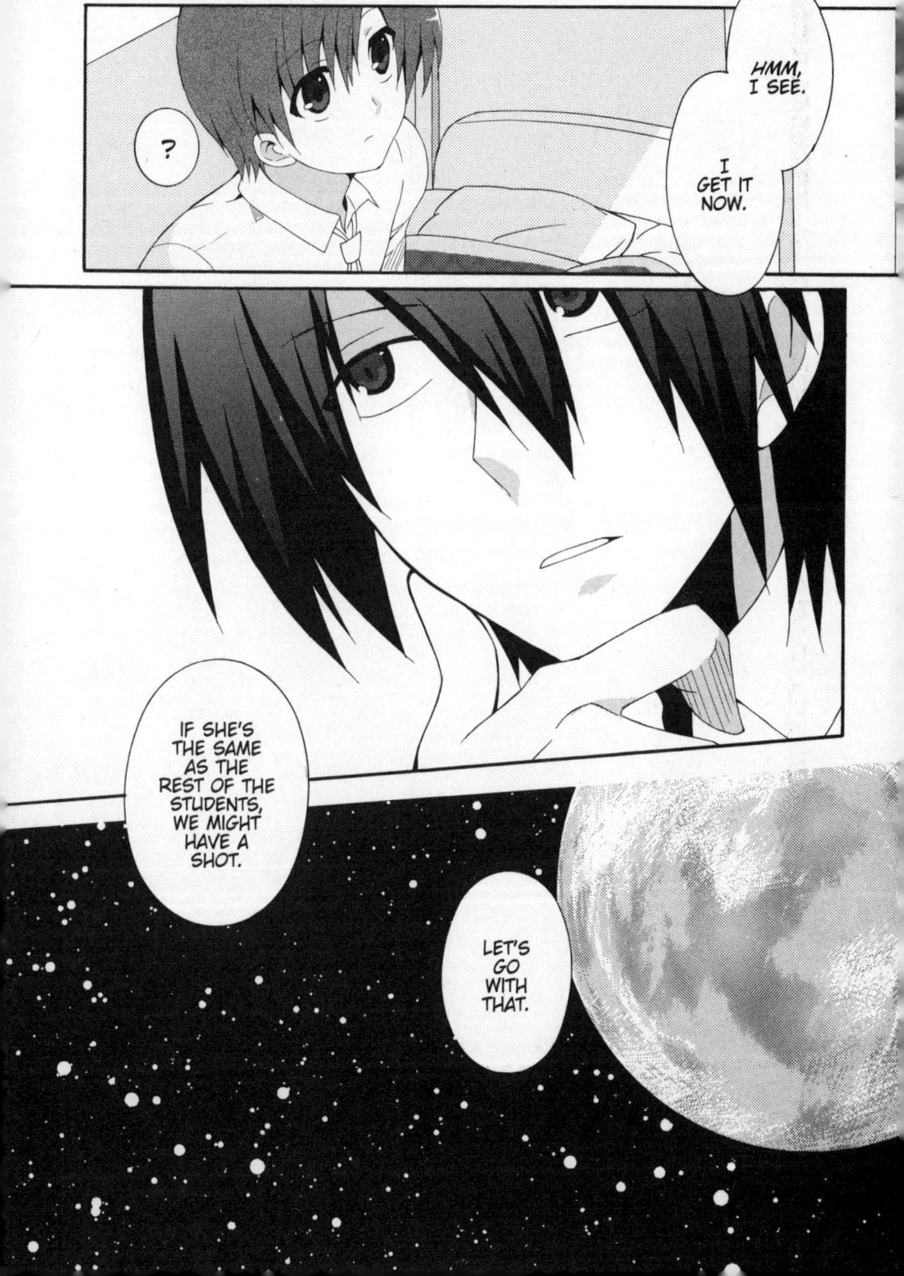
HMM, I SEE.
I GET IT NOW.
?
IF SHE'S THE SAME AS THE REST OF THE STUDENTS, WE MIGHT HAVE A SHOT.
LET'S GO WITH THAT.

Angel Beats!
Heaven's Door

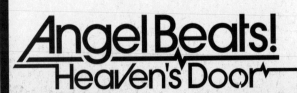

So relaxing...
KAPPOOOOON

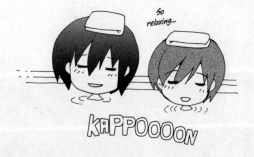

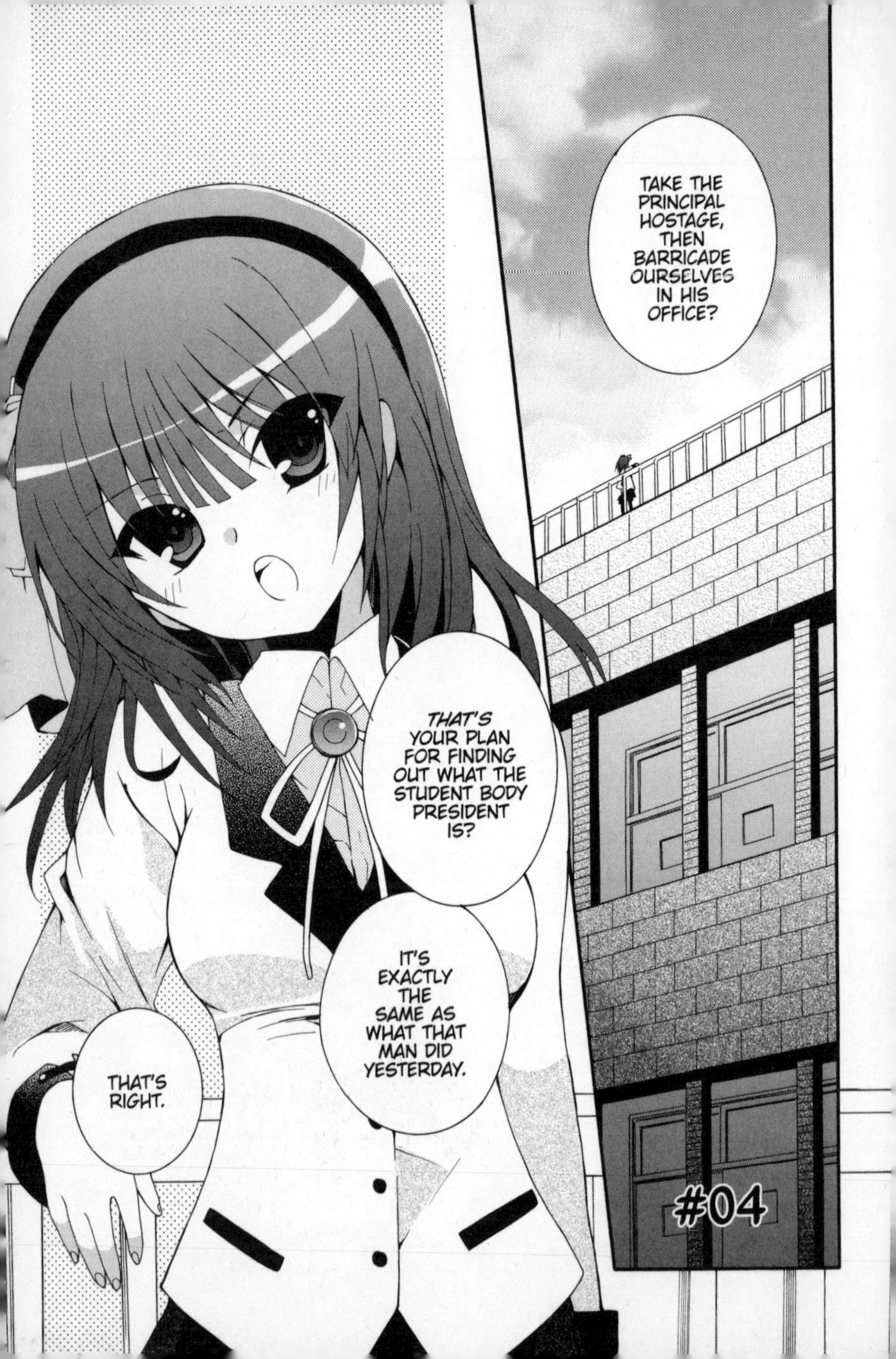
TAKE THE PRINCIPAL HOSTAGE, THEN BARRICADE OURSELVES IN HIS OFFICE?
#04
THAT'S YOUR PLAN FOR FINDING OUT WHAT THE STUDENT BODY PRESIDENT IS?
IT'S EXACTLY THE SAME AS WHAT THAT MAN DID YESTERDAY.
THAT'S RIGHT.

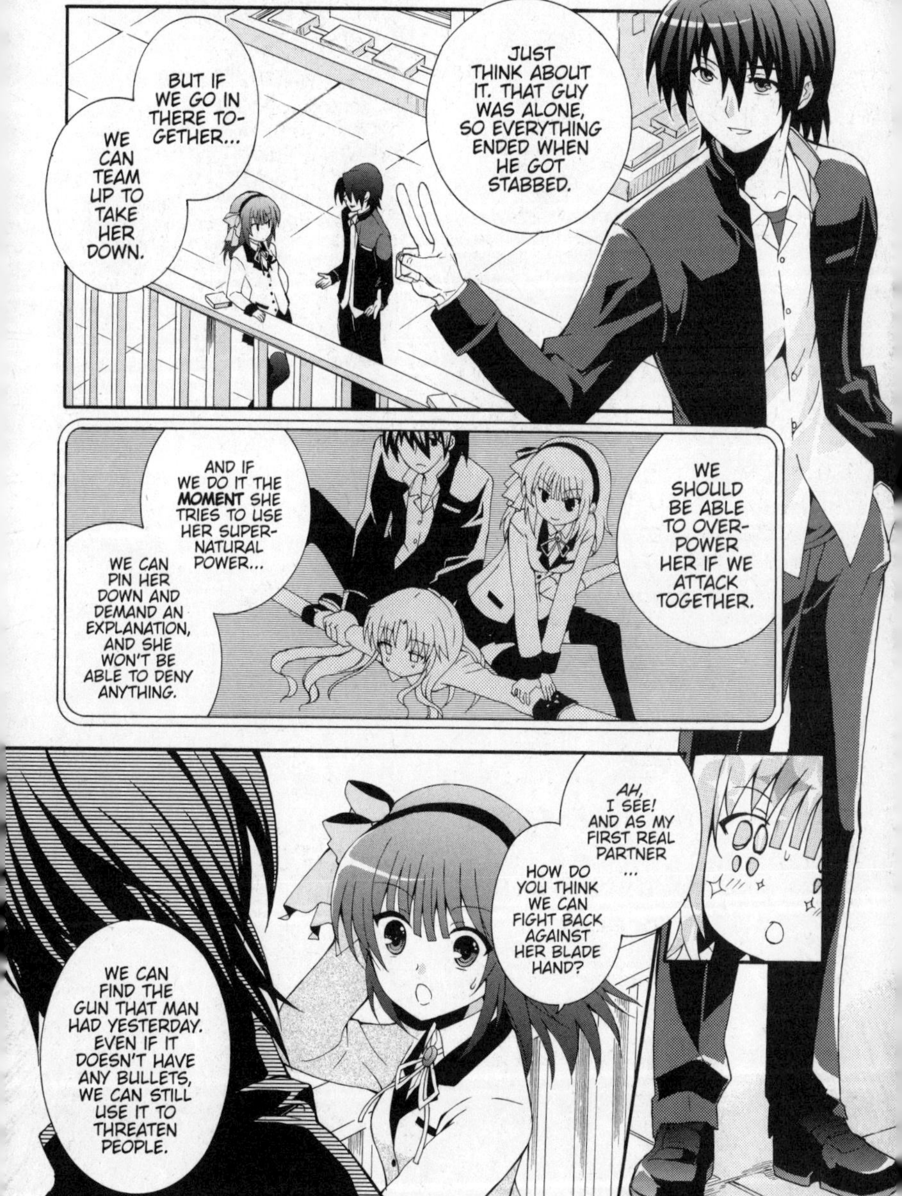
JUST THINK ABOUT IT. THAT GUY WAS ALONE, SO EVERYTHING ENDED WHEN HE GOT STABBED.
BUT IF WE GO IN THERE TO-GETHER...
WE CAN TEAM UP TO TAKE HER DOWN.
WE SHOULD BE ABLE TO OVER-POWER HER IF WE ATTACK TOGETHER.
AND IF WE DO IT THE MOMENT SHE TRIES TO USE HER SUPER-NATURAL POWER...
WE CAN PIN HER DOWN AND DEMAND AN EXPLANATION, AND SHE WON'T BE ABLE TO DENY ANYTHING.
AH, I SEE! AND AS MY FIRST REAL PARTNER ...
HOW DO YOU THINK WE CAN FIGHT BACK AGAINST HER BLADE HAND?
WE CAN FIND THE GUN THAT MAN HAD YESTERDAY. EVEN IF IT DOESN'T HAVE ANY BULLETS, WE CAN STILL USE IT TO THREATEN PEOPLE.

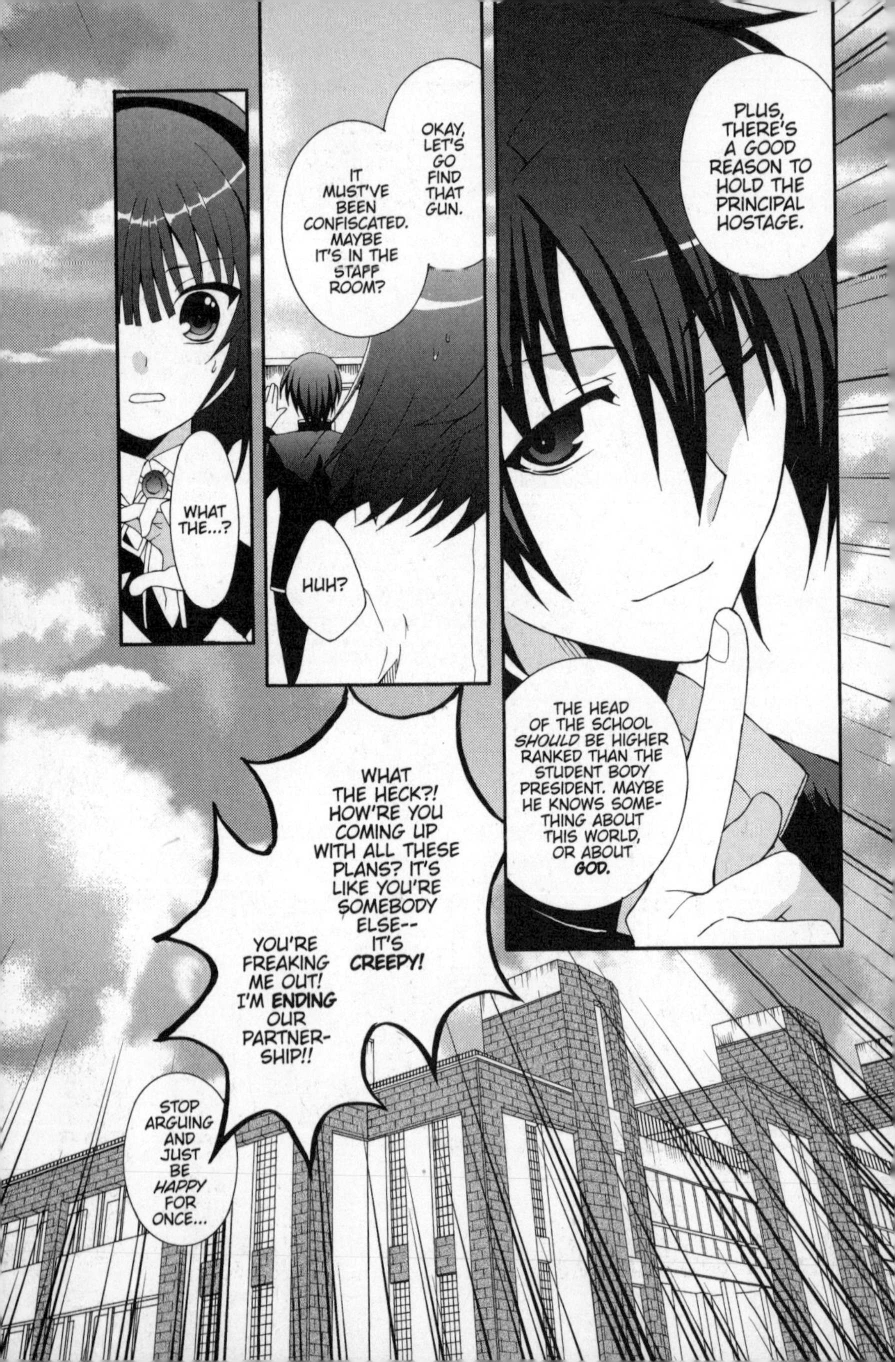
PLUS, THERE'S A GOOD REASON TO HOLD THE PRINCIPAL HOSTAGE.
THE HEAD OF THE SCHOOL *SHOULD* BE HIGHER RANKED THAN THE STUDENT BODY PRESIDENT. MAYBE HE KNOWS SOME-THING ABOUT THIS WORLD, OR ABOUT **GOD.**
OKAY, LET'S GO FIND THAT GUN.
IT MUST'VE BEEN CONFISCATED. MAYBE IT'S IN THE STAFF ROOM?
HUH?
WHAT THE...?
WHAT THE HECK?! HOW'RE YOU COMING UP WITH ALL THESE PLANS? IT'S LIKE YOU'RE SOMEBODY ELSE-- IT'S **CREEPY!**
YOU'RE FREAKING ME OUT! I'M **ENDING** OUR PARTNER-SHIP!!
STOP ARGUING AND JUST BE *HAPPY* FOR ONCE...

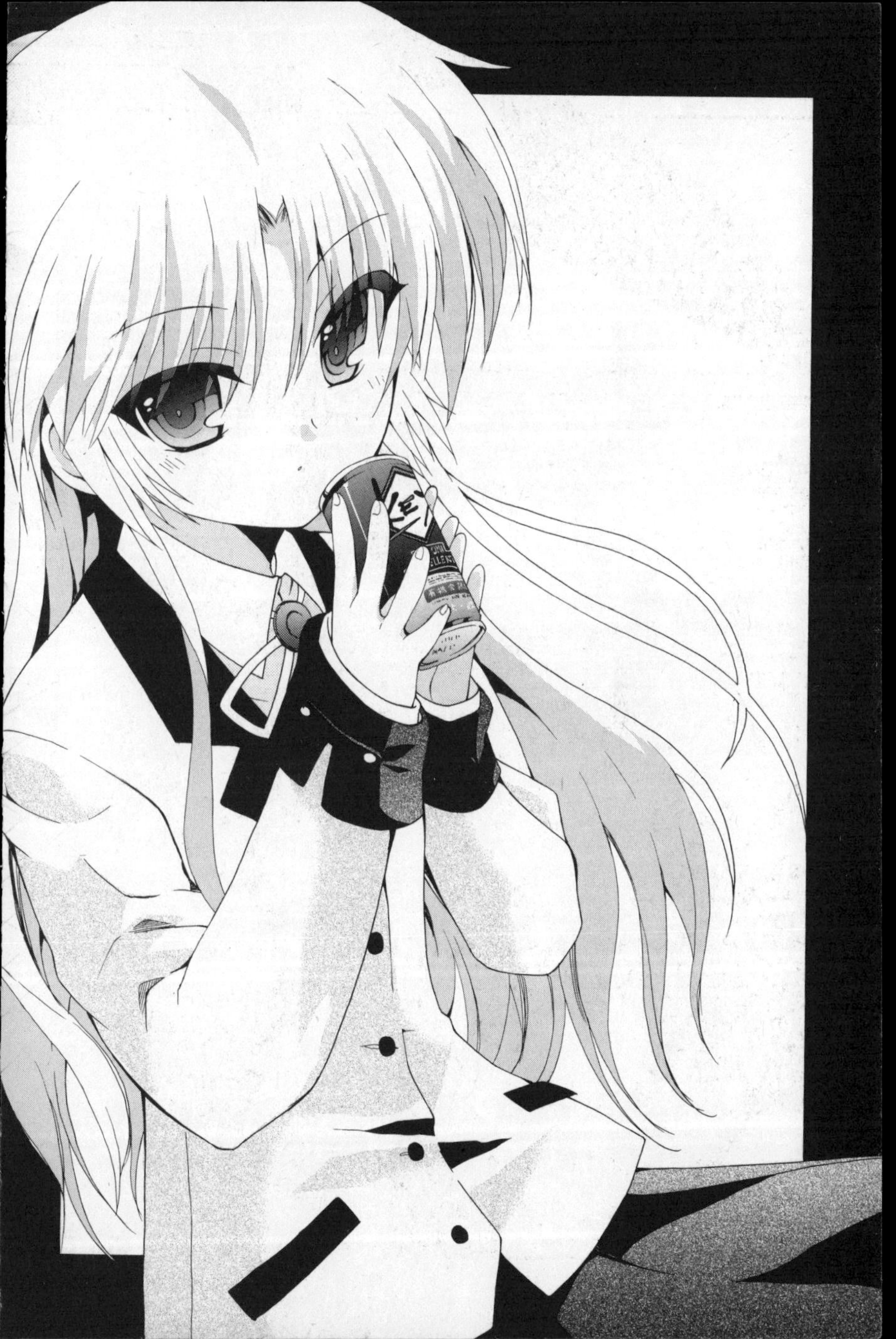

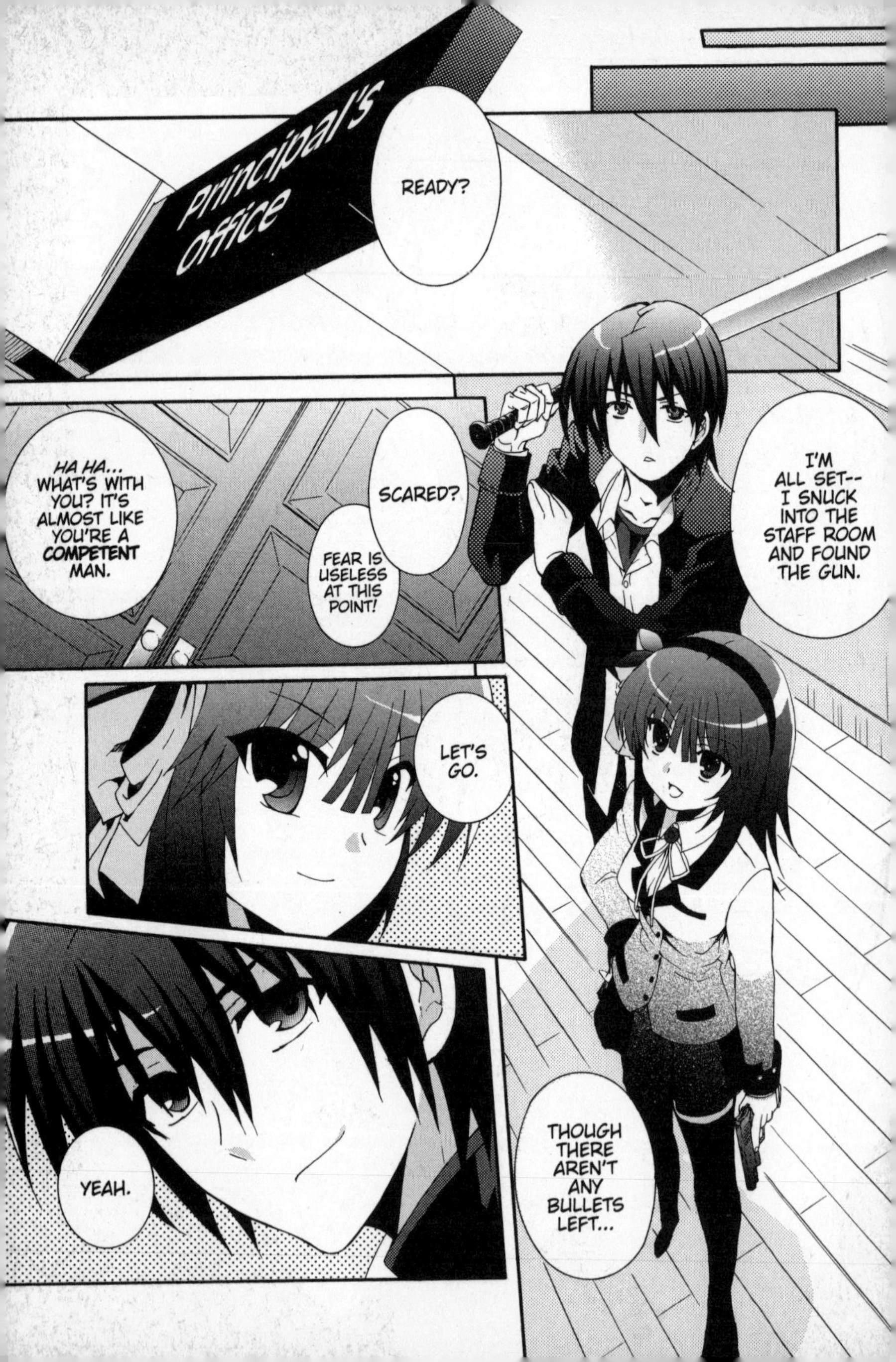
Principal's office
READY?
I'M ALL SET-- I SNUCK INTO THE STAFF ROOM AND FOUND THE GUN.
THOUGH THERE AREN'T ANY BULLETS LEFT...
SCARED?
FEAR IS USELESS AT THIS POINT!
HA HA... WHAT'S WITH YOU? IT'S ALMOST LIKE YOU'RE A COMPETENT MAN.
LET'S GO.
YEAH.

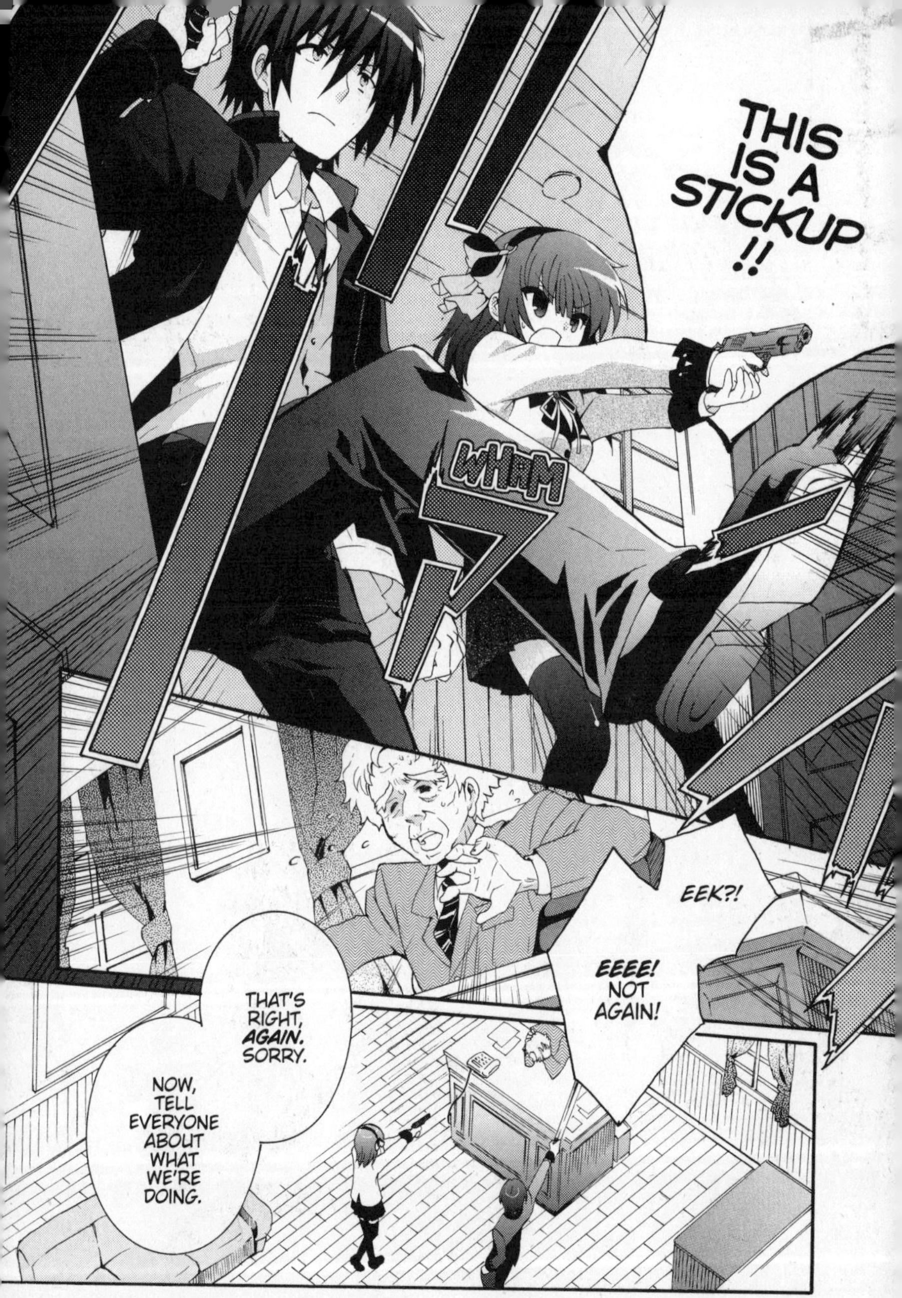
THIS IS A STICKUP!!
WHAM
EEK?!
EEEE! NOT AGAIN!
THAT'S RIGHT, AGAIN. SORRY.
NOW, TELL EVERYONE ABOUT WHAT WE'RE DOING.

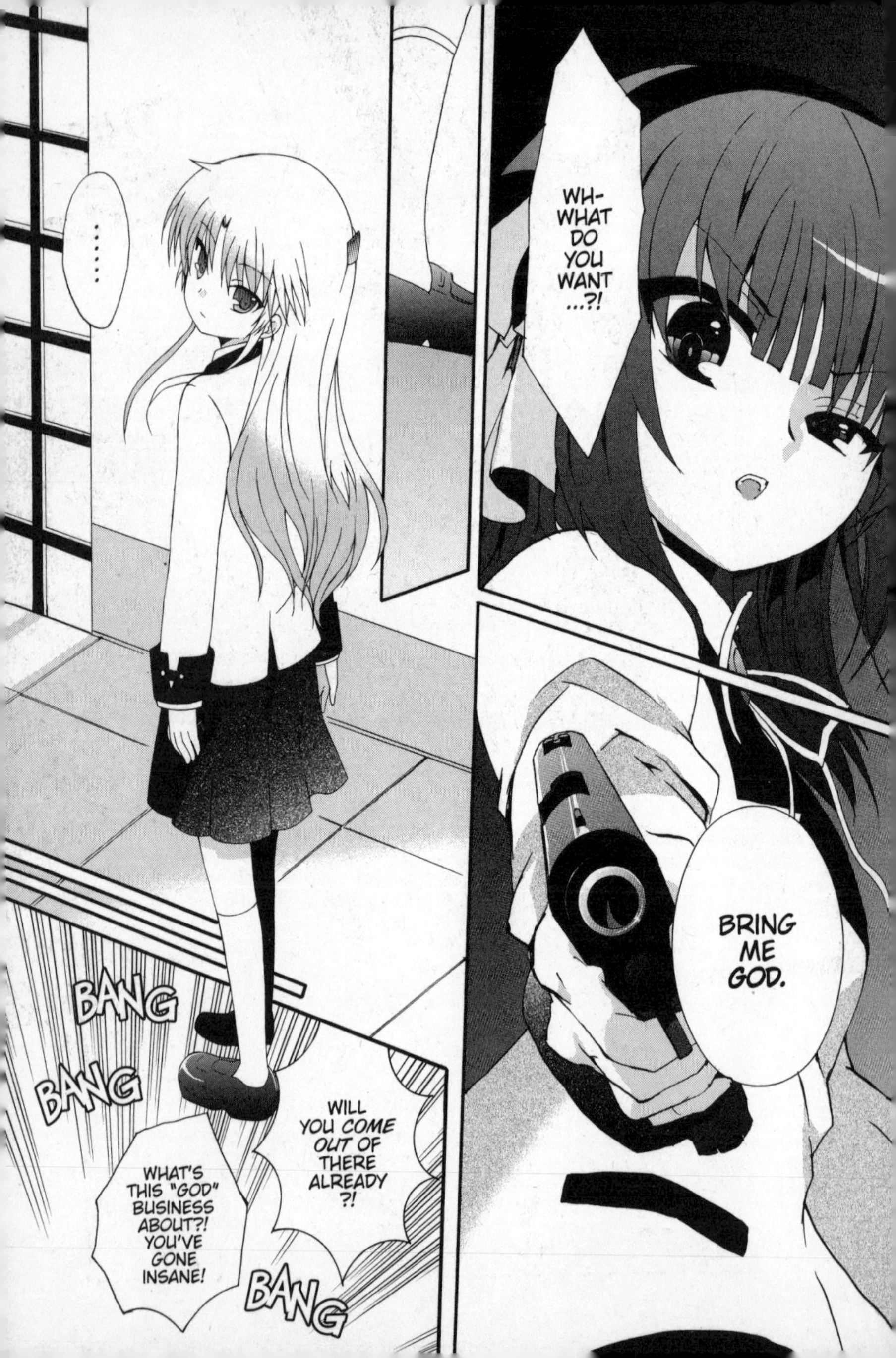
WH- WHAT DO YOU WANT ...?!
BRING ME GOD.
......
BANG
BANG
WILL YOU COME OUT OF THERE ALREADY ?!
WHAT'S THIS "GOD" BUSINESS ABOUT?! YOU'VE GONE INSANE!
BANG

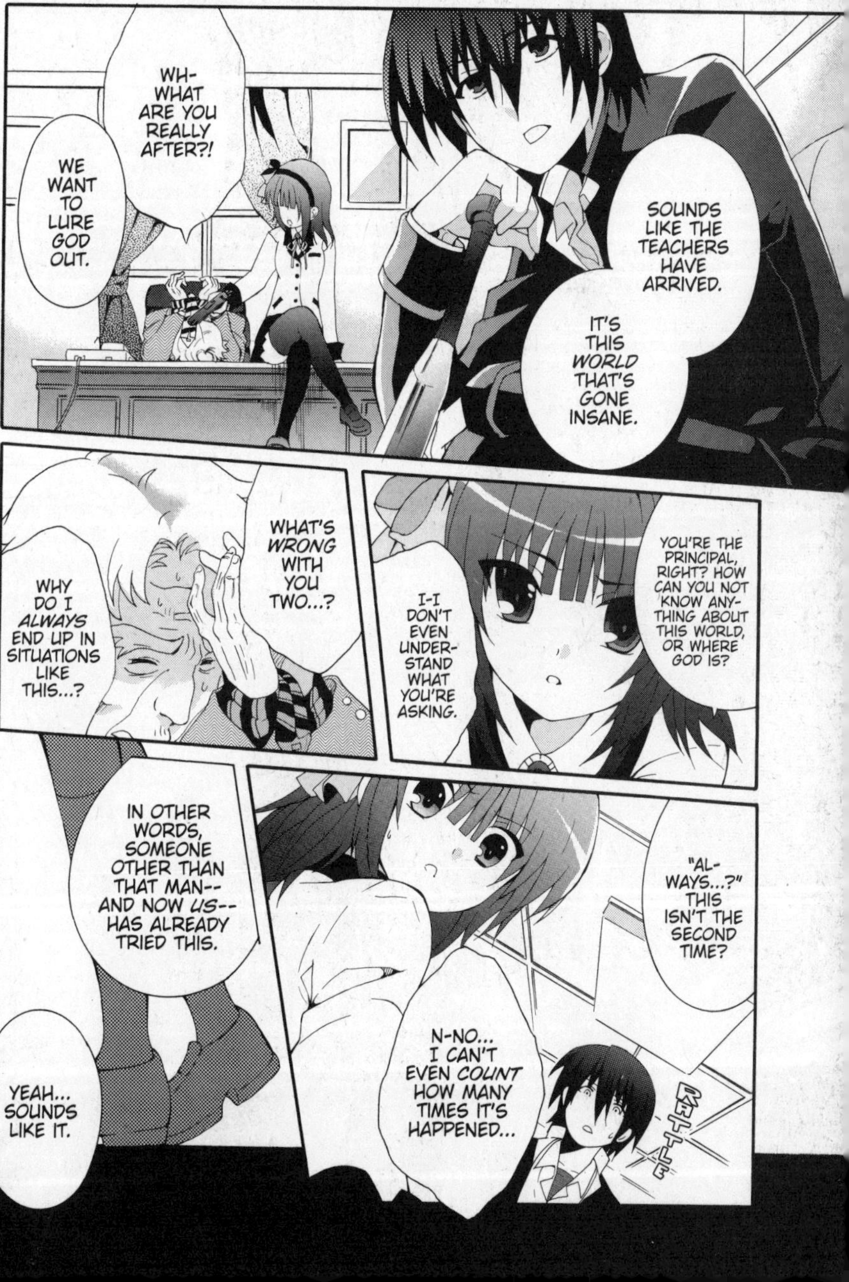
SOUNDS LIKE THE TEACHERS HAVE ARRIVED.
IT'S THIS *WORLD* THAT'S GONE INSANE.
WH- WHAT ARE YOU REALLY AFTER?!
WE WANT TO LURE GOD OUT.
YOU'RE THE PRINCIPAL, RIGHT? HOW CAN YOU NOT KNOW ANY-THING ABOUT THIS WORLD, OR WHERE GOD IS?
I-I DON'T EVEN UNDER-STAND WHAT YOU'RE ASKING.
WHAT'S *WRONG* WITH YOU TWO...?
WHY DO I *ALWAYS* END UP IN SITUATIONS LIKE THIS...?
"AL-WAYS...?" THIS ISN'T THE SECOND TIME?
N-NO... I CAN'T EVEN *COUNT* HOW MANY TIMES IT'S HAPPENED...
RATTLE
IN OTHER WORDS, SOMEONE OTHER THAN THAT MAN-- AND NOW *US*-- HAS ALREADY TRIED THIS.
YEAH... SOUNDS LIKE IT.

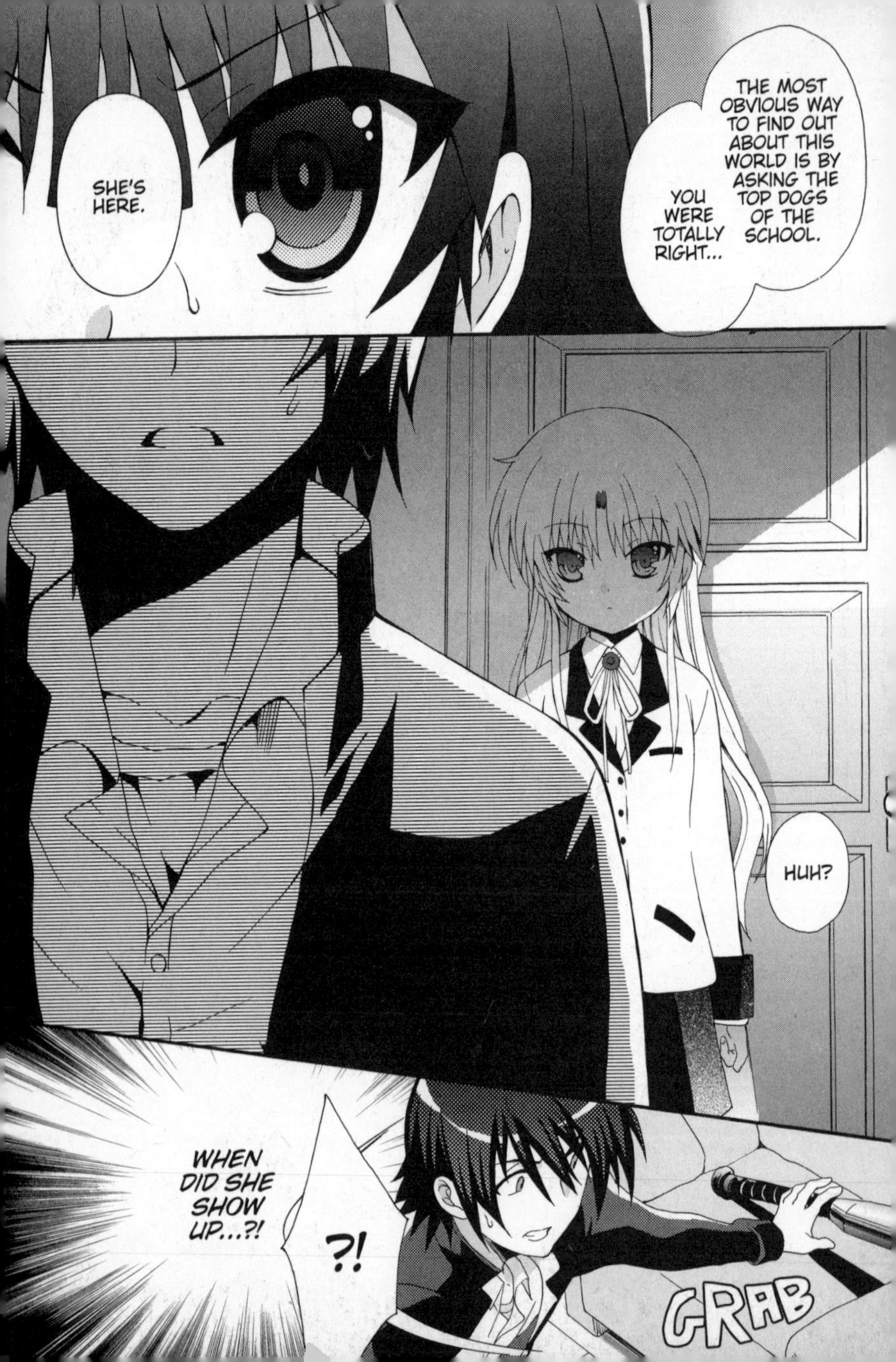
THE MOST OBVIOUS WAY TO FIND OUT ABOUT THIS WORLD IS BY ASKING THE TOP DOGS OF THE SCHOOL.
YOU WERE TOTALLY RIGHT...
SHE'S HERE.
HUH?
?!
WHEN DID SHE SHOW UP...?!
GRAB

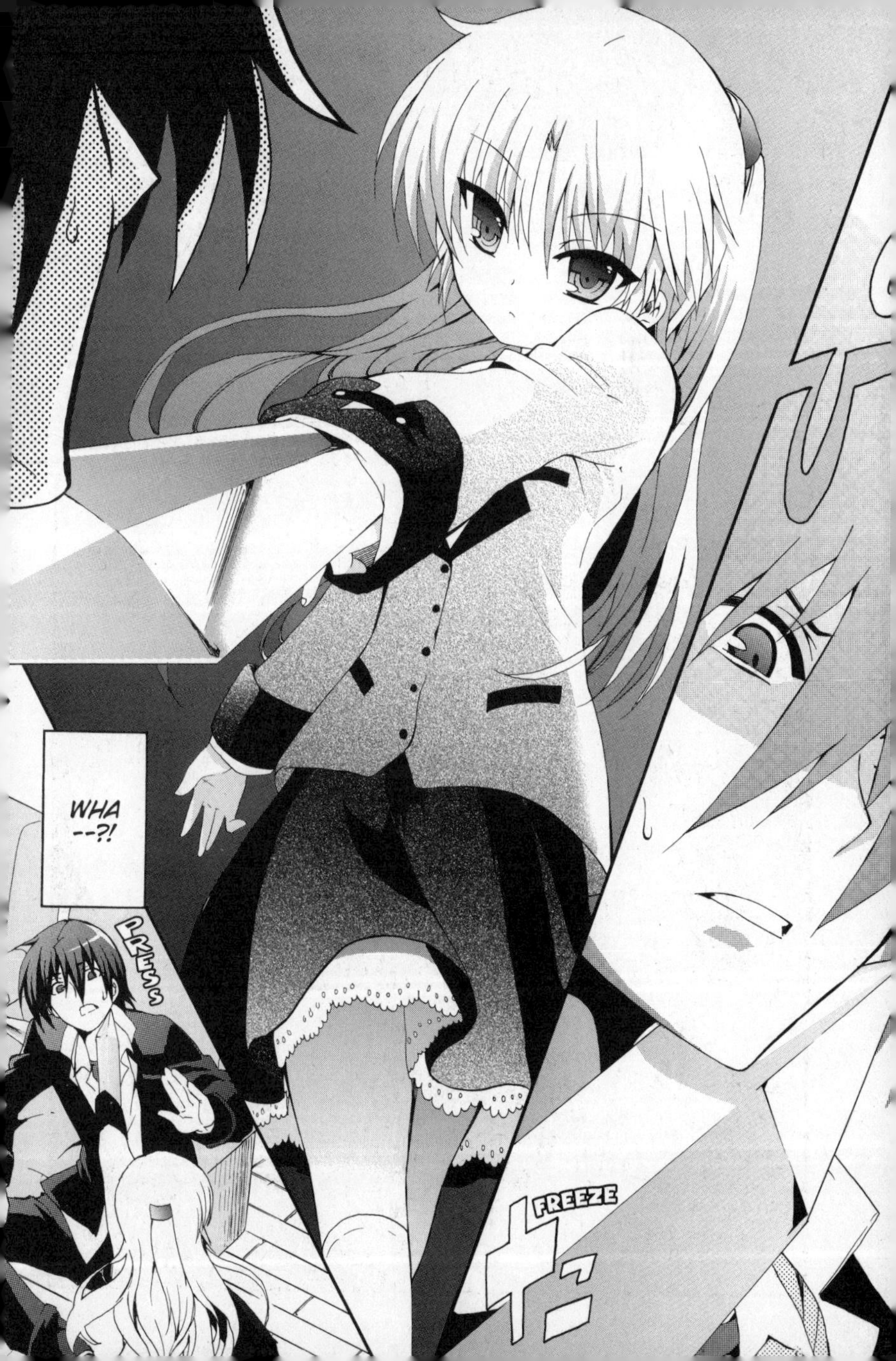
FREEZE
WHA --?!
PRESS

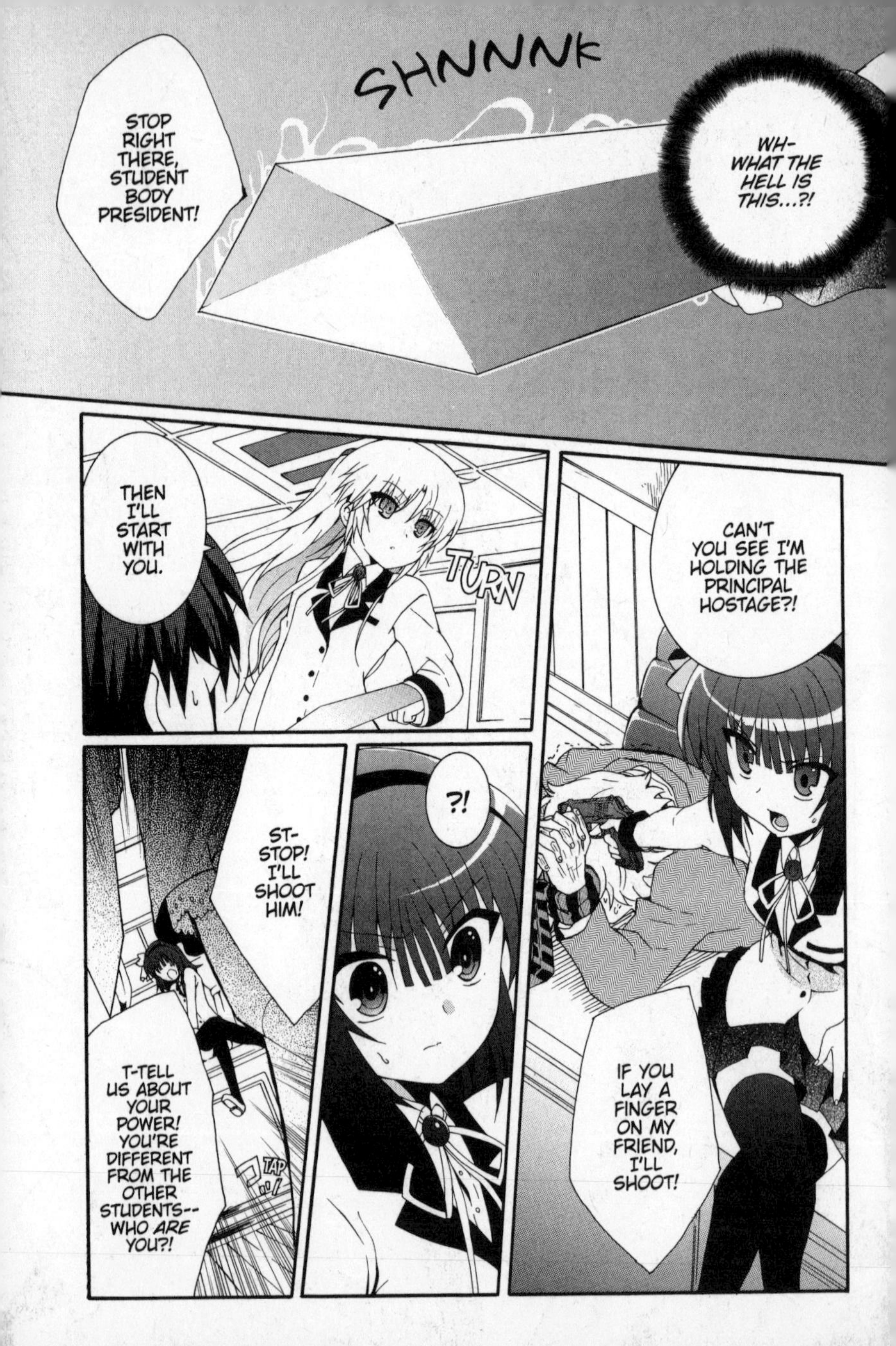
WH- WHAT THE HELL IS THIS...?!
SHNNNK
STOP RIGHT THERE, STUDENT BODY PRESIDENT!
CAN'T YOU SEE I'M HOLDING THE PRINCIPAL HOSTAGE?!
IF YOU LAY A FINGER ON MY FRIEND, I'LL SHOOT!
THEN I'LL START WITH YOU.
TURN
?!
ST- STOP! I'LL SHOOT HIM!
T-TELL US ABOUT YOUR POWER! YOU'RE DIFFERENT FROM THE OTHER STUDENTS-- WHO *ARE* YOU?!
TAP

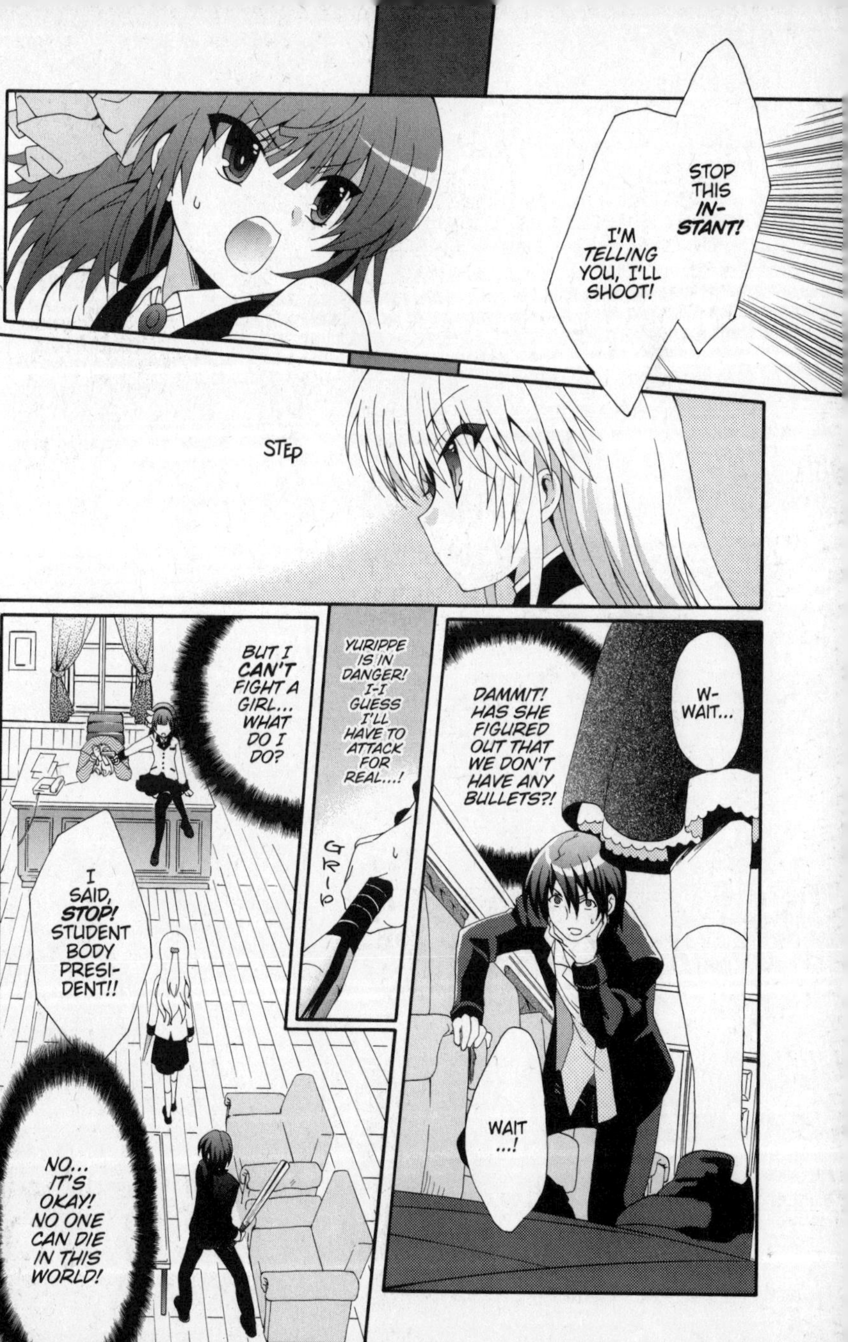
STOP THIS INSTANT!
I'M TELLING YOU, I'LL SHOOT!
STEP
W-WAIT...
DAMMIT! HAS SHE FIGURED OUT THAT WE DON'T HAVE ANY BULLETS?!
WAIT ...!
YURIPPE IS IN DANGER! I-I GUESS I'LL HAVE TO ATTACK FOR REAL...!
GRIP
BUT I CAN'T FIGHT A GIRL... WHAT DO I DO?
I SAID, STOP! STUDENT BODY PRESIDENT!!
NO... IT'S OKAY! NO ONE CAN DIE IN THIS WORLD!

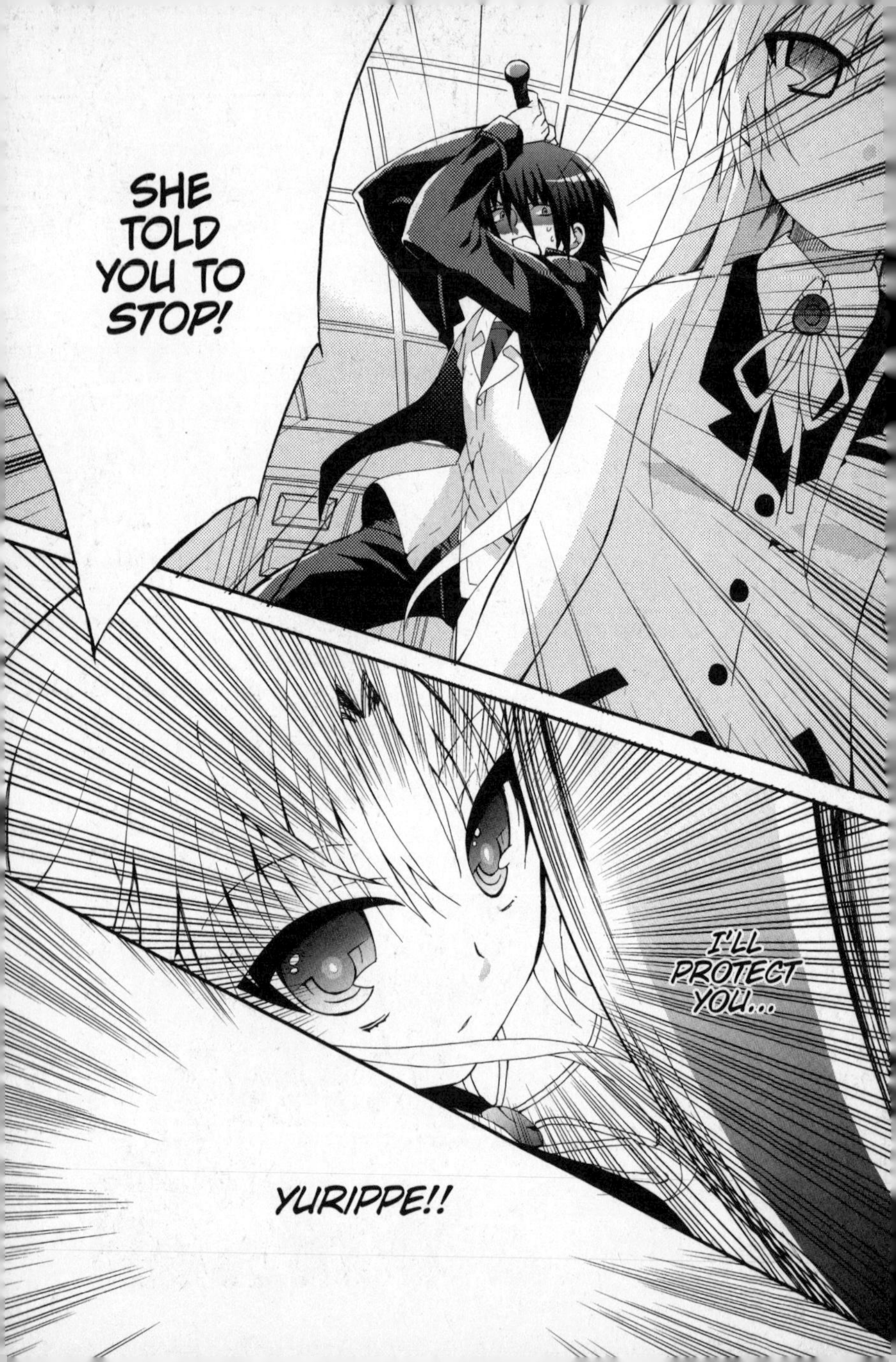
SHE TOLD YOU TO STOP!
I'LL PROTECT YOU...
YURIPPE!!

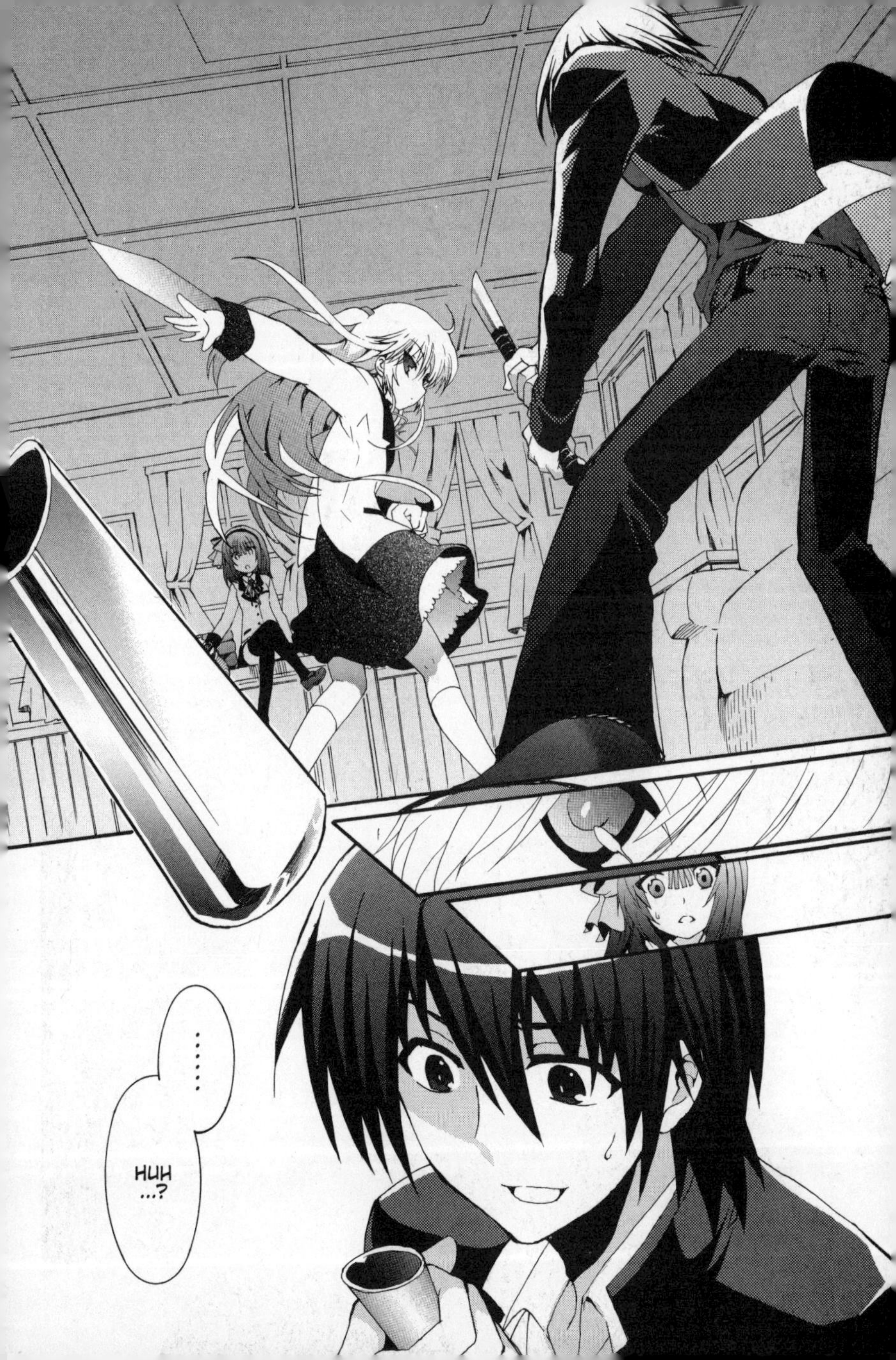
......
HUH ...?

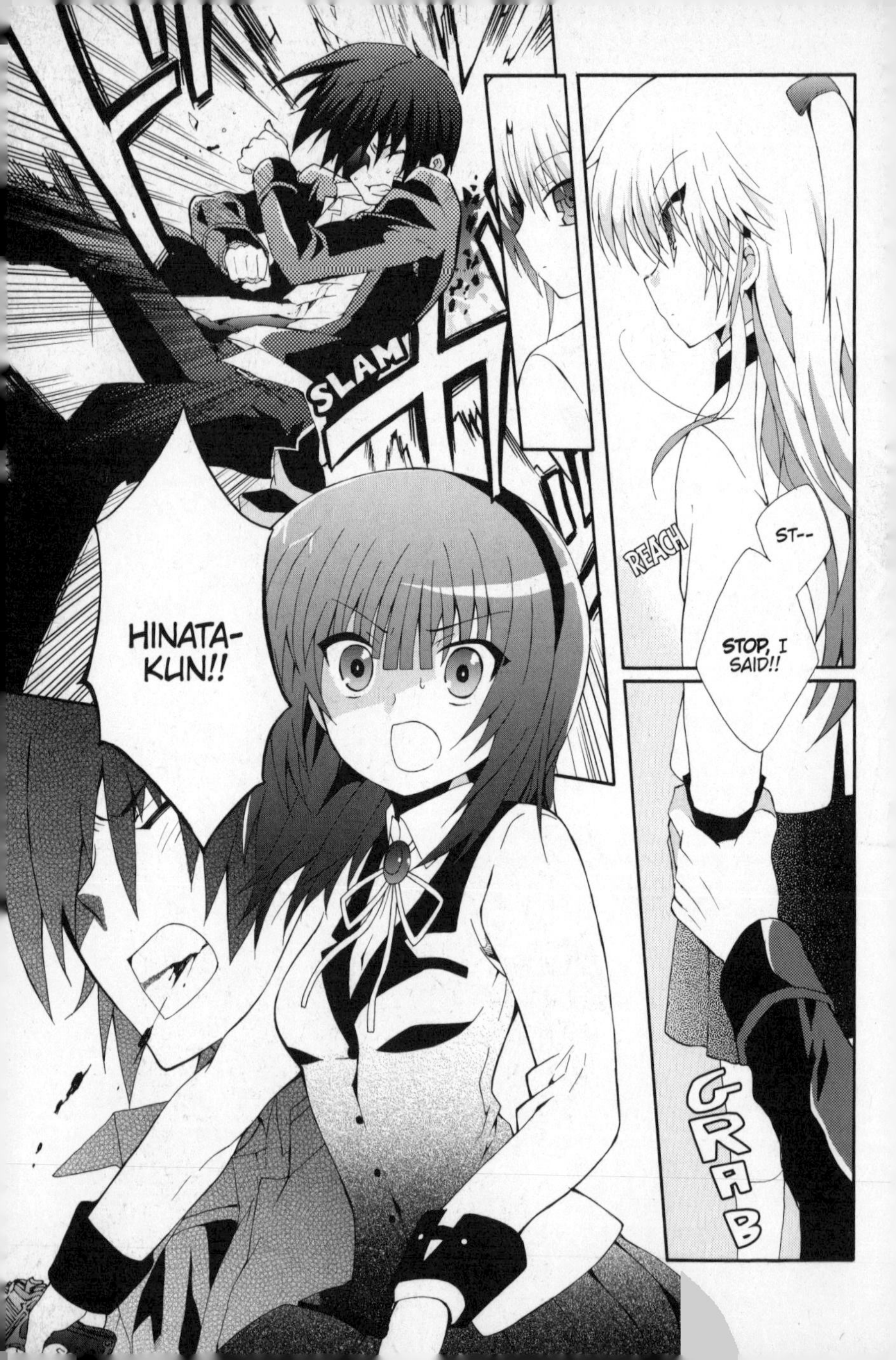
ST--
REACH
STOP, I SAID!!
SLAM
GRAB
HINATA-KUN!!

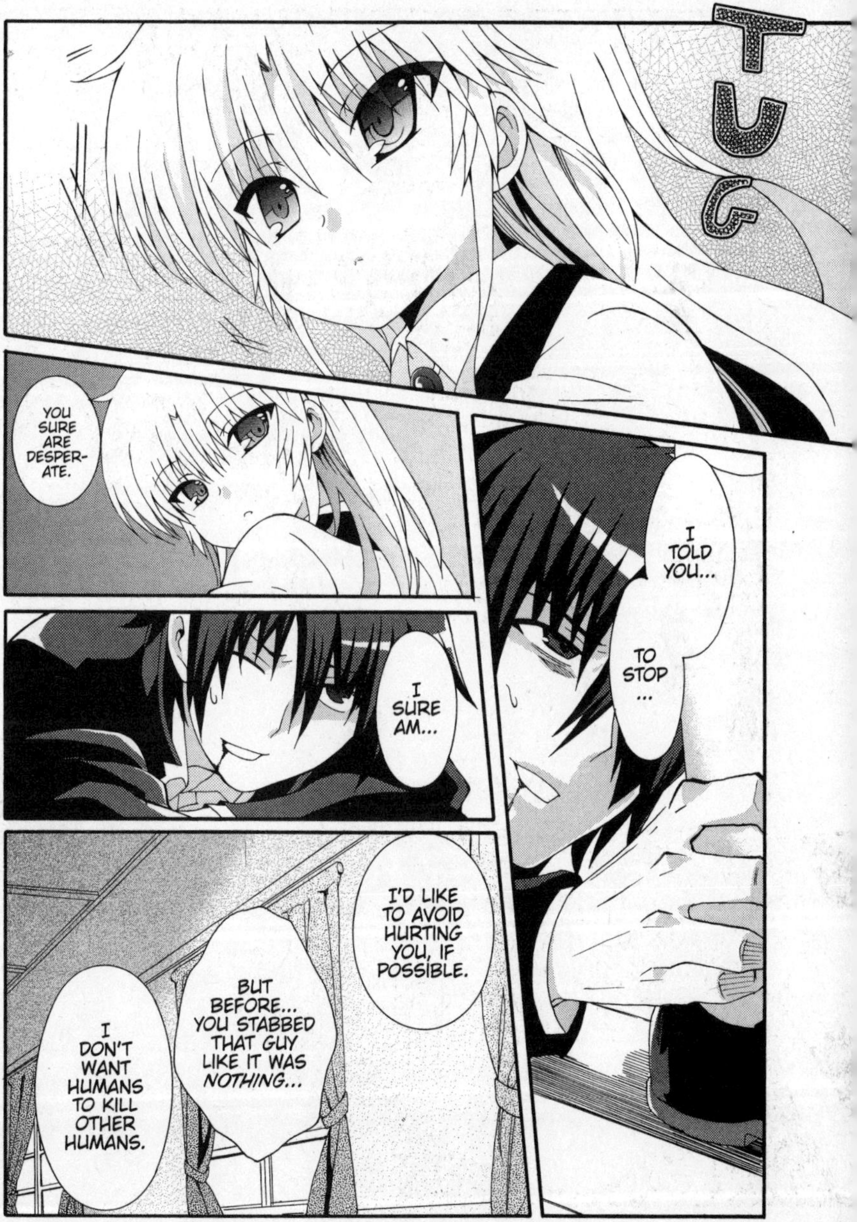
TUG
I TOLD YOU...
TO STOP...
YOU SURE ARE DESPERATE.
I SURE AM...
I'D LIKE TO AVOID HURTING YOU, IF POSSIBLE.
BUT BEFORE... YOU STABBED THAT GUY LIKE IT WAS *NOTHING*...
I DON'T WANT HUMANS TO KILL OTHER HUMANS.

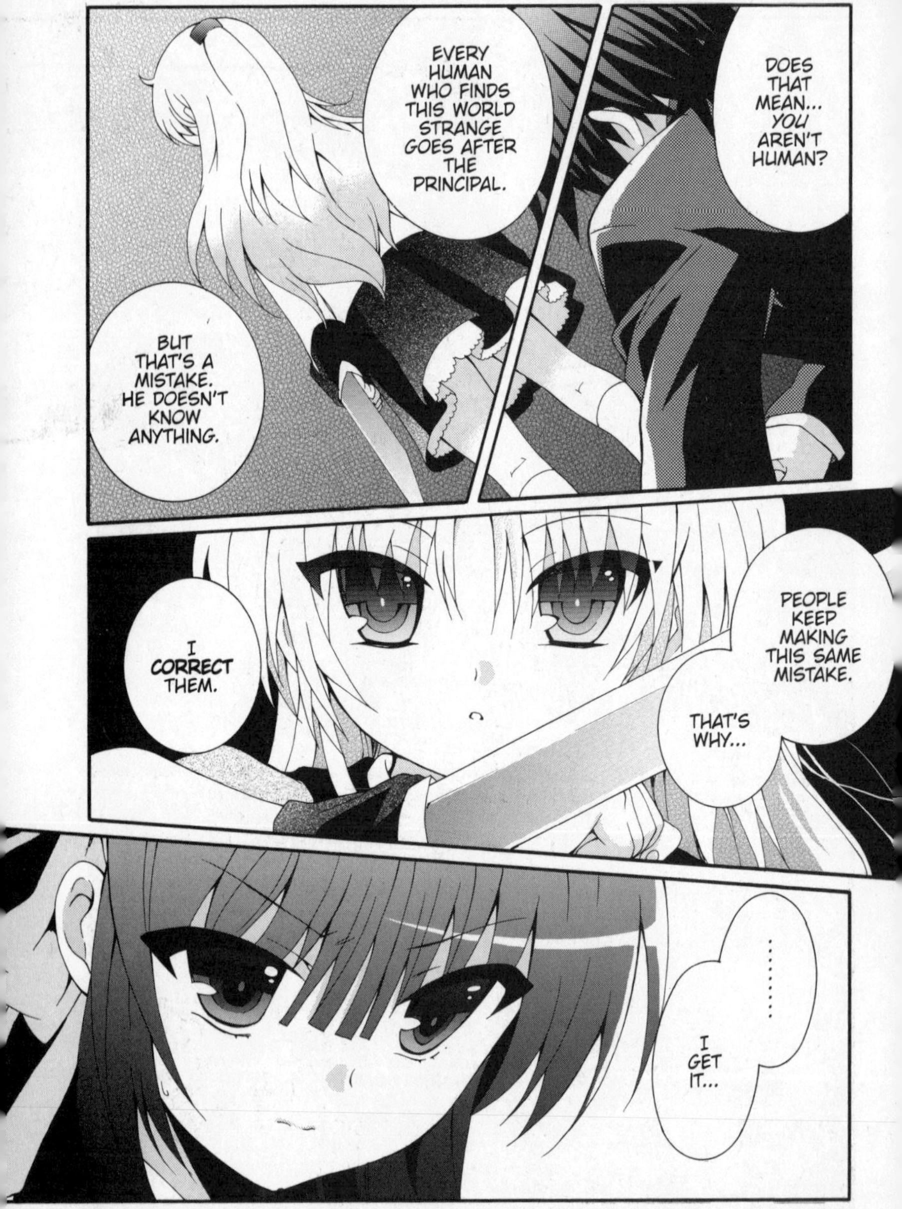
DOES THAT MEAN... *YOU* AREN'T HUMAN?
EVERY HUMAN WHO FINDS THIS WORLD STRANGE GOES AFTER THE PRINCIPAL.
BUT THAT'S A MISTAKE. HE DOESN'T KNOW ANYTHING.
PEOPLE KEEP MAKING THIS SAME MISTAKE.
THAT'S WHY...
I **CORRECT** THEM.
......
I GET IT...

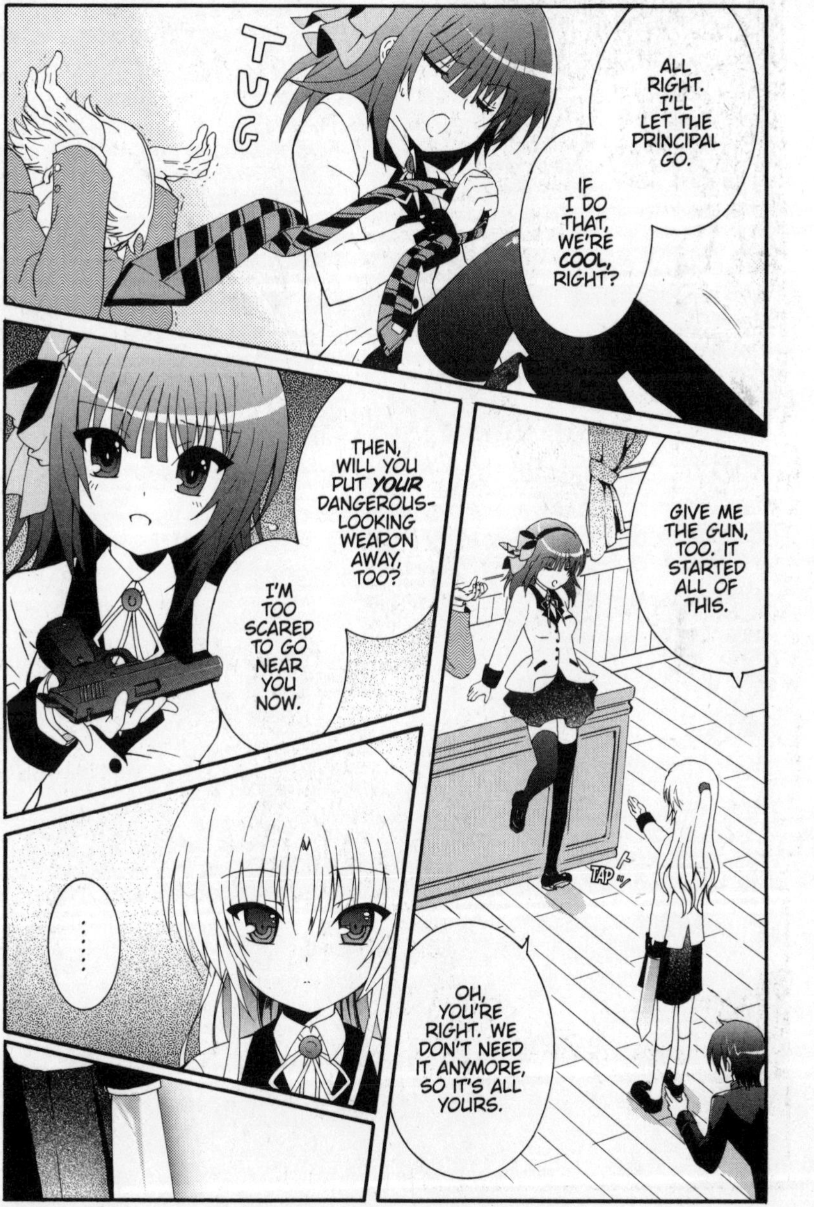
ALL RIGHT. I'LL LET THE PRINCIPAL GO.
IF I DO THAT, WE'RE COOL, RIGHT?
TUG
GIVE ME THE GUN, TOO. IT STARTED ALL OF THIS.
TAP
OH, YOU'RE RIGHT. WE DON'T NEED IT ANYMORE, SO IT'S ALL YOURS.
THEN, WILL YOU PUT YOUR DANGEROUS-LOOKING WEAPON AWAY, TOO?
I'M TOO SCARED TO GO NEAR YOU NOW.
......

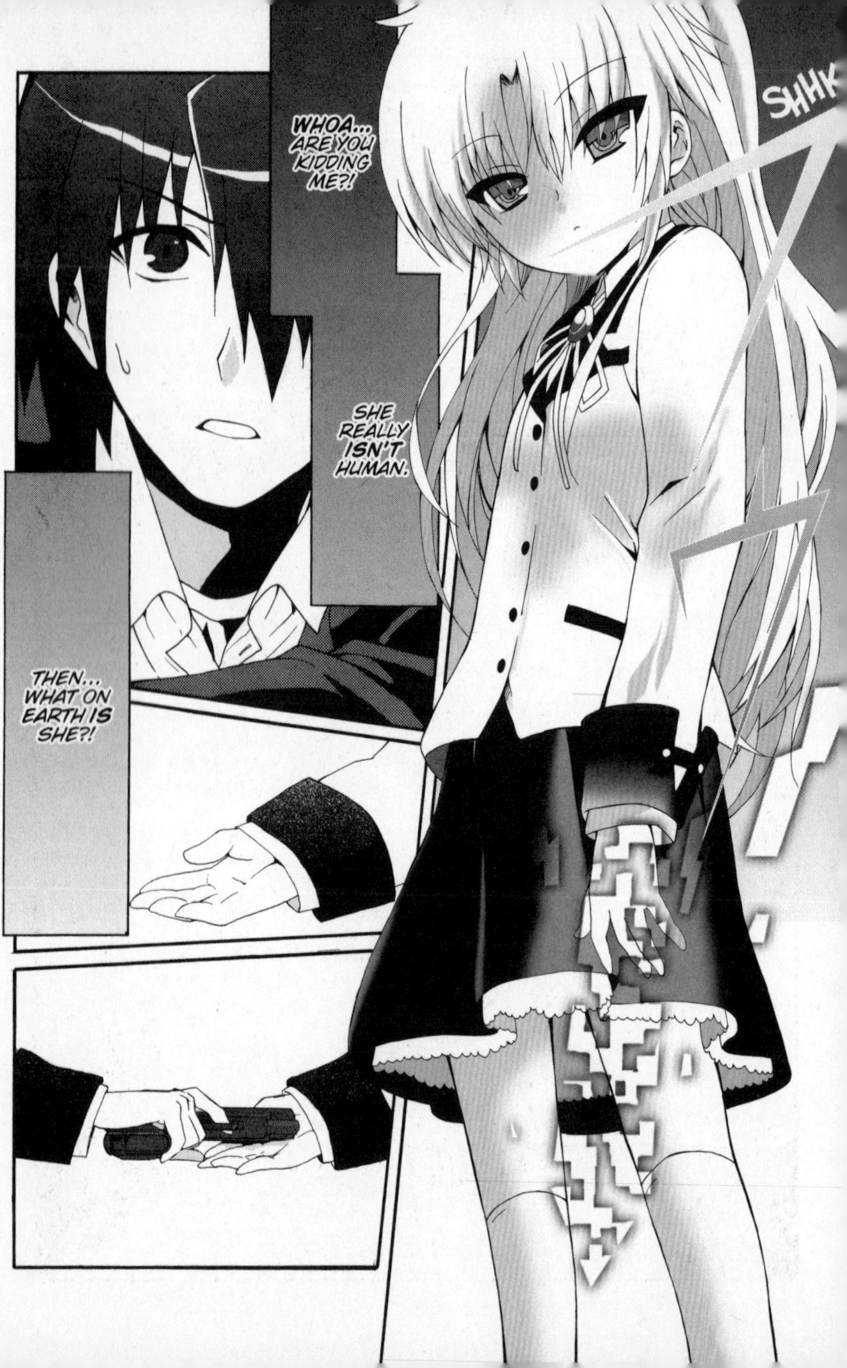
SHHK
WHOA... ARE YOU KIDDING ME?!
SHE REALLY ISN'T HUMAN.
THEN... WHAT ON EARTH IS SHE?!

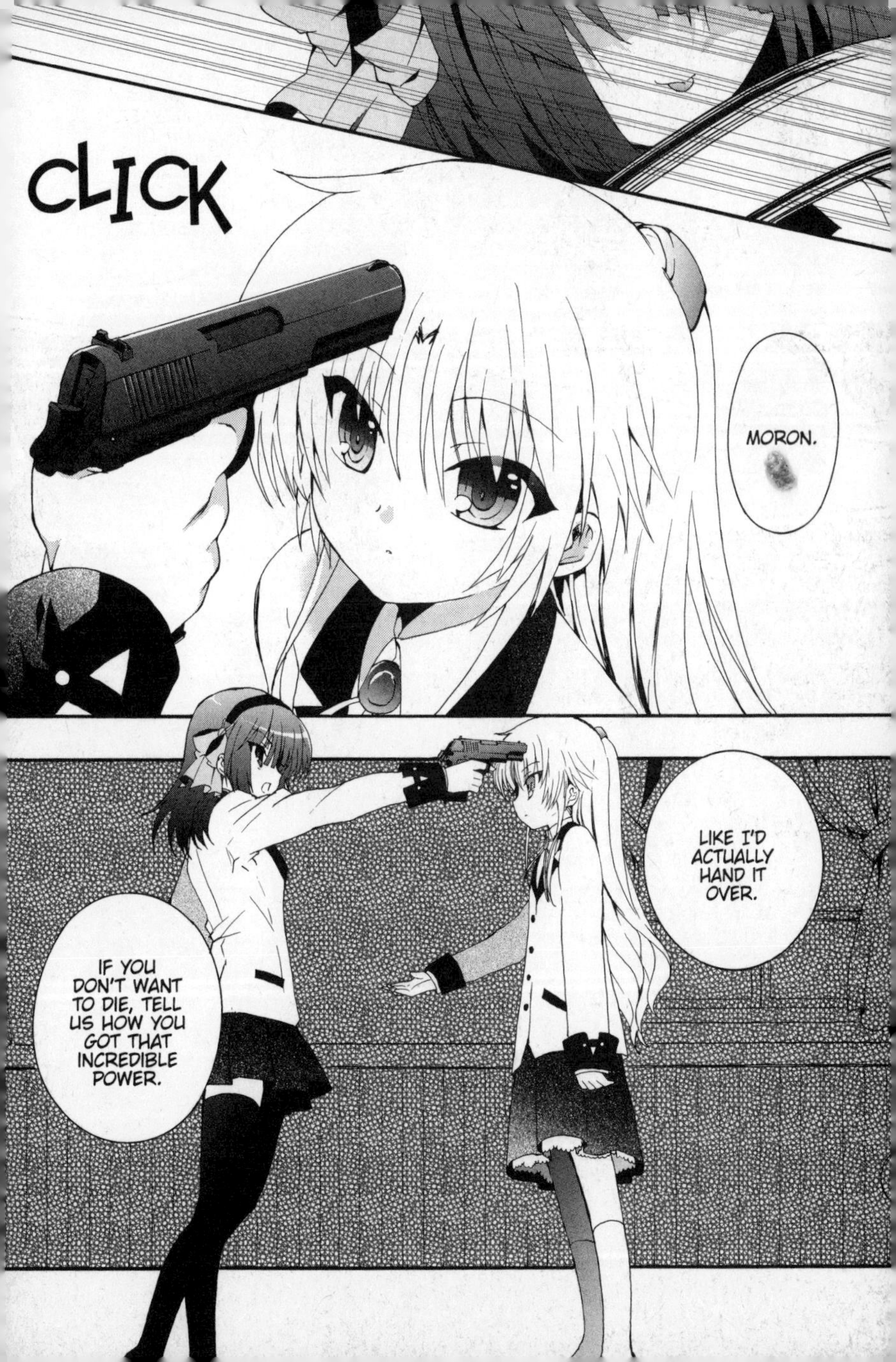
CLICK
MORON.
LIKE I'D ACTUALLY HAND IT OVER.
IF YOU DON'T WANT TO DIE, TELL US HOW YOU GOT THAT INCREDIBLE POWER.

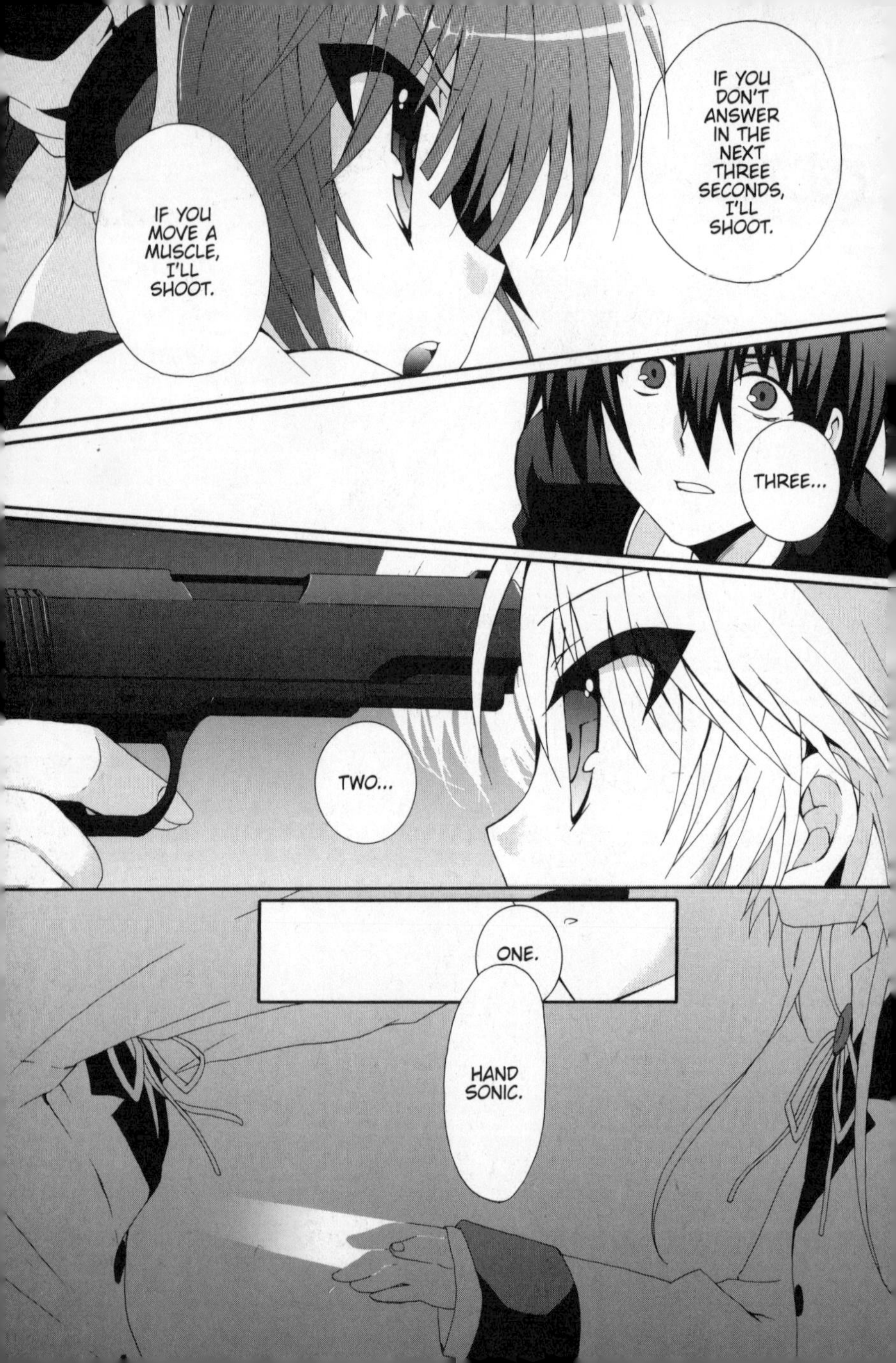
IF YOU DON'T ANSWER IN THE NEXT THREE SECONDS, I'LL SHOOT.
IF YOU MOVE A MUSCLE, I'LL SHOOT.
THREE...
TWO...
ONE.
HAND SONIC.

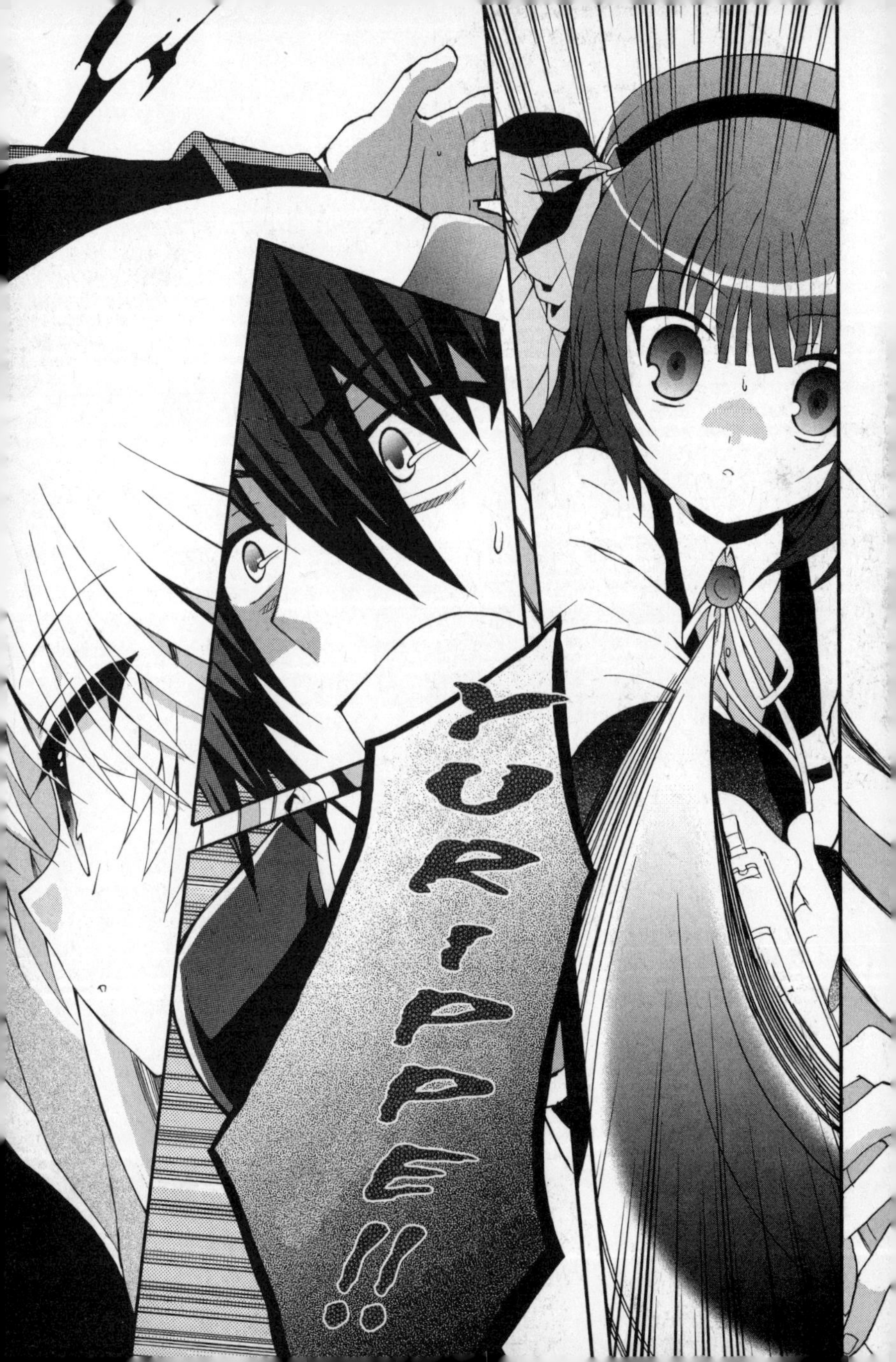
SURIPPE!!

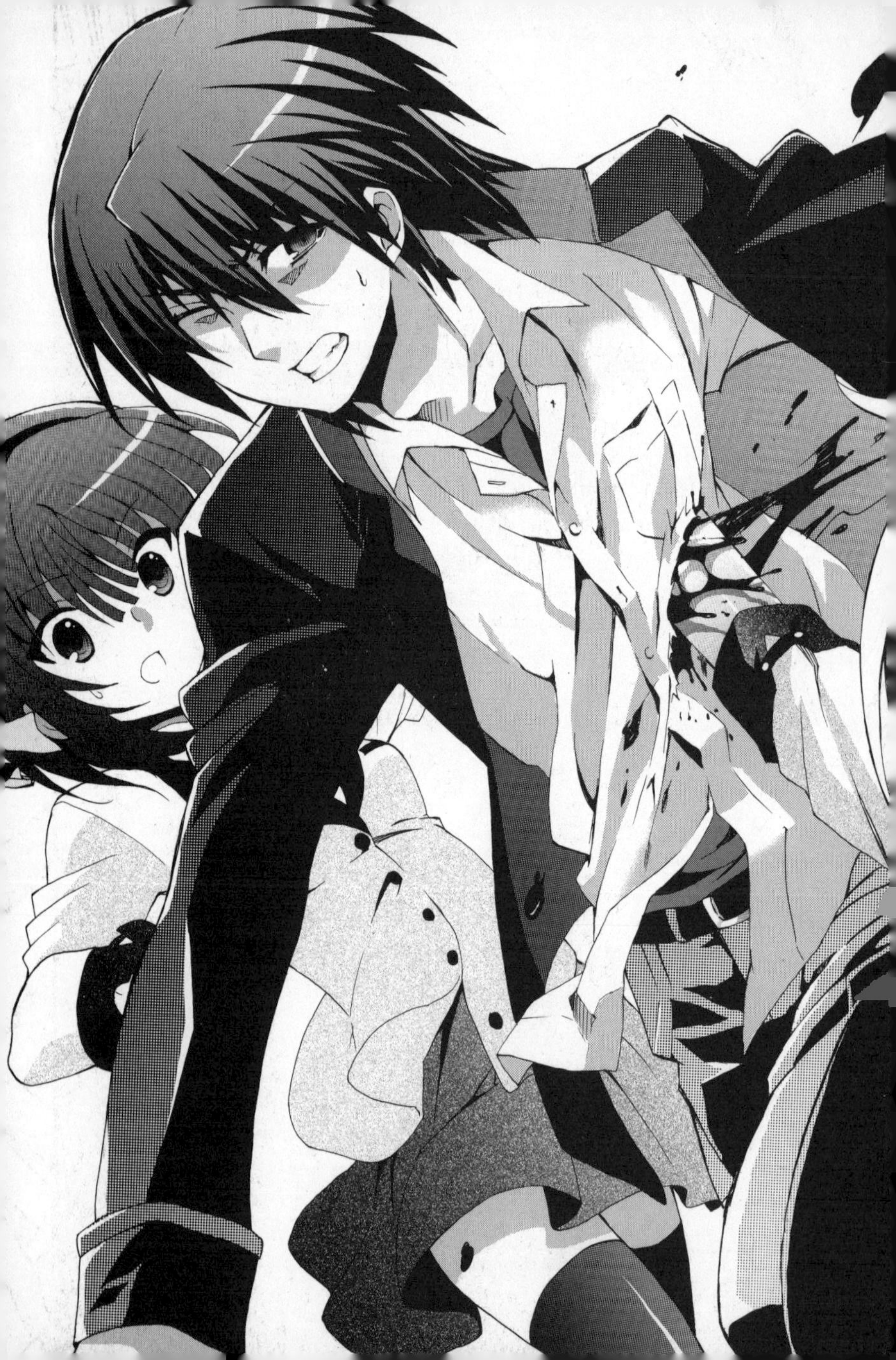

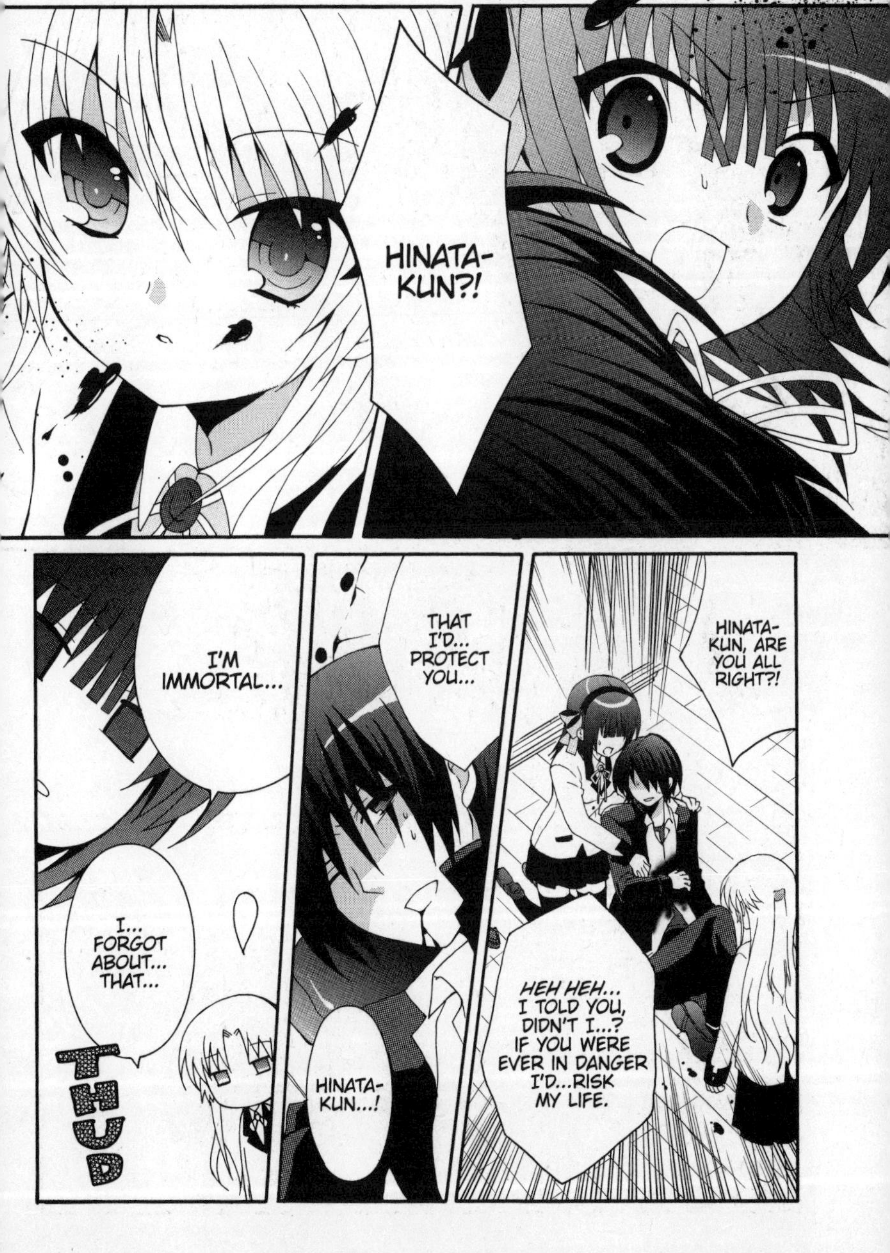
HINATA-KUN?!
HINATA-KUN, ARE YOU ALL RIGHT?!
HEH HEH... I TOLD YOU, DIDN'T I...? IF YOU WERE EVER IN DANGER I'D...RISK MY LIFE.
THAT I'D... PROTECT YOU...
HINATA-KUN...!
I'M IMMORTAL...
I... FORGOT ABOUT... THAT...
THUD

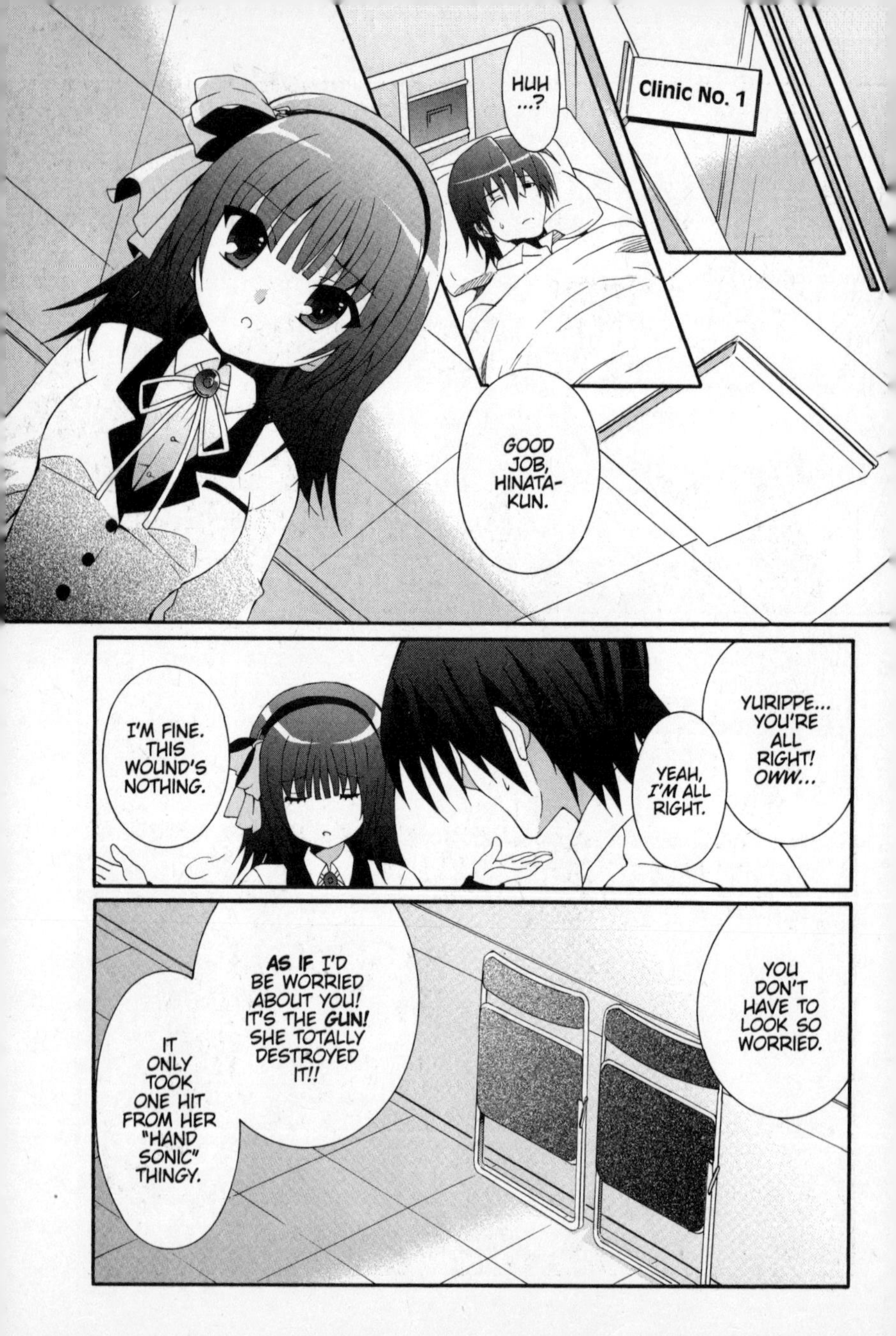
Clinic No. 1
HUH ...?
GOOD JOB, HINATA-KUN.
YURIPPE... YOU'RE ALL RIGHT! OWW...
YEAH, I'M ALL RIGHT.
I'M FINE. THIS WOUND'S NOTHING.
YOU DON'T HAVE TO LOOK SO WORRIED.
AS IF I'D BE WORRIED ABOUT YOU! IT'S THE GUN! SHE TOTALLY DESTROYED IT!!
IT ONLY TOOK ONE HIT FROM HER "HAND SONIC" THINGY.

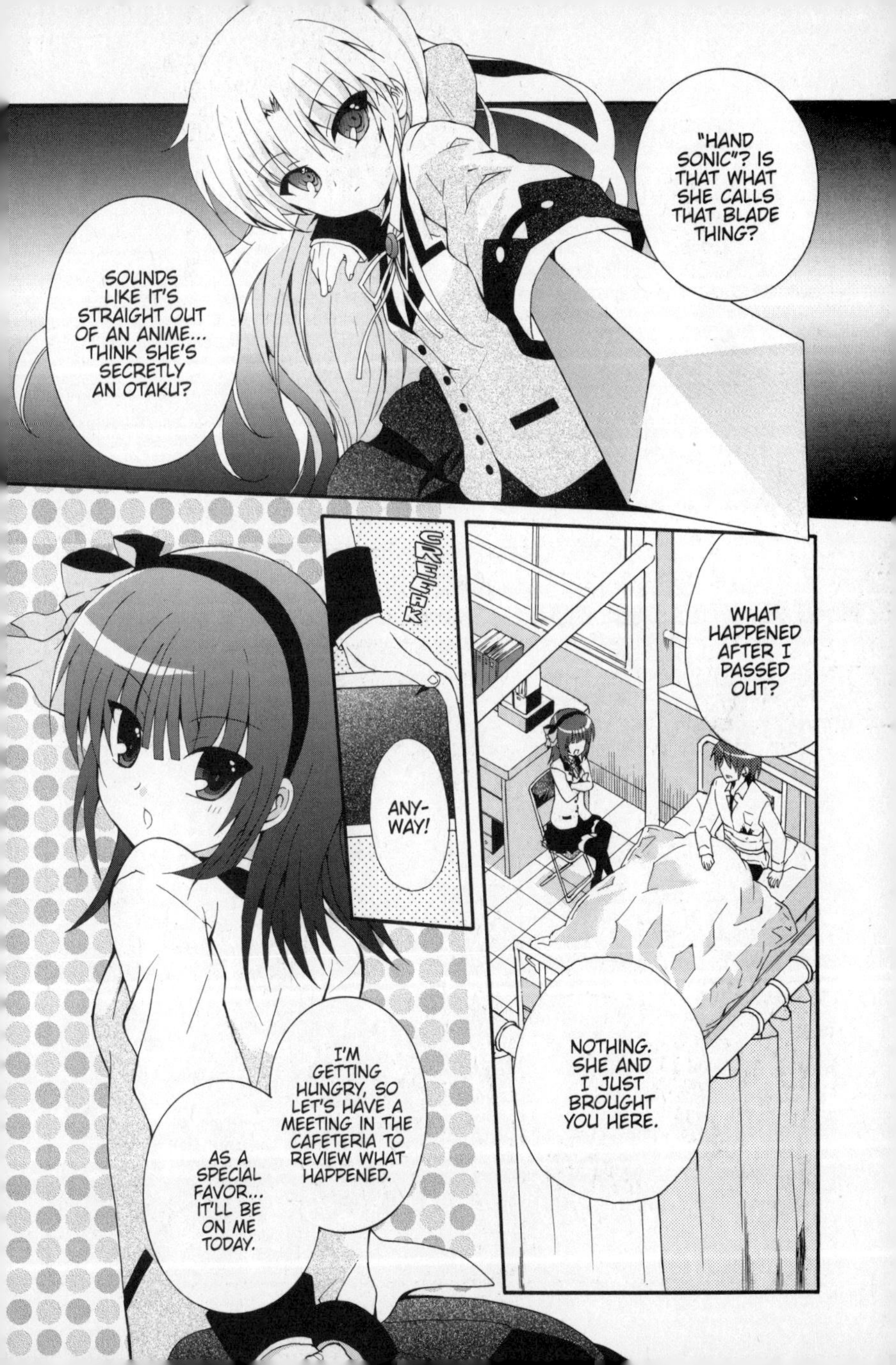
"HAND SONIC"? IS THAT WHAT SHE CALLS THAT BLADE THING?
SOUNDS LIKE IT'S STRAIGHT OUT OF AN ANIME... THINK SHE'S SECRETLY AN OTAKU?
WHAT HAPPENED AFTER I PASSED OUT?
NOTHING. SHE AND I JUST BROUGHT YOU HERE.
CREEEAK
ANY-WAY!
I'M GETTING HUNGRY, SO LET'S HAVE A MEETING IN THE CAFETERIA TO REVIEW WHAT HAPPENED.
AS A SPECIAL FAVOR... IT'LL BE ON ME TODAY.

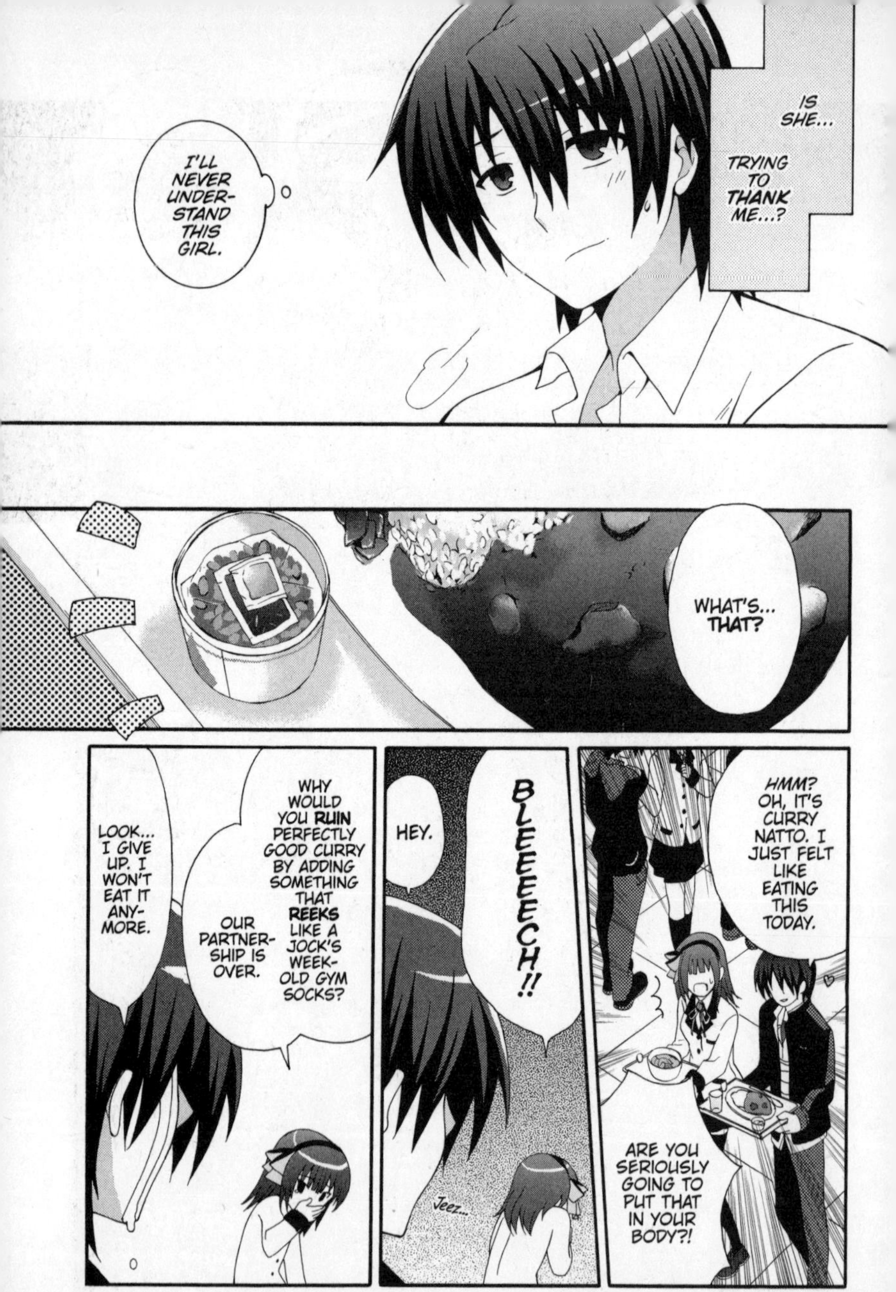
IS SHE... TRYING TO THANK ME...?
I'LL NEVER UNDERSTAND THIS GIRL.
WHAT'S... THAT?
HMM? OH, IT'S CURRY NATTO. I JUST FELT LIKE EATING THIS TODAY.
ARE YOU SERIOUSLY GOING TO PUT THAT IN YOUR BODY?!
BLEEEECH!!
HEY.
Jeez...
WHY WOULD YOU RUIN PERFECTLY GOOD CURRY BY ADDING SOMETHING THAT REEKS LIKE A JOCK'S WEEK-OLD GYM SOCKS?
OUR PARTNERSHIP IS OVER.
LOOK... I GIVE UP. I WON'T EAT IT ANYMORE.

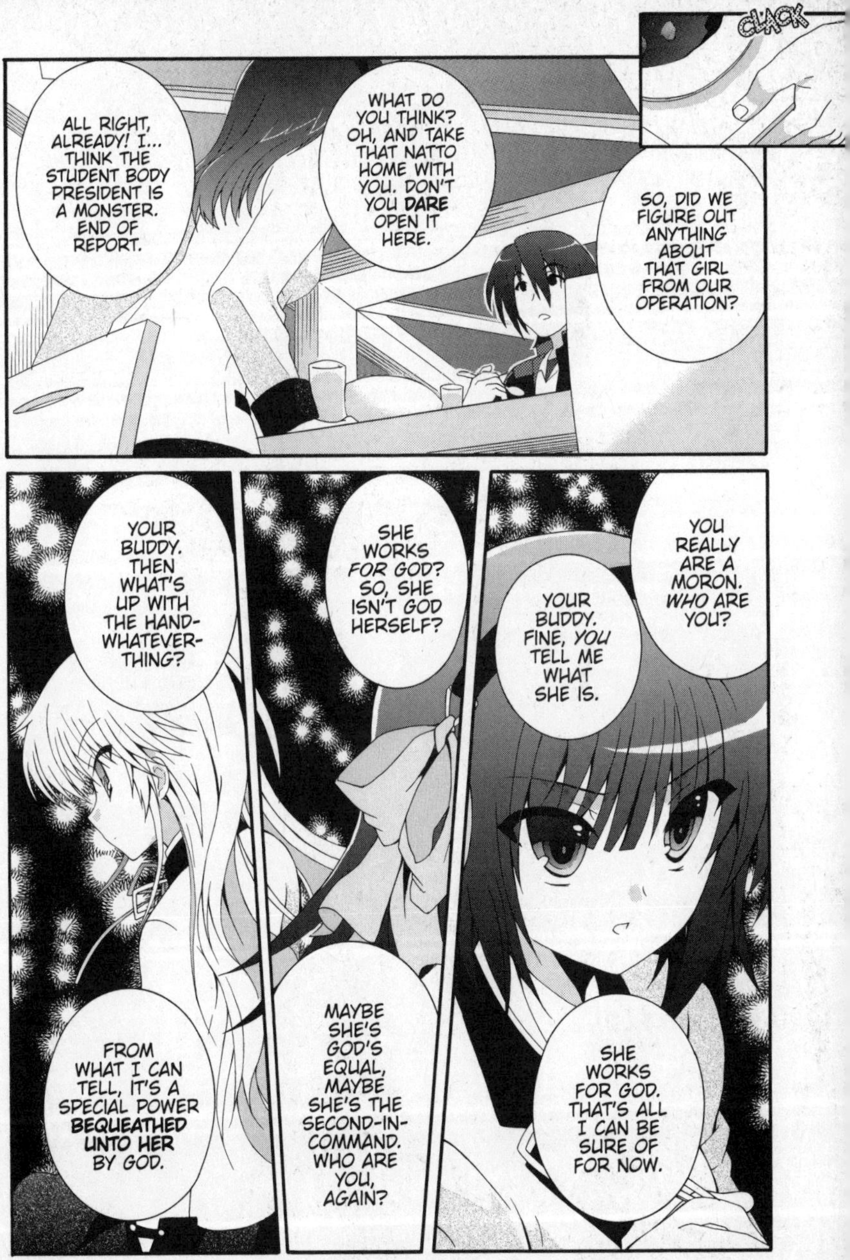
CLACK
SO, DID WE FIGURE OUT ANYTHING ABOUT THAT GIRL FROM OUR OPERATION?
WHAT DO YOU THINK? OH, AND TAKE THAT NATTO HOME WITH YOU. DON'T YOU **DARE** OPEN IT HERE.
ALL RIGHT, ALREADY! I... THINK THE STUDENT BODY PRESIDENT IS A MONSTER. END OF REPORT.
YOU REALLY ARE A MORON. *WHO ARE* YOU?
YOUR BUDDY. FINE, *YOU* TELL ME WHAT SHE IS.
SHE WORKS FOR GOD. THAT'S ALL I CAN BE SURE OF FOR NOW.
SHE WORKS *FOR GOD*? SO, SHE ISN'T GOD HERSELF?
MAYBE SHE'S GOD'S EQUAL, MAYBE SHE'S THE SECOND-IN-COMMAND. WHO ARE YOU, AGAIN?
YOUR BUDDY. THEN WHAT'S UP WITH THE HAND-WHATEVER-THING?
FROM WHAT I CAN TELL, IT'S A SPECIAL POWER **BEQUEATHED UNTO HER** BY GOD.

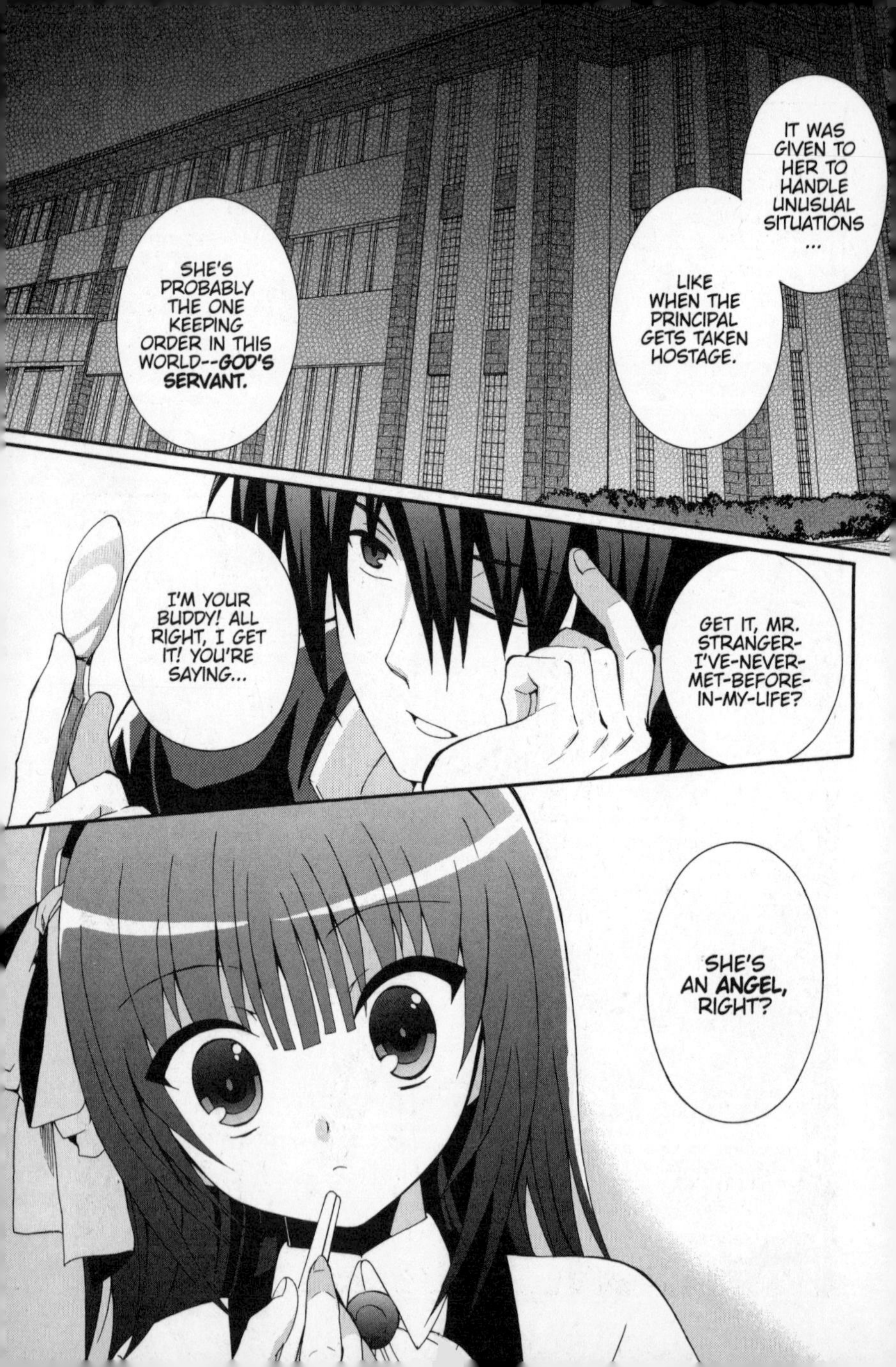
IT WAS GIVEN TO HER TO HANDLE UNUSUAL SITUATIONS ...
LIKE WHEN THE PRINCIPAL GETS TAKEN HOSTAGE.
SHE'S PROBABLY THE ONE KEEPING ORDER IN THIS WORLD--**GOD'S SERVANT.**
GET IT, MR. STRANGER-I'VE-NEVER-MET-BEFORE-IN-MY-LIFE?
I'M YOUR BUDDY! ALL RIGHT, I GET IT! YOU'RE SAYING...
SHE'S AN **ANGEL,** RIGHT?

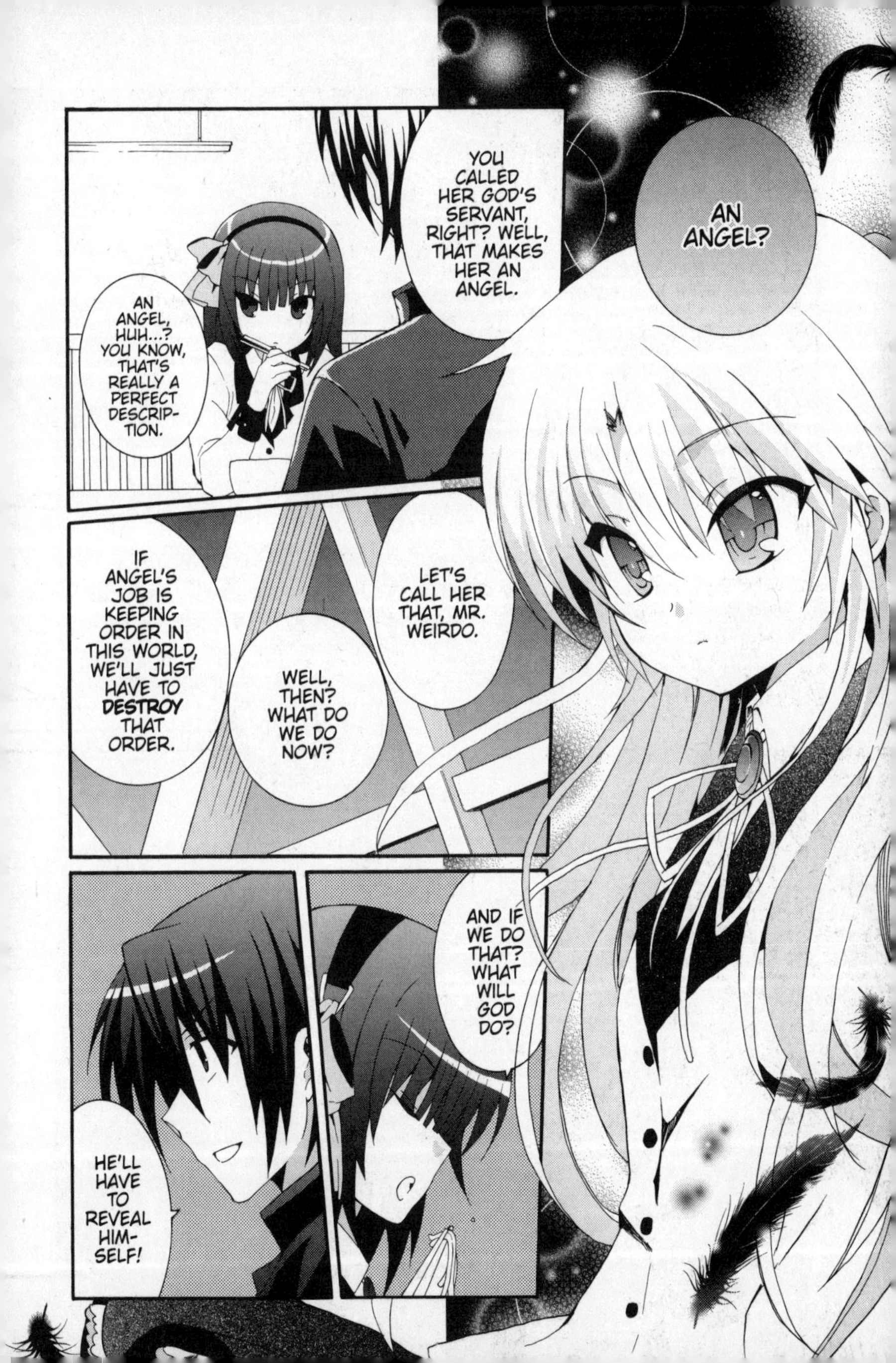
AN ANGEL?
YOU CALLED HER GOD'S SERVANT, RIGHT? WELL, THAT MAKES HER AN ANGEL.
AN ANGEL, HUH...? YOU KNOW, THAT'S REALLY A PERFECT DESCRIPTION.
LET'S CALL HER THAT, MR. WEIRDO.
WELL, THEN? WHAT DO WE DO NOW?
IF ANGEL'S JOB IS KEEPING ORDER IN THIS WORLD, WE'LL JUST HAVE TO **DESTROY** THAT ORDER.
AND IF WE DO THAT? WHAT WILL GOD DO?
HE'LL HAVE TO REVEAL HIMSELF!

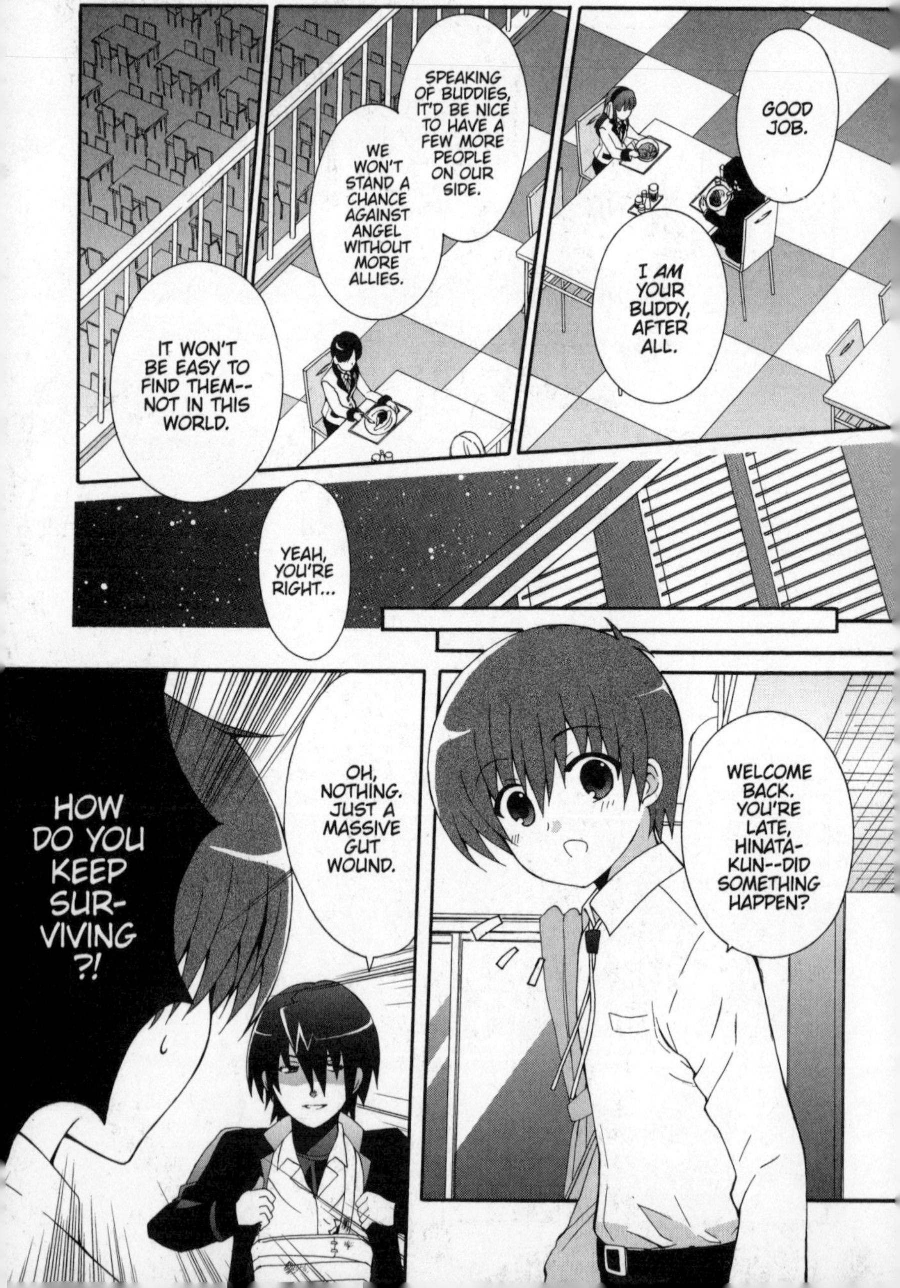
GOOD JOB.
I AM YOUR BUDDY, AFTER ALL.
SPEAKING OF BUDDIES, IT'D BE NICE TO HAVE A FEW MORE PEOPLE ON OUR SIDE.
WE WON'T STAND A CHANCE AGAINST ANGEL WITHOUT MORE ALLIES.
IT WON'T BE EASY TO FIND THEM-- NOT IN THIS WORLD.
YEAH, YOU'RE RIGHT...
WELCOME BACK. YOU'RE LATE, HINATA-KUN--DID SOMETHING HAPPEN?
OH, NOTHING. JUST A MASSIVE GUT WOUND.
HOW DO YOU KEEP SUR-VIVING?!

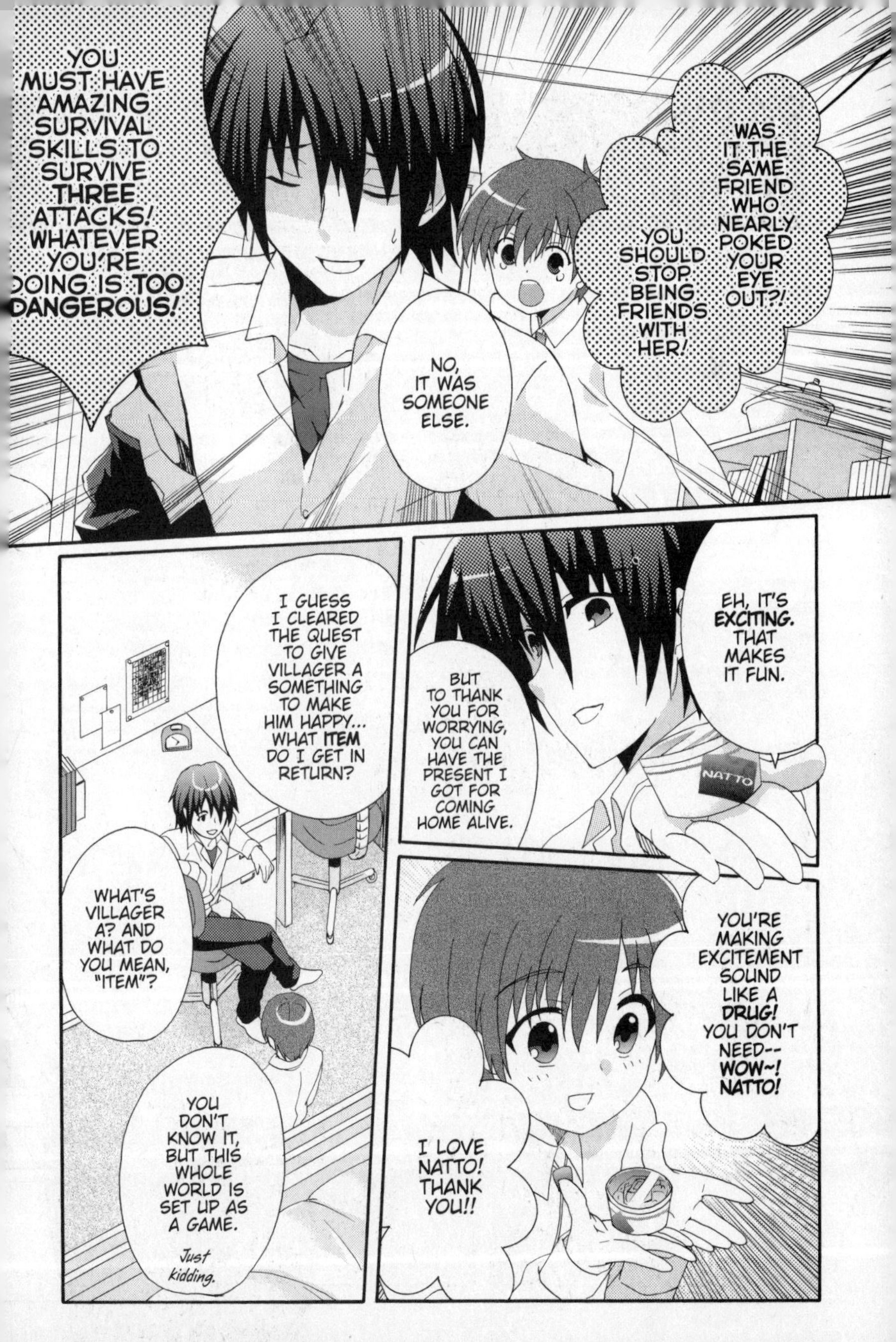
WAS IT THE SAME FRIEND WHO NEARLY POKED YOUR EYE OUT?!
YOU SHOULD STOP BEING FRIENDS WITH HER!
YOU MUST HAVE AMAZING SURVIVAL SKILLS TO SURVIVE THREE ATTACKS! WHATEVER YOU'RE DOING IS TOO DANGEROUS!
NO, IT WAS SOMEONE ELSE.
EH, IT'S EXCITING. THAT MAKES IT FUN.
BUT TO THANK YOU FOR WORRYING, YOU CAN HAVE THE PRESENT I GOT FOR COMING HOME ALIVE.
NATTO
YOU'RE MAKING EXCITEMENT SOUND LIKE A DRUG! YOU DON'T NEED-- WOW~! NATTO!
I LOVE NATTO! THANK YOU!!
I GUESS I CLEARED THE QUEST TO GIVE VILLAGER A SOMETHING TO MAKE HIM HAPPY... WHAT ITEM DO I GET IN RETURN?
WHAT'S VILLAGER A? AND WHAT DO YOU MEAN, "ITEM"?
YOU DON'T KNOW IT, BUT THIS WHOLE WORLD IS SET UP AS A GAME.
Just kidding.

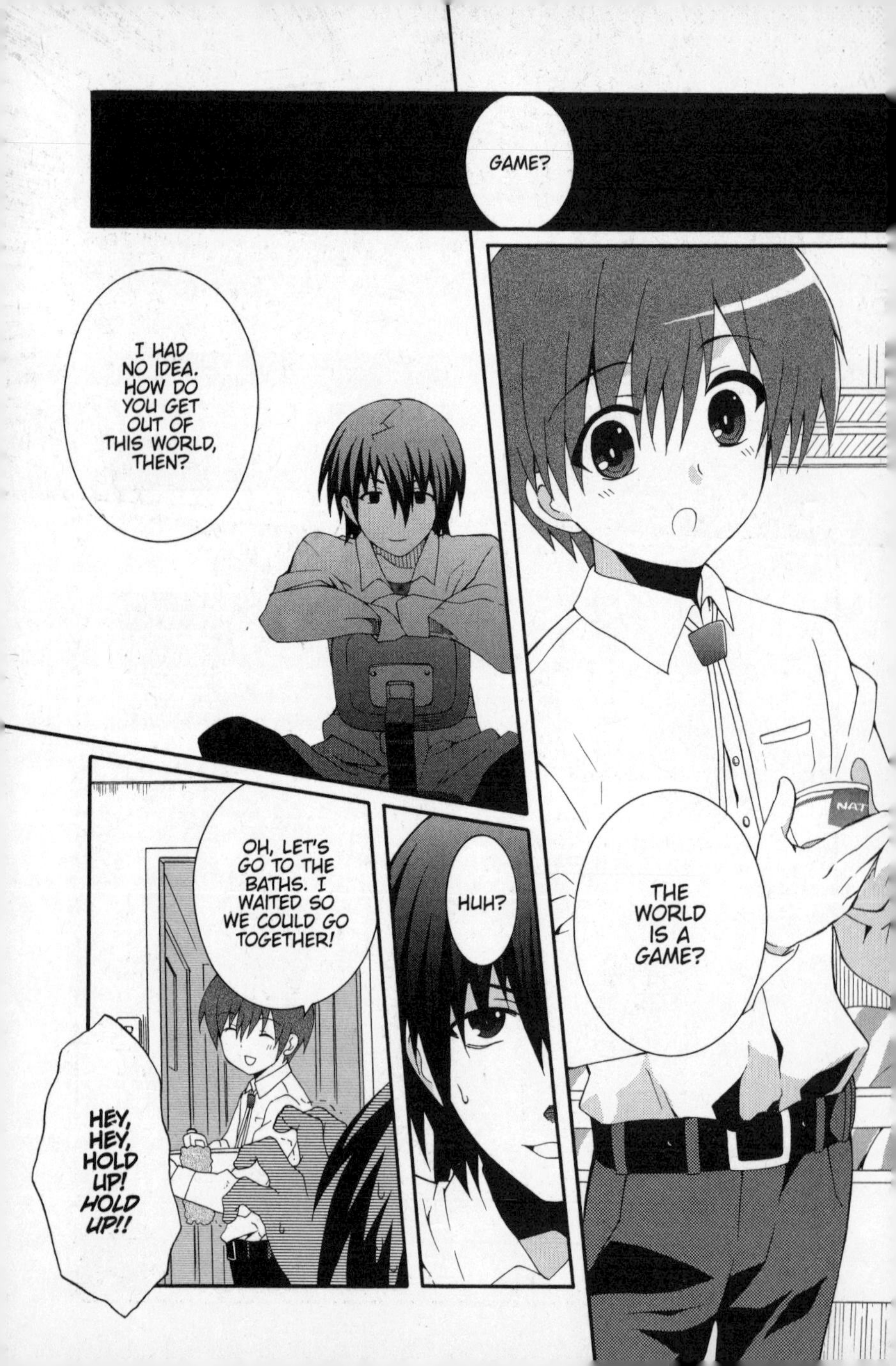
GAME?
THE WORLD IS A GAME?
I HAD NO IDEA. HOW DO YOU GET OUT OF THIS WORLD, THEN?
HUH?
OH, LET'S GO TO THE BATHS. I WAITED SO WE COULD GO TOGETHER!
HEY, HEY, HOLD UP! HOLD UP!!

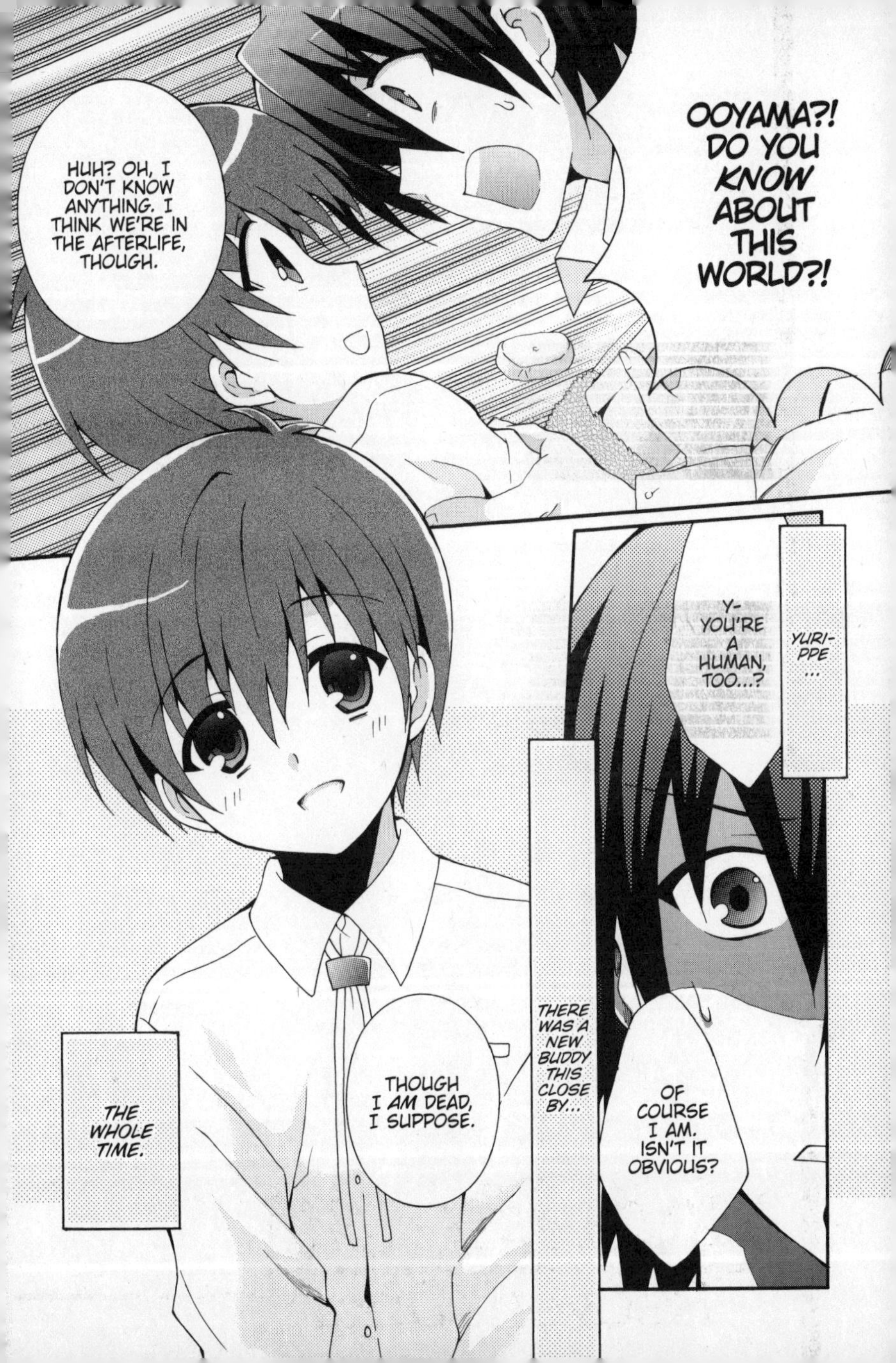
OOYAMA?! DO YOU KNOW ABOUT THIS WORLD?!
HUH? OH, I DON'T KNOW ANYTHING. I THINK WE'RE IN THE AFTERLIFE, THOUGH.
YURIPPE...
Y-YOU'RE A HUMAN, TOO...?
OF COURSE I AM. ISN'T IT OBVIOUS?
THOUGH I AM DEAD, I SUPPOSE.
THERE WAS A NEW BUDDY THIS CLOSE BY...
THE WHOLE TIME.

Angel Beats!
Heaven's Door

I
found
one...

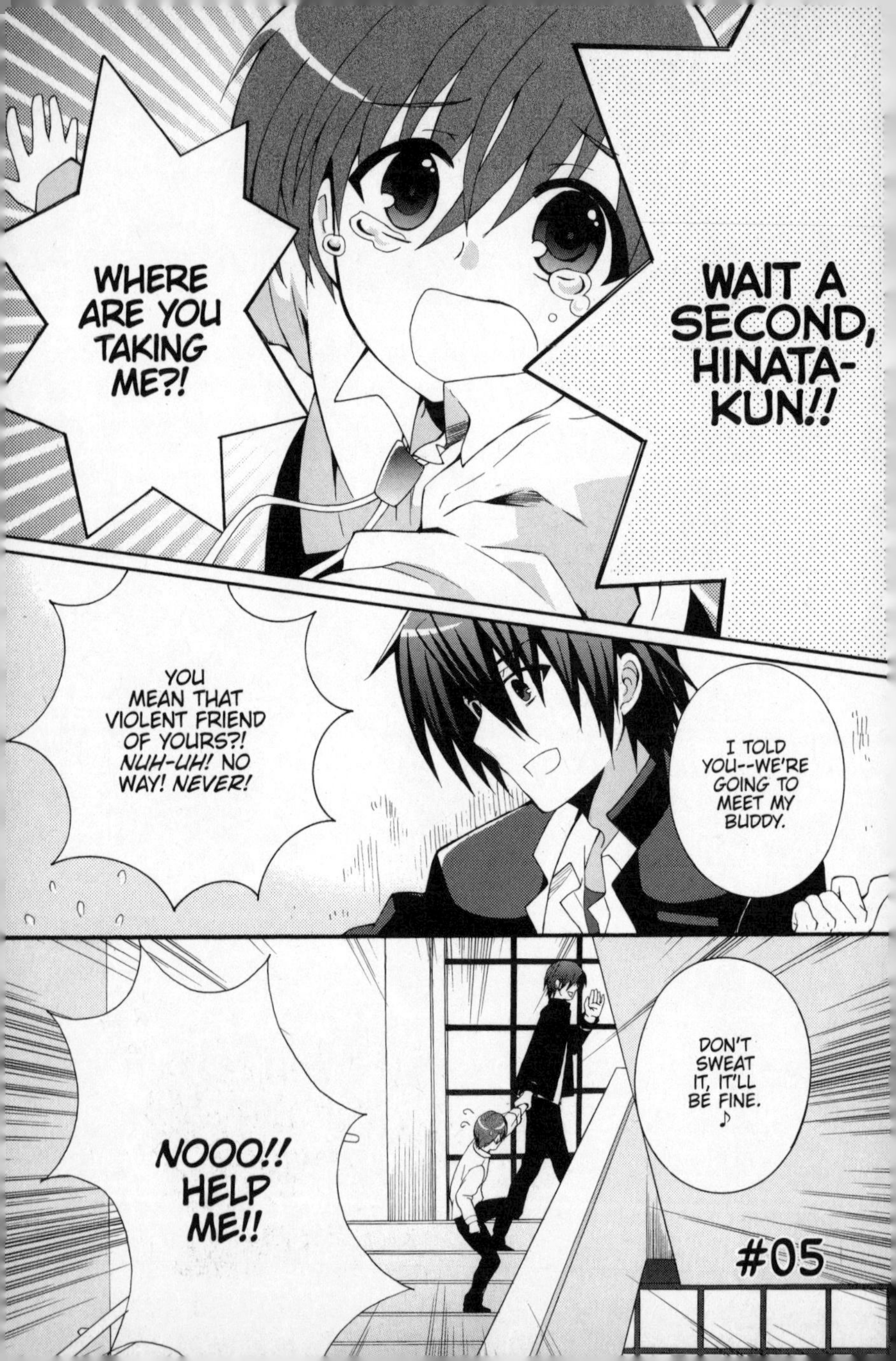
WAIT A SECOND, HINATA-KUN!!
WHERE ARE YOU TAKING ME?!
I TOLD YOU--WE'RE GOING TO MEET MY BUDDY.
YOU MEAN THAT VIOLENT FRIEND OF YOURS?! NUH-UH! NO WAY! NEVER!
DON'T SWEAT IT, IT'LL BE FINE. ♪
NOOO!! HELP ME!!
#05

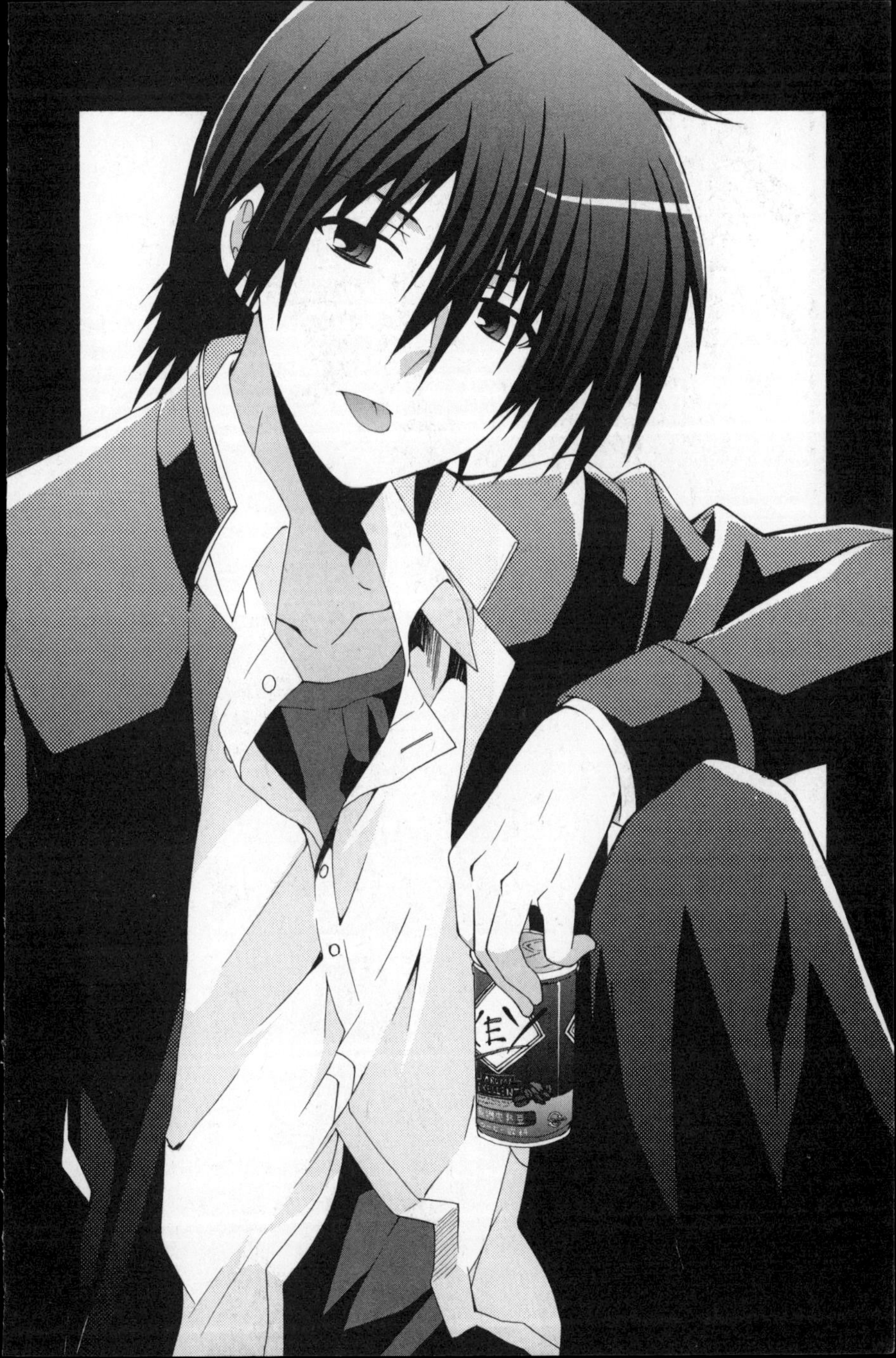

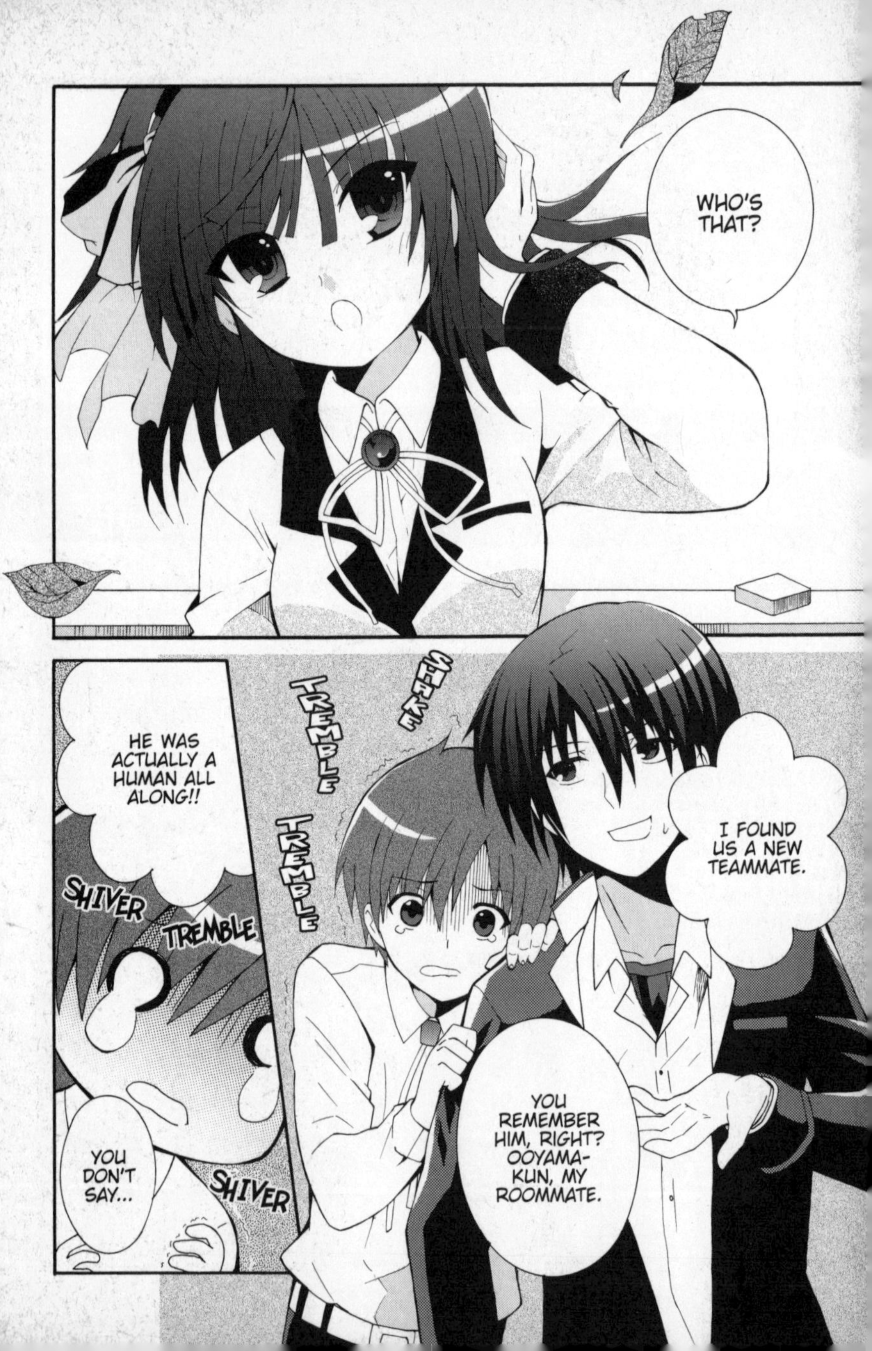
WHO'S THAT?
I FOUND US A NEW TEAMMATE.
SHAKE
TREMBLE
TREMBLE
YOU REMEMBER HIM, RIGHT? OOYAMA-KUN, MY ROOMMATE.
HE WAS ACTUALLY A HUMAN ALL ALONG!!
SHIVER
TREMBLE
YOU DON'T SAY...
SHIVER

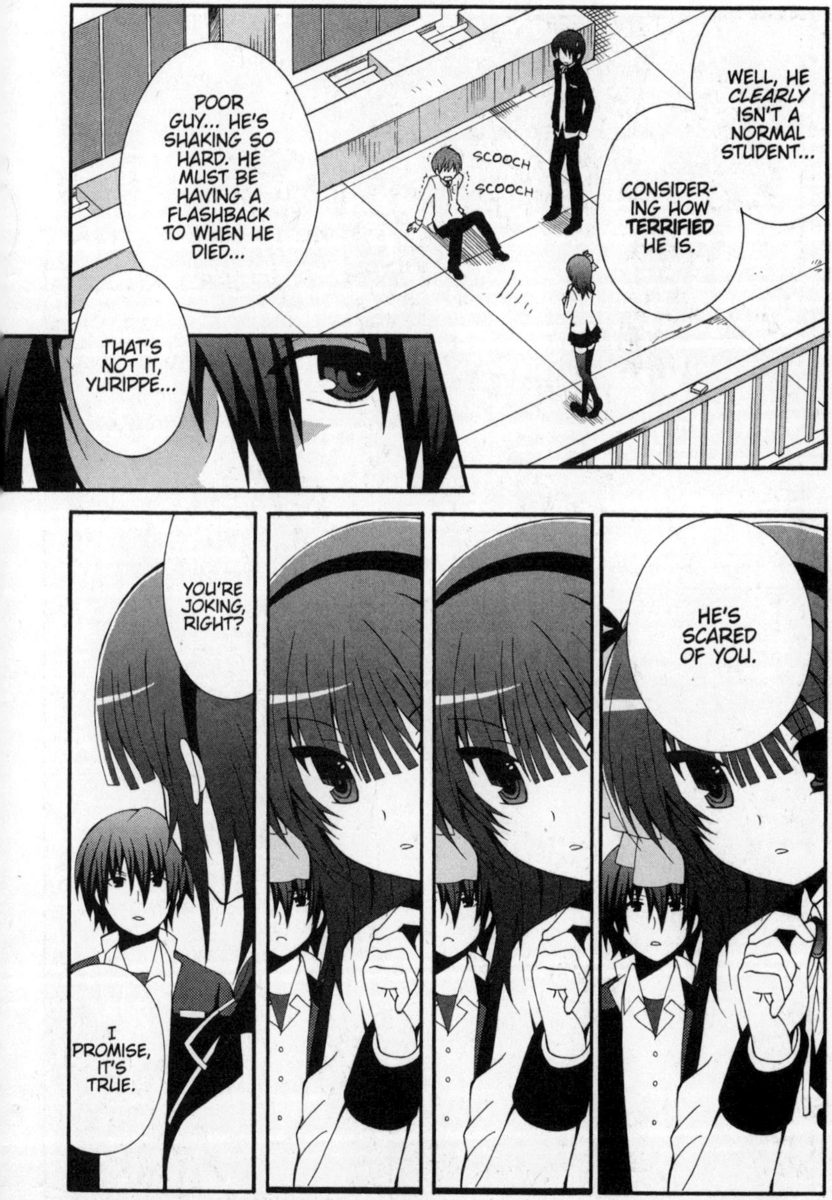
WELL, HE CLEARLY ISN'T A NORMAL STUDENT...
CONSIDER-ING HOW TERRIFIED HE IS.
SCOOCH
SCOOCH
POOR GUY... HE'S SHAKING SO HARD. HE MUST BE HAVING A FLASHBACK TO WHEN HE DIED...
THAT'S NOT IT, YURIPPE...
HE'S SCARED OF YOU.
YOU'RE JOKING, RIGHT?
I PROMISE, IT'S TRUE.

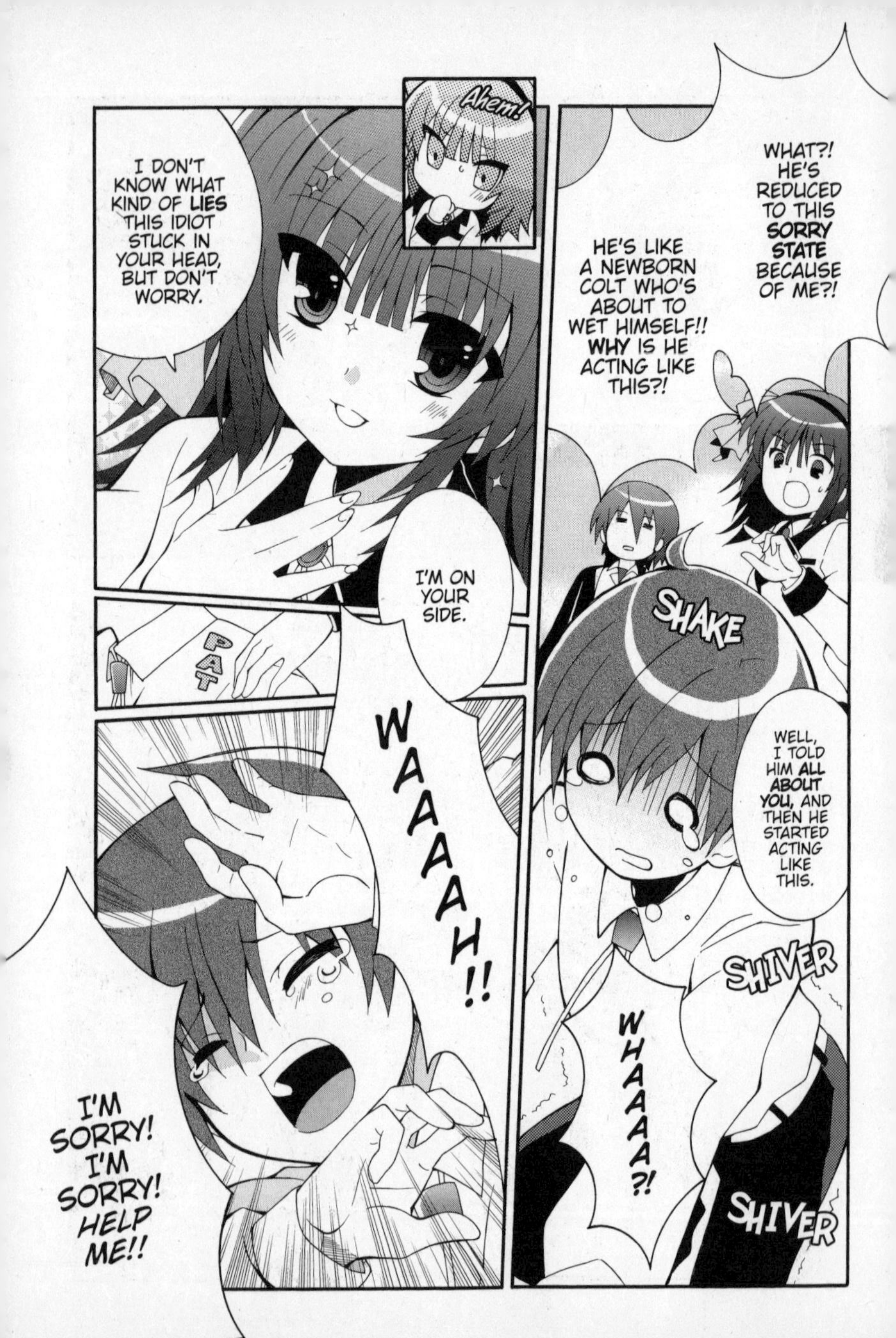
WHAT?! HE'S REDUCED TO THIS **SORRY STATE** BECAUSE OF ME?!
HE'S LIKE A NEWBORN COLT WHO'S ABOUT TO WET HIMSELF!! **WHY** IS HE ACTING LIKE THIS?!
SHAKE
WELL, I TOLD HIM **ALL ABOUT YOU,** AND THEN HE STARTED ACTING LIKE THIS.
SHIVER
WHAAAAA?!
SHIVER
Ahem!
I DON'T KNOW WHAT KIND OF **LIES** THIS IDIOT STUCK IN YOUR HEAD, BUT DON'T WORRY.
I'M ON YOUR SIDE.
PAT
WAAAAAH!!
I'M SORRY! I'M SORRY! HELP ME!!

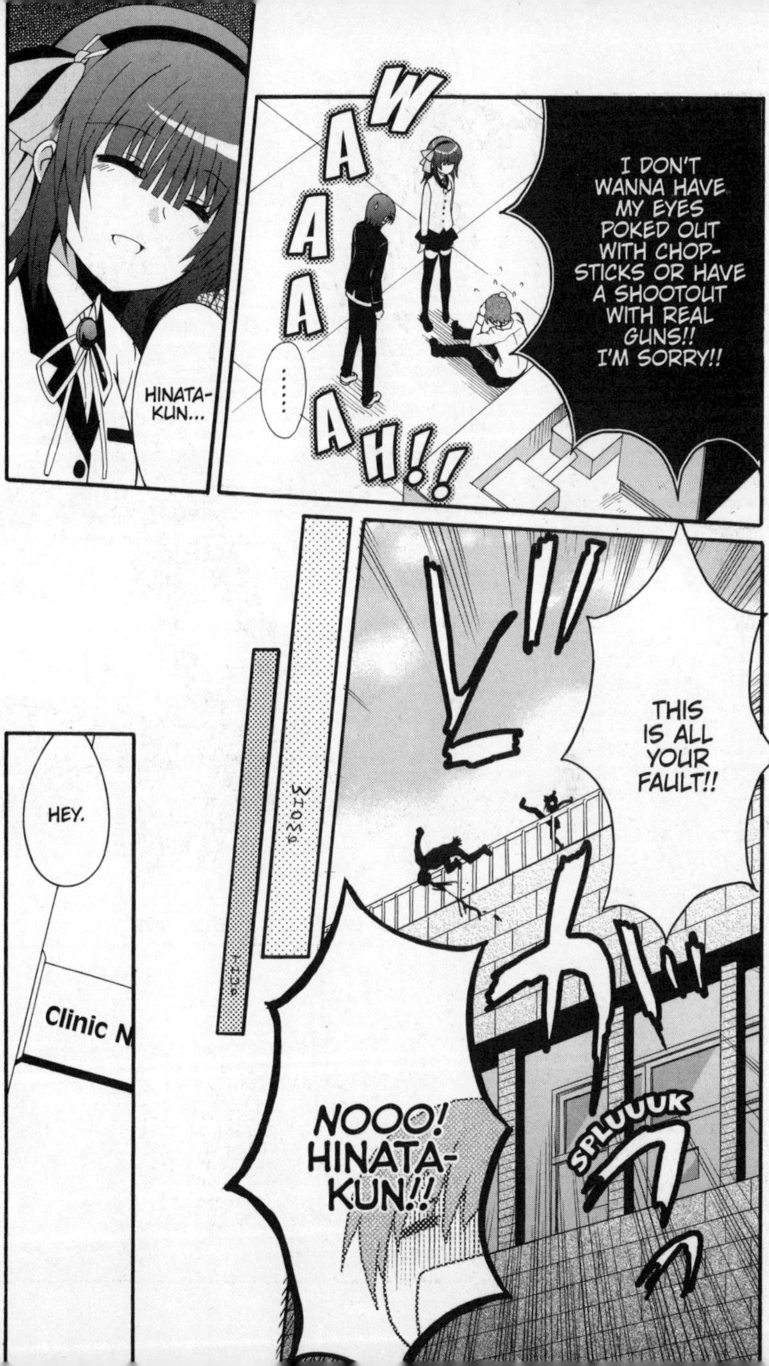

I DON'T WANNA HAVE MY EYES POKED OUT WITH CHOP-STICKS OR HAVE A SHOOTOUT WITH REAL GUNS!! I'M SORRY!!
WAAAAAH!!
......
HINATA-KUN...
THIS IS ALL YOUR FAULT!!
NOOO! HINATA-KUN!!
SPLUUUK
WHOMP
THUD
HEY.
Clinic M

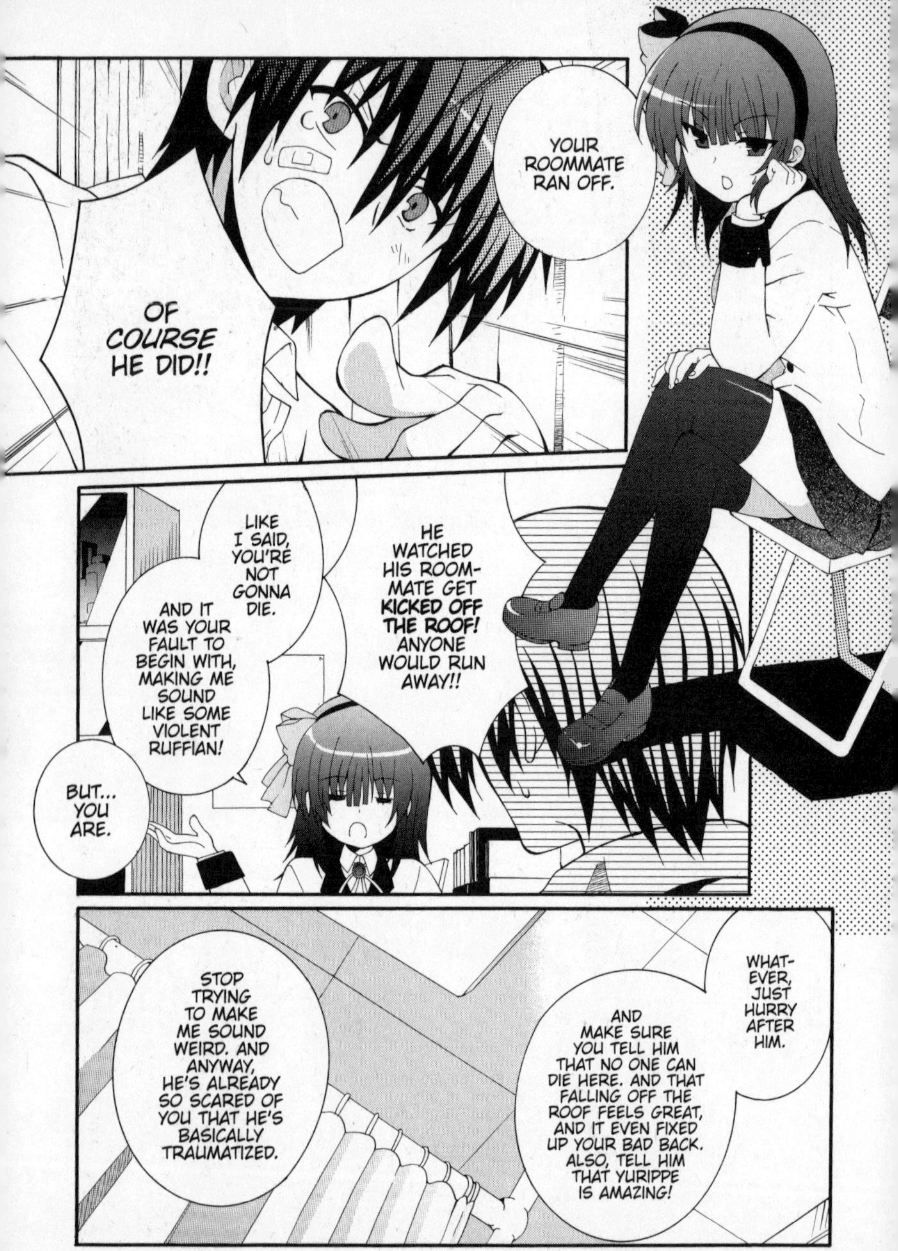
YOUR ROOMMATE RAN OFF.
OF COURSE HE DID!!
HE WATCHED HIS ROOM-MATE GET **KICKED OFF THE ROOF!** ANYONE WOULD RUN AWAY!!
LIKE I SAID, YOU'RE NOT GONNA DIE.
AND IT WAS YOUR FAULT TO BEGIN WITH, MAKING ME SOUND LIKE SOME VIOLENT RUFFIAN!
BUT... YOU ARE.
WHAT-EVER, JUST HURRY AFTER HIM.
AND MAKE SURE YOU TELL HIM THAT NO ONE CAN DIE HERE. AND THAT FALLING OFF THE ROOF FEELS GREAT, AND IT EVEN FIXED UP YOUR BAD BACK. ALSO, TELL HIM THAT YURIPPE IS AMAZING!
STOP TRYING TO MAKE ME SOUND WEIRD. AND ANYWAY, HE'S ALREADY SO SCARED OF YOU THAT HE'S BASICALLY TRAUMATIZED.

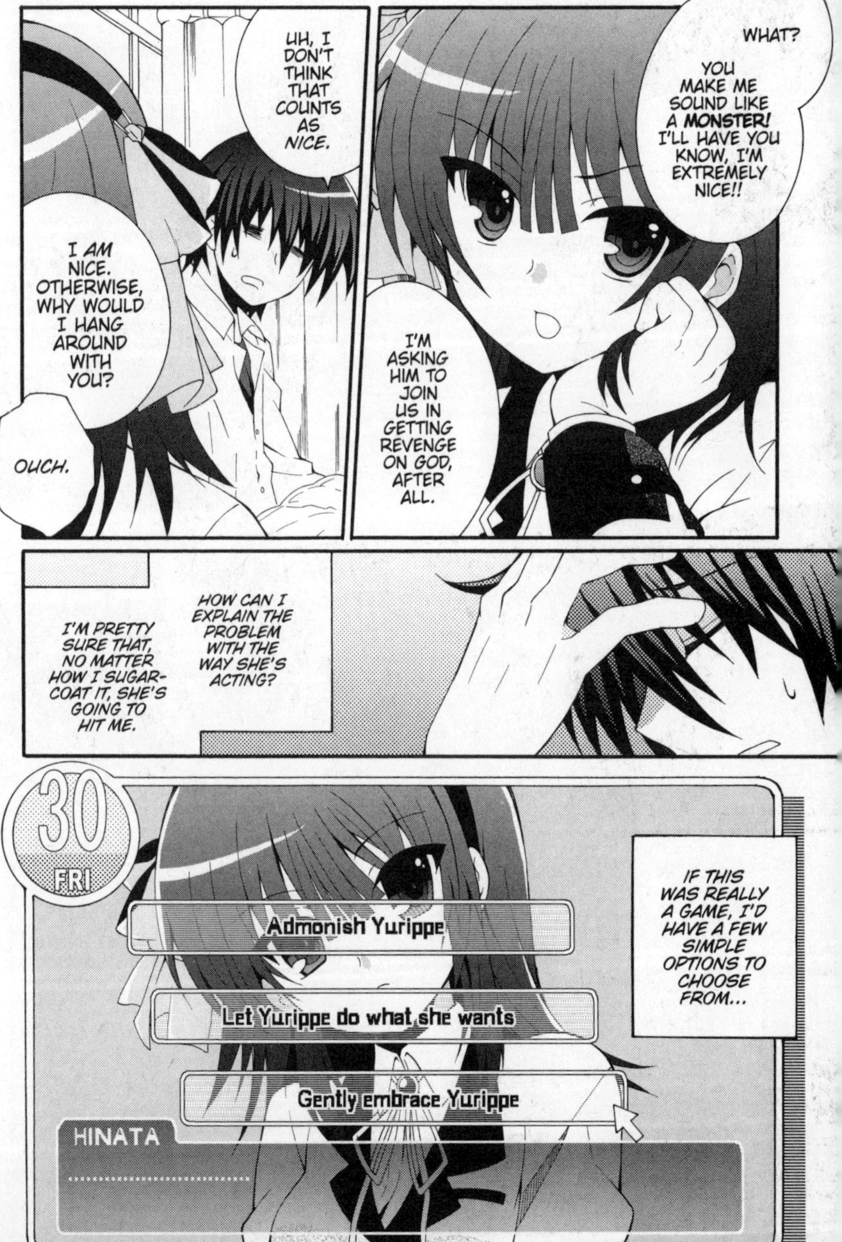
WHAT?
YOU MAKE ME SOUND LIKE A **MONSTER!** I'LL HAVE YOU KNOW, I'M EXTREMELY NICE!!
I'M ASKING HIM TO JOIN US IN GETTING REVENGE ON GOD, AFTER ALL.
UH, I DON'T THINK THAT COUNTS AS *NICE.*
I *AM* NICE. OTHERWISE, WHY WOULD I HANG AROUND WITH YOU?
OUCH.
HOW CAN I EXPLAIN THE PROBLEM WITH THE WAY SHE'S ACTING?
I'M PRETTY SURE THAT, NO MATTER HOW I SUGAR-COAT IT, SHE'S GOING TO HIT ME.
IF THIS WAS REALLY A GAME, I'D HAVE A FEW SIMPLE OPTIONS TO CHOOSE FROM...
30
FRI
Admonish Yurippe
Let Yurippe do what she wants
Gently embrace Yurippe
HINATA
....

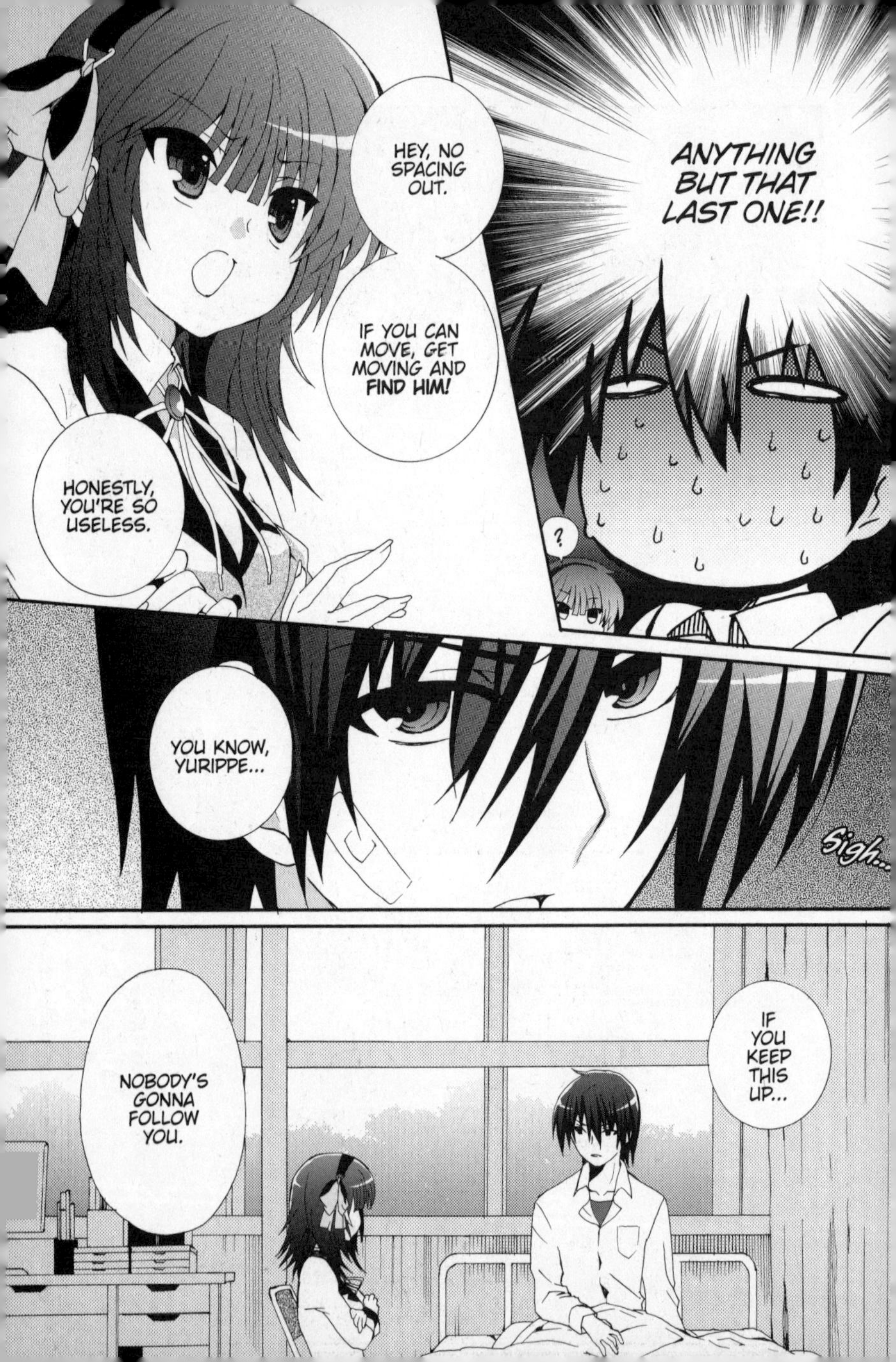
ANYTHING BUT THAT LAST ONE!!
?
HEY, NO SPACING OUT.
IF YOU CAN MOVE, GET MOVING AND FIND HIM!
HONESTLY, YOU'RE SO USELESS.
Sigh...
YOU KNOW, YURIPPE...
IF YOU KEEP THIS UP...
NOBODY'S GONNA FOLLOW YOU.

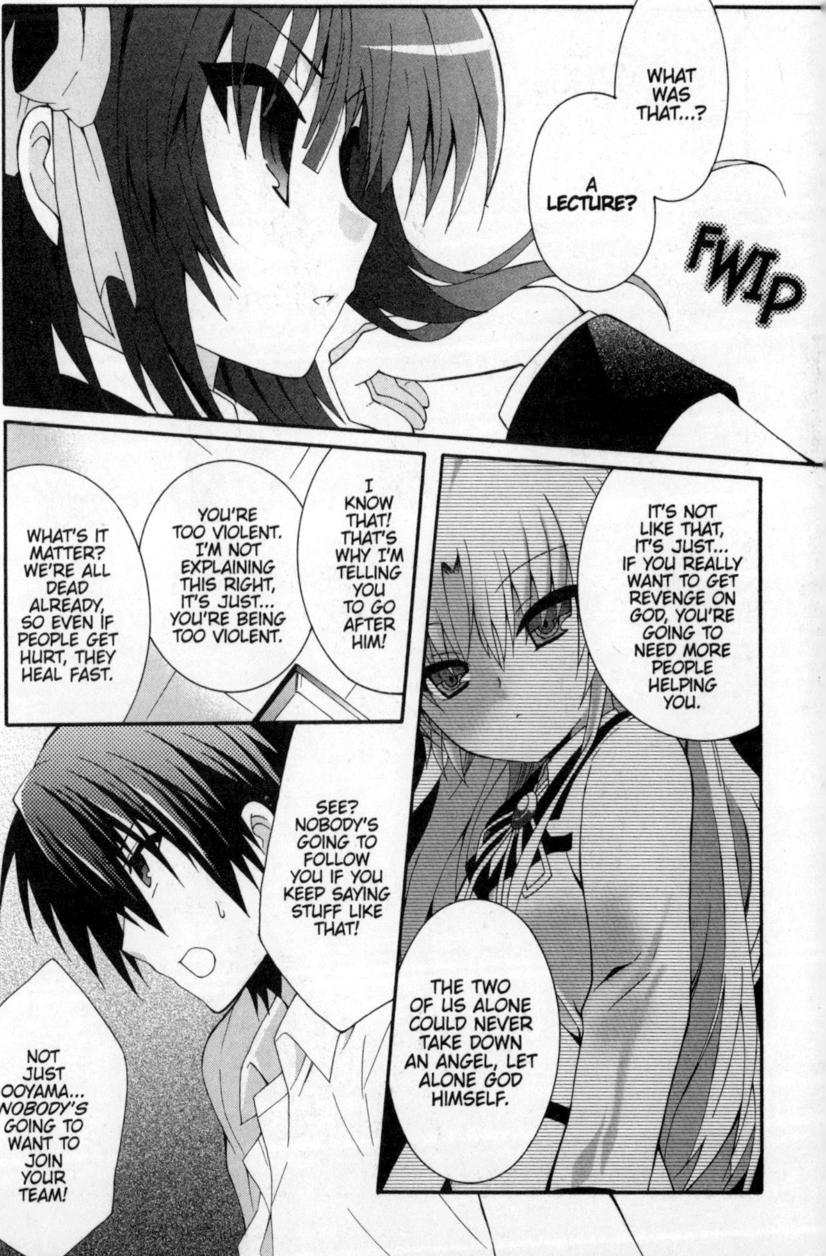
WHAT WAS THAT...?
A LECTURE?
FWIP
IT'S NOT LIKE THAT, IT'S JUST... IF YOU REALLY WANT TO GET REVENGE ON GOD, YOU'RE GOING TO NEED MORE PEOPLE HELPING YOU.
THE TWO OF US ALONE COULD NEVER TAKE DOWN AN ANGEL, LET ALONE GOD HIMSELF.
I KNOW THAT! THAT'S WHY I'M TELLING YOU TO GO AFTER HIM!
YOU'RE TOO VIOLENT. I'M NOT EXPLAINING THIS RIGHT, IT'S JUST... YOU'RE BEING TOO VIOLENT.
WHAT'S IT MATTER? WE'RE ALL DEAD ALREADY, SO EVEN IF PEOPLE GET HURT, THEY HEAL FAST.
SEE? NOBODY'S GOING TO FOLLOW YOU IF YOU KEEP SAYING STUFF LIKE THAT!
NOT JUST OOYAMA... NOBODY'S GOING TO WANT TO JOIN YOUR TEAM!

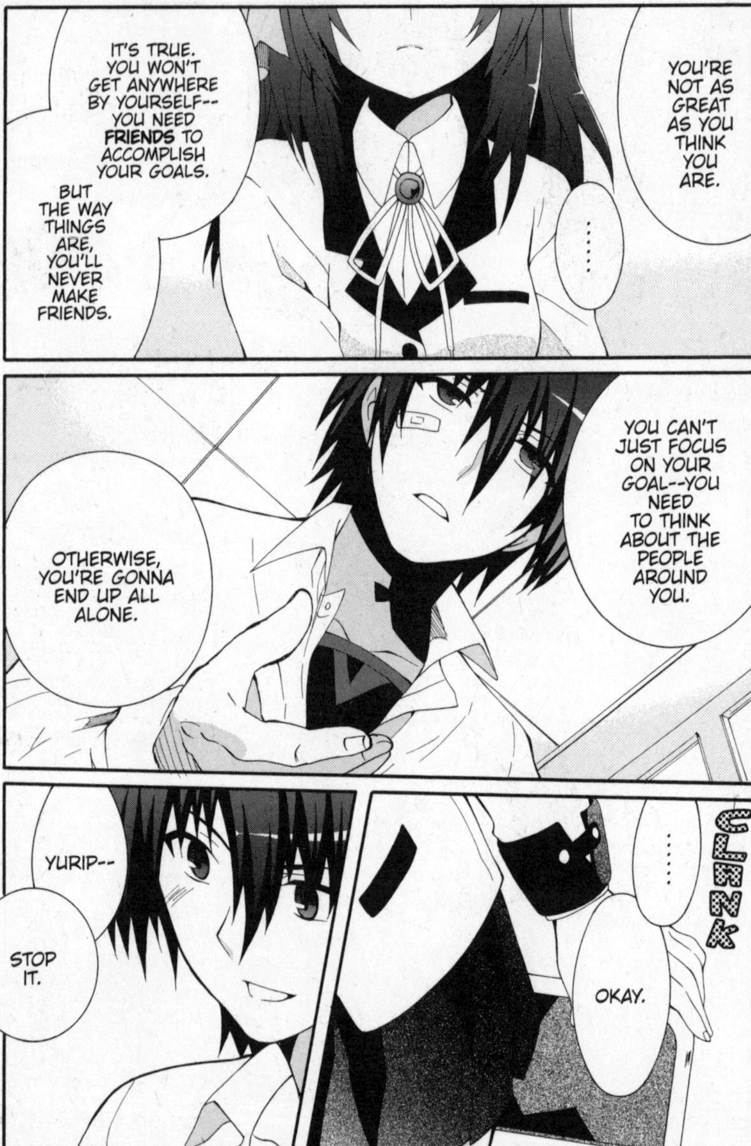
YOU'RE NOT AS GREAT AS YOU THINK YOU ARE.
......
IT'S TRUE. YOU WON'T GET ANYWHERE BY YOURSELF--YOU NEED **FRIENDS** TO ACCOMPLISH YOUR GOALS.
BUT THE WAY THINGS ARE, YOU'LL NEVER MAKE FRIENDS.
YOU CAN'T JUST FOCUS ON YOUR GOAL--YOU NEED TO THINK ABOUT THE PEOPLE AROUND YOU.
OTHERWISE, YOU'RE GONNA END UP ALL ALONE.
CLINK
......
OKAY.
YURIP--
STOP IT.

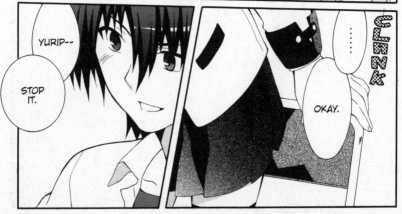

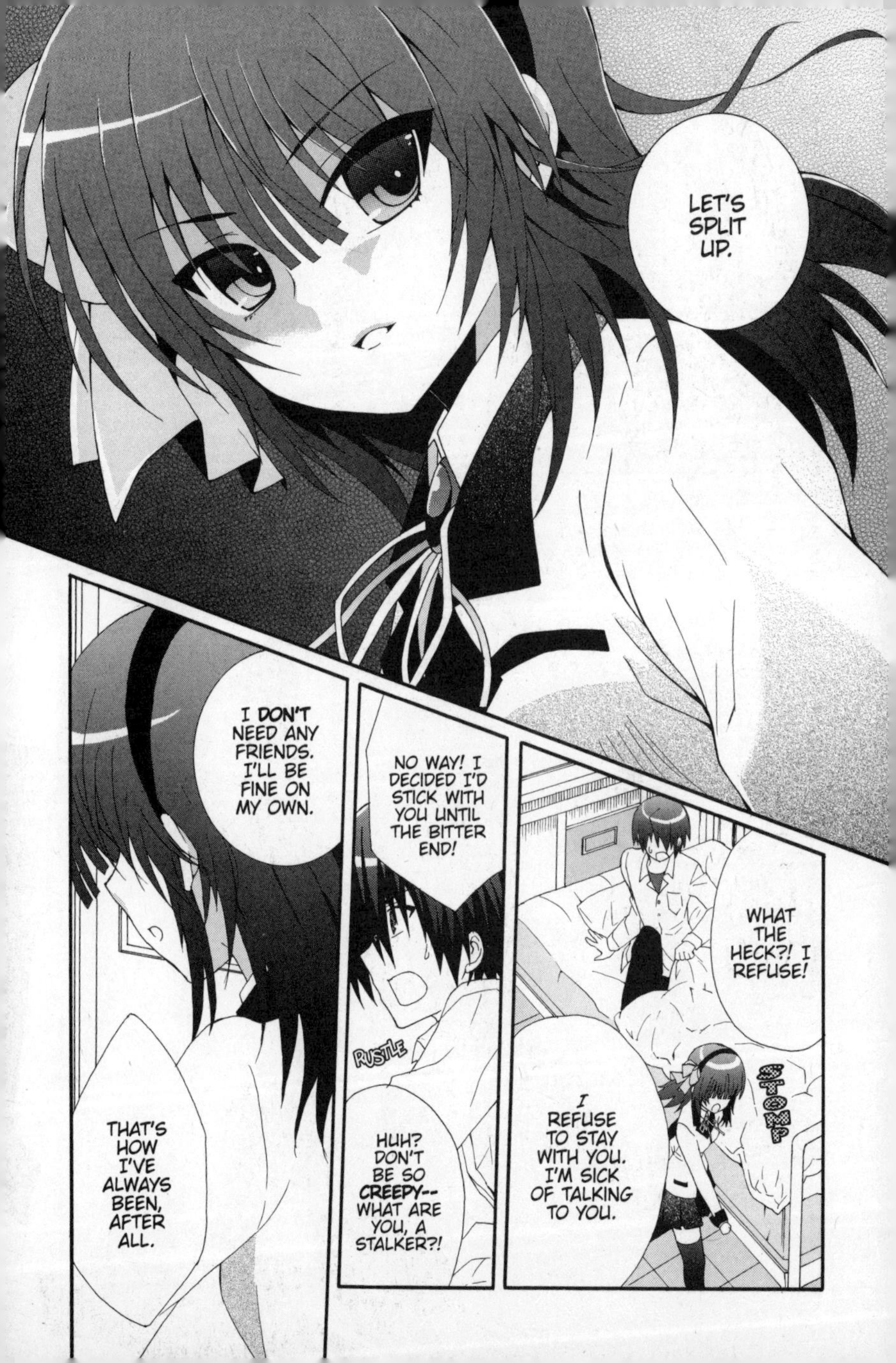
LET'S SPLIT UP.
WHAT THE HECK?! I REFUSE!
STOMP
I REFUSE TO STAY WITH YOU. I'M SICK OF TALKING TO YOU.
NO WAY! I DECIDED I'D STICK WITH YOU UNTIL THE BITTER END!
RUSTLE
HUH? DON'T BE SO **CREEPY**-- WHAT ARE YOU, A STALKER?!
I **DON'T** NEED ANY FRIENDS. I'LL BE FINE ON MY OWN.
THAT'S HOW I'VE ALWAYS BEEN, AFTER ALL.

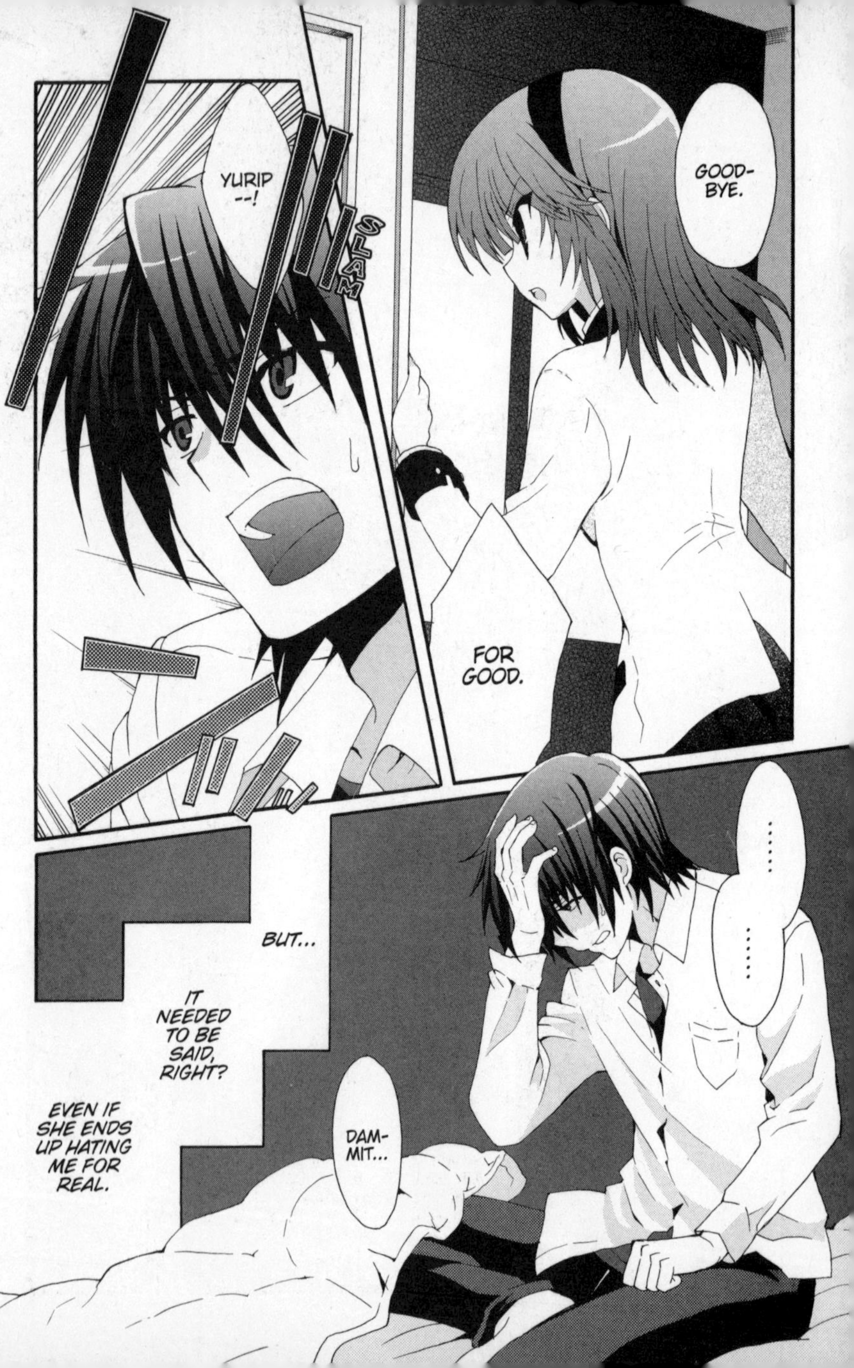
GOOD-BYE.
FOR GOOD.
YURIP--!
SLAM
......
......
BUT...
IT NEEDED TO BE SAID, RIGHT?
DAM-MIT...
EVEN IF SHE ENDS UP HATING ME FOR REAL.

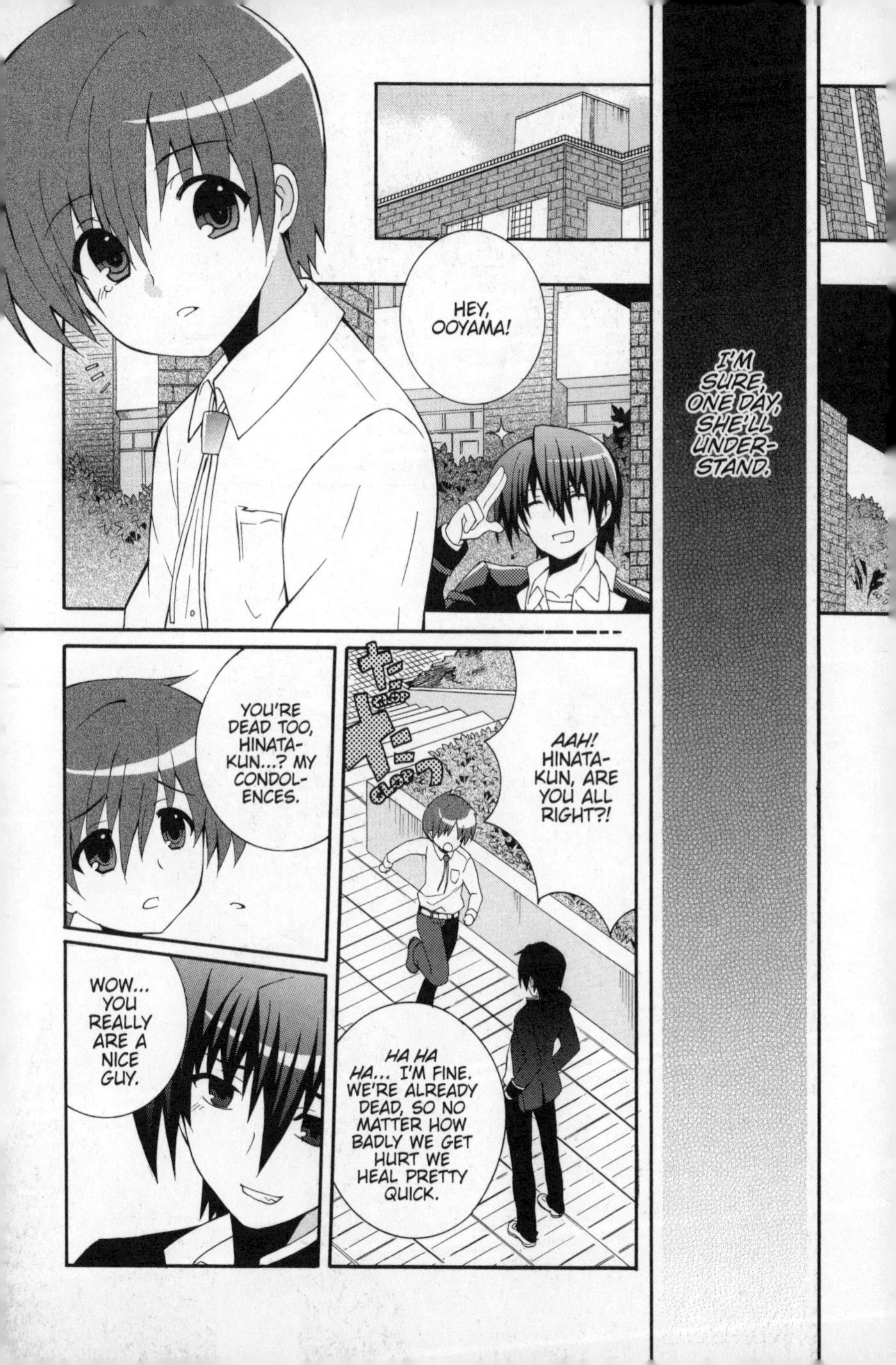
I'M SURE, ONE DAY, SHE'LL UNDER-STAND.
HEY, OOYAMA!
AAH! HINATA-KUN, ARE YOU ALL RIGHT?!
HA HA HA... I'M FINE. WE'RE ALREADY DEAD, SO NO MATTER HOW BADLY WE GET HURT WE HEAL PRETTY QUICK.
YOU'RE DEAD TOO, HINATA-KUN...? MY CONDOL-ENCES.
WOW... YOU REALLY ARE A NICE GUY.

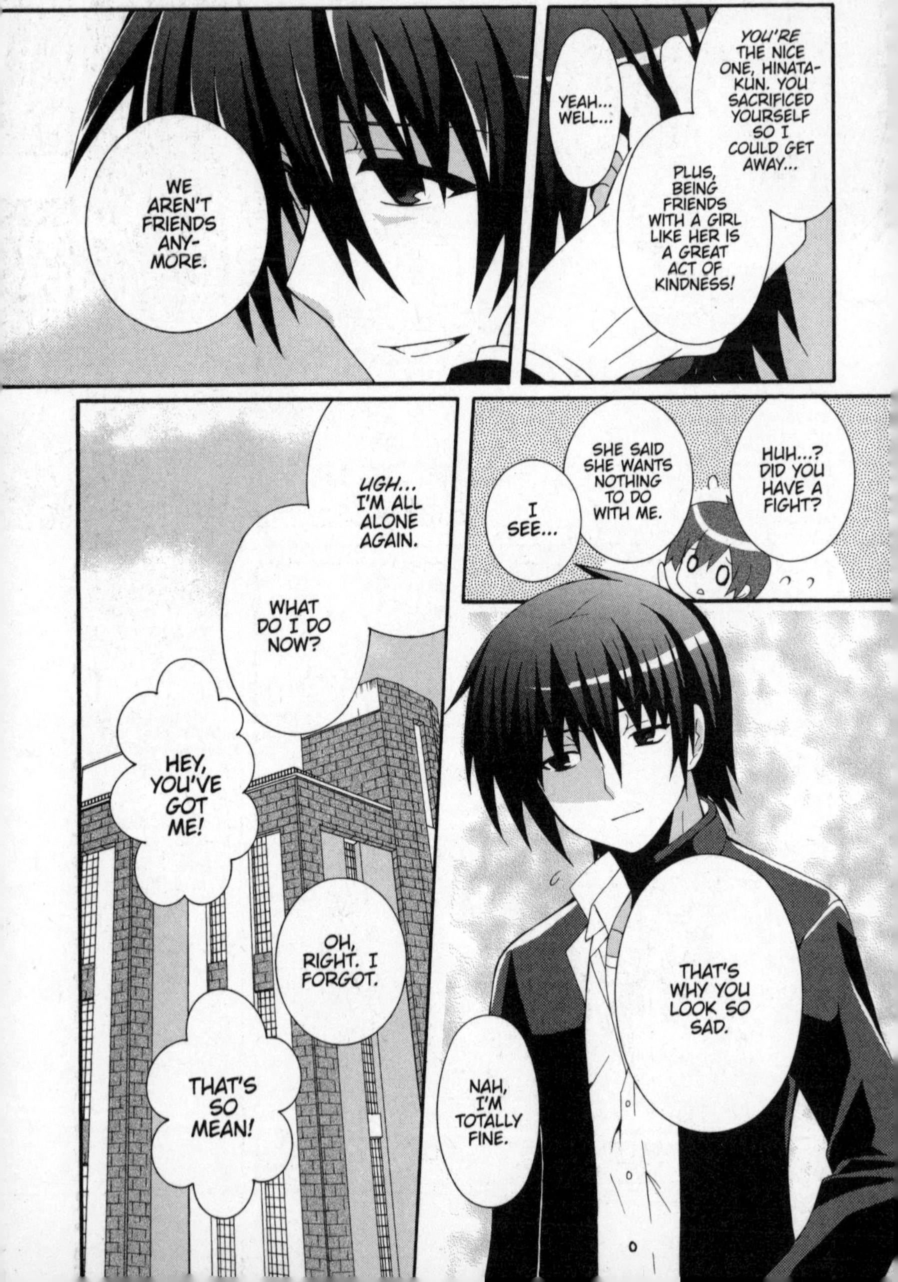
YOU'RE THE NICE ONE, HINATA-KUN. YOU SACRIFICED YOURSELF SO I COULD GET AWAY...
YEAH... WELL...
PLUS, BEING FRIENDS WITH A GIRL LIKE HER IS A GREAT ACT OF KINDNESS!
WE AREN'T FRIENDS ANY-MORE.
HUH...? DID YOU HAVE A FIGHT?
SHE SAID SHE WANTS NOTHING TO DO WITH ME.
I SEE...
THAT'S WHY YOU LOOK SO SAD.
NAH, I'M TOTALLY FINE.
UGH... I'M ALL ALONE AGAIN.
WHAT DO I DO NOW?
HEY, YOU'VE GOT ME!
OH, RIGHT. I FORGOT.
THAT'S SO MEAN!

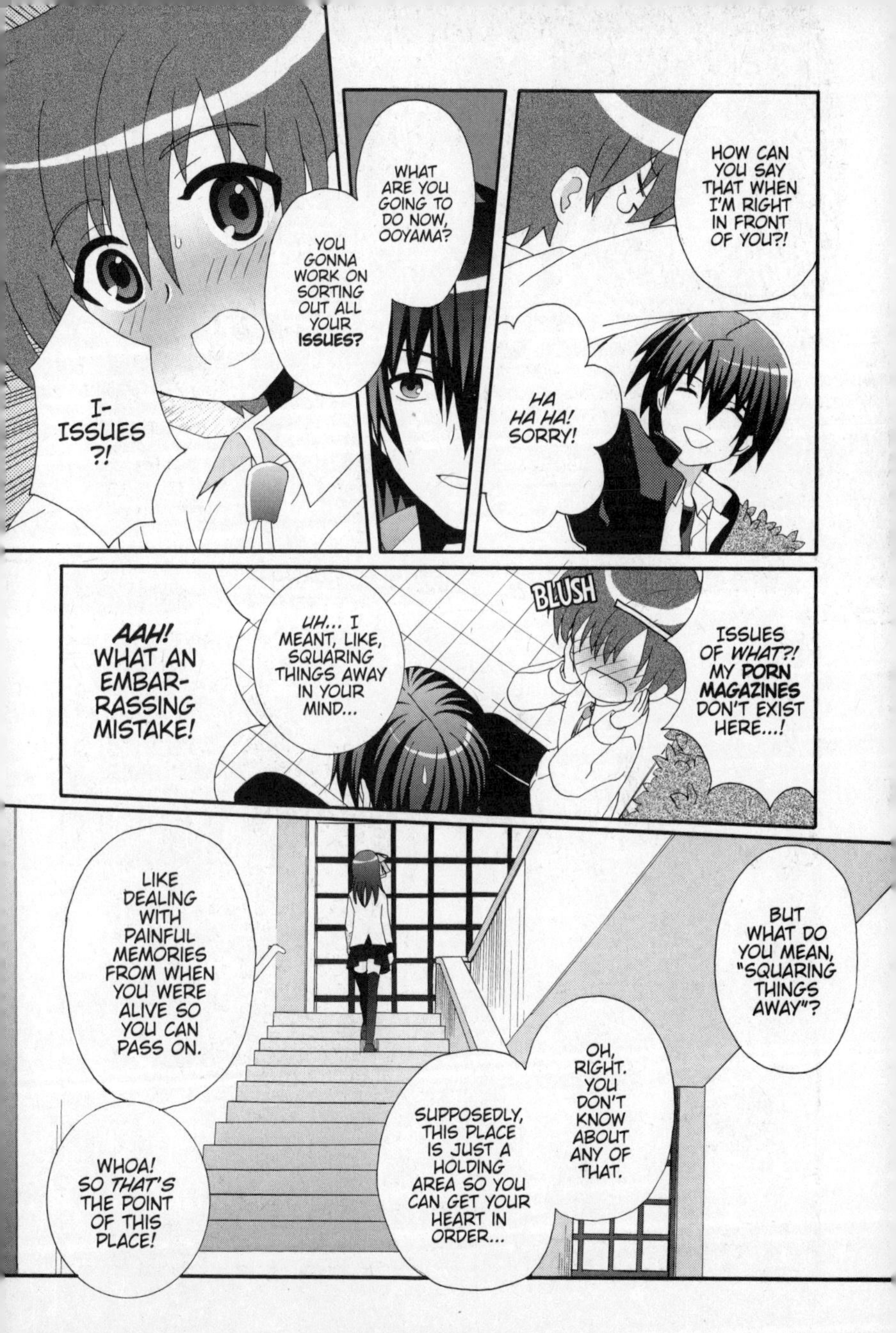
HOW CAN YOU SAY THAT WHEN I'M RIGHT IN FRONT OF YOU?!
HA HA HA! SORRY!
WHAT ARE YOU GOING TO DO NOW, OOYAMA?
YOU GONNA WORK ON SORTING OUT ALL YOUR **ISSUES?**
I- ISSUES ?!
BLUSH
ISSUES OF *WHAT?!* MY **PORN** ***MAGAZINES*** DON'T EXIST HERE...!
UH... I MEANT, LIKE, SQUARING THINGS AWAY IN YOUR MIND...
AAH! WHAT AN EMBAR-RASSING MISTAKE!
BUT WHAT DO YOU MEAN, "SQUARING THINGS AWAY"?
OH, RIGHT. YOU DON'T KNOW ABOUT ANY OF THAT.
SUPPOSEDLY, THIS PLACE IS JUST A HOLDING AREA SO YOU CAN GET YOUR HEART IN ORDER...
LIKE DEALING WITH PAINFUL MEMORIES FROM WHEN YOU WERE ALIVE SO YOU CAN PASS ON.
WHOA! SO *THAT'S* THE POINT OF THIS PLACE!

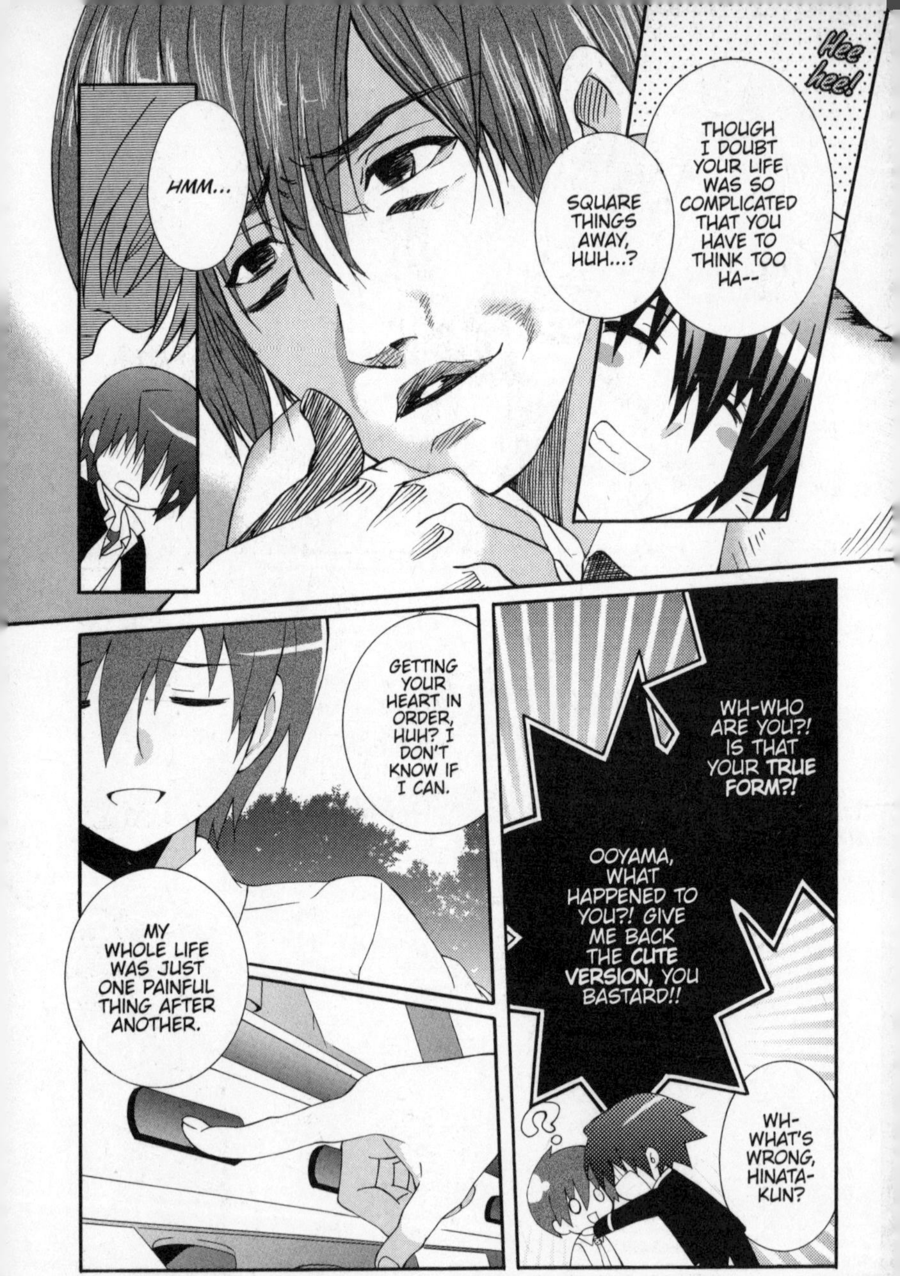
SQUARE THINGS AWAY, HUH...?
THOUGH I DOUBT YOUR LIFE WAS SO COMPLICATED THAT YOU HAVE TO THINK TOO HA--
Hee hee!
HMM...
WH-WHO ARE YOU?! IS THAT YOUR **TRUE FORM?!**
OOYAMA, WHAT HAPPENED TO YOU?! GIVE ME BACK THE **CUTE VERSION,** YOU BASTARD!!
WH- WHAT'S WRONG, HINATA-KUN?
GETTING YOUR HEART IN ORDER, HUH? I DON'T KNOW IF I CAN.
MY WHOLE LIFE WAS JUST ONE PAINFUL THING AFTER ANOTHER.

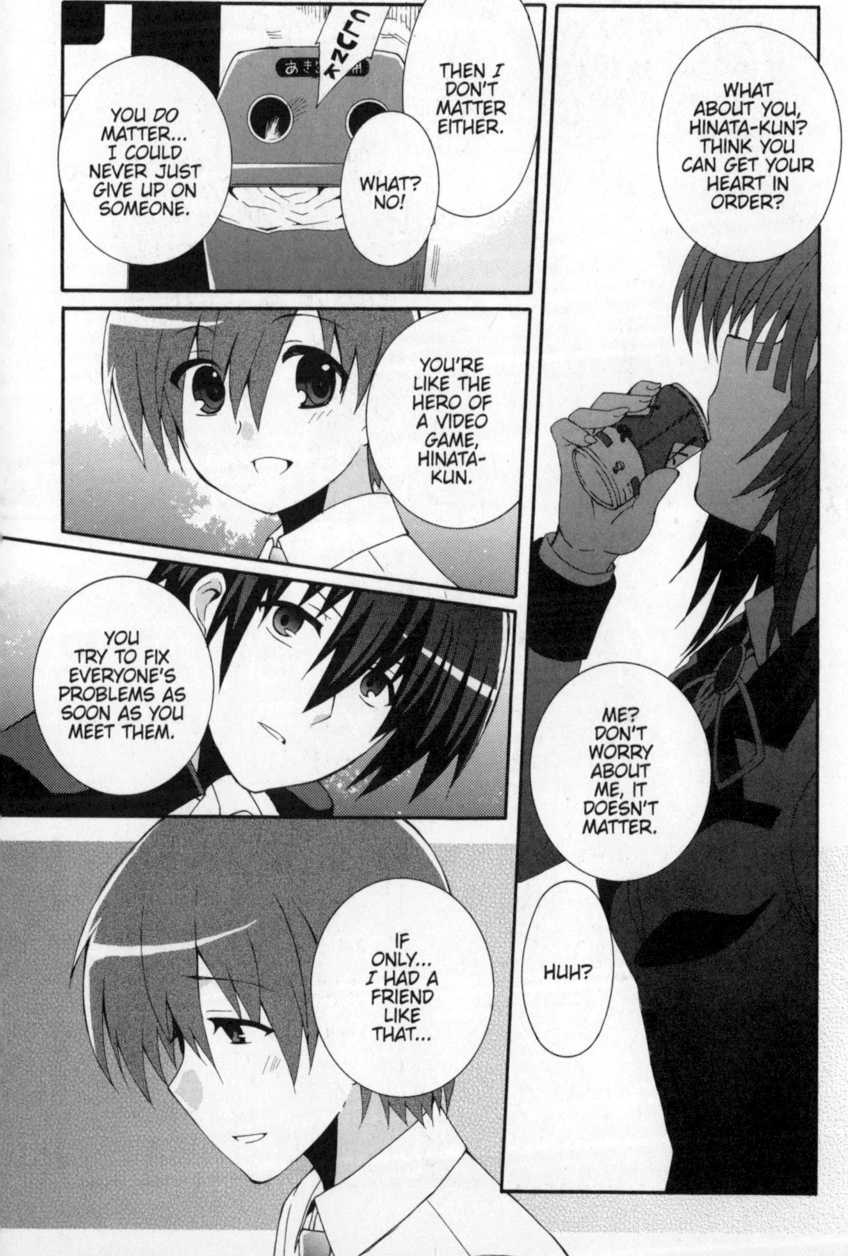
WHAT ABOUT YOU, HINATA-KUN? THINK YOU CAN GET YOUR HEART IN ORDER?
ME? DON'T WORRY ABOUT ME, IT DOESN'T MATTER.
HUH?
THEN *I* DON'T MATTER EITHER.
CLUNK
WHAT? NO!
YOU DO MATTER... I COULD NEVER JUST GIVE UP ON SOMEONE.
YOU'RE LIKE THE HERO OF A VIDEO GAME, HINATA-KUN.
YOU TRY TO FIX EVERYONE'S PROBLEMS AS SOON AS YOU MEET THEM.
IF ONLY... *I* HAD A FRIEND LIKE THAT...

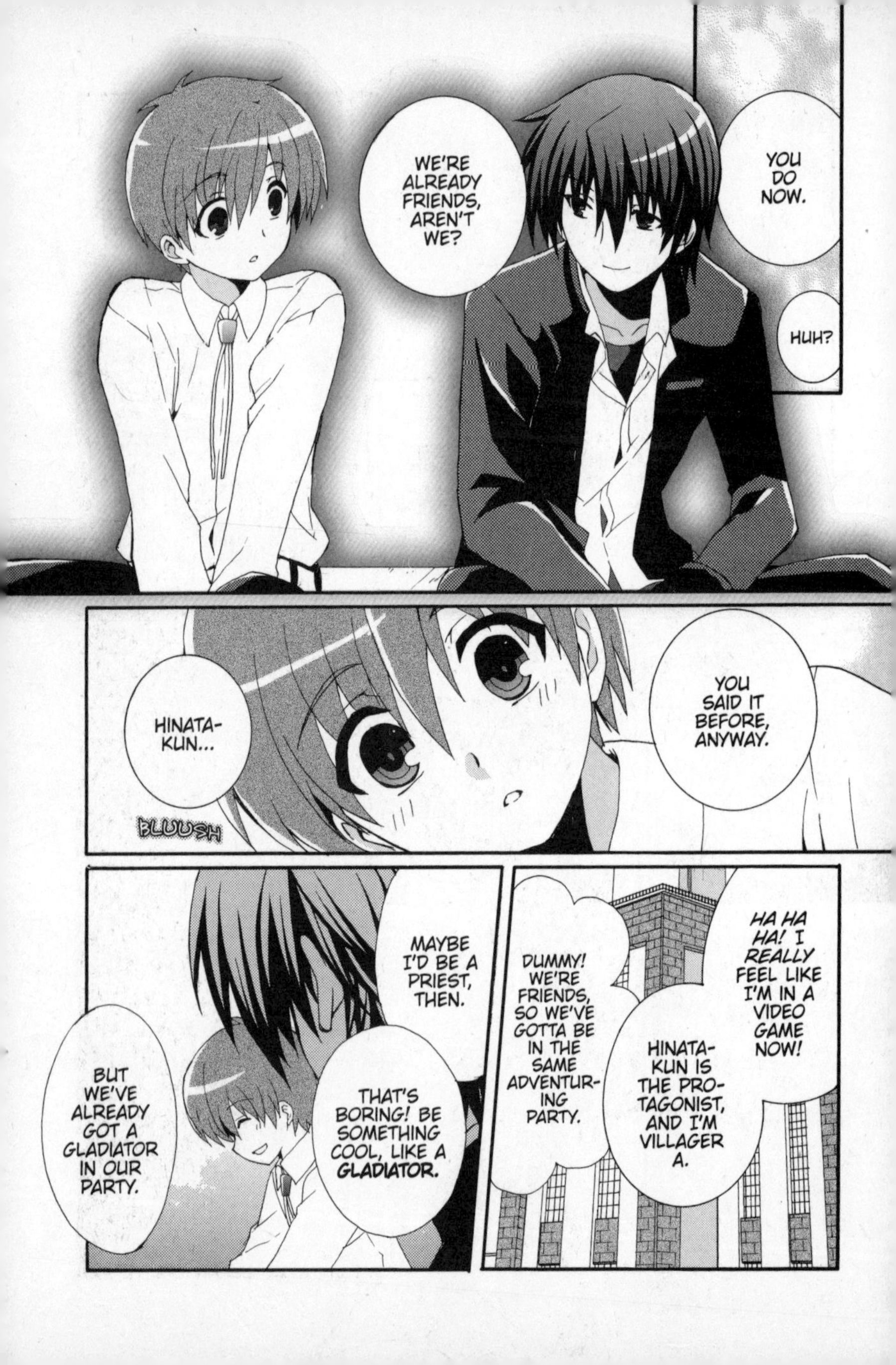

YOU DO NOW.
HUH?
WE'RE ALREADY FRIENDS, AREN'T WE?
YOU SAID IT BEFORE, ANYWAY.
HINATA-KUN...
BLUUSH
HA HA HA! I *REALLY* FEEL LIKE I'M IN A VIDEO GAME NOW!
HINATA-KUN IS THE PROTAGONIST, AND I'M VILLAGER A.
DUMMY! WE'RE FRIENDS, SO WE'VE GOTTA BE IN THE SAME ADVENTURING PARTY.
MAYBE I'D BE A PRIEST, THEN.
THAT'S BORING! BE SOMETHING COOL, LIKE A **GLADIATOR**.
BUT WE'VE ALREADY GOT A GLADIATOR IN OUR PARTY.

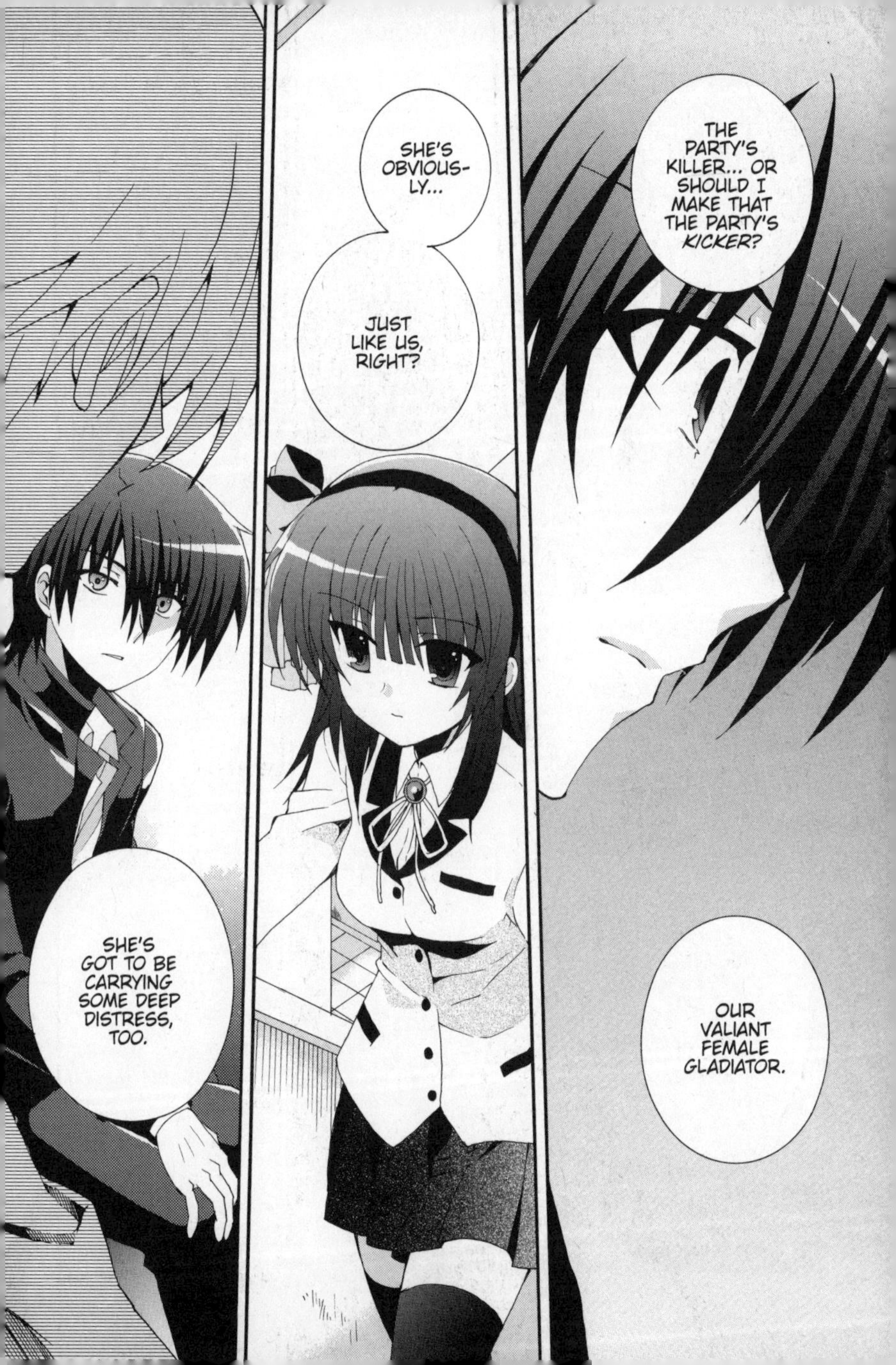
THE PARTY'S KILLER... OR SHOULD I MAKE THAT THE PARTY'S *KICKER?*
OUR VALIANT FEMALE GLADIATOR.
SHE'S OBVIOUS-LY...
JUST LIKE US, RIGHT?
SHE'S GOT TO BE CARRYING SOME DEEP DISTRESS, TOO.

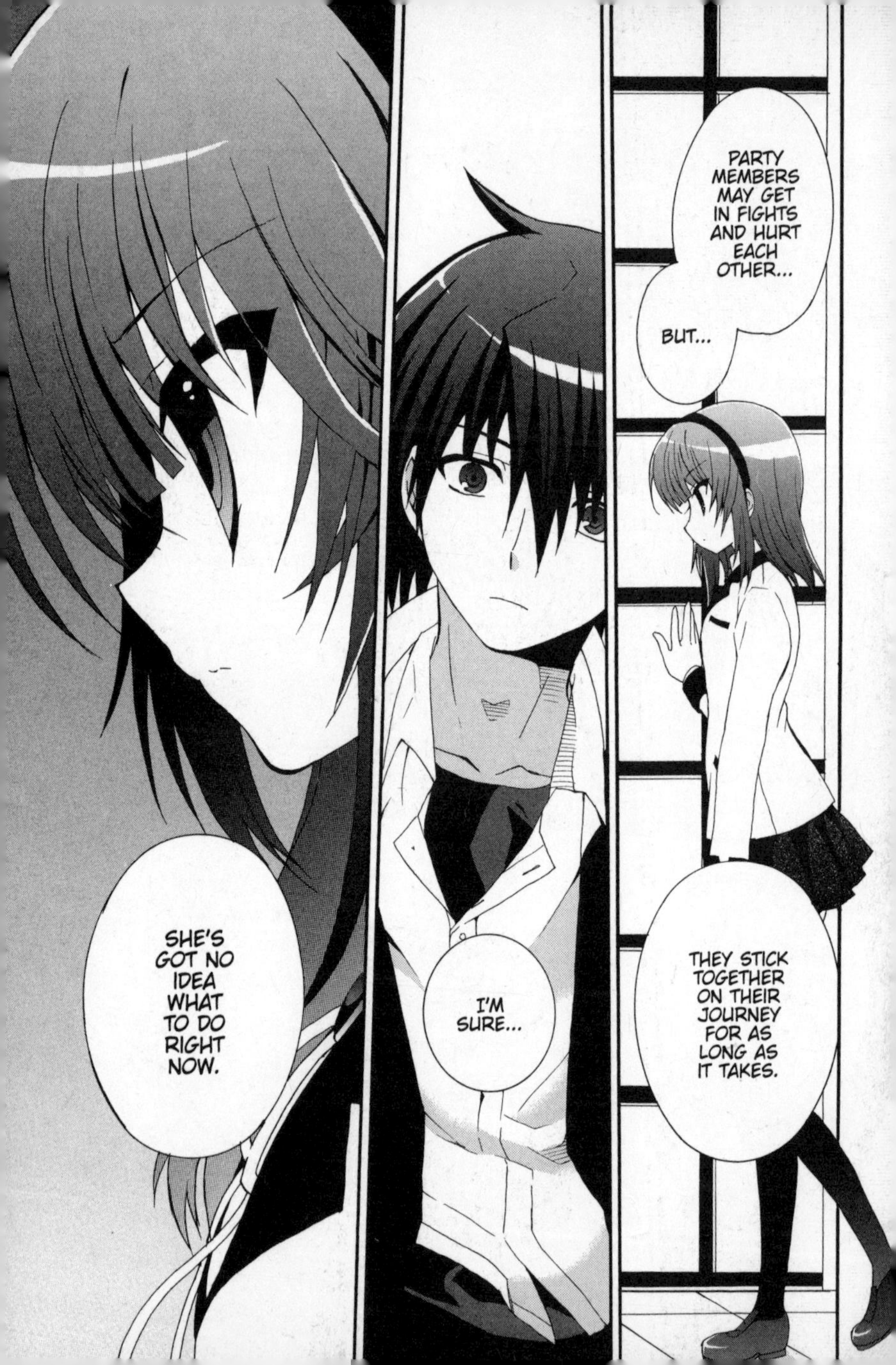
PARTY MEMBERS MAY GET IN FIGHTS AND HURT EACH OTHER... BUT...
THEY STICK TOGETHER ON THEIR JOURNEY FOR AS LONG AS IT TAKES.
I'M SURE...
SHE'S GOT NO IDEA WHAT TO DO RIGHT NOW.

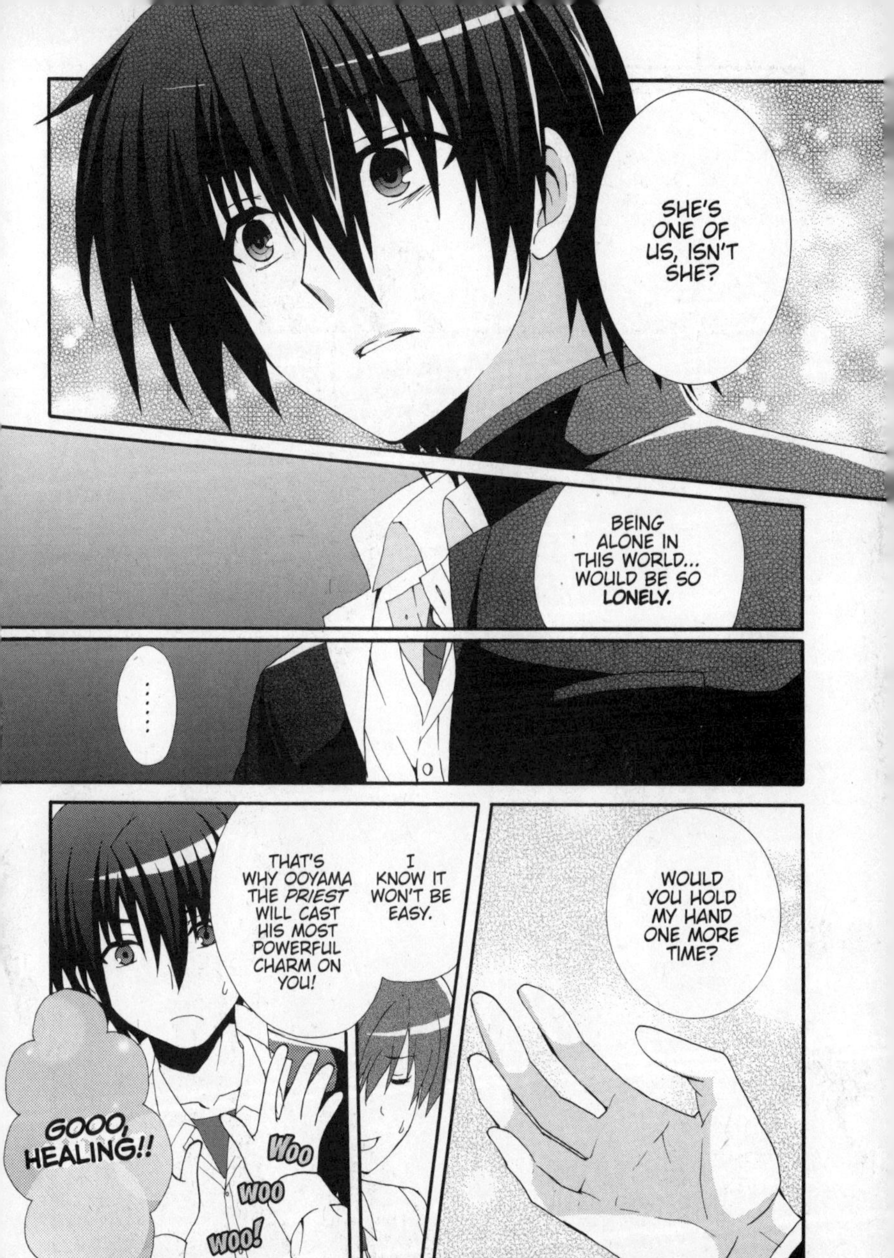
SHE'S ONE OF US, ISN'T SHE?
BEING ALONE IN THIS WORLD... WOULD BE SO **LONELY.**
......
WOULD YOU HOLD MY HAND ONE MORE TIME?
I KNOW IT WON'T BE EASY.
THAT'S WHY OOYAMA THE *PRIEST* WILL CAST HIS MOST POWERFUL CHARM ON YOU!
GOOO, HEALING!!
Woo woo woo!

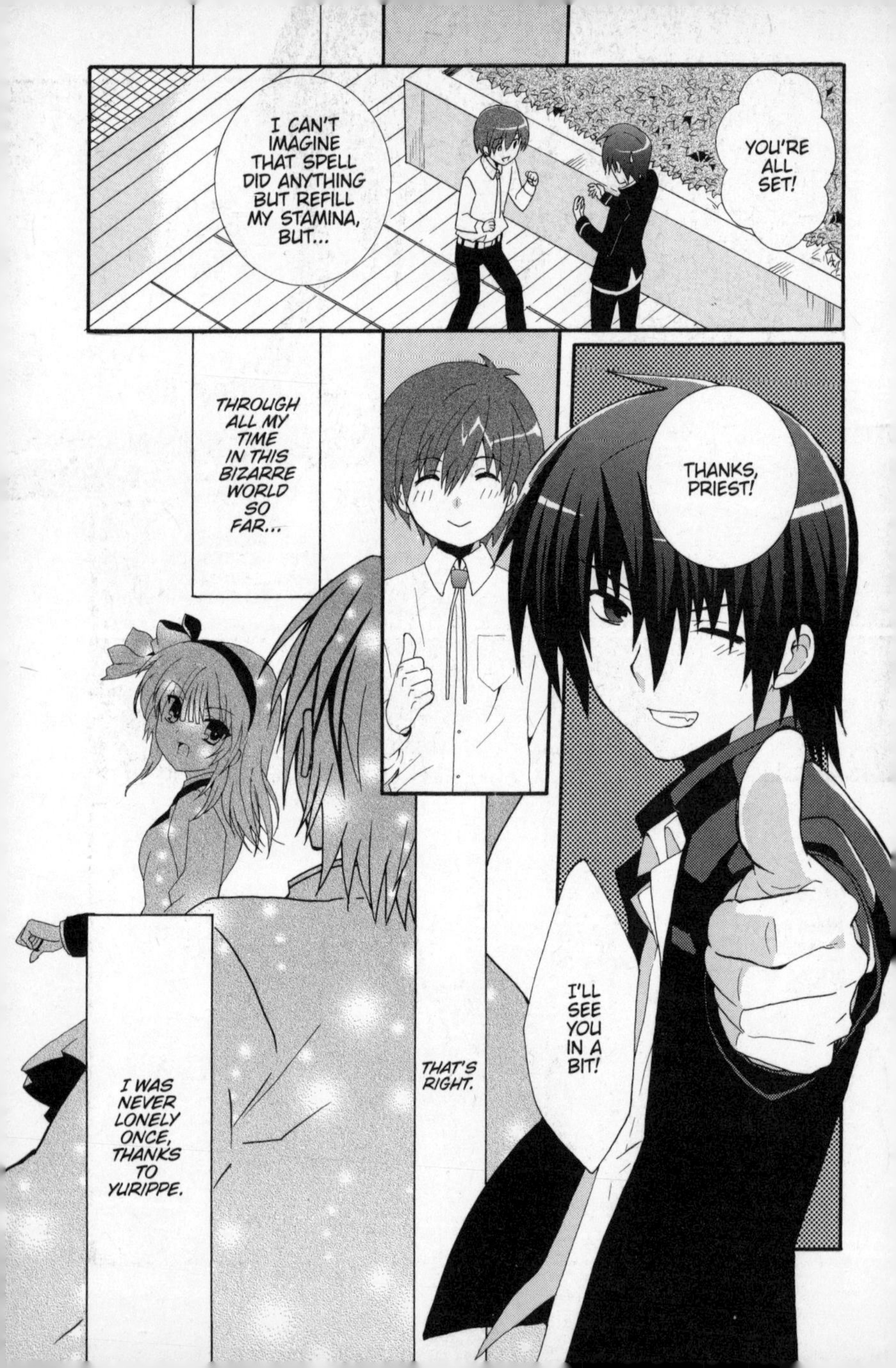
YOU'RE ALL SET!
I CAN'T IMAGINE THAT SPELL DID ANYTHING BUT REFILL MY STAMINA, BUT...
THANKS, PRIEST!
I'LL SEE YOU IN A BIT!
THROUGH ALL MY TIME IN THIS BIZARRE WORLD SO FAR...
THAT'S RIGHT.
I WAS NEVER LONELY ONCE, THANKS TO YURIPPE.

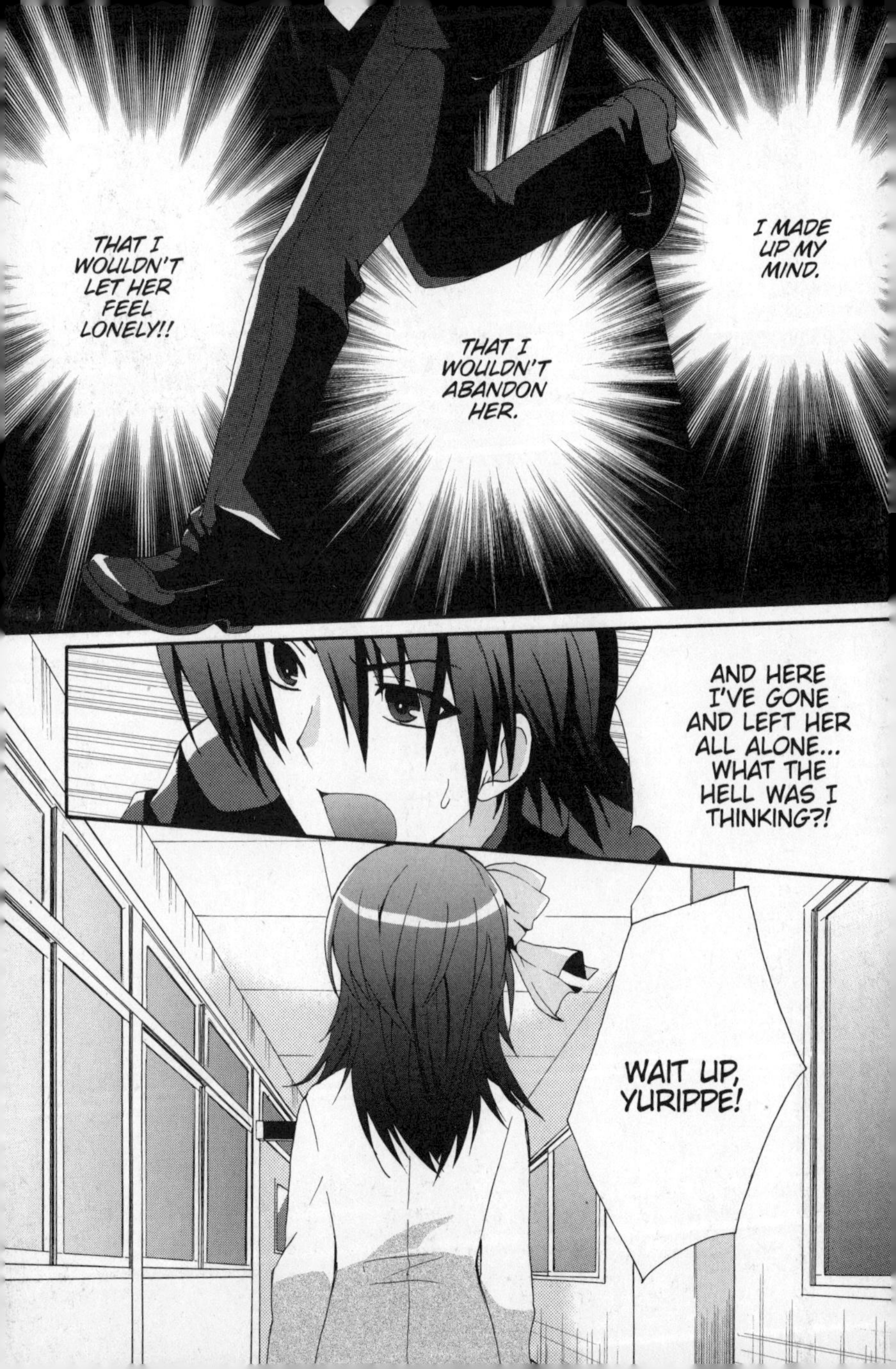
I MADE UP MY MIND.
THAT I WOULDN'T ABANDON HER.
THAT I WOULDN'T LET HER FEEL LONELY!!
AND HERE I'VE GONE AND LEFT HER ALL ALONE... WHAT THE HELL WAS I THINKING?!
WAIT UP, YURIPPE!

Angel Beats!
Heaven's Door

Whatever! I don't need anyone!

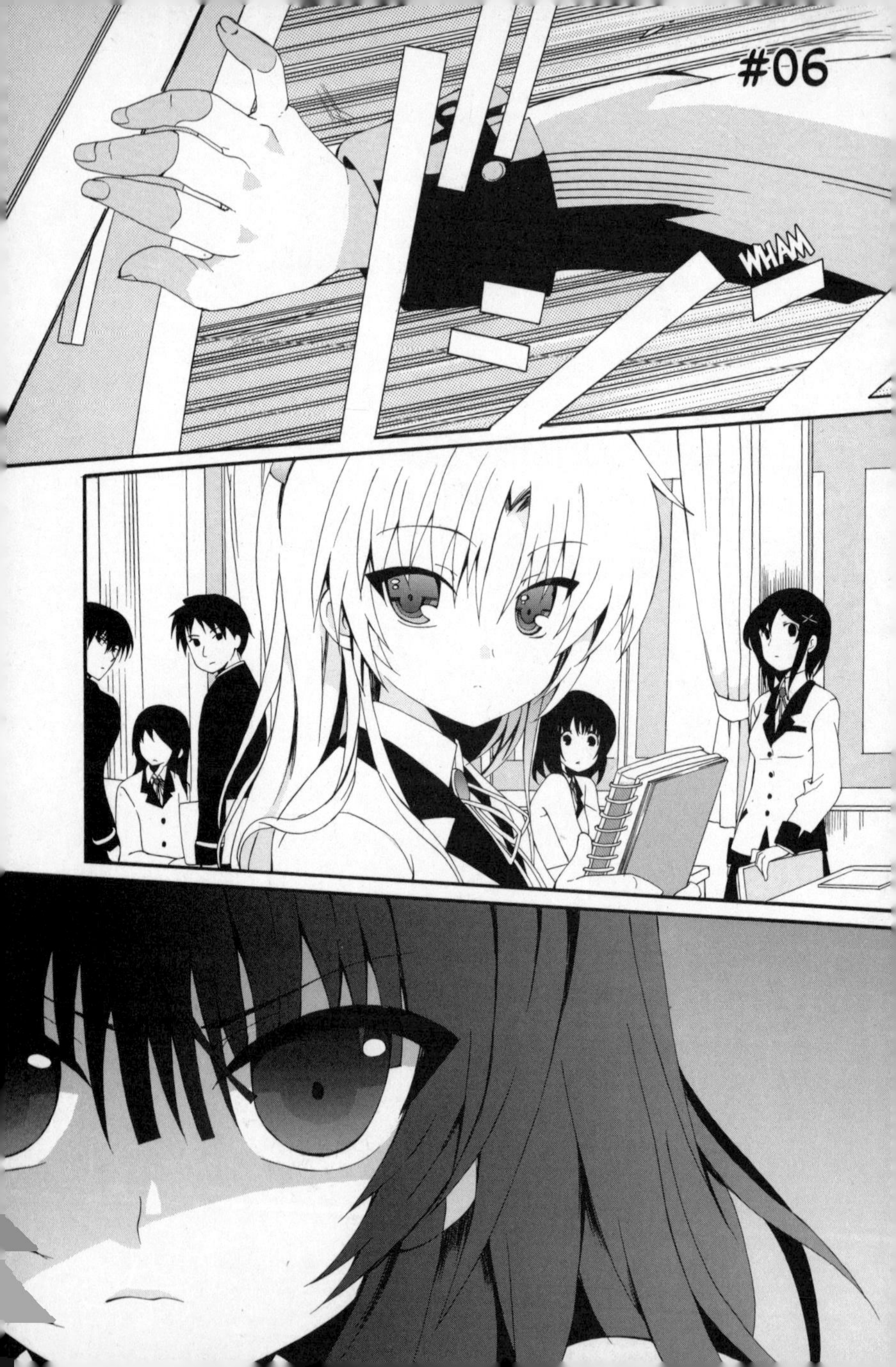
#06
WHAM

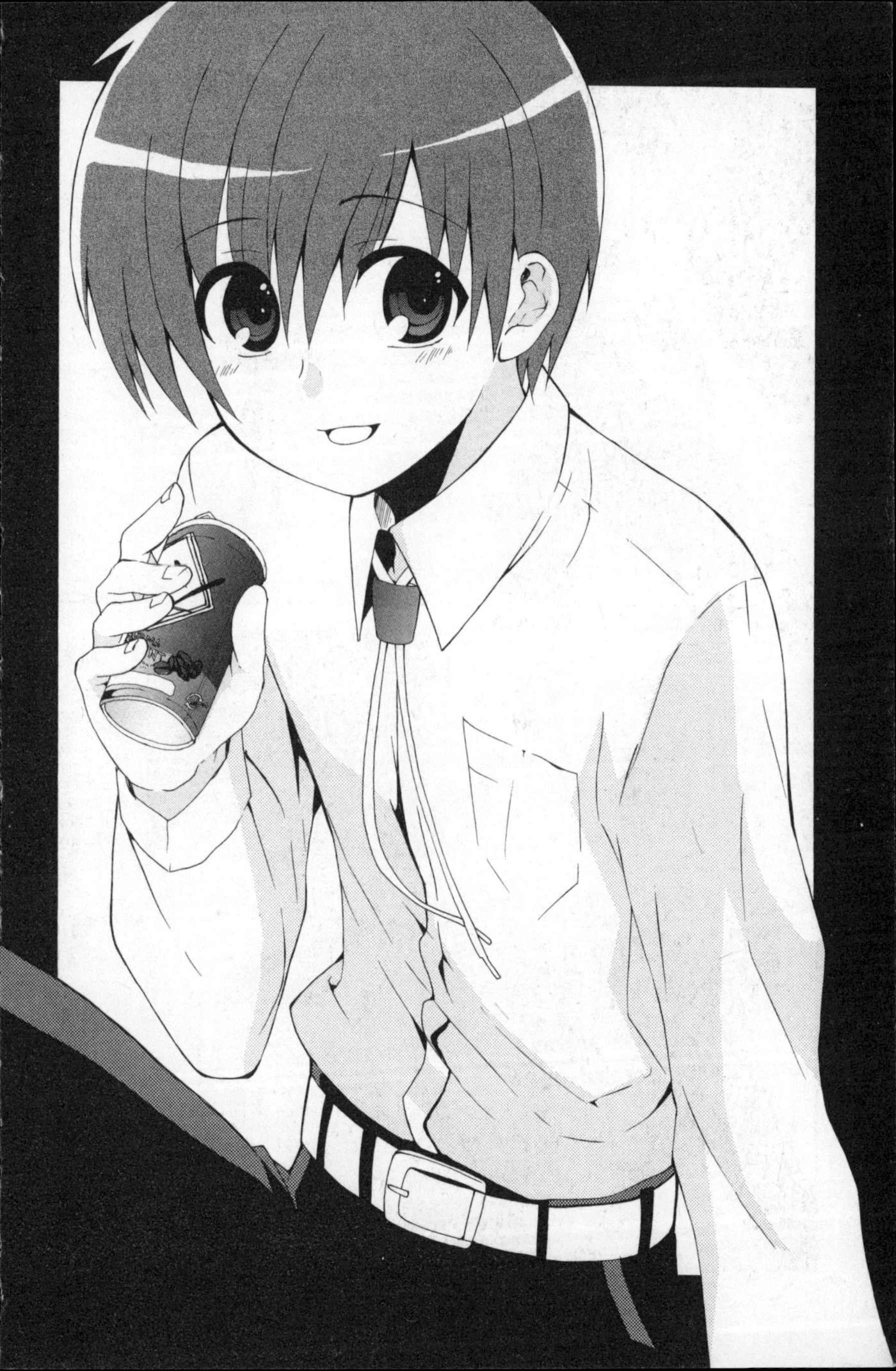

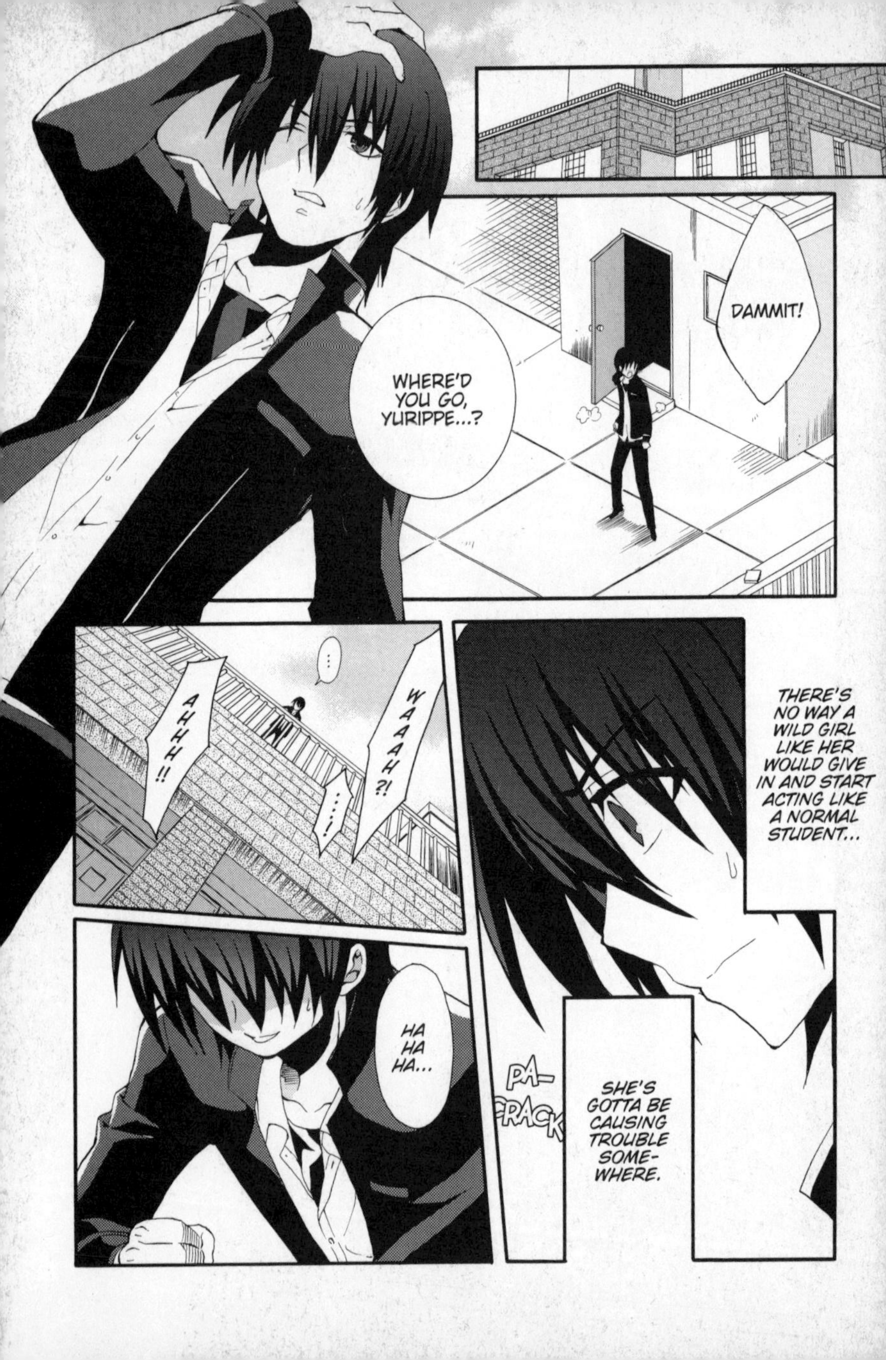
DAMMIT!
WHERE'D YOU GO, YURIPPE...?
THERE'S NO WAY A WILD GIRL LIKE HER WOULD GIVE IN AND START ACTING LIKE A NORMAL STUDENT...
SHE'S GOTTA BE CAUSING TROUBLE SOME-WHERE.
PA-CRACK
WAAAAH?!
...
...!
AHHH!!
HA HA HA...

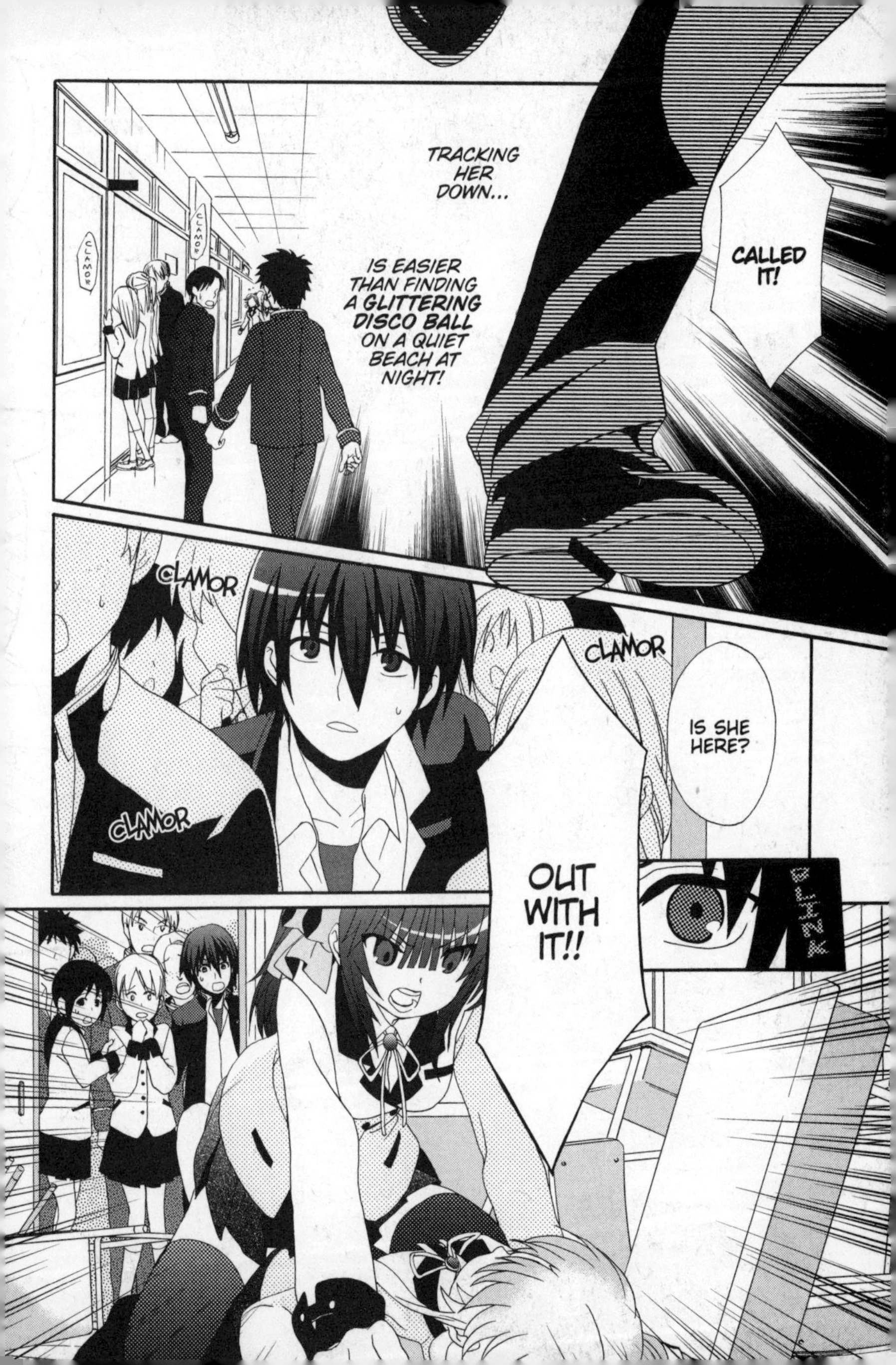
CALLED IT!
TRACKING HER DOWN...
IS EASIER THAN FINDING A GLITTERING DISCO BALL ON A QUIET BEACH AT NIGHT!
CLAMOR
CLAMOR
CLAMOR
IS SHE HERE?
CLAMOR
CLAMOR
BLINK
OUT WITH IT!!

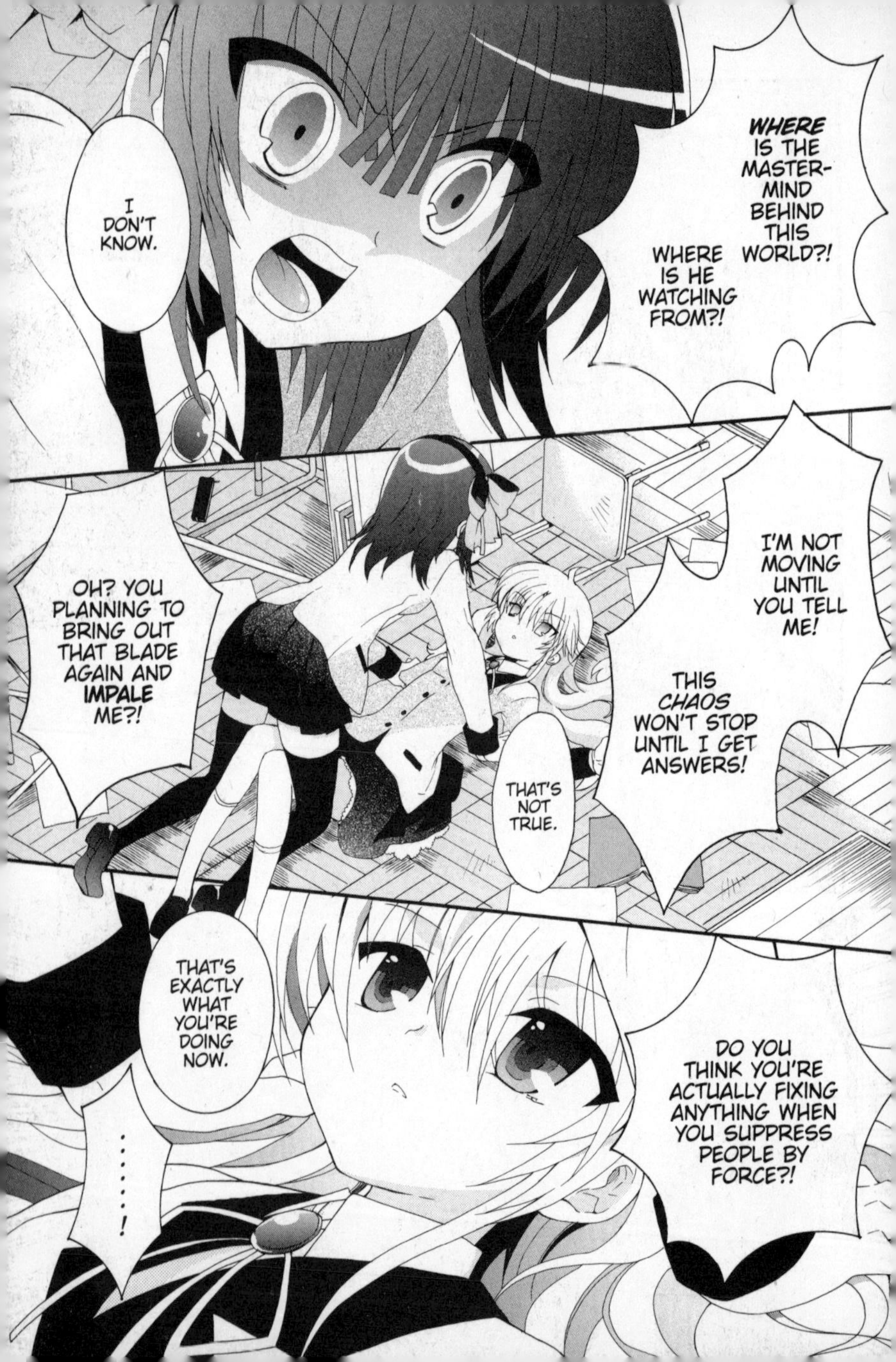

WHERE IS THE MASTER-MIND BEHIND THIS WORLD?!
WHERE IS HE WATCHING FROM?!
I DON'T KNOW.
I'M NOT MOVING UNTIL YOU TELL ME!
THIS *CHAOS* WON'T STOP UNTIL I GET ANSWERS!
THAT'S NOT TRUE.
OH? YOU PLANNING TO BRING OUT THAT BLADE AGAIN AND **IMPALE** ME?!
DO YOU THINK YOU'RE ACTUALLY FIXING ANYTHING WHEN YOU SUPPRESS PEOPLE BY FORCE?!
THAT'S EXACTLY WHAT YOU'RE DOING NOW.
......!

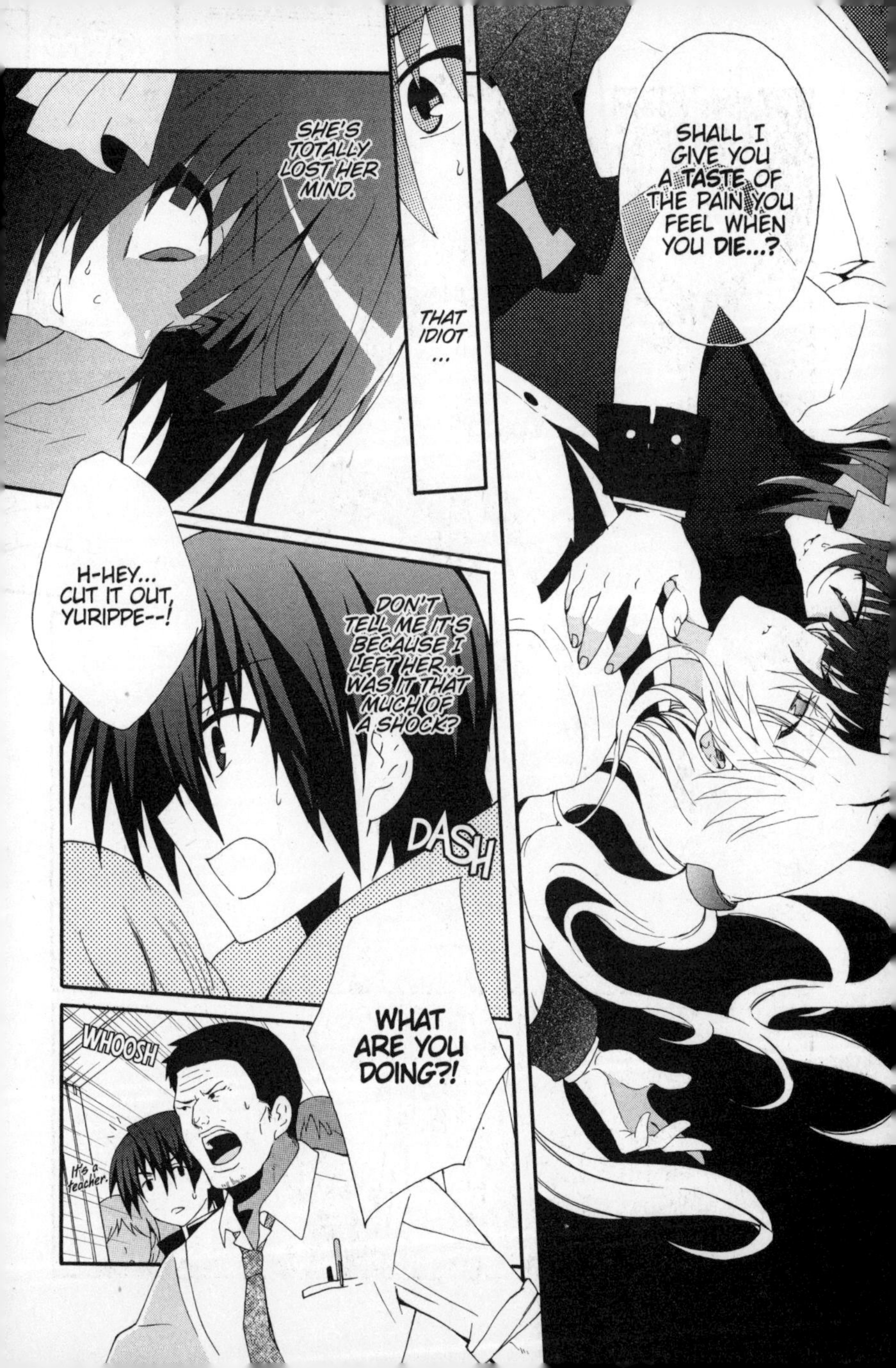

SHALL I GIVE YOU A TASTE OF THE PAIN YOU FEEL WHEN YOU DIE...?
THAT IDIOT ...
SHE'S TOTALLY LOST HER MIND.
H-HEY... CUT IT OUT, YURIPPE--!
DON'T TELL ME IT'S BECAUSE I LEFT HER... WAS IT THAT MUCH OF A SHOCK?
DASH
WHAT ARE YOU DOING?!
WHOOSH
It's a teacher.

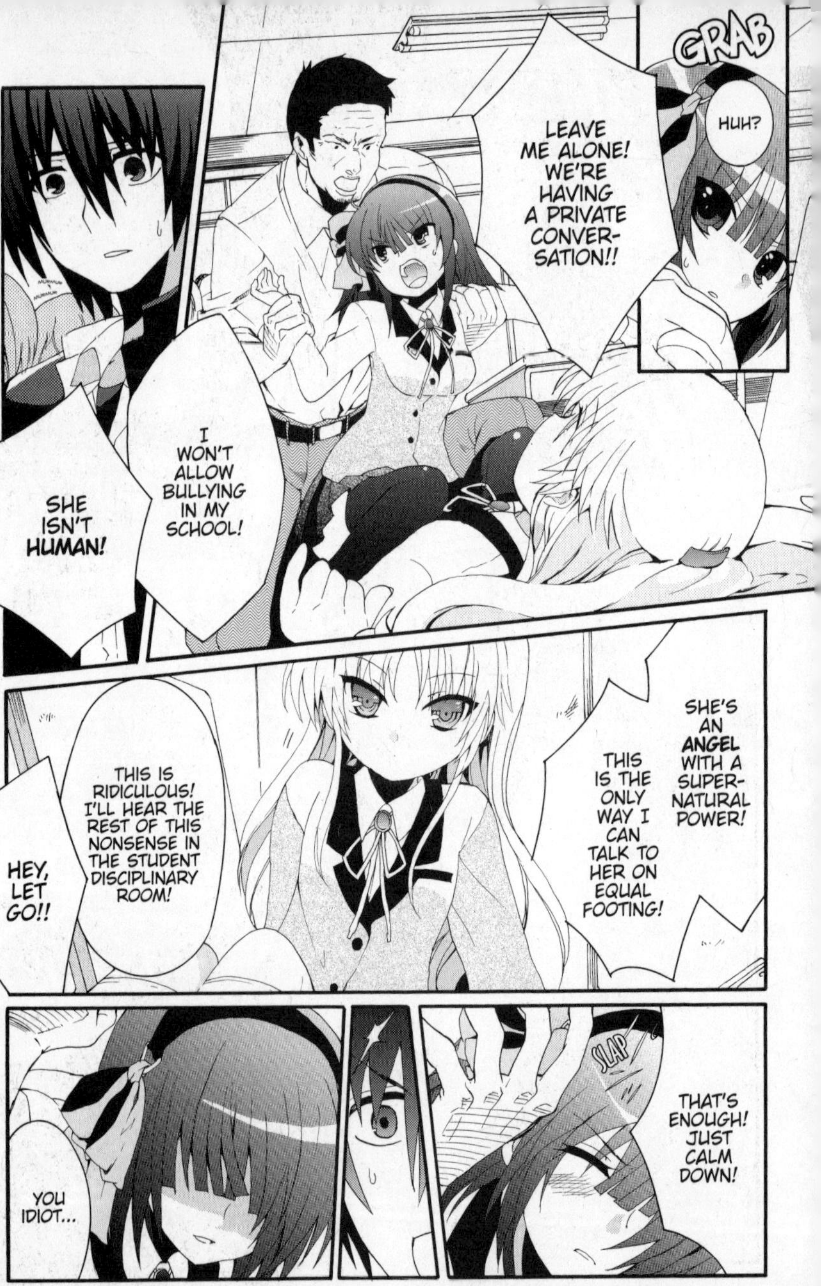
GRAB
HUH?
LEAVE ME ALONE! WE'RE HAVING A PRIVATE CONVER-SATION!!
I WON'T ALLOW BULLYING IN MY SCHOOL!
SHE ISN'T HUMAN!
SHE'S AN ANGEL WITH A SUPER-NATURAL POWER!
THIS IS THE ONLY WAY I CAN TALK TO HER ON EQUAL FOOTING!
THIS IS RIDICULOUS! I'LL HEAR THE REST OF THIS NONSENSE IN THE STUDENT DISCIPLINARY ROOM!
HEY, LET GO!!
SLAP
THAT'S ENOUGH! JUST CALM DOWN!
YOU IDIOT...

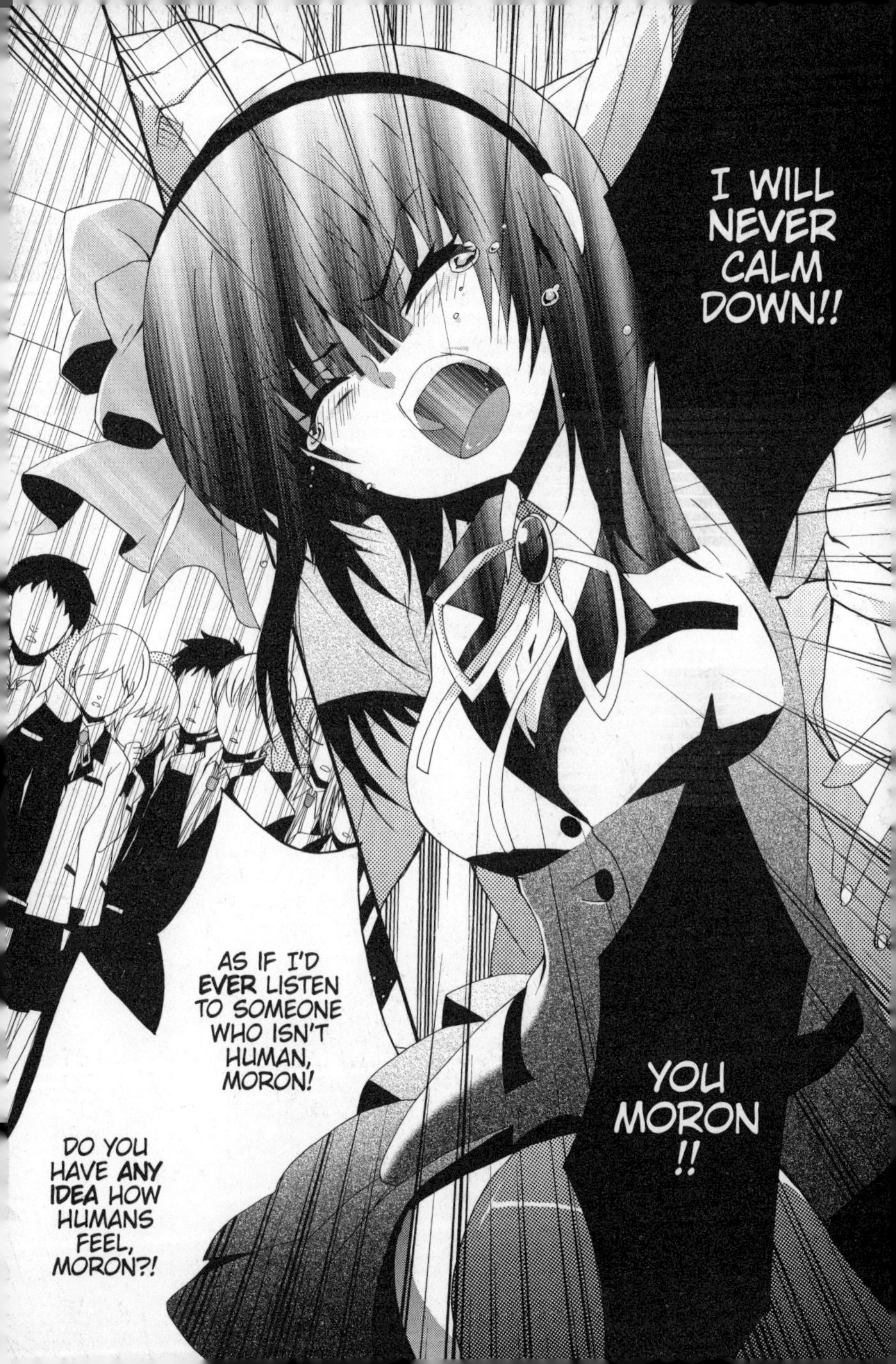
I WILL NEVER CALM DOWN!!
YOU MORON !!
AS IF I'D EVER LISTEN TO SOMEONE WHO ISN'T HUMAN, MORON!
DO YOU HAVE ANY IDEA HOW HUMANS FEEL, MORON?!

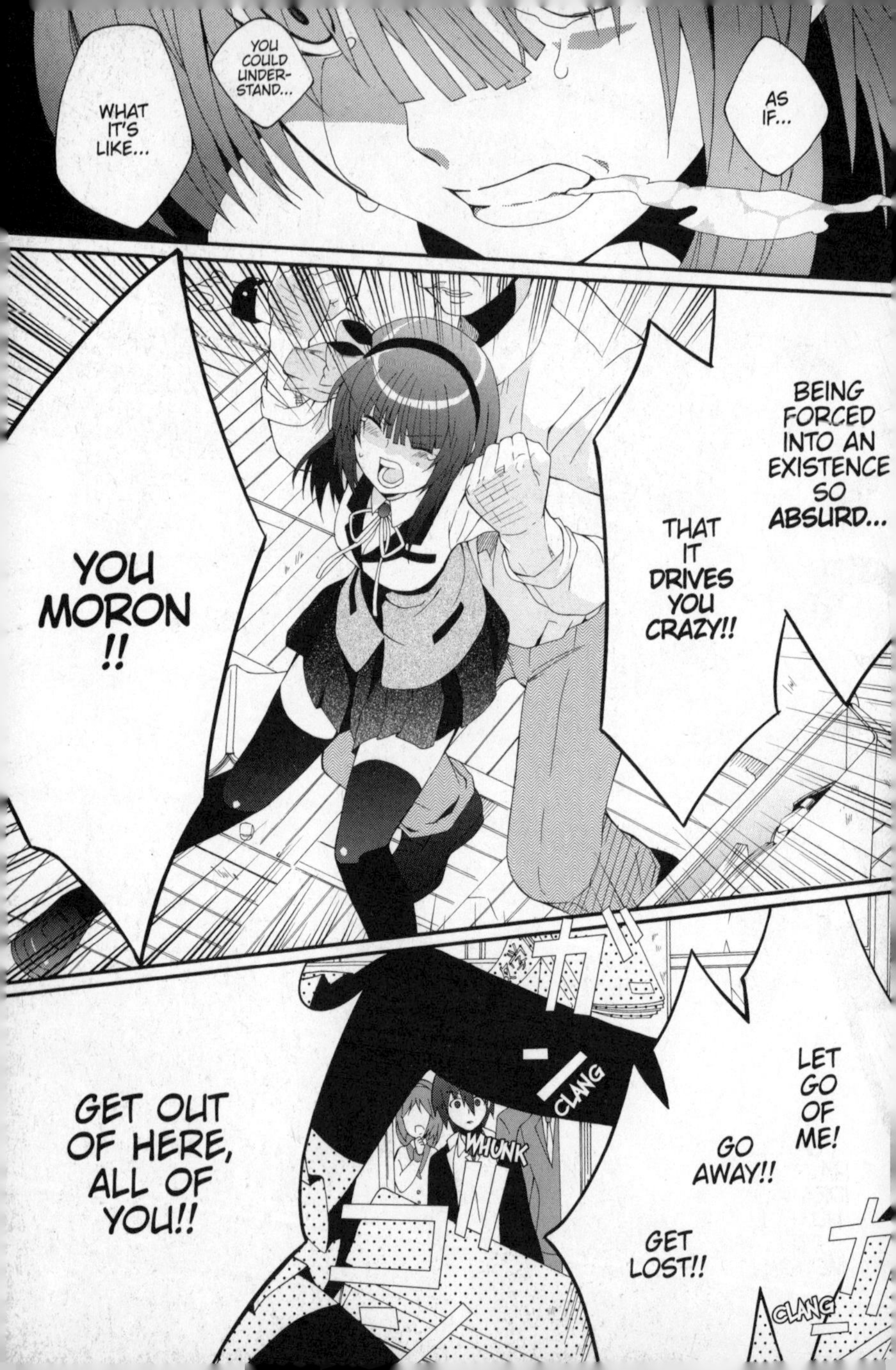
AS IF...
YOU COULD UNDER-STAND...
WHAT IT'S LIKE...
BEING FORCED INTO AN EXISTENCE SO ABSURD...
THAT IT DRIVES YOU CRAZY!!
YOU MORON !!
LET GO OF ME!
CLANG
GO AWAY!!
WHUNK
GET LOST!!
CLANG
GET OUT OF HERE, ALL OF YOU!!

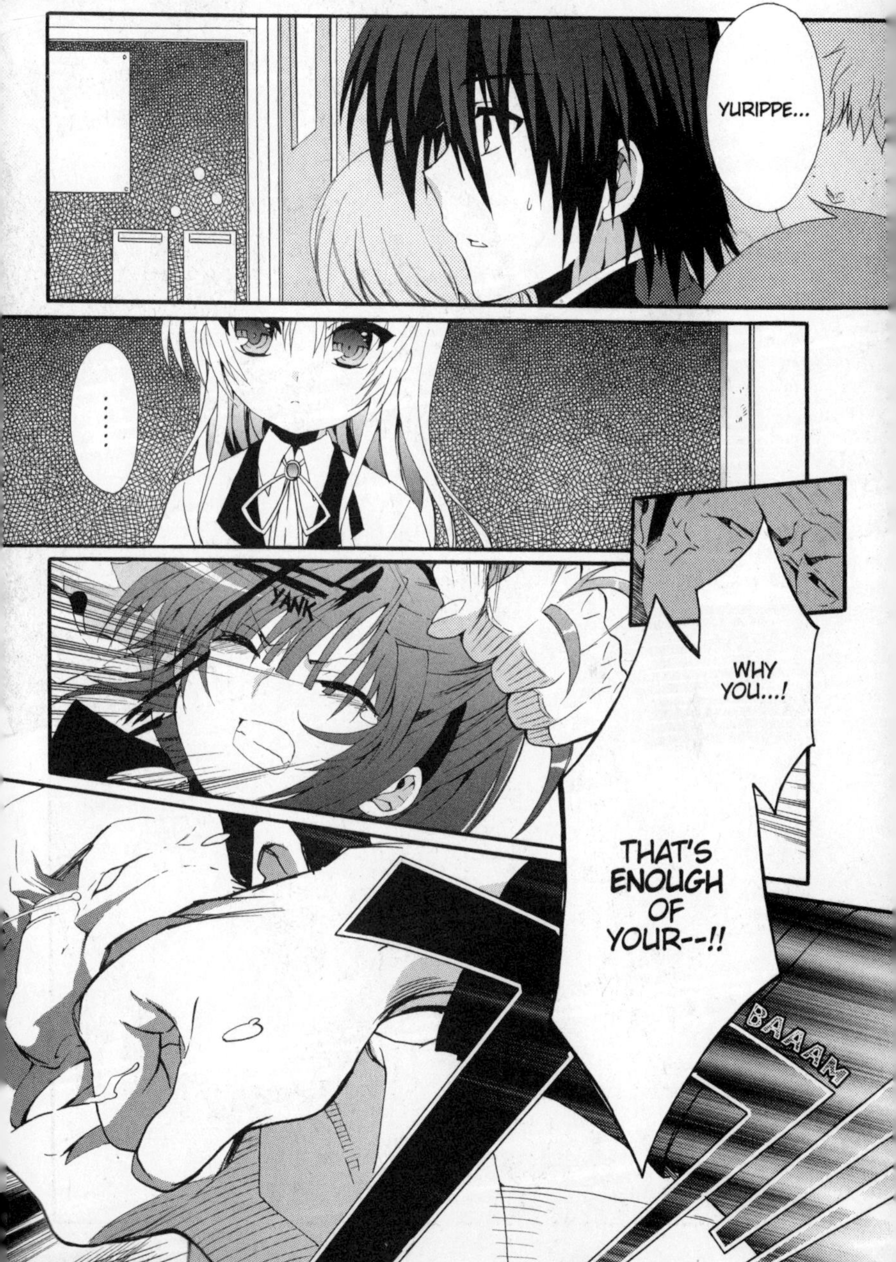
YURIPPE...
......
WHY YOU...!
YANK
THAT'S ENOUGH OF YOUR--!!
BAAAAM

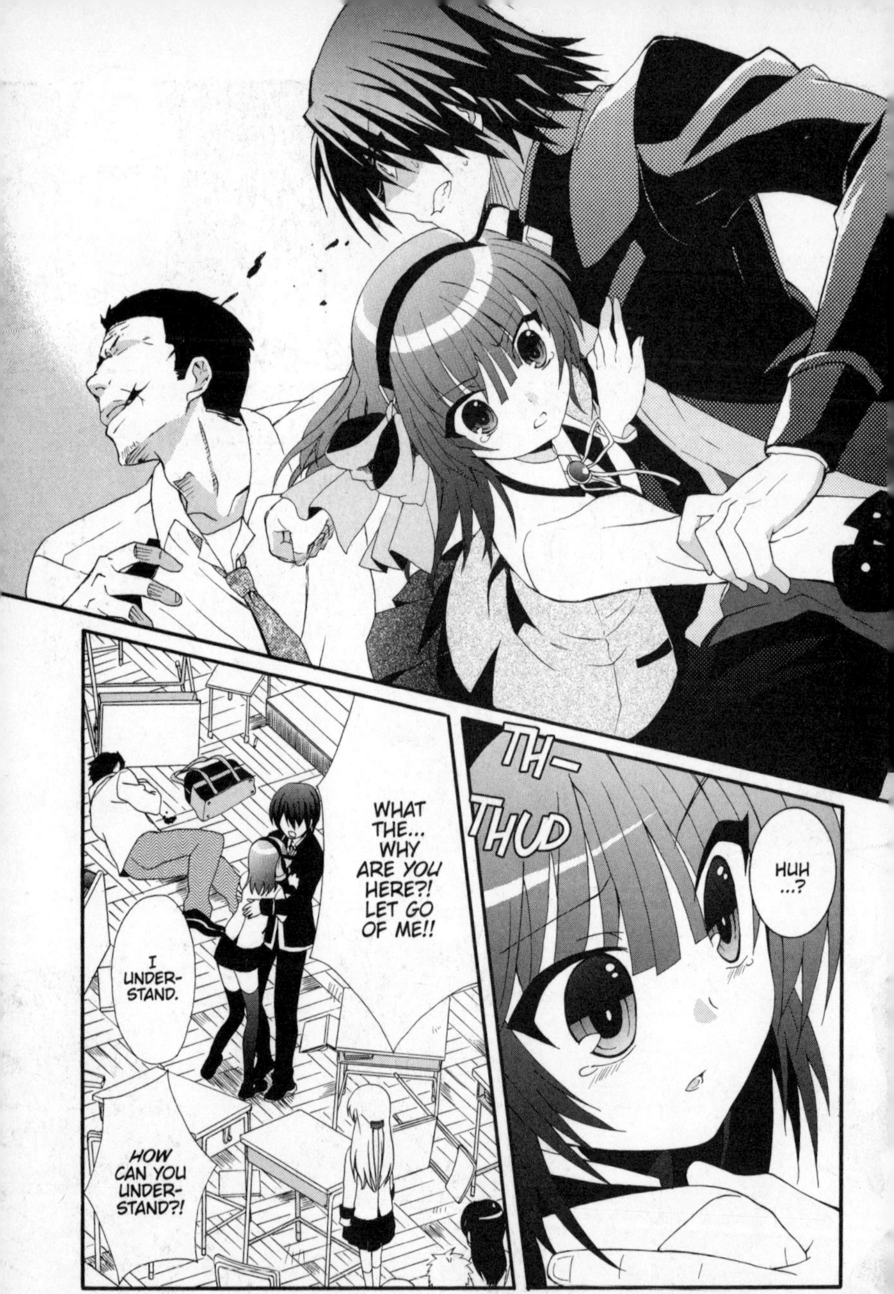
TH-THUD
HUH ...?
WHAT THE... WHY ARE YOU HERE?! LET GO OF ME!!
I UNDER-STAND.
HOW CAN YOU UNDER-STAND?!

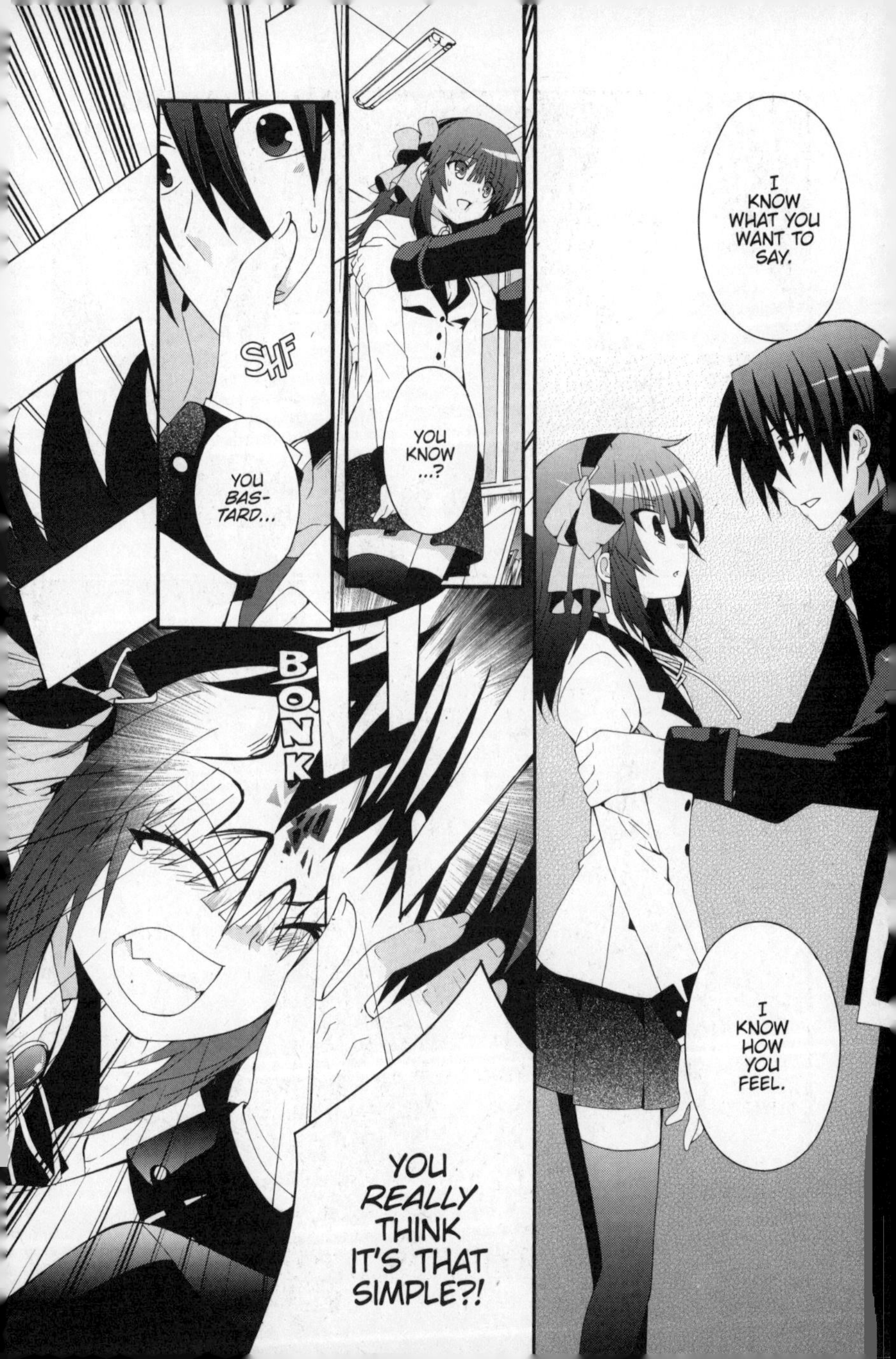
I KNOW WHAT YOU WANT TO SAY.
I KNOW HOW YOU FEEL.
YOU KNOW ...?
SHF
YOU BASTARD...
BONK
YOU REALLY THINK IT'S THAT SIMPLE?!

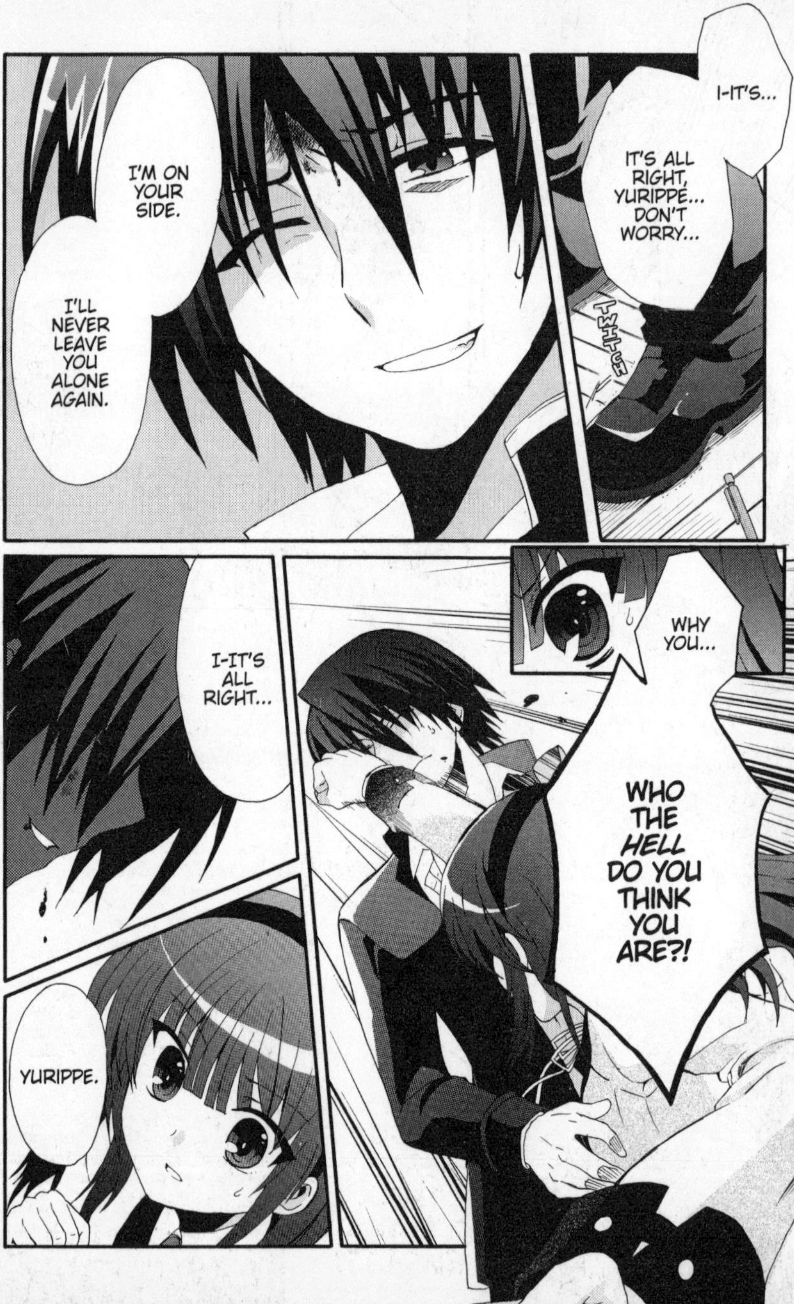
I-IT'S...
IT'S ALL RIGHT, YURIPPE... DON'T WORRY...
TWITCH
I'M ON YOUR SIDE.
I'LL NEVER LEAVE YOU ALONE AGAIN.
WHY YOU...
WHO THE *HELL* DO YOU THINK YOU ARE?!
I-IT'S ALL RIGHT...
YURIPPE.

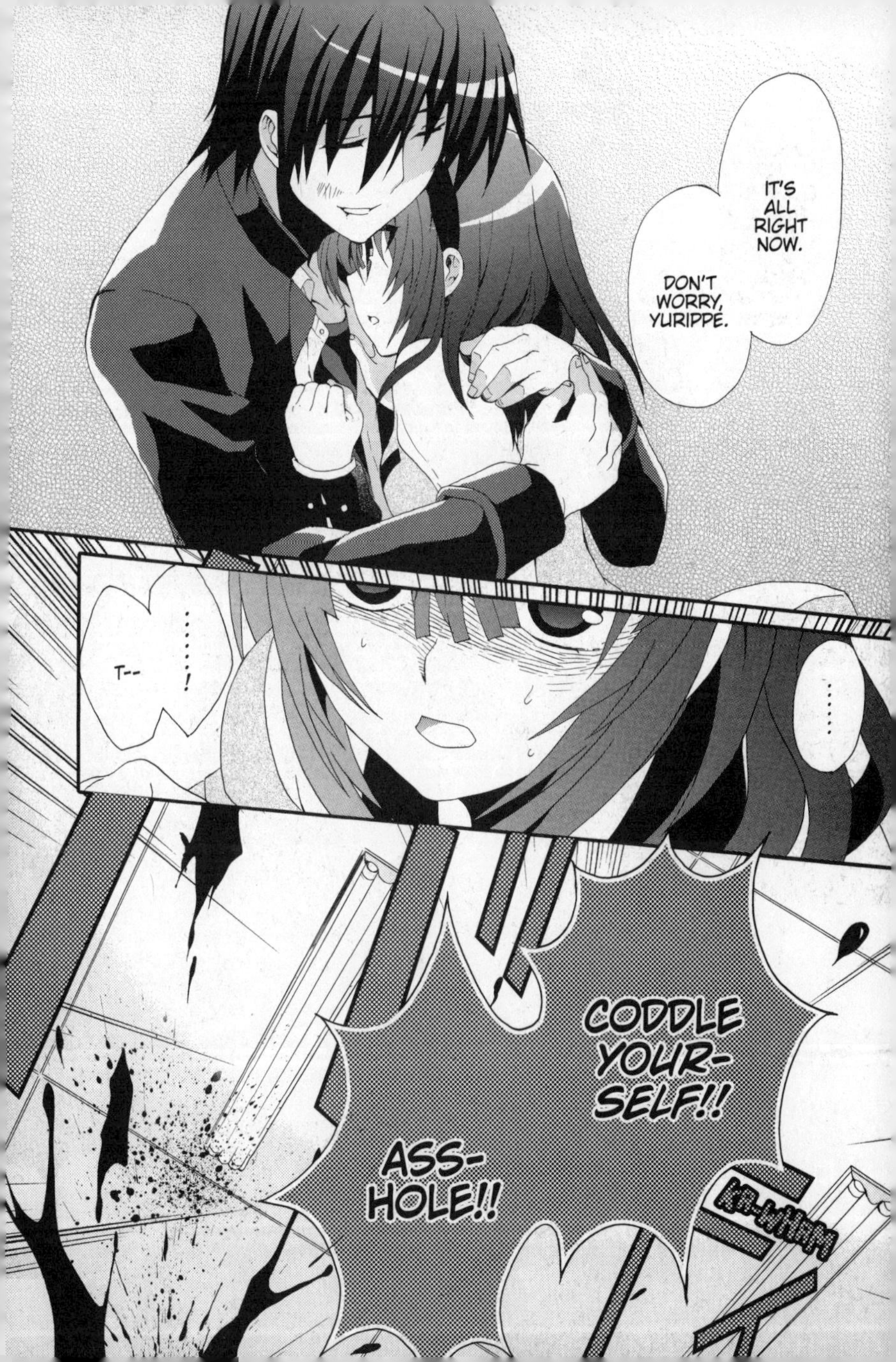
IT'S ALL RIGHT NOW.
DON'T WORRY, YURIPPE.
……
T--……!
CODDLE YOUR-SELF!!
ASS-HOLE!!

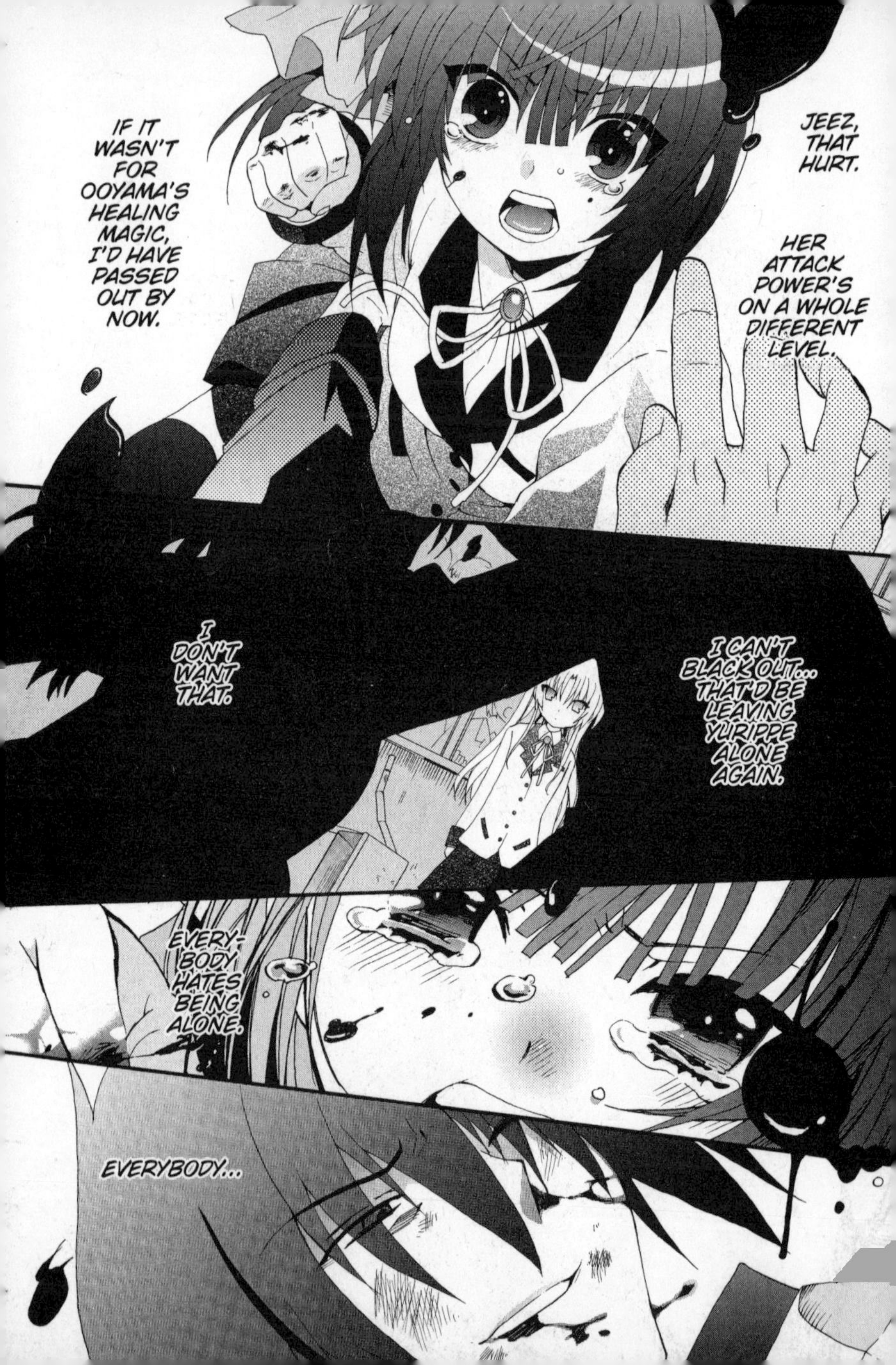
JEEZ, THAT HURT.
HER ATTACK POWER'S ON A WHOLE DIFFERENT LEVEL.
IF IT WASN'T FOR OOYAMA'S HEALING MAGIC, I'D HAVE PASSED OUT BY NOW.
I CAN'T BLACK OUT... THAT'D BE LEAVING YURIPPE ALONE AGAIN.
I DON'T WANT THAT.
EVERY-BODY HATES BEING ALONE.
EVERYBODY...

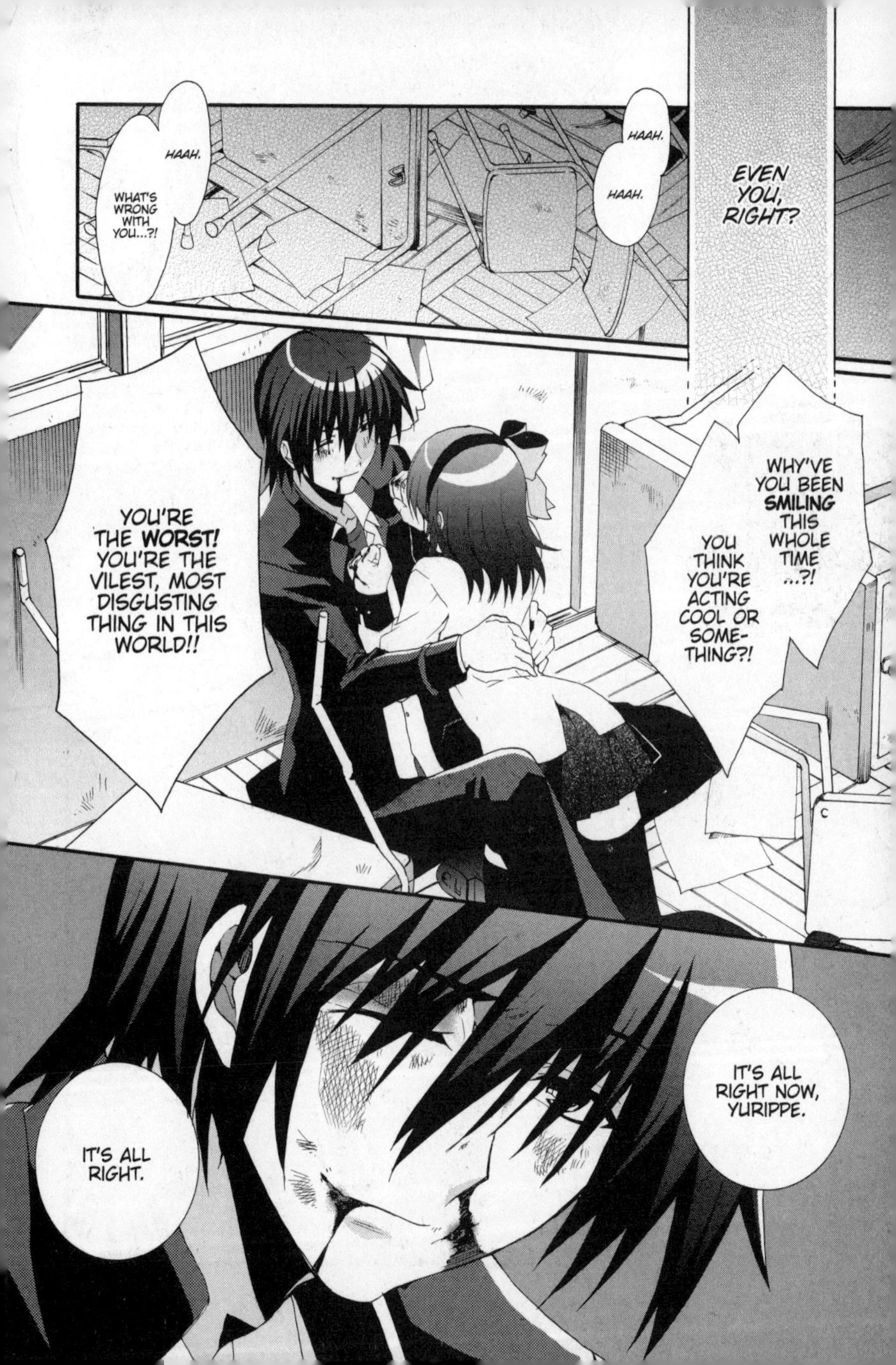
EVEN YOU, RIGHT?
HAAH.
HAAH.
HAAH.
WHAT'S WRONG WITH YOU...?!
WHY'VE YOU BEEN SMILING THIS WHOLE TIME ...?!
YOU THINK YOU'RE ACTING COOL OR SOME-THING?!
YOU'RE THE WORST! YOU'RE THE VILEST, MOST DISGUSTING THING IN THIS WORLD!!
IT'S ALL RIGHT NOW, YURIPPE.
IT'S ALL RIGHT.

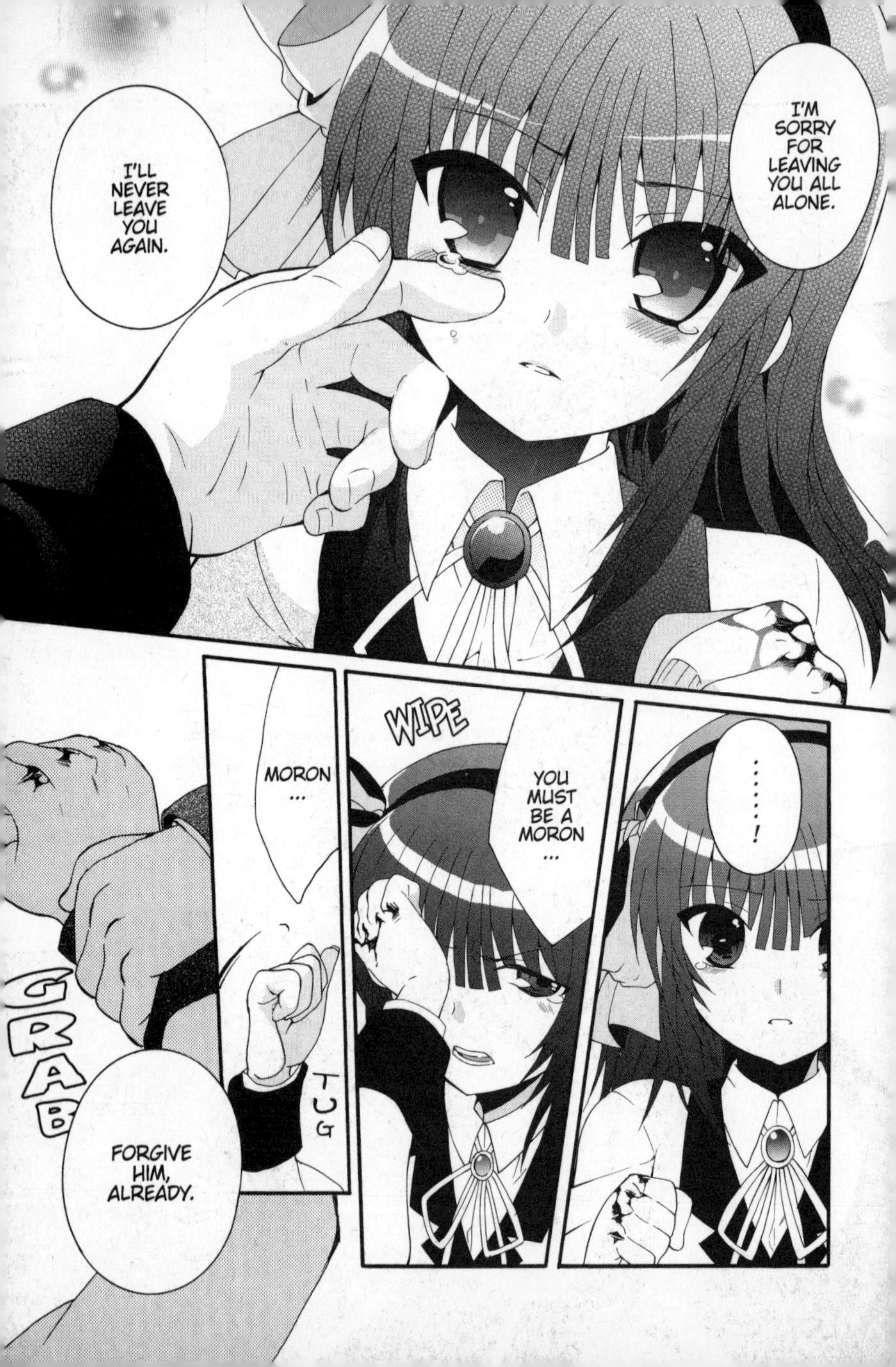
I'M SORRY FOR LEAVING YOU ALL ALONE.
I'LL NEVER LEAVE YOU AGAIN.
......!
YOU MUST BE A MORON ...
WIPE
MORON ...
TUG
GRAB
FORGIVE HIM, ALREADY.

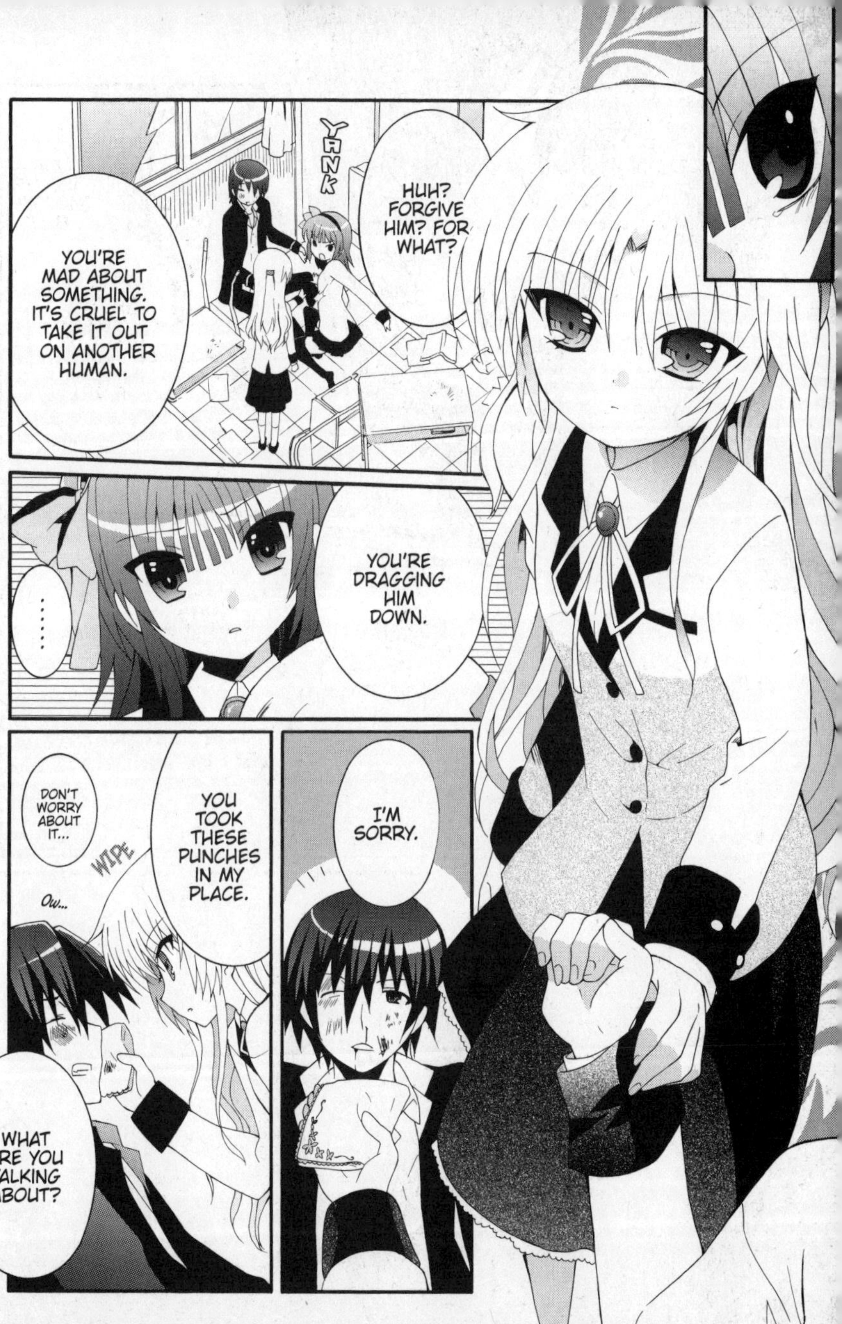

HUH? FORGIVE HIM? FOR WHAT?
YANK
YOU'RE MAD ABOUT SOMETHING. IT'S CRUEL TO TAKE IT OUT ON ANOTHER HUMAN.
YOU'RE DRAGGING HIM DOWN.
......
I'M SORRY.
YOU TOOK THESE PUNCHES IN MY PLACE.
DON'T WORRY ABOUT IT...
WIPE
Ow...
WHAT ARE YOU TALKING ABOUT?

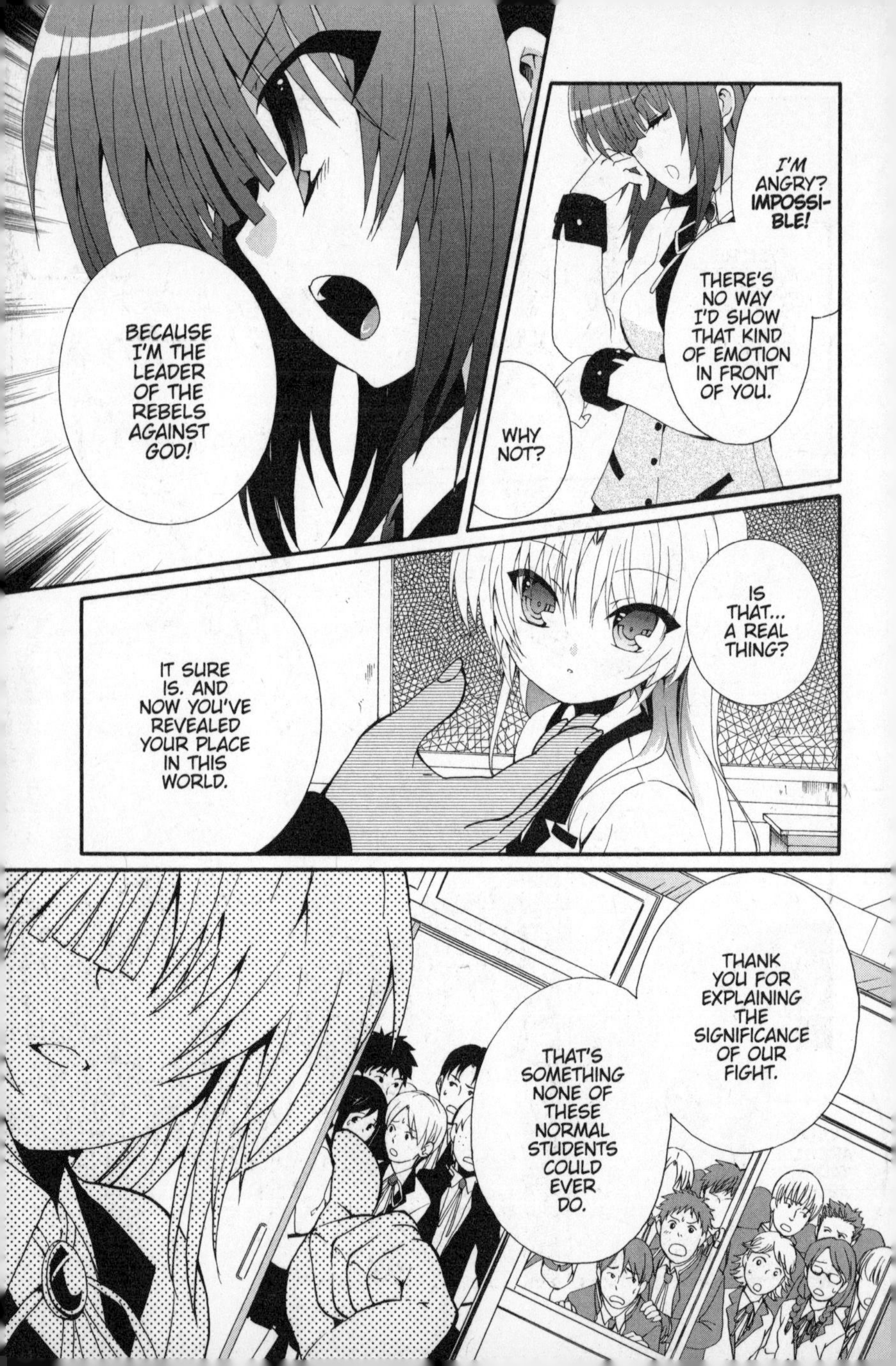
I'M ANGRY? IMPOSSIBLE!
THERE'S NO WAY I'D SHOW THAT KIND OF EMOTION IN FRONT OF YOU.
WHY NOT?
BECAUSE I'M THE LEADER OF THE REBELS AGAINST GOD!
IS THAT... A REAL THING?
IT SURE IS. AND NOW YOU'VE REVEALED YOUR PLACE IN THIS WORLD.
THANK YOU FOR EXPLAINING THE SIGNIFICANCE OF OUR FIGHT.
THAT'S SOMETHING NONE OF THESE NORMAL STUDENTS COULD EVER DO.

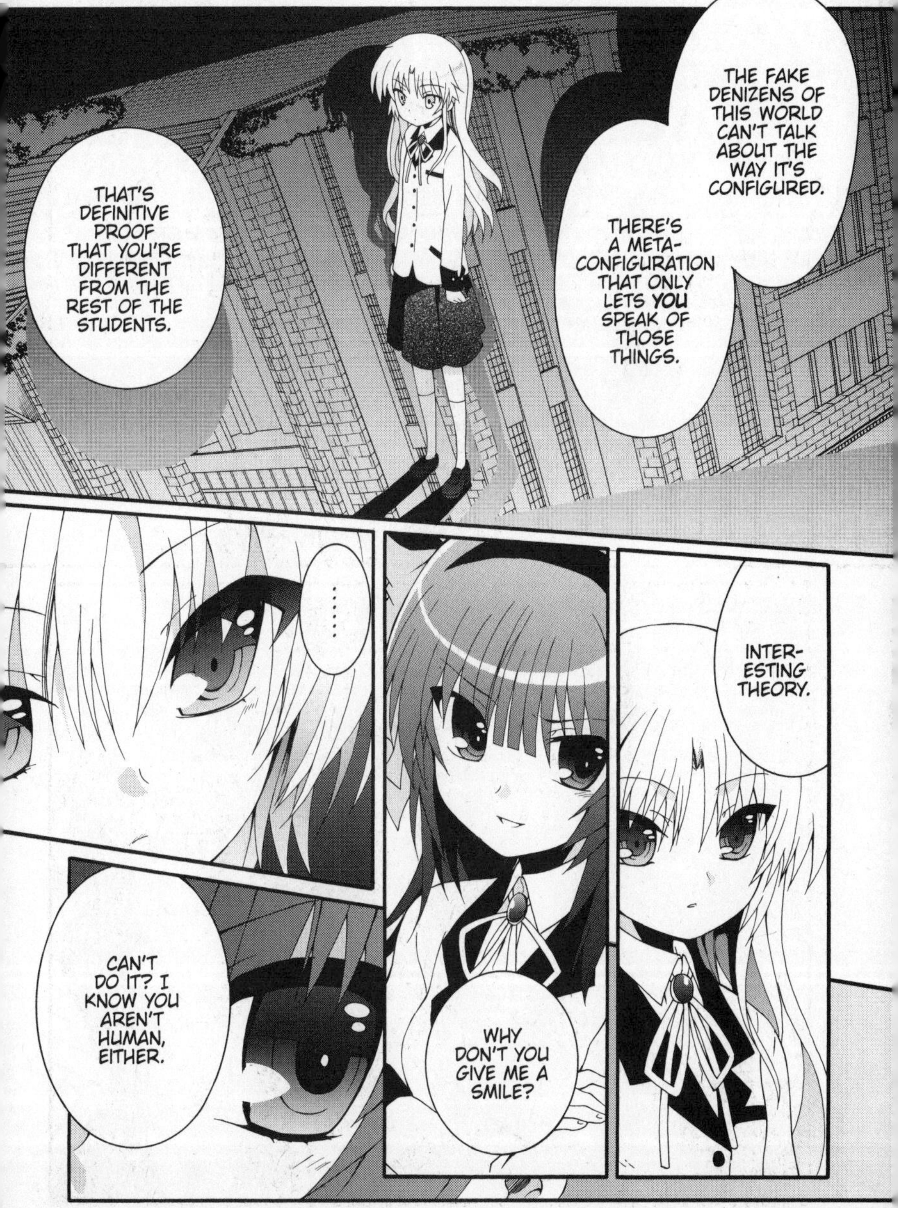
THE FAKE DENIZENS OF THIS WORLD CAN'T TALK ABOUT THE WAY IT'S CONFIGURED.
THERE'S A META-CONFIGURATION THAT ONLY LETS **YOU** SPEAK OF THOSE THINGS.
THAT'S DEFINITIVE PROOF THAT YOU'RE DIFFERENT FROM THE REST OF THE STUDENTS.
INTER-ESTING THEORY.
WHY DON'T YOU GIVE ME A SMILE?
......
CAN'T DO IT? I KNOW YOU AREN'T HUMAN, EITHER.

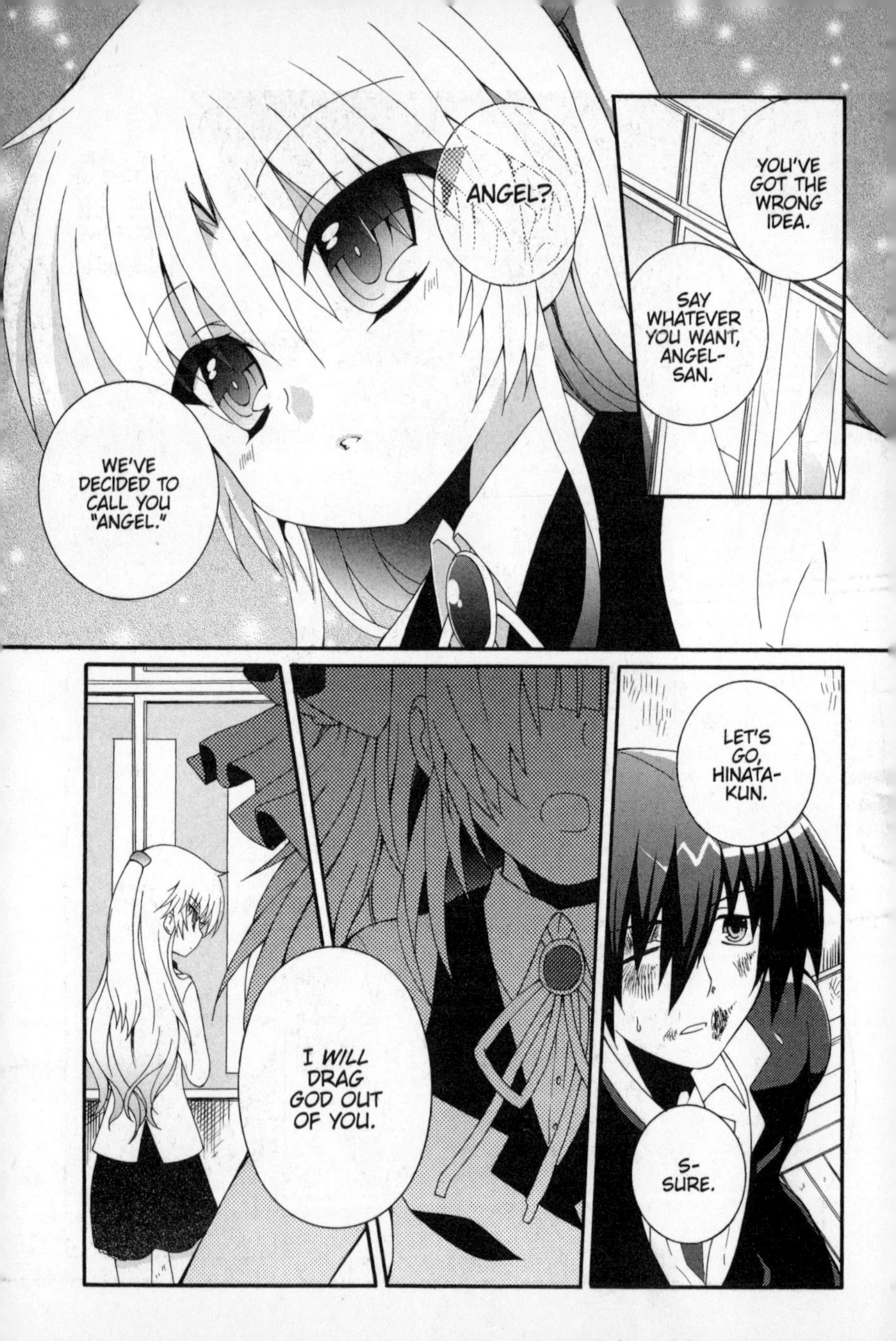
ANGEL?
WE'VE DECIDED TO CALL YOU "ANGEL."
YOU'VE GOT THE WRONG IDEA.
SAY WHATEVER YOU WANT, ANGEL-SAN.
LET'S GO, HINATA-KUN.
S-SURE.
I *WILL* DRAG GOD OUT OF YOU.

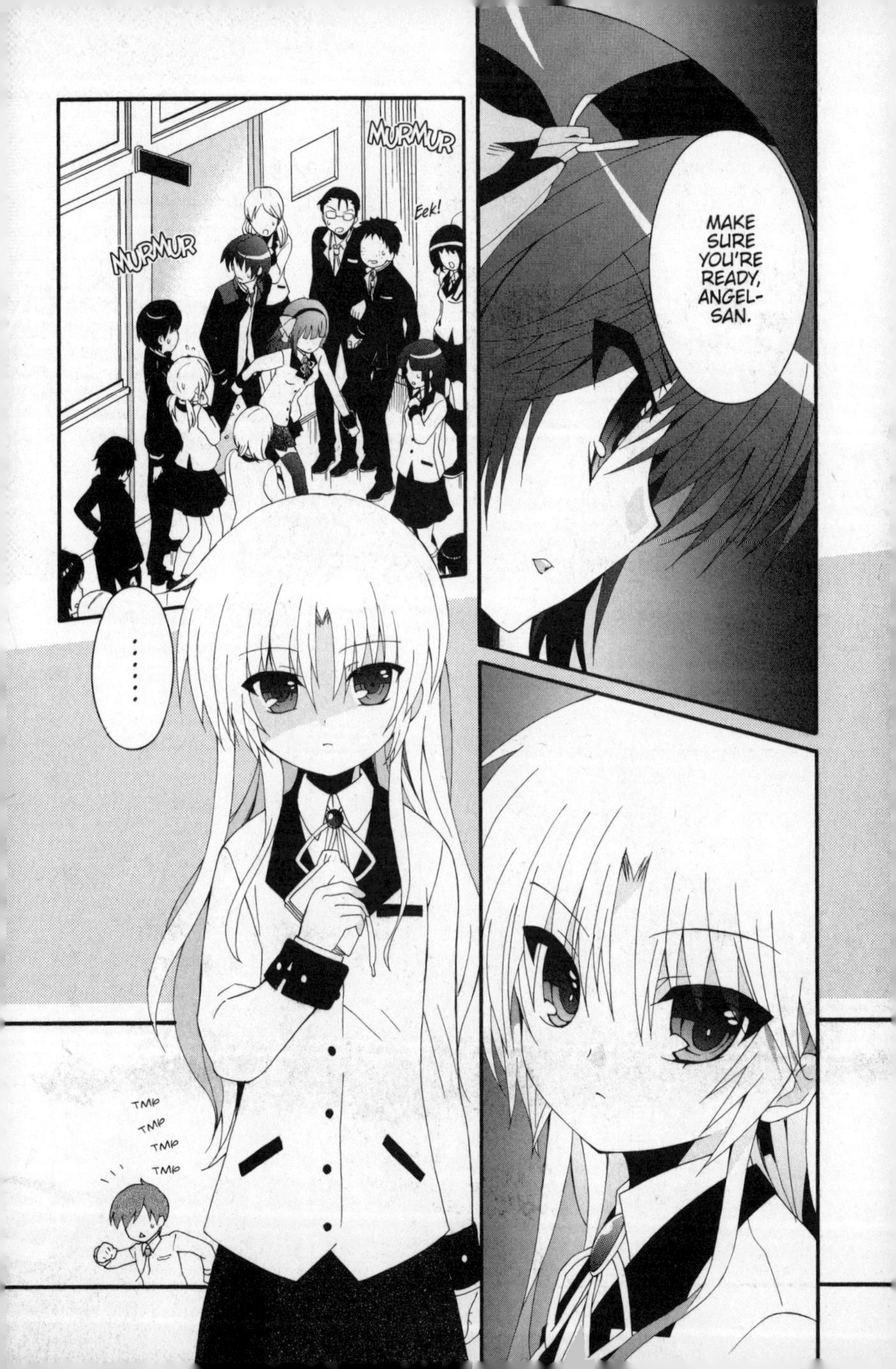
MAKE SURE YOU'RE READY, ANGEL-SAN.
MURMUR
Eek!
MURMUR
......
TMP
TMP
TMP
TMP

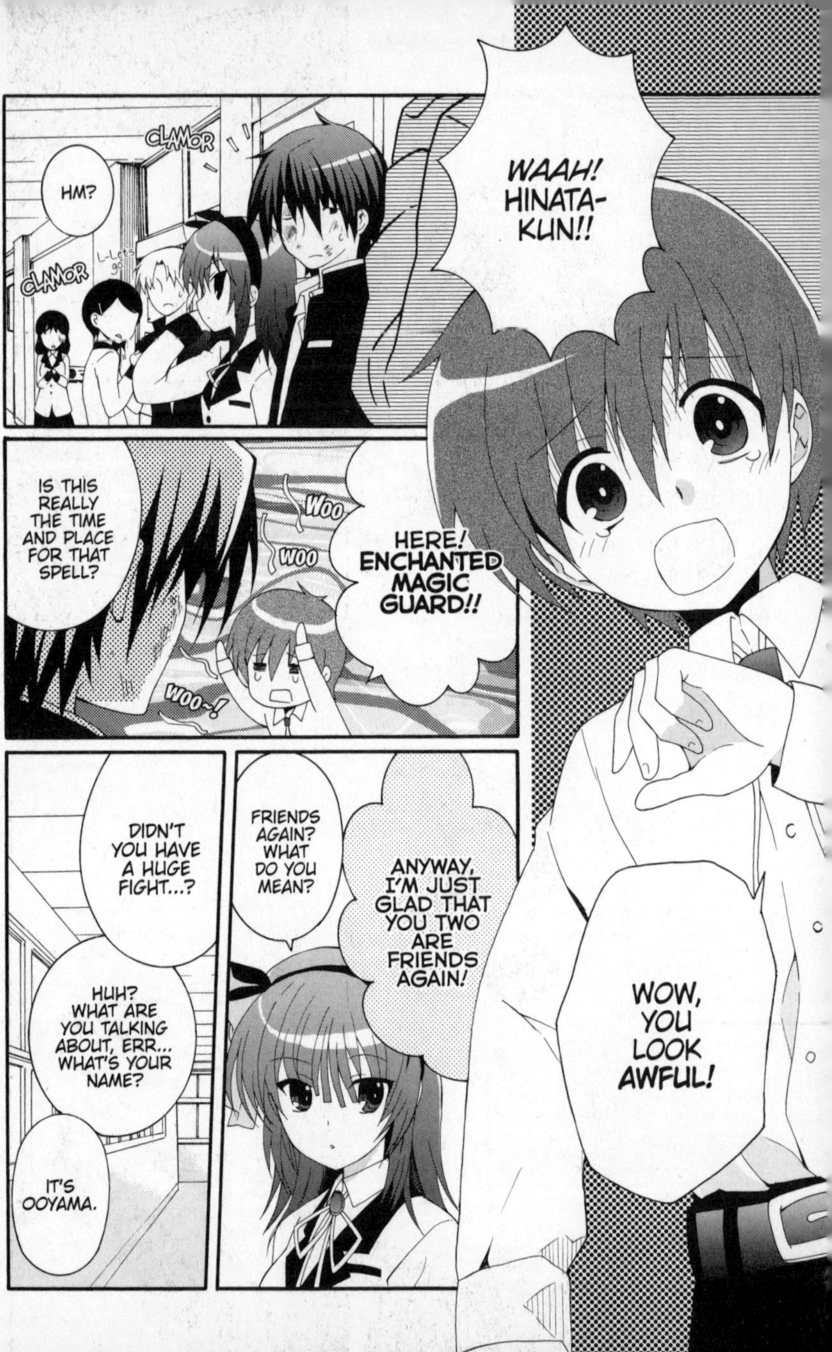
WAAH! HINATA-KUN!!
WOW, YOU LOOK AWFUL!
CLAMOR
HM?
L-Lets go!
CLAMOR
HERE! ENCHANTED MAGIC GUARD!!
Woo
WOO
woo~!
IS THIS REALLY THE TIME AND PLACE FOR THAT SPELL?
ANYWAY, I'M JUST GLAD THAT YOU TWO ARE FRIENDS AGAIN!
FRIENDS AGAIN? WHAT DO YOU MEAN?
DIDN'T YOU HAVE A HUGE FIGHT...?
HUH? WHAT ARE YOU TALKING ABOUT, ERR... WHAT'S YOUR NAME?
IT'S OOYAMA.

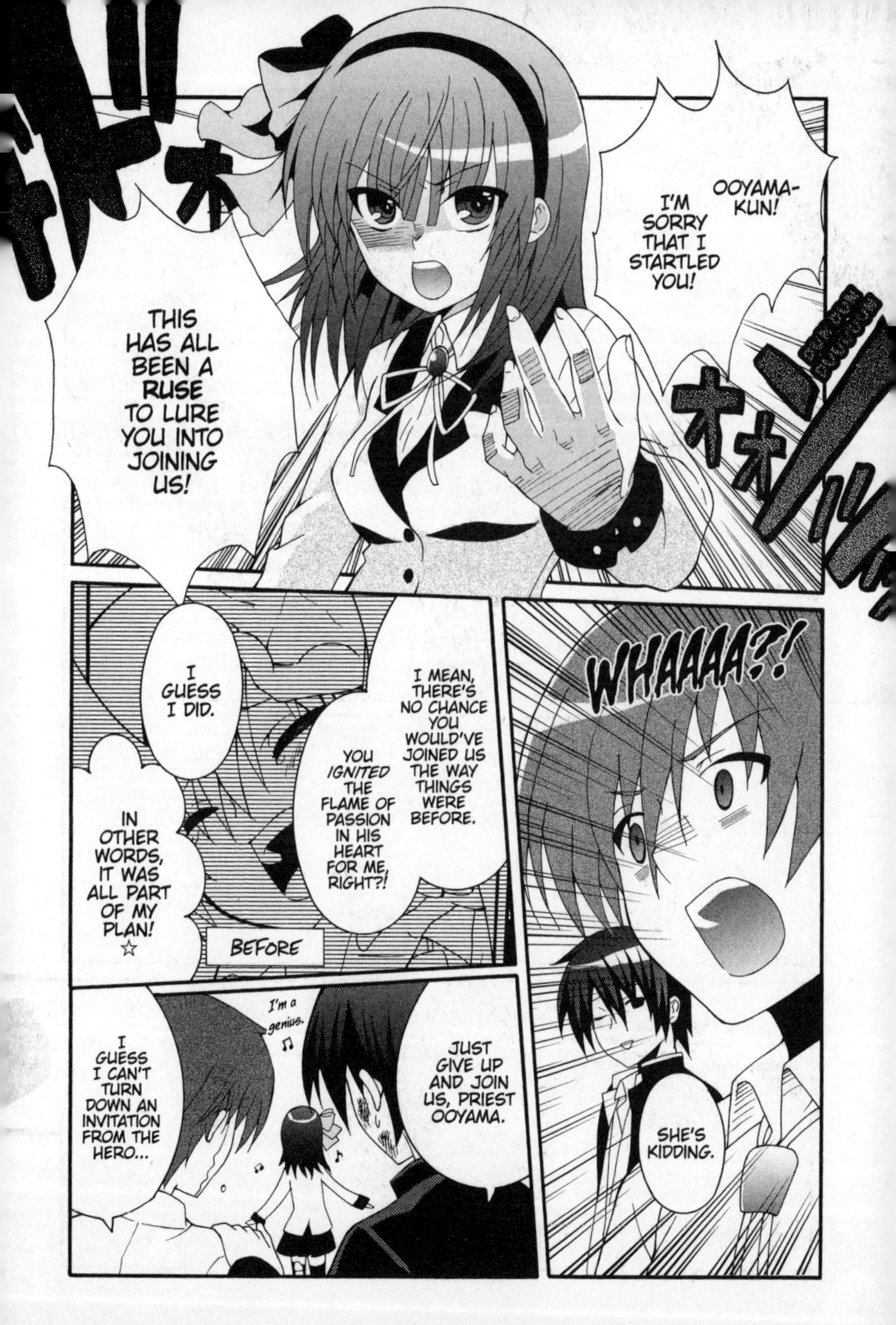
OOYAMA-KUN!
I'M SORRY THAT I STARTLED YOU!
THIS HAS ALL BEEN A RUSE TO LURE YOU INTO JOINING US!
WHAAAA?!
SHE'S KIDDING.
I MEAN, THERE'S NO CHANCE YOU WOULD'VE JOINED US THE WAY THINGS WERE BEFORE.
YOU IGNITED THE FLAME OF PASSION IN HIS HEART FOR ME, RIGHT?!
I GUESS I DID.
IN OTHER WORDS, IT WAS ALL PART OF MY PLAN! ☆
BEFORE
JUST GIVE UP AND JOIN US, PRIEST OOYAMA.
I'm a genius.
I GUESS I CAN'T TURN DOWN AN INVITATION FROM THE HERO...

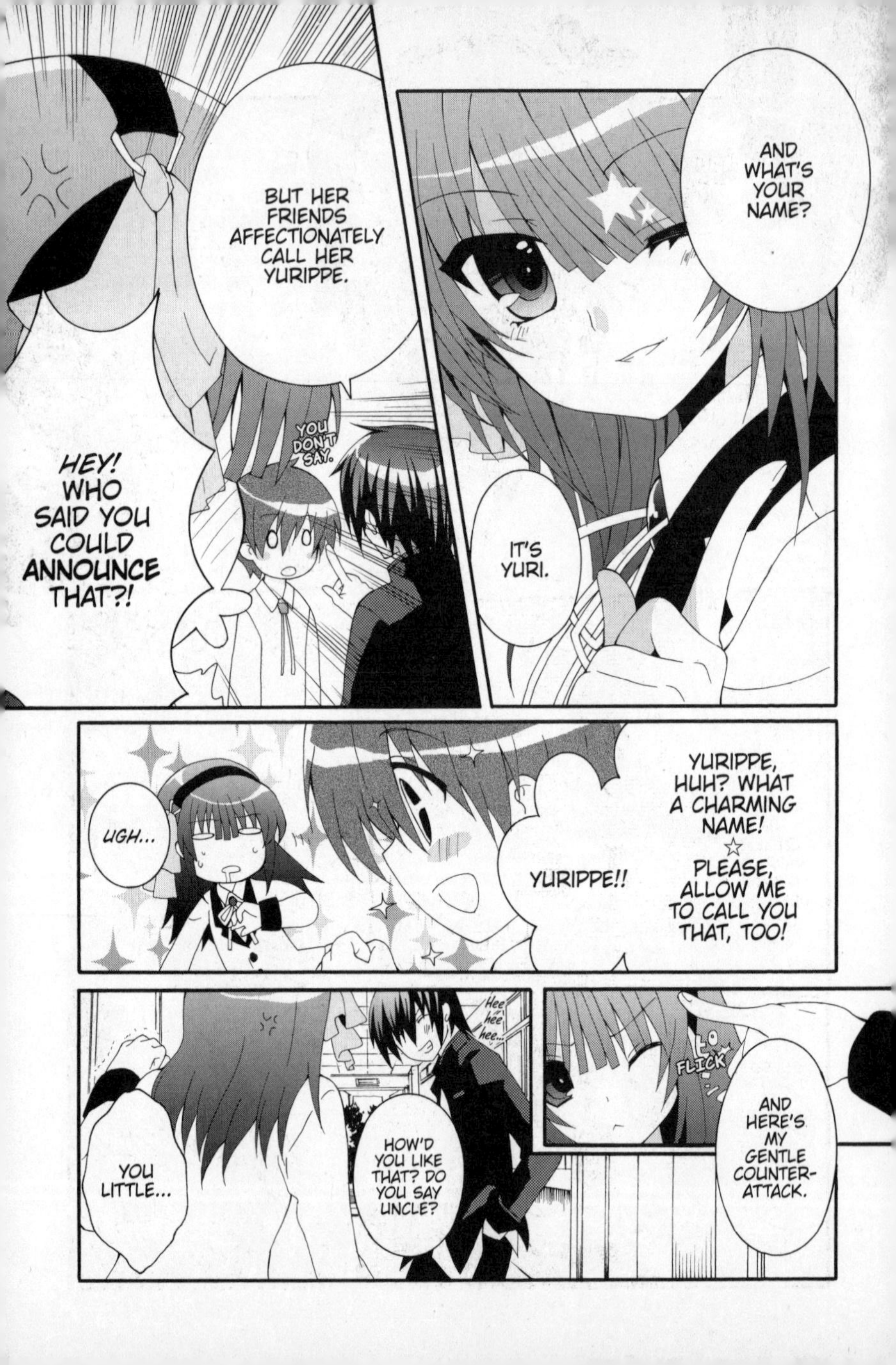

AND WHAT'S YOUR NAME?
IT'S YURI.
BUT HER FRIENDS AFFECTIONATELY CALL HER YURIPPE.
YOU DON'T SAY.
HEY! WHO SAID YOU COULD ANNOUNCE THAT?!
YURIPPE, HUH? WHAT A CHARMING NAME! ☆ PLEASE, ALLOW ME TO CALL YOU THAT, TOO!
YURIPPE!!
UGH...
FLICK
AND HERE'S MY GENTLE COUNTER-ATTACK.
Hee hee hee...
HOW'D YOU LIKE THAT? DO YOU SAY UNCLE?
YOU LITTLE...

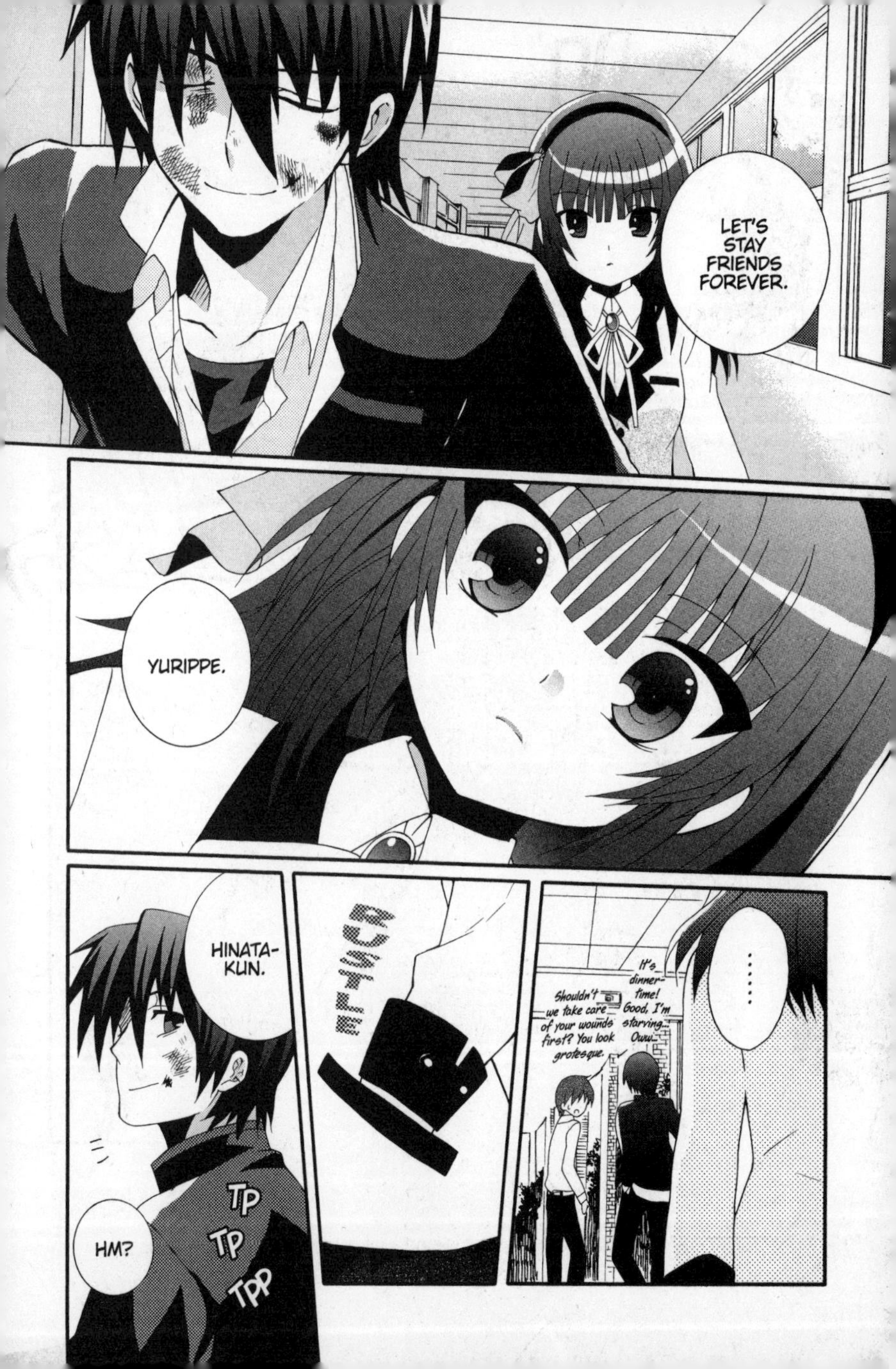
LET'S STAY FRIENDS FOREVER.
YURIPPE.
......
It's dinner-time! Good, I'm starving... Owww...
Shouldn't we take care of your wounds first? You look grotesque.
RUSTLE
HINATA-KUN.
HM?
TP
TP
TPP

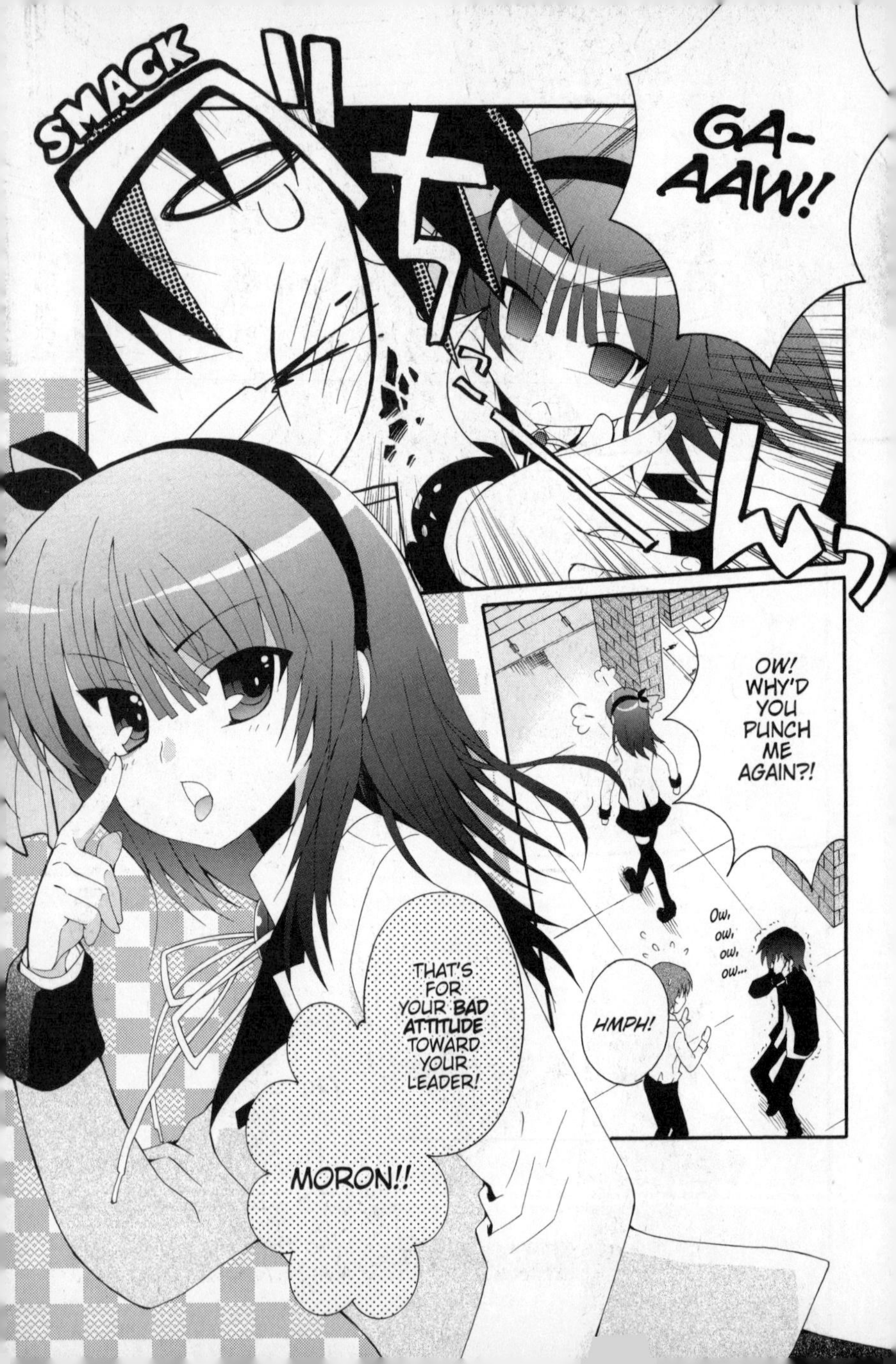
GA-AAW!
SMACK!!
OW! WHY'D YOU PUNCH ME AGAIN?!
Ow, ow, ow, ow...
HMPH!
THAT'S FOR YOUR BAD ATTITUDE TOWARD YOUR LEADER!
MORON!!

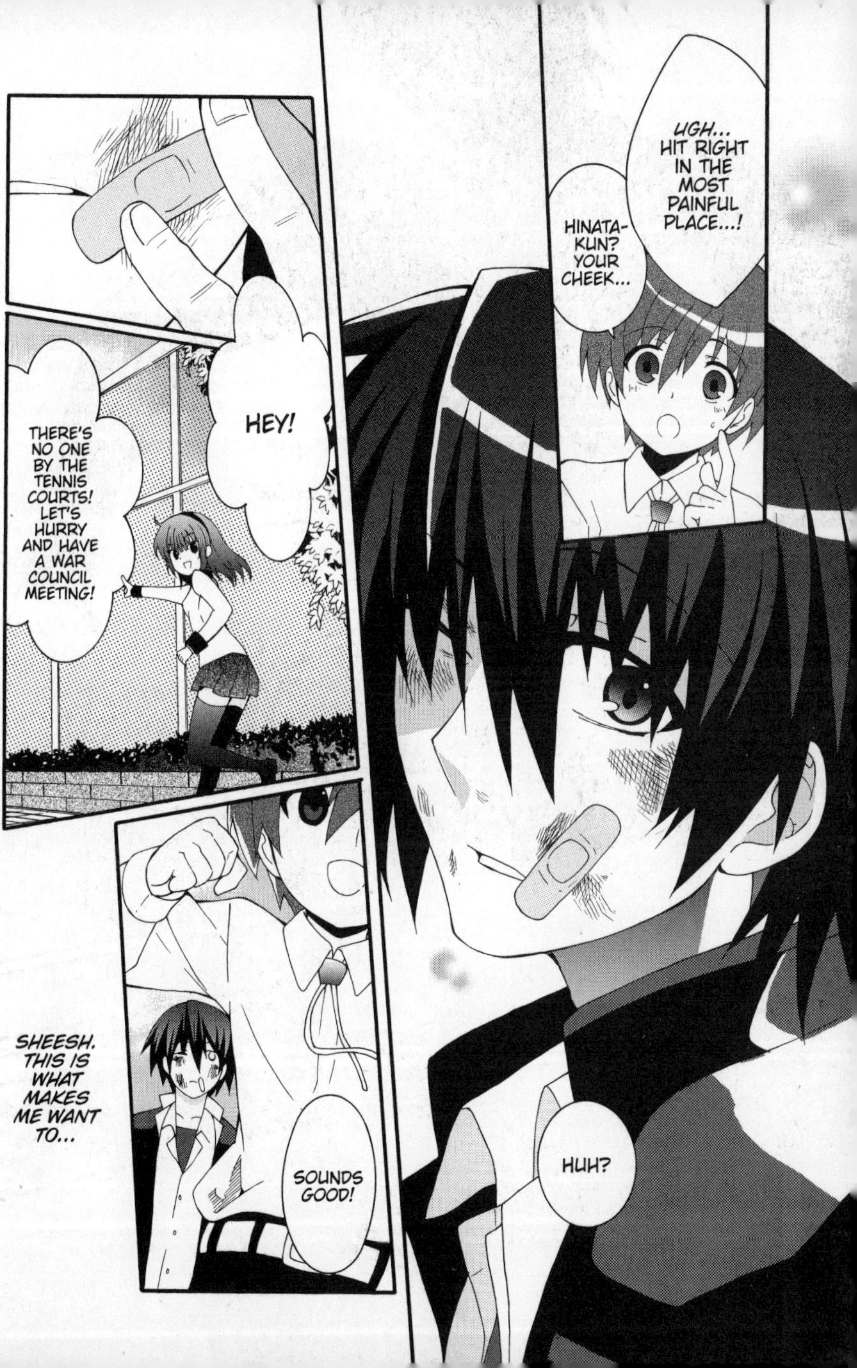
UGH... HIT RIGHT IN THE MOST PAINFUL PLACE...!
HINATA-KUN? YOUR CHEEK...
HUH?
HEY!
THERE'S NO ONE BY THE TENNIS COURTS! LET'S HURRY AND HAVE A WAR COUNCIL MEETING!
SOUNDS GOOD!
SHEESH. THIS IS WHAT MAKES ME WANT TO...

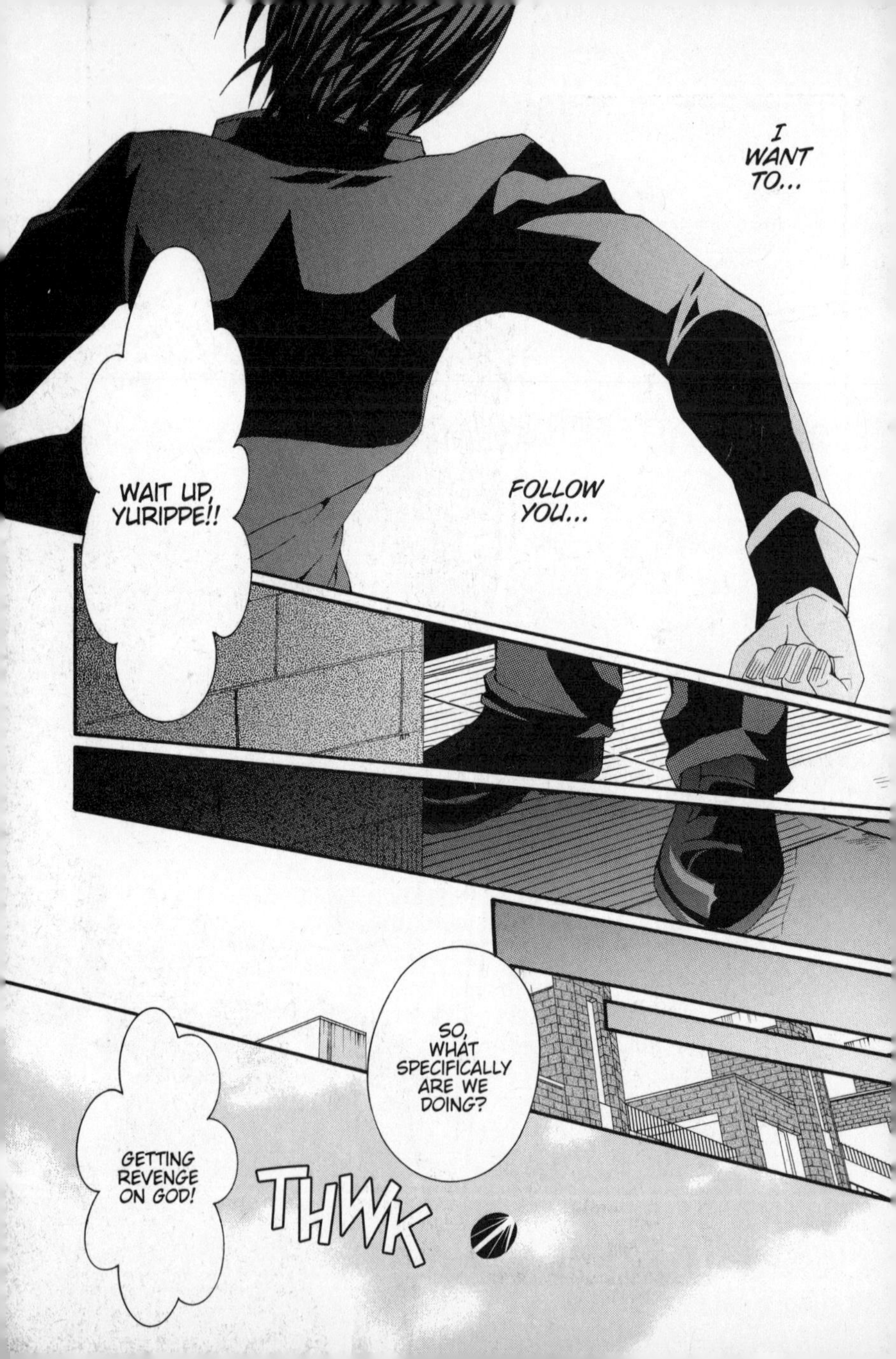
I WANT TO...
FOLLOW YOU...
WAIT UP, YURIPPE!!
SO, WHAT SPECIFICALLY ARE WE DOING?
THWK
GETTING REVENGE ON GOD!

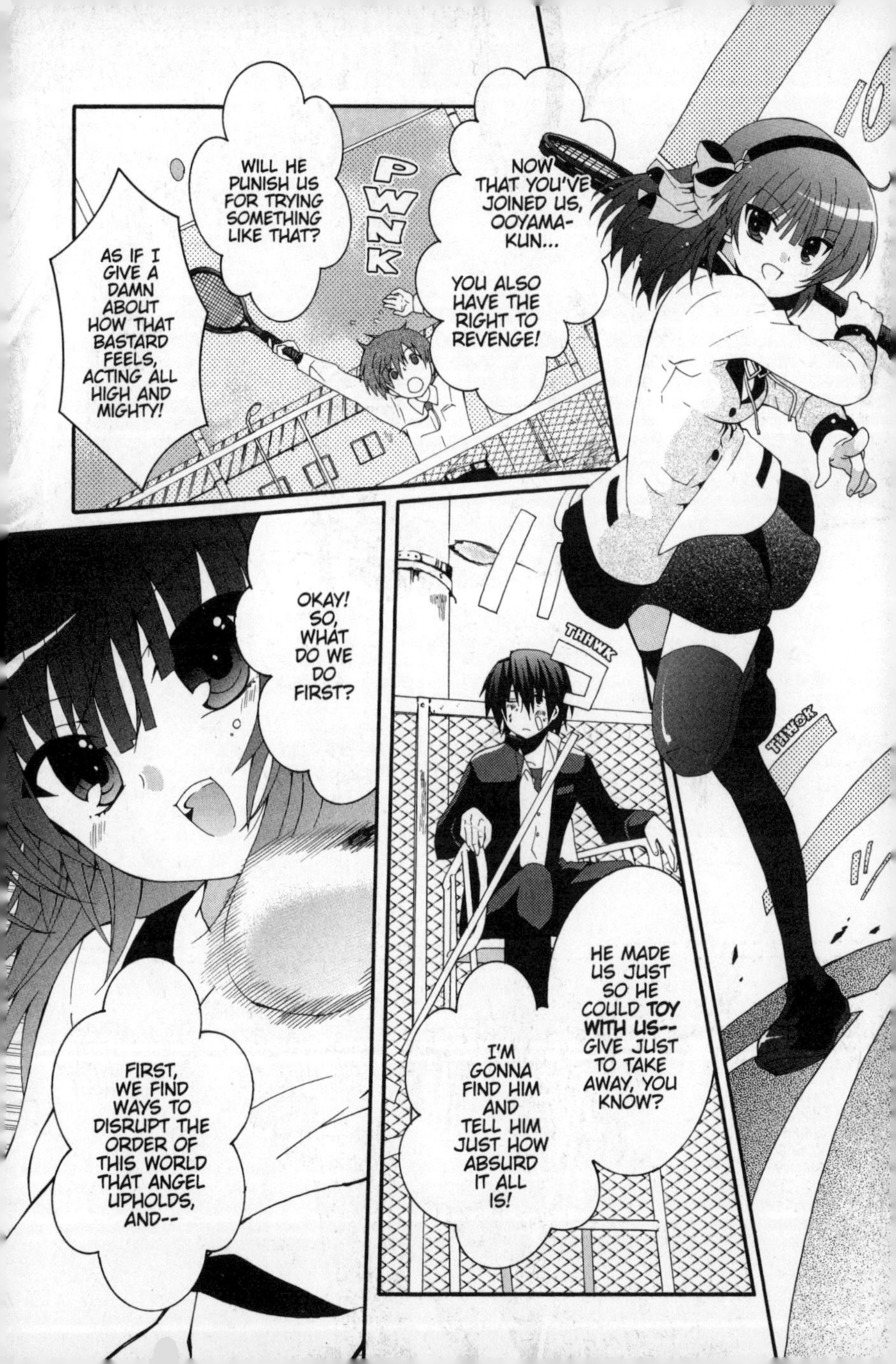
NOW THAT YOU'VE JOINED US, OOYAMA-KUN...
YOU ALSO HAVE THE RIGHT TO REVENGE!
PWNK
WILL HE PUNISH US FOR TRYING SOMETHING LIKE THAT?
AS IF I GIVE A DAMN ABOUT HOW THAT BASTARD FEELS, ACTING ALL HIGH AND MIGHTY!
THWOK
THHWK
HE MADE US JUST SO HE COULD TOY WITH US-- GIVE JUST TO TAKE AWAY, YOU KNOW?
I'M GONNA FIND HIM AND TELL HIM JUST HOW ABSURD IT ALL IS!
OKAY! SO, WHAT DO WE DO FIRST?
FIRST, WE FIND WAYS TO DISRUPT THE ORDER OF THIS WORLD THAT ANGEL UPHOLDS, AND--

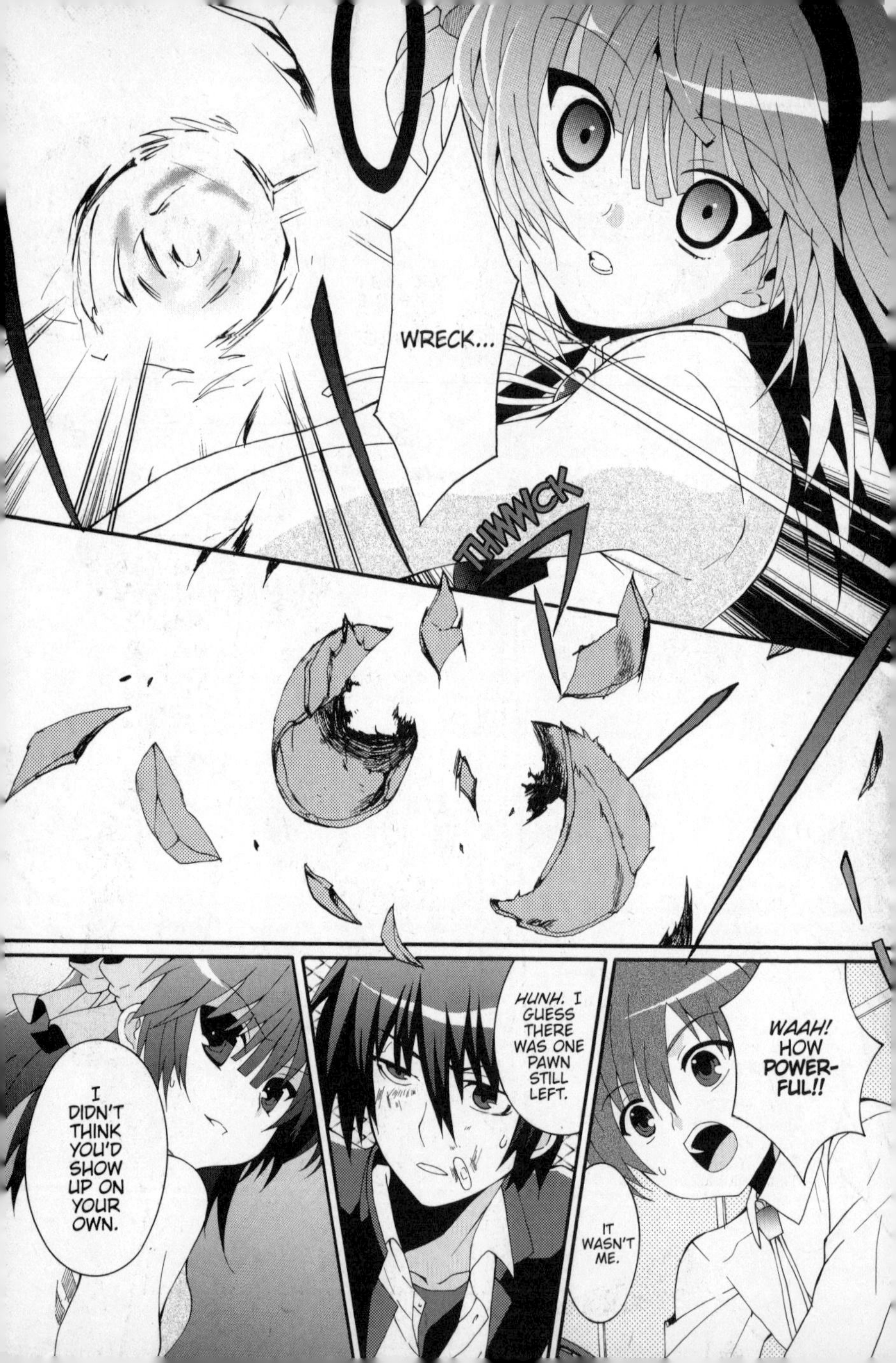
WRECK...
THWWCK
WAAH! HOW POWER-FUL!!
IT WASN'T ME.
HUNH. I GUESS THERE WAS ONE PAWN STILL LEFT.
I DIDN'T THINK YOU'D SHOW UP ON YOUR OWN.

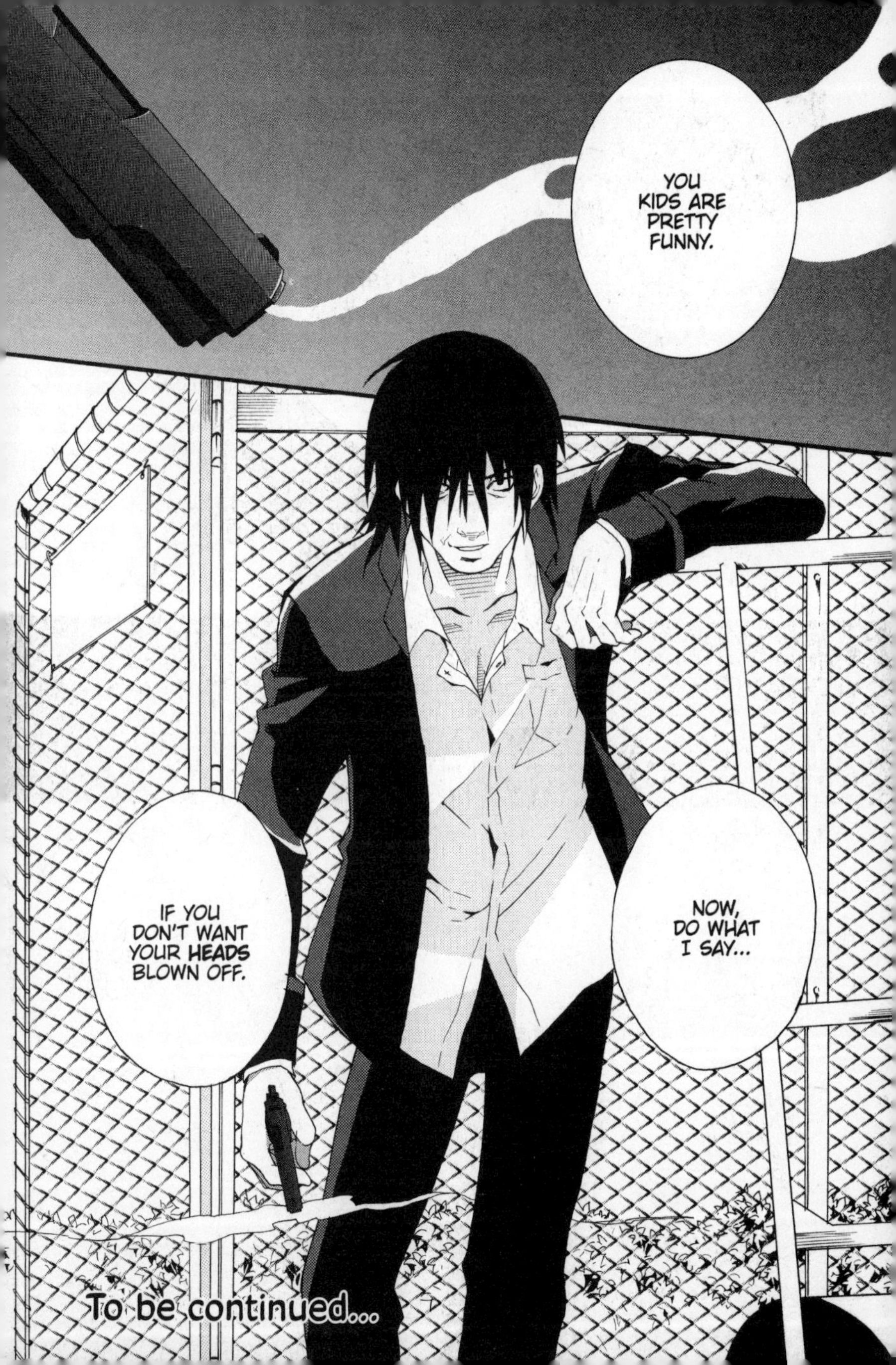
YOU KIDS ARE PRETTY FUNNY.
NOW, DO WHAT I SAY...
IF YOU DON'T WANT YOUR **HEADS** BLOWN OFF.
To be continued...

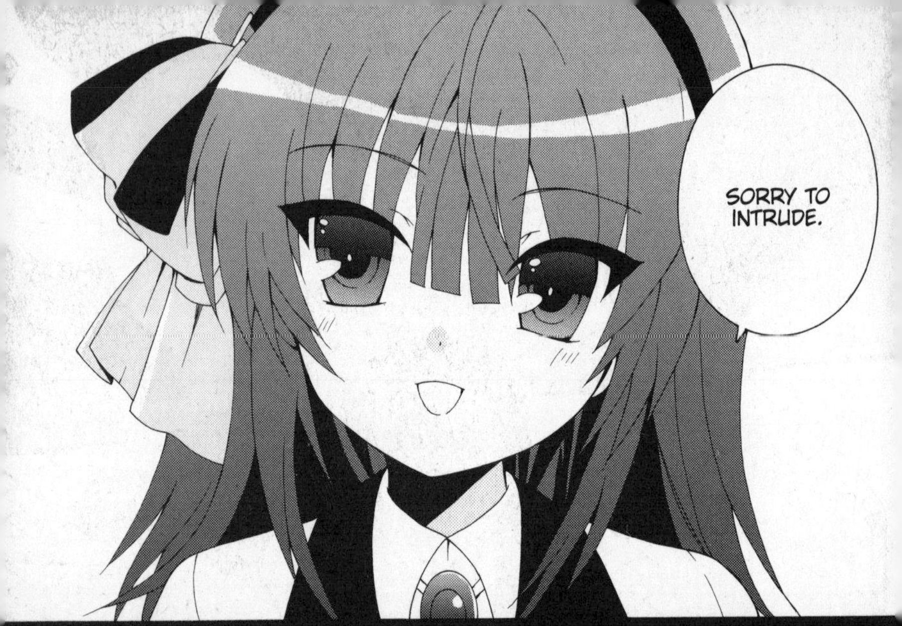
SORRY TO INTRUDE.

Bonus Manga: Farewell, Sadness

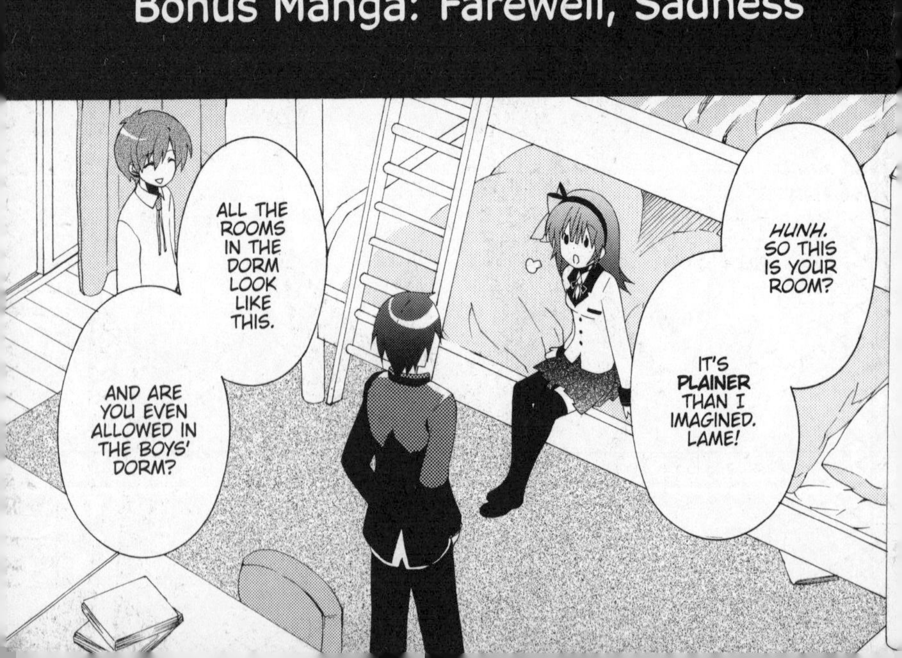
HUNH. SO THIS IS YOUR ROOM?
IT'S **PLAINER** THAN I IMAGINED. LAME!
ALL THE ROOMS IN THE DORM LOOK LIKE THIS.
AND ARE YOU EVEN ALLOWED IN THE BOYS' DORM?

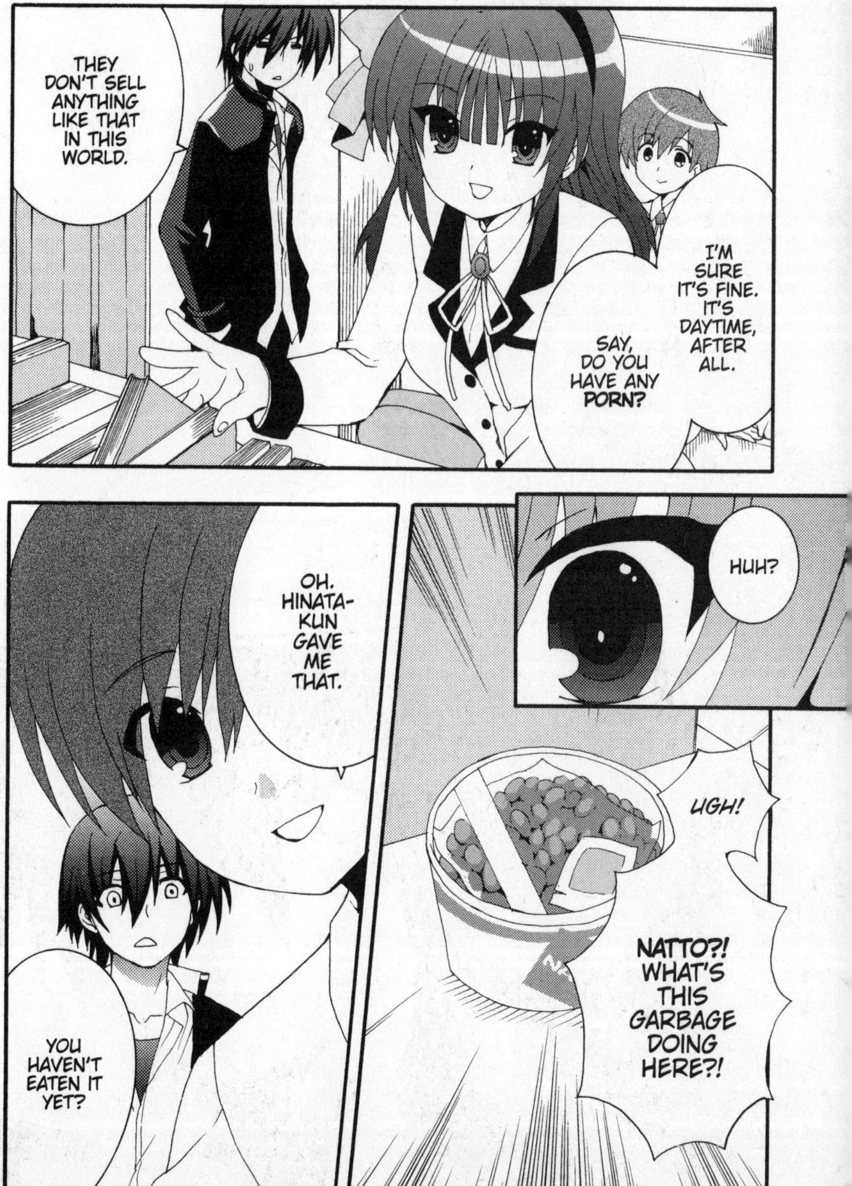
I'M SURE IT'S FINE. IT'S DAYTIME, AFTER ALL.
SAY, DO YOU HAVE ANY PORN?
THEY DON'T SELL ANYTHING LIKE THAT IN THIS WORLD.
HUH?
UGH!
NATTO?! WHAT'S THIS GARBAGE DOING HERE?!
OH. HINATA-KUN GAVE ME THAT.
YOU HAVEN'T EATEN IT YET?

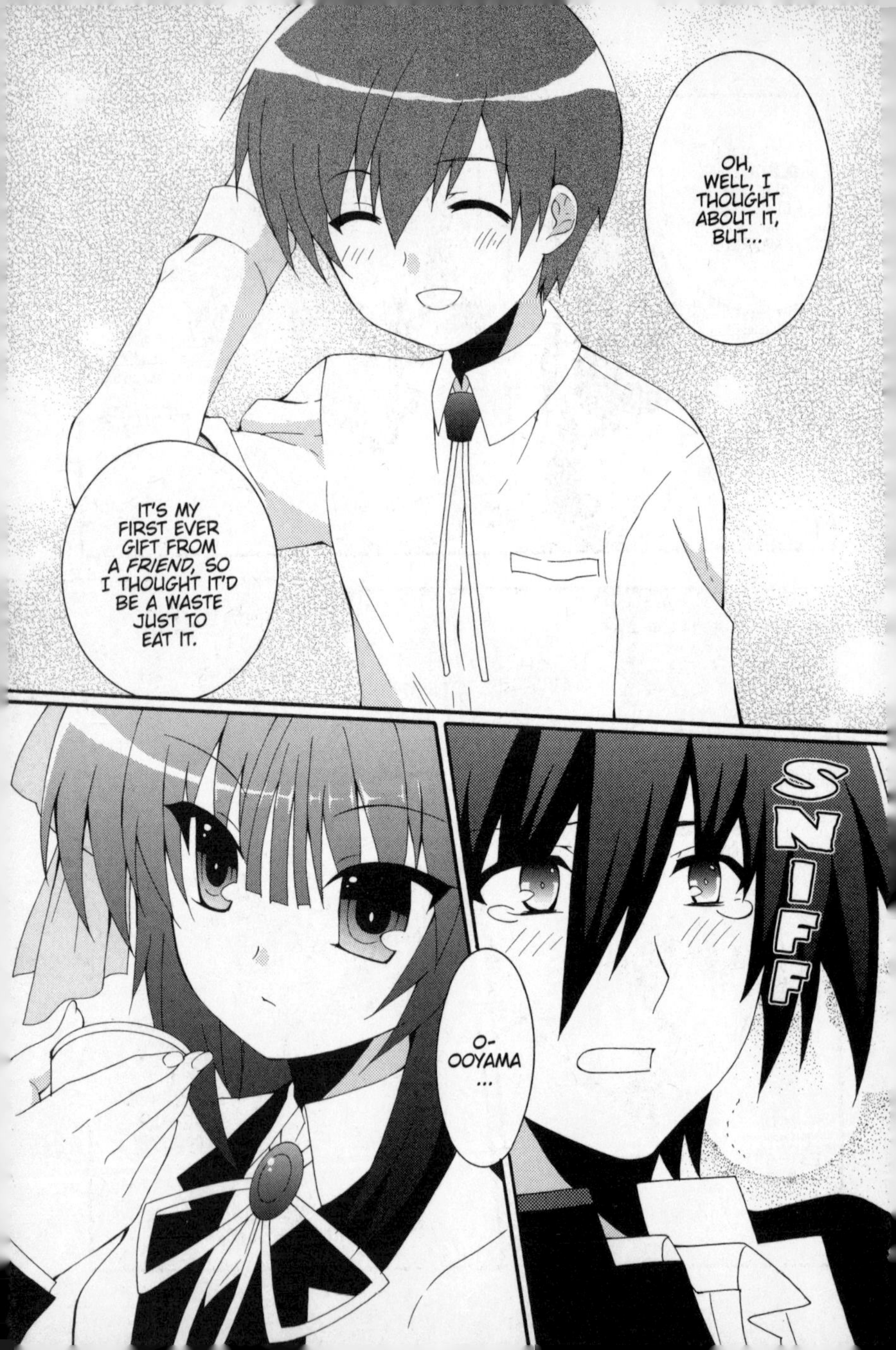
OH, WELL, I THOUGHT ABOUT IT, BUT...
IT'S MY FIRST EVER GIFT FROM A *FRIEND*, SO I THOUGHT IT'D BE A WASTE JUST TO EAT IT.
SNIFF
O-OOYAMA...

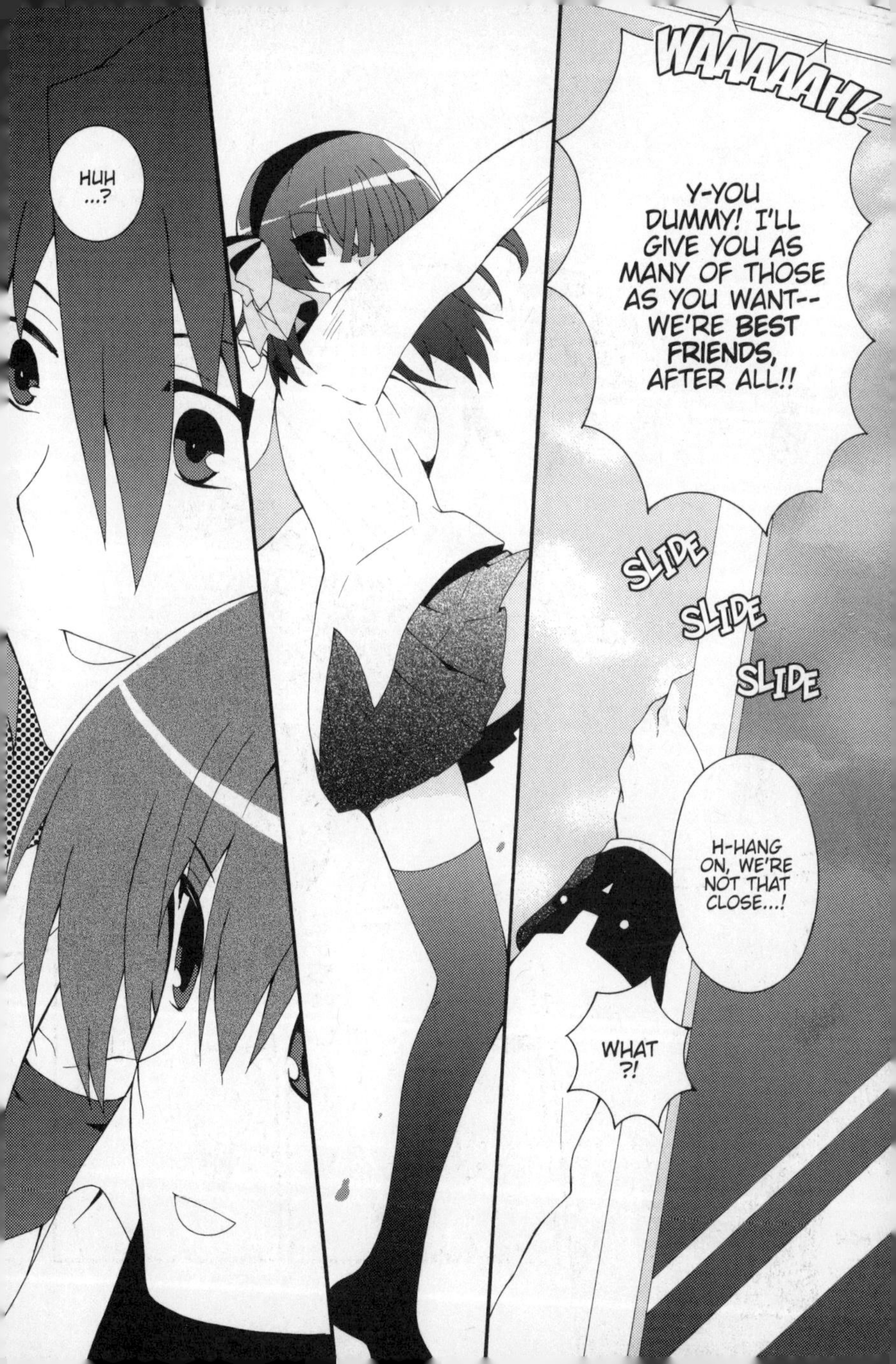
WAAAAAH!
Y-YOU DUMMY! I'LL GIVE YOU AS MANY OF THOSE AS YOU WANT--WE'RE BEST FRIENDS, AFTER ALL!!
SLIDE
SLIDE
SLIDE
H-HANG ON, WE'RE NOT THAT CLOSE...!
WHAT ?!
HUH ...?

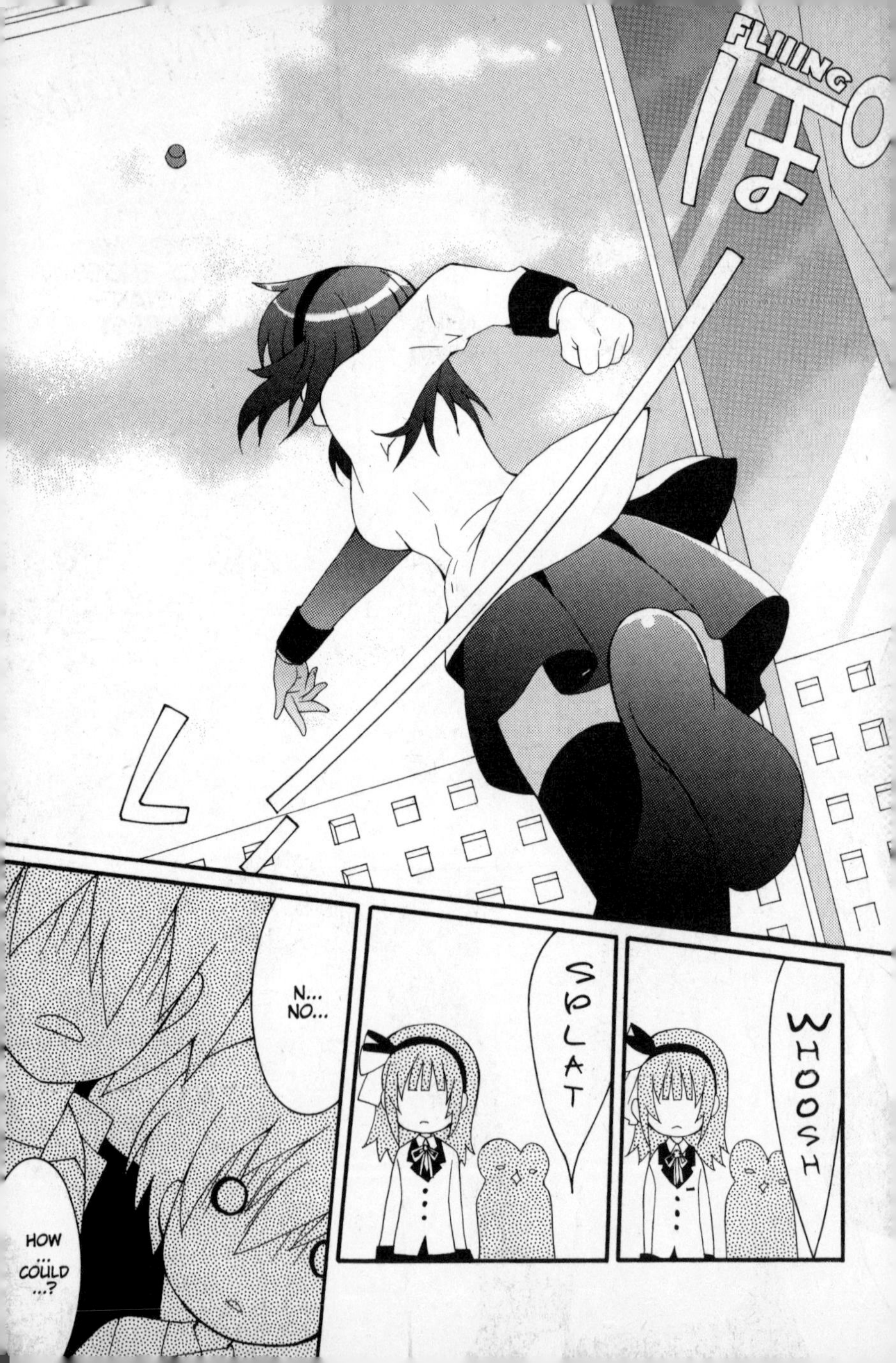
FLIIING
WHOOSH
SPLAT
N... NO...
HOW ... COULD ...?

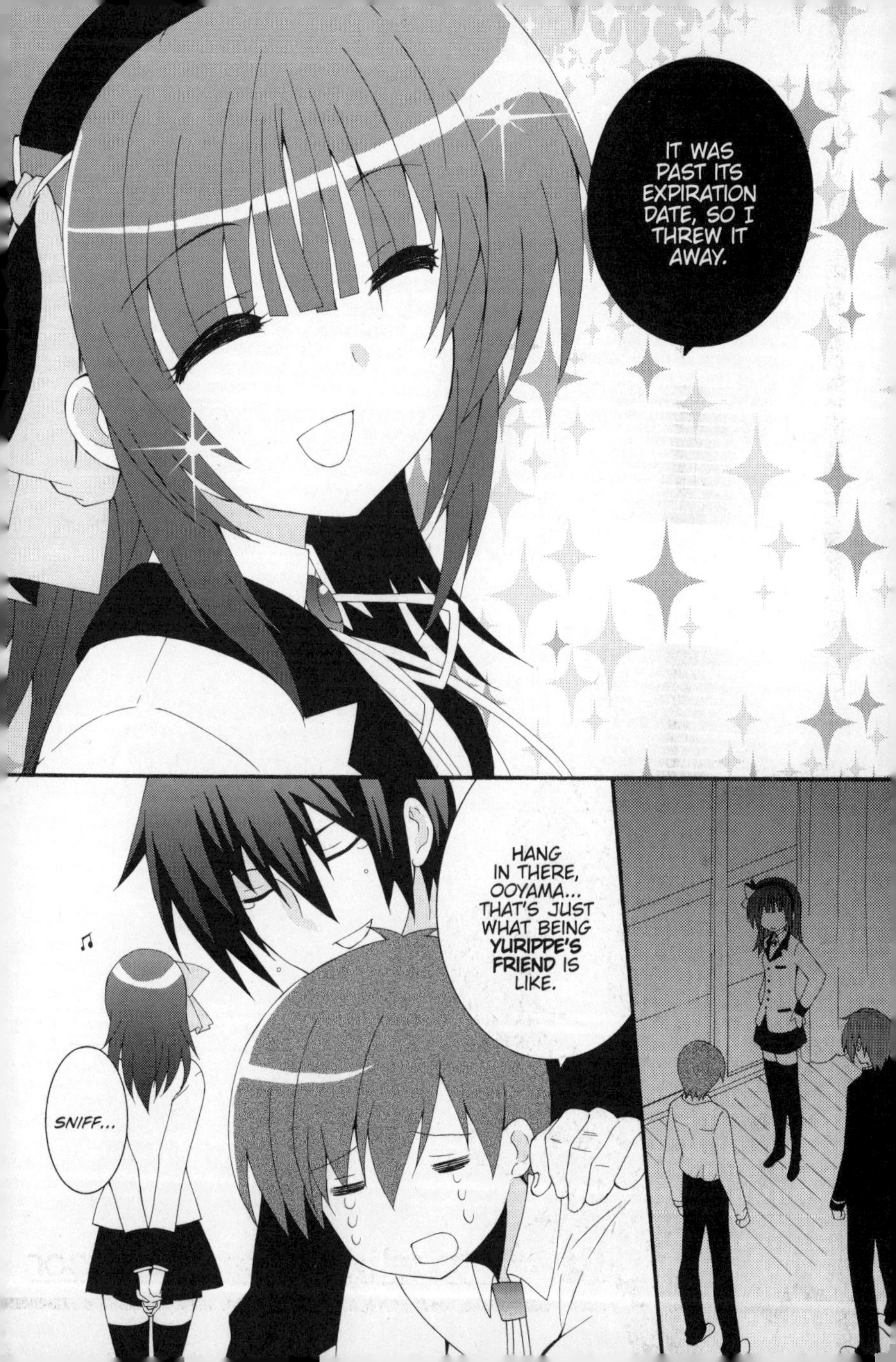
IT WAS PAST ITS EXPIRATION DATE, SO I THREW IT AWAY.
HANG IN THERE, OOYAMA... THAT'S JUST WHAT BEING **YURIPPE'S FRIEND** IS LIKE.
♪
SNIFF...

Angel Beats! Heaven's Door

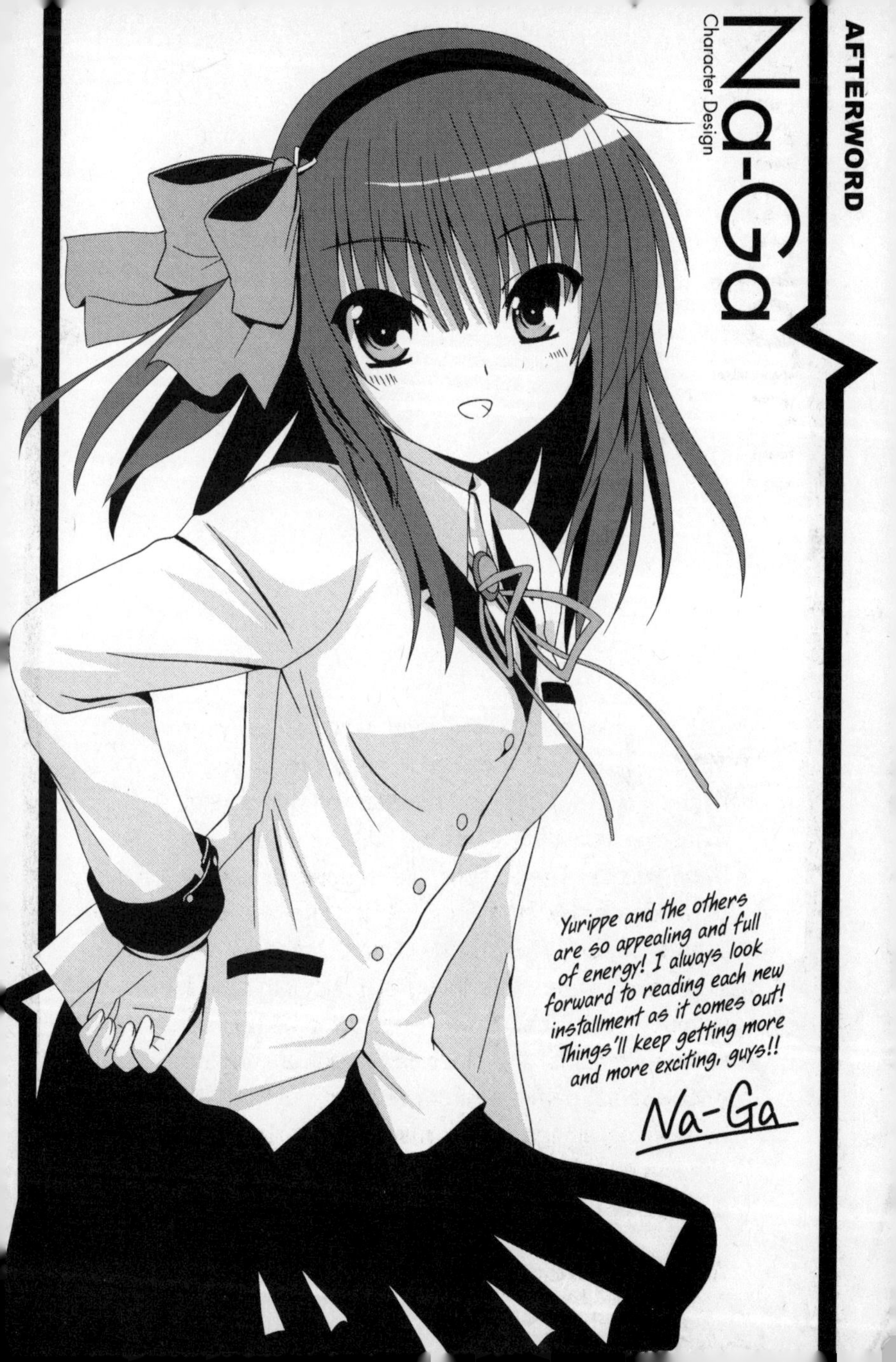
AFTERWORD
Na-Ga
Character Design
Yurippe and the others are so appealing and full of energy! I always look forward to reading each new installment as it comes out! Things'll keep getting more and more exciting, guys!!
Na-Ga

AFTERWORD

Original Story

MaedaJun

Isn't it strange that the one who wrote your endorsement is also writing an afterword for you?! I'd just like to say that so I can start off with a joke. I was the one who came up with the *"Heaven's Door"* subtitle. The episode title for episode 12 was *"Knockin' on Heaven's Door,"* which I chose since it implies "heading towards the climax," but really that was more of an afterthought. I just thought it sounded cool (heh). Now, I need to come up with some material for the other SSS members for the Angel Beats! game, so from here on out I'll really be working alongside this manga's serialization. I imagine it'll be a long journey. Asami-san, let's both dedicate our lives to *Angel Beats!* for a while!

Angel Beats! rocks! Cheers!

Hello there. I'm Yuriko Asami, the writer for *Angel Beats! Heaven's Door.*

I've been in love with *Angel Beats!* since I first laid eyes on the characters and descriptions on the official website, so I'm a big fan--I bought all the blu-rays and CDs with my own money. I even have multiple copies of each, so I have one for home and one for the car. No matter how I feel when I watch it, it soothes me.

I never imagined that a simple fan like me would be asked to draw the manga. It's very nerve-racking every month, but it's also really fun.

I still think I have a long way to go as an artist, but I hope I can express the fun of *Angel Beats!* in manga form, if even just a little. I'll try my hardest, so please keep supporting me! I look forward to writing for you!

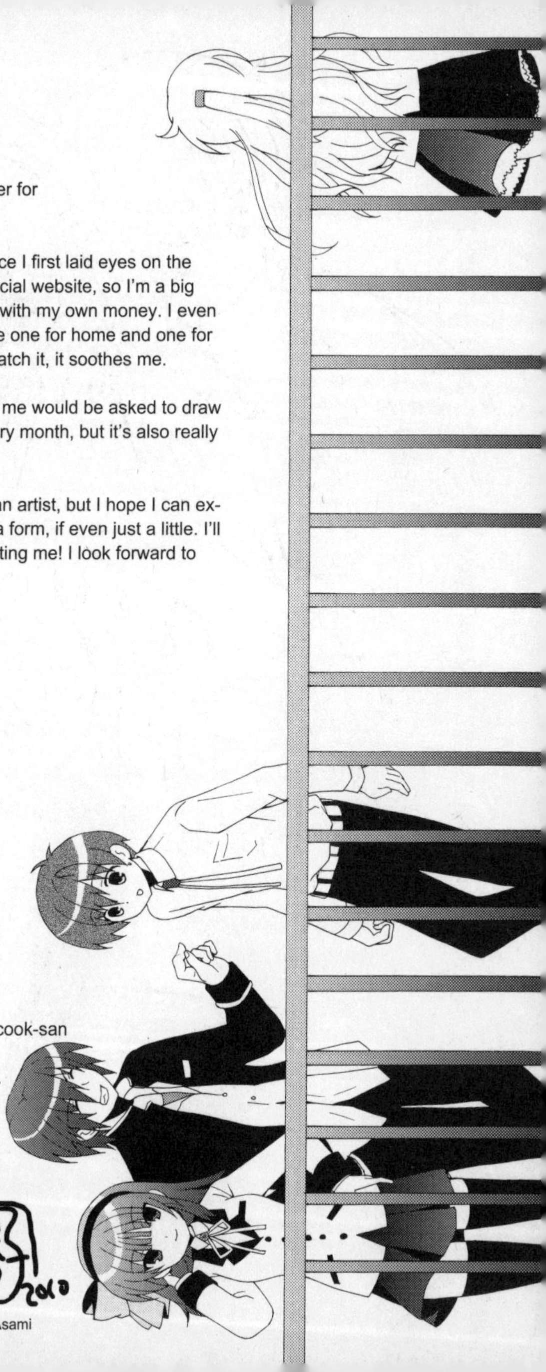

Special Thanks

■ Maeda-sama

■ Na-Ga-sama

■ The staff of the anime

■ My editor, Yokoyama-sama

☐ Oniko-san, Migiwa Banri-san, pyXcook-san

☐ Everyone who picked up this book.

Thank you so much!

Yuriko Asami

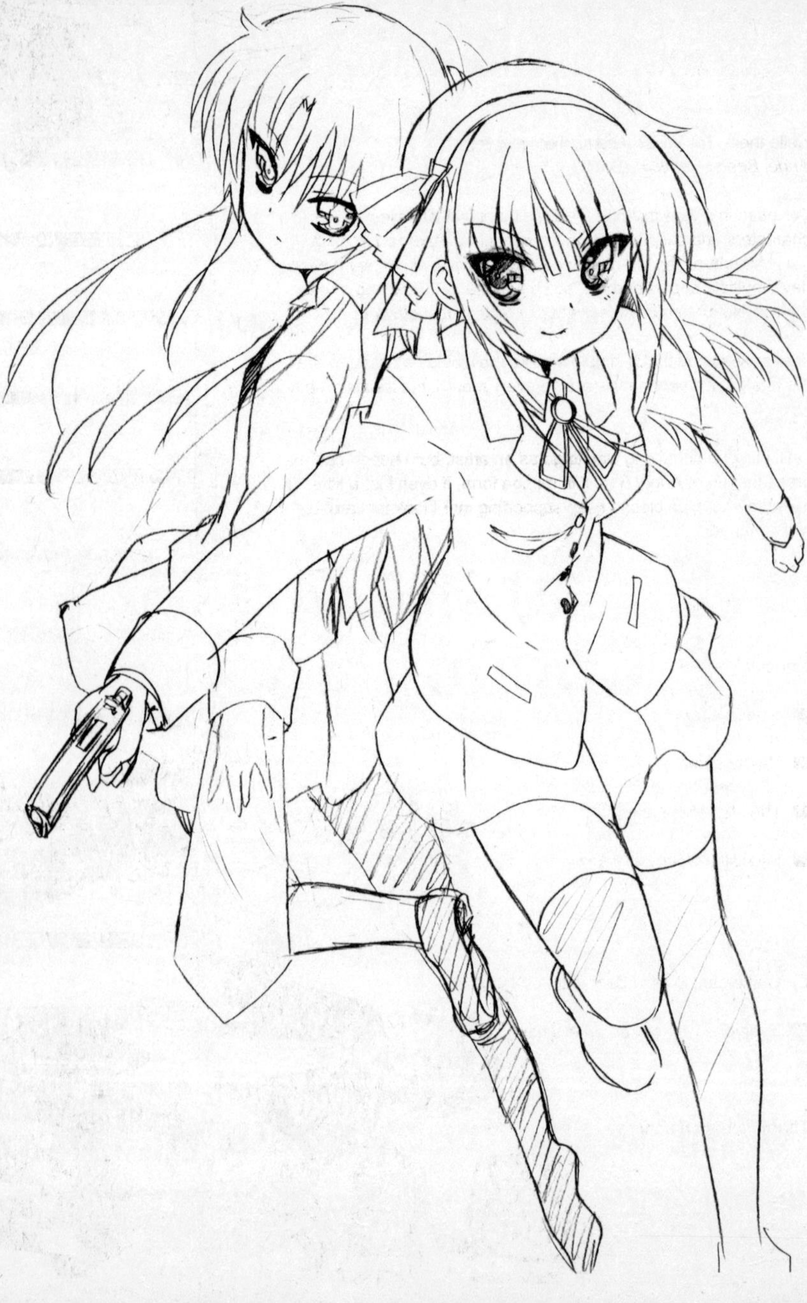

—————— !!

Let's get along...

**This challenge will deliver
the final blow!!**

You realize that what you just said
isn't an explanation, right?!

[Volume 2
Coming Soon!!]

Of course...
Th-think about it.

Why?

Why is an Angel here?

Why?

What is the truth about Heaven?

NEXT VOLUME

Do you know the truth about us——

1, 2, 3, 4, 5, 6, 7, 8, 9...10!!

**What the hell
are we doing?!**

Angel Beats! Heaven's Door

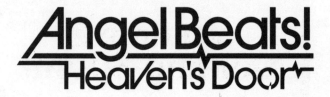

Leave the rest to me.

That's right. We'll be going to a
paradise for just the two of us.

SEVEN SEAS ENTERTAINMENT PRESENTS

story by **JUN MAEDA** / art by **YURIKO ASAMI** / original character design by **NA-GA**

TRANSLATION
Ryan Peterson

ADAPTATION
Rebecca Scoble

LETTERING AND LAYOUT
Jennifer Skarupa

COVER DESIGN
Nicky Lim

PROOFREADER
Lianne Sentar

PRODUCTION MANAGER
Lissa Pattillo

EDITOR-IN-CHIEF
Adam Arnold

PUBLISHER
Jason DeAngelis

ANGEL BEATS! HEAVEN'S DOOR VOL. 1

Edited by ASCII MEDIA WORKS.
First published in Japan in 2010 by KADOKAWA CORPORATION, Tokyo.
English translation rights arranged with KADOKAWA CORPORATION, Tokyo.

ISBN: 978-1-626921-89-4

Printed in Canada

First Printing: February 2016

10 9 8 7 6 5 4 3 2 1

FOLLOW US ONLINE: ***www.gomanga.com***

READING DIRECTIONS

This book reads from ***right to left***, Japanese style. If this is your first time reading manga, you start reading from the top right panel on each page and take it from there. If you get lost, just follow the numbered diagram here. It may seem backwards at first, but you'll get the hang of it! Have fun!!

1
2
3
4
5
6
7
8
9

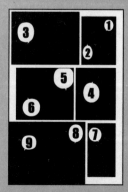